Optimized C++

Kurt Guntheroth

Beijing · Boston · Farnham · Sebastopol · Tokyo

Optimized C++

by Kurt Guntheroth

Copyright © 2016 Kurt Guntheroth. All rights reserved.

Printed in the United States of America.

Published by O'Reilly Media, Inc., 1005 Gravenstein Highway North, Sebastopol, CA 95472.

O'Reilly books may be purchased for educational, business, or sales promotional use. Online editions are also available for most titles (*http://safaribooksonline.com*). For more information, contact our corporate/institutional sales department: 800-998-9938 or *corporate@oreilly.com*.

Editors: Meghan Blanchette and Andy Oram	**Indexer:** Judy McConville
Acquisition Editor: Meghan Blanchette	**Interior Designer:** David Futato
Production Editor: Nicole Shelby	**Cover Designer:** Randy Comer
Copyeditor: Rachel Head	**Illustrator:** Rebecca Demarest
Proofreader: Jasmine Kwityn	

April 2016: First Edition

Revision History for the First Edition
2016-04-27: First Release

See *http://oreilly.com/catalog/errata.csp?isbn=9781491922064* for release details.

The O'Reilly logo is a registered trademark of O'Reilly Media, Inc. *Optimized C++*, the cover image, and related trade dress are trademarks of O'Reilly Media, Inc.

978-1-491-92206-4

[LSI]

Everyone thanks their spouse for helping make a book possible. It's trite, I know. My wife Renee Ostler made this book possible by giving me permission to take months off work, by giving me time and space to focus on writing, and by staying up late asking me questions about optimizing C++ code, even though she wasn't particularly engaged by the topic, just to show her support. She made this project important to her because it was important to me. No author could ask for more.

Table of Contents

Preface

Hi. My name is Kurt, and I'm a code-aholic.

I have been writing software for over 35 years. I've never worked at Microsoft, or Google, Facebook, Apple, or anywhere else famous. But beyond a few short vacations, I have written code every day of that time. I have spent the last 20 years almost exclusively writing C++ and talking to other very bright developers about C++. This is my qualification to write a book about optimizing C++ code. I have also written *a lot* of English prose, including specifications, comments, manuals, notes, and blog posts (*http://oldhandsblog.blogspot.com*). It has amazed me from time to time that only half of the bright, competent developers I have worked with can string two grammatical English sentences together.

One of my favorite quotes comes by way of a letter from Sir Isaac Newton, in which he writes, "If I have seen farther, it is by standing on the shoulders of giants." I too have stood on the shoulders of giants, and particularly have read their book: elegant little books, like Brian Kernighan and Dennis Ritchie's *The C Programming Language*; smart, ahead-of-the-curve books, like Scott Meyers's *Effective C++* series; challenging, mind-expanding books, like Andrei Alexandrescu's *Modern C++ Design*; careful, precise books, like Bjarne Stroustrup and Margaret Ellis's *The Annotated C++ Reference Manual*. For most of my career, it never crossed my mind that I might someday write a book. Then one day, quite suddenly, I found I needed to write this one.

So why write a book about performance tuning in C++?

At the dawn of the 21st century, C++ was under assault. Fans of C pointed to C++ programs whose performance was inferior to supposedly equivalent code written in C. Famous corporations with big marketing budgets touted proprietary object-oriented languages, claiming C++ was too hard to use, and that their tools were the future. Universities settled on Java for teaching because it came with a free toolchain. As a result of all this buzz, big companies made big-money bets on coding websites and operating systems in Java or C# or PHP. C++ seemed to be on the wane. It was an uncomfortable time for anyone who believed C++ was a powerful, useful tool.

Then a funny thing happened. Processor cores stopped getting faster, but workloads kept growing. Those same companies began hiring C++ programmers to solve their scaling issues. The cost of rewriting code from scratch in C++ became less than the cost of the electricity going into their data centers. All of a sudden, C++ was popular again.

Uniquely among programming languages in wide use in early 2016, C++ offers developers a continuum of implementation choices, ranging from hands-off, automated support to fine manual control. C++ empowers developers to take control of performance trade-offs. This control makes optimization possible.

There are not many books on optimization of C++ code. One of the few is Bulka and Mayhew's meticulously researched but now somewhat dated *Optimizing C++*. The authors appear to have had similar career experiences to mine, and discovered many of the same principles. For readers who are interested in another take on the issues in this book, their book is a good place to start. Also, Scott Meyers, among many others, covers avoiding copy construction extensively and well.

There are enough different things to know about optimization to fill 10 books. I have tried to pick and choose things that seemed to occur frequently in my own work, or that offered the biggest performance wins. To the many readers with their own performance tuning war stories who may wonder why I've said nothing about strategies that worked miracles for them, all I can say is, *so little time, so much to tell*.

I welcome your errata, comments, and favorite optimization strategies at *antelope_book@guntheroth.com*.

I love the craft of software development. I enjoy endlessly practicing the *kata* of each new loop or interface. At the corner of Sonnet and Science, writing code is a skill so esoteric, an art form so internal, that almost nobody but another practitioner can appreciate it. There is beauty in an elegantly coded function, and wisdom in a powerful idiom well used. Sadly, though, for every epic software poem like Stepanov's Standard Template Library, there are 10,000 drab tomes of uninspired code.

The root purpose of this book is to give every reader permission to think a little harder about the beauty of well-tuned software. Take it and run with it. See farther!

Apology for the Code in This Book

Although I have been writing and optimizing C++ code for over 20 years, most of the code appearing in this book was developed specifically *for* this book. Like all new code, it surely contains defects. I offer my apologies.

I have developed for Windows, Linux, and various embedded systems over the years. The code presented in this book was developed on Windows. The code and the book no doubt show a Windows bias. The lessons of how to optimize C++ code that are illustrated using Visual Studio on Windows apply equally to Linux, Mac OS X, or any other C++ environment. However, the precise timings of different optimizations depend on the compiler and standard library implementation, and the processor on which the code is tested. Optimization is an experimental science. Taking optimization advice on faith is fraught with negative surprises.

I am aware that compatibility with various other compilers, and with other Unix and embedded systems, can be challenging, and I apologize if the code does not compile on your favorite system. Since this book is not about cross-system compatibility, I have erred on the side of presenting simple code.

The curly-brace indentation style shown here is not my favorite:

```
if (bool_condition) {
    controlled_statement();
}
```

However, because it has the advantage of putting the most lines possible on the printed page, I have chosen to use it for the examples throughout this book.

Using Code Examples

Supplemental material (code examples, sample solutions, etc.) is available for download at *www.guntheroth.com*.

This book is here to help you get your job done. In general, if example code is offered with this book, you may use it in your programs and documentation. You do not need to contact us for permission unless you're reproducing a significant portion of the code. For example, writing a program that uses several chunks of code from this book does not require permission. Selling or distributing a CD-ROM of examples from O'Reilly books does require permission. Answering a question by citing this book and quoting example code does not require permission. Incorporating a significant amount of example code from this book into your product's documentation does require permission.

We appreciate, but do not require, attribution. An attribution usually includes the title, author, publisher, and ISBN. For example: "*Optimized C++* by Kurt Guntheroth (O'Reilly). Copyright 2016 Kurt Guntheroth, 978-1-491-92206-4."

If you feel your use of code examples falls outside fair use or the permission given above, feel free to contact us at *permissions@oreilly.com*.

Conventions Used in This Book

The following typographical conventions are used in this book:

Plain text
> Used for menu titles, menu options, menu buttons, and keyboard accelerators (such as Alt and Control).

Italic
> Indicates new terms, URLs, email addresses, pathnames, filenames, and file extensions.

`Constant width`
> Used for program listings, as well as within paragraphs to refer to program elements such as variable or function names, databases, data types, environment variables, statements, and keywords.

## CHAPTER 1

An Overview of Optimization

The world has a stupendous appetite for computation. Whether the code you are writing runs on a watch, phone, tablet, workstation, supercomputer, or planet-spanning network of data centers, there are many programs that must run flat-out all the time. So it may not be enough merely to accurately convert the cool idea in your head into lines of code. It may not be enough even to comb the code for defects until it runs correctly all the time. Your application may be sluggish on the kind of hardware your customers can afford. Your hardware team may have saddled you with a tiny processor to meet their power consumption goals. You may be battling a competitor over throughput or frames per second. Or you may be building out to planetary scale and just slightly nervous about boiling the oceans. Enter optimization.

This book is about optimization—specifically, optimizing C++ programs, with particular reference to patterns of behavior of C++ code. Some of the techniques in this book are applicable to other programming languages, but I have made no attempt to explain the techniques in a universal way. Some optimizations that are effective on C++ code have no effect or are simply not possible in other languages.

This book is about taking correct code that embodies best practices of C++ design, and changing it into correct code that still embodies good C++ design but also runs faster and consumes fewer resources on pretty much any computer. Many opportunities for optimization occur because some C++ features, used casually, run slowly and consume many resources. Such code, while correct, is ill-considered, given just a little general knowledge about modern microprocessor devices or a little thought about the costs of various C++ constructs. Other optimizations are available because of the fine control C++ offers over memory management and copying.

This book is *not* about laboriously coding assembly language subroutines, counting clock cycles, or learning how many instructions Intel's latest silicon stylings can dispatch concurrently. There exist developers who work with a single platform (the

Xbox is a good example) for several years, and have the time and the need to master these dark arts. However, the great majority of developers target phones, tablets, or PCs, which contain an endless variety of microprocessor chips—some of which have not yet even been designed. Developers of software embedded into products also face a variety of processors with widely varying architectures. Attempting to learn processor arcana will make most developers crazy and paralyze them with indecision. I don't recommend this path. Processor-dependent optimization is simply not fruitful for most applications, which must by definition run on a variety of processors.

This book is likewise *not* about learning the fastest operating system–dependent way to do some operation on Windows, and again on Linux, OS X, and every embedded operating system. It is about what you can do in C++, including with the C++ standard library. Breaking out of C++ to perform an optimization may make it hard for peers to review or comment on the optimized code. It's not an action to be taken lightly.

This book is about learning *how* to optimize. Any static catalog of techniques or functions is doomed, as new algorithms are discovered and new language features become available. Instead, this book provides several running examples of how code may be improved incrementally, so that the reader becomes familiar with the code tuning process and develops the mindset that makes optimization fruitful.

This book is about optimizing the coding process as well. Developers mindful of the runtime cost of their code can write code that is efficient from the start. With practice, writing fast code usually takes no longer than writing slow code.

Finally, this book is about performing miracles; about checking in a change and later hearing a colleague exclaim in surprise, "Wow, what happened? It just started right up. Who fixed something?" Optimization is something you can also do to your status as a developer and your personal pride in your craft.

Optimization Is Part of Software Development

Optimization is a coding activity. In traditional software development processes, optimization takes place after Code Complete, during the integration and testing phase of a project, when the performance of a whole program can be observed. In an Agile development process, one or more sprints may be allocated to optimization after a feature with performance goals is coded, or as needed to meet performance targets.

The goal of optimization is to improve the behavior of a correct program so that it also meets customer needs for speed, throughput, memory footprint, power consumption, and so on. Optimization is thus as important to the development process as coding features is. Unacceptably poor performance is the same kind of problem for users as bugs and missing features.

One important difference between bug fixing and performance tuning is that performance is a continuous variable. A feature is either coded, or it is not. A bug is either present or absent. However, performance can be very bad or very good or somewhere in between. Optimization is also an iterative process in which each time the slowest part of the program is improved, a new slowest part appears.

Optimization is very much an experimental science, calling for a scientific mindset to a greater degree than some other coding tasks. To be successful at optimization requires observing behavior, forming testable hypotheses based on these observations, and performing experiments that result in measurements that either support or refute the hypotheses. Experienced developers often believe they have valid experience and valid intuitions about optimal code. But unless they frequently test their intuitions, they will frequently be wrong. My personal experiences writing the test programs for this book revealed several results that contradicted my intuitions. Experimentation, rather than intuition, is a theme of this book.

Optimization Is Effective

It is difficult for developers to reason about the effects of individual coding decisions on the overall performance of a large program. Thus, practically all complete programs contain significant opportunities for optimization. Even code produced by experienced teams with plenty of time can often be sped up by a factor of 30%–100%. For more rushed or less experienced teams, I have seen performance improvements of 3 to 10 times. A speedup of more than 10x by tweaking code is less likely. However, selection of a better algorithm or data structure can be the difference between whether a feature can be deployed or is infeasibly slow.

It's OK to Optimize

Many treatments of optimization begin with a stern warning: *don't*! Don't optimize, and if you have to optimize, don't do it until the end of the project, and don't do any more optimizing than you must. For instance, famous computer scientist Donald Knuth said of optimization:

> We should forget about small efficiencies, say about 97 percent of the time: premature optimization is the root of all evil.
>
> —Donald Knuth, *Structured Programming with go to Statements*, ACM Computing Surveys 6(4), December 1974, p268. CiteSeerX: 10.1.1.103.6084 (*http://bit.ly/ knuth-1974*)

Or this from William A. Wulf:

> More computing sins are committed in the name of efficiency (without necessarily achieving it) than for any other single reason—including blind stupidity.
>
> —"A Case Against the GOTO," *Proceedings of the 25th National ACM Conference* (1972): 796

The advice not to optimize has become received wisdom, unquestioned even by many experienced coders, who wince reflexively when conversation turns to performance tuning. I think cynical promotion of this advice has been used too often to excuse weak development habits and avoid the small amount of analysis that might result in vastly faster code. I also think uncritical acceptance of this advice is responsible for a lot of wasted CPU cycles, a lot of frustrated user-hours, and too much time spent reworking code that should have been more efficient from the start.

My advice is less dogmatic. It is OK to optimize. It is OK to learn efficient programming idioms, and to apply them all the time, even if you don't know what code is performance-critical. These idioms are good C++. You won't be disrespected by your peers for having used them. If somebody asks why you didn't write something "simple" and inefficient, you may say, "It takes the same amount of time to write efficient code as slow, wasteful code. Why would anyone choose deliberately to write inefficient code?"

What's not OK is to make no progress for days because you can't decide which algorithm will be better, when you don't know that it matters. What's not OK is to spend weeks coding something in assembler because you guess it *might* be time-critical, then spoil the whole effort by calling your code as a function when the C++ compiler might have inlined it for you. What's not OK is to demand that your team code half their program in C because "everybody knows C is faster," when you do not in fact know either that C really is faster, or that C++ isn't fast. In other words, all the best practices of software development still apply. Optimization isn't an excuse to break the rules.

It's not OK to waste a bunch of extra time on optimization when you don't know where you have performance problems. Chapter 3 introduces the 90/10 rule, the notion that only about 10% of a program's code is performance-critical. It is thus neither necessary nor helpful to change every line of a program in order to improve the program's performance. Since only 10% of the program has a significant impact on performance, your chances of picking a good starting point at random are poor. Chapter 3 provides tools to help determine where the hot spots in the code are.

When I was in college, my professors warned that optimal algorithms might have a higher startup cost than simple ones. They should therefore only be used on large data sets. Although that's possibly true for some esoteric algorithms, my experience is that optimal algorithms for simple searching and sorting tasks take little time to set up, and they give a performance improvement even on small data sets.

I have also been advised to develop programs using whatever algorithm is easiest to code, and then go back and optimize it if the program runs too slowly. While it is undeniably good advice to continue making progress, once you have coded an optimal search or sort a couple of times, it is no more difficult to get running than a slower algorithm. You might as well do it right the first time and debug only one algorithm.

Received wisdom is, in fact, probably the single greatest enemy of performance improvement efforts. For instance, "everybody knows" that an optimal sort algorithm runs in $O(n \ log \ n)$ time, where n is the size of the data set (see "Time Cost of Algorithms" on page 92 for a brief review of the big-O notation and time cost). This received wisdom is valuable to the extent that it keeps developers from believing their $O(n^2)$ insertion sort is optimal, but not so good if it prevents them from checking the literature to find out that radix sort is faster at $O(n \ log_r \ n)$ (where r is the radix or number of sorting buckets), that flashsort has even faster $O(n)$ performance on randomly distributed data, or that quicksort, which received wisdom makes the benchmark against which other sorts are measured, has painfully bad $O(n^2)$ worst-case performance. Aristotle said that women had fewer teeth than men (*The History of Animals*, Book II, part 1 (*http://bit.ly/aristotle-animals*)), a bit of received wisdom that stood for 1,500 years before someone was curious enough to count the teeth in a few mouths. The antidote to received wisdom is the scientific method, in the form of experimentation. Chapter 3 covers instruments to measure software performance and experiments to validate optimizations.

There is also received wisdom in the software development world that optimization is not relevant. The reasoning goes that even if your code runs slowly today, each new year brings faster processors, solving your performance problems for free through the passage of time. Like most received wisdom, this nugget of thought was never really true. It might have seemed true in the 1980s and 1990s, when desktop computers and standalone applications dominated the development scene and single-core processors doubled in speed every 18 months. But while today's multicore processors continue to become more powerful in the aggregate, the performance of individual cores improves only gradually, or sometimes even declines. Programs today must also run on mobile platforms, where battery life and heat dissipation constrain the instruction execution rate. Furthermore, while time may bring new customers with faster computers, it does nothing to improve the performance of existing hardware. Existing customers' workloads are all that is increasing with time. The only speed upgrade an existing customer will ever get from your company comes from optimizing subsequent releases. Optimization keeps your program fresh.

A Nanosecond Here, a Nanosecond There

A billion here, a billion there, pretty soon you're talking real money.

—Frequently misattributed to Senator Everett Dirkson (1898–1969), who claims he never said this, though he admits saying a lot of things like it

Desktop computers are astonishingly fast. They can dispatch a new instruction every nanosecond (or better). That's every 10^{-9} seconds! It is seductively appealing to believe that optimization cannot possibly matter when a computer is so fast.

The problem with this way of thinking is that the faster the processor is, the faster wasted instructions pile up. If 50% of the instructions executed by a program are unnecessary, that program can be made to run twice as fast by removing them, no matter how rapidly each unnecessary instruction is executed.

Your colleagues who say "efficiency doesn't matter" may also mean it doesn't matter for certain applications, which are human response–bound and run on desktop computers that are already very fast. Efficiency matters very much on small embedded and mobile processors with memory, power, or speed constraints. It also matters on servers running flat-out on big computers. Another way to say this is that efficiency matters for any application that must contend for constrained resources (memory, power, CPU cycles). Efficiency matters a great deal, too, any time your workload is big enough to be spread across multiple computers. In this case, efficiency can be the difference between spending on 100 servers or cloud instances versus 500 or 1,000.

In 50 years, computer performance has improved by six orders of magnitude. And yet, here we are talking about optimization. If the past is any guide, optimization will likely remain relevant far into the future.

Summary of Strategies for Optimizing C++ Code

Round up the usual suspects.

—Capt. Louis Renault (Claude Rains), *Casablanca*, 1942

The mix of features in C++ provides a continuum of implementation choices ranging from hands-off automation and expressiveness on one hand, to increasingly fine control over performance on the other hand. It is this degree of choice that makes it possible to tune C++ programs to meet requirements for performance.

C++ has its "usual suspects" for optimization hot spots, including function calls, memory allocation, and loops. The following is a summary list of ways to improve the performance of C++ programs, which is also an outline of this book. The advice is shockingly simple. All of it has been published before. But of course, the devil is in the details. The examples and heuristics in this book will help you better recognize optimization opportunities when you see them.

Use a Better Compiler, Use Your Compiler Better

C++ compilers are complex software artifacts. Each compiler makes different decisions about what machine code to generate for C++ statements. They see different opportunities for optimization. They will produce different executables from the same source code. If you are squeezing the last iota of performance from your code, it may be worthwhile to try several compilers to see if one produces a faster executable for your code.

The most important advice about which C++ compiler to pick is *use a compiler conforming to C++11*. C++11 implements rvalue references and move semantics that eliminate many copy operations that were unavoidable with previous C++ versions. (Move semantics are discussed in "Implement Move Semantics" on page 137.)

Sometimes *using a better compiler* means *using your compiler better*. For instance, if your application seems sluggish, have a look at the compiler switches to see if the optimizer is turned on. This seems totally obvious, but I can't count the number of times I have given this advice to people who subsequently admitted that, yes, their code ran much faster when compiled with optimization turned on. In many cases, you need go no further. The compiler alone may make your program several times faster if you ask it nicely.

By default, most compilers don't turn on any optimizations. Compile times are slightly shorter without the optimization pass. This was a big deal in the 1990s, but nowadays compilers and computers are so fast that the extra cost is insignificant. Debugging is also simpler with the optimizer turned off because the flow of execution exactly follows the source code. The optimizer may move code out of loops, remove some function calls, and remove some variables altogether. Some compilers won't emit debug symbols at all when optimization is turned on. Other compilers are more generous, but understanding what the program is doing by watching the flow of execution in the debugger can be challenging. Many compilers allow individual optimizations to be turned on and off in a debug build without affecting debugging too much. Just turning on function inlining can have a significant impact on a C++ program because good C++ style includes writing many small member functions to access the member variables of each class.

The documentation that comes with a C++ compiler contains an extensive description of the optimization flags and pragmas available. This documentation is like the owner's manual that comes with a new car. You can get in your new car and drive it without reading the manual, but there is a lot of information there that might help you use this big, complicated tool more effectively.

If you are lucky enough to be developing for the x86 architecture on Windows or Linux, you have a choice of several excellent compilers under very active development. Microsoft pushed out three versions of Visual C++ in the five years before this book was written. GCC releases more than one version a year.

As of early 2016, there is reasonable consensus that Intel's C++ compiler generates the tightest code on both Linux and Windows, that the GNU C++ compiler GCC has lower performance but excellent standards conformance, and that Microsoft's Visual C++ is in between. I would love to help your decision making by producing a little chart that says Intel C++ generates code that is so many percent faster than GCC, but it depends on your code, and on who has just pushed out a souped-up release. Intel C++ costs over a thousand dollars, but offers a 30-day free trial. There are free express versions of Visual C++. On Linux, GCC is always free. It is inexpensive to perform a little experiment, trying each compiler on your code to see if any give a performance advantage.

Use Better Algorithms

The biggest bang for the optimization buck comes from choosing an optimal algorithm. Optimization efforts can improve the performance of a program in a dramatic fashion. They can put zip into code that seemed sluggish before, just as upgrading your PC makes applications run faster. Unfortunately, just like upgrading your PC, most optimizations improve performance by at most a constant factor. Many optimization efforts give an improvement of 30%–100%. If you are lucky, you might triple your performance. But a quantum leap in performance is unlikely—unless you can locate a more efficient algorithm.

Optimization War Story

Back in the days of 8-inch floppies and 1 MHz processors, a certain developer designed a program to manage radio stations. One aspect of this program was to produce a sorted log of the songs played each day. The trouble was, it took about 27 hours to sort a day's worth of data, which was obviously unacceptable. To get this important sort to run faster, the developer resorted to heroic feats. He reverse engineered the computer and hacked into the microcode by undocumented means. He microcoded an in-memory sort that reduced run time to a still-unacceptable 17 hours. Desperate, he called the computer manufacturer, for whom I worked, for assistance.

I asked the developer what sorting algorithm he was using. He said, "Merge sort." Merge sort is a member of the family of optimal comparison sorting algorithms. How many records was he sorting? "A few thousand," he replied. This made no sense. The system he was using should have been able to sort his data in less than an hour.

I thought to ask the developer to describe his sort algorithm in detail. I can no longer recall the tortured words that followed, but it turned out the developer had implemented an insertion sort. Insertion sort is a poor choice, taking time proportional to the square of the number of records to be sorted (see "Time Cost of Sorting Algorithms" on page 99). He knew there was something called merge sort, and that it was optimal. He had found a way to describe his insertion sort using the words "merge" and "sort."

I coded a very conventional sort routine for this customer, using a real merge sort. It sorted his data in 45 minutes.

It is foolish to struggle heroically to optimize a bad algorithm. Learning and using optimal algorithms for searching and sorting is a broad path to optimal code. An inefficient search or sort routine can completely dominate the running time of a program. Code tweaking cuts run time by a constant factor. Switching to a more optimal algorithm can cut run time by a factor that grows bigger the bigger your data set is. Even on small data sets of a dozen items an optimal search or sort can save a bunch of time if the data is searched frequently. Chapter 5, *Optimize Algorithms* contains some guidance on what optimal algorithms look like.

Chances to use optimal algorithms come in all sizes, from compact little closed-form computations, to tight keyword search functions, to complex data structures and massive programs. There are many excellent books covering this subject. Whole careers can be spent studying it. I regret that I can only touch lightly on the topic of optimal algorithms in this book.

"Optimization Patterns" on page 100 covers several important techniques for improving performance; these include *precomputation* (moving computation from run time to link, compile, or design time), *lazy computation* (moving computation toward the point where a sometimes unused result is actually needed), and *caching* (saving and reusing expensive computations). Chapter 7, *Optimize Hot Statements* adds many examples of these techniques in practice.

Use Better Libraries

The standard C++ template and runtime libraries that come with a C++ compiler must be maintainable, general, and very robust. It may come as a surprise to developers that these libraries are not necessarily tuned for speed. It may come as an even greater surprise that even after 30 years of C++, the libraries that come with commercial C++ compilers still contain bugs, and may not conform to the current C++ standard, or even to the standard in force when the compiler was released. This complicates the task of measuring or recommending optimizations, and makes nonportable any optimization experience developers believe they have. Chapter 8, *Use Better Libraries* covers these issues.

Mastery of the C++ standard library is a critical skill for the optimizing developer. This book provides recommendations for algorithms for searching and sorting (Chapter 9, *Optimize Searching and Sorting*), optimal idioms of use of container classes (Chapter 10, *Optimize Data Structures*), I/O (Chapter 11, *Optimize I/O*), concurrency (Chapter 12, *Optimize Concurrency*), and memory management (Chapter 13, *Optimize Memory Management*).

There are open source libraries for important functions like memory management (see "High-Performance Memory Managers" on page 333) that provide sophisticated implementations that can be faster and more capable than what's provided by a vendor's C++ runtime library. The advantage of these alternative libraries is that they may be easy to drop into an existing project, and provide an immediate speed improvement.

There are many publicly available libraries from the Boost project (*http://www.boost.org*) and Google Code (*https://code.google.com*), among many others, that provide libraries for things such as I/O, windowing, string handling (see "Adopt a novel string implementation" on page 85) and concurrency (see "Concurrency Libraries" on page 320) that are not drop-in replacements for the standard libraries but offer improved performance and added features. These libraries gain part of their speed advantage from making different design trade-offs than the ones made for the standard library.

Finally, it is possible to develop a project-specific library that relaxes some of the safety and robustness constraints of the standard library in exchange for a speed advantage. All these topics are covered in Chapter 8, *Use Better Libraries*.

Function calls are expensive in several ways (see "Cost of Function Calls" on page 161). Good function library APIs provide functions that reflect the idioms of use of these APIs, so that the user doesn't have to make unnecessarily frequent calls to the most fundamental functions. For instance, an API that gets characters and provides only a `get_char()` function requires the user to spend a function call for each character needed. If the API also provides a `get_buffer()` function, the API can avoid the expense of calling a function for each character.

Function and class libraries are good places to hide the complexity that sometimes comes with highly tuned programs. Libraries should pay your program back for the cost of calling into them by doing work with maximum efficiency. Library functions are quite likely to be at the bottom of deeply nested calling chains, where the effect of improved performance is magnified.

Reduce Memory Allocation and Copying

Reducing calls into the memory manager is such an effective optimization that a developer can be a successful optimizer knowing only this one trick. While the cost of most C++ language features is at most a few instructions, the cost of each call into the memory manager is measured in thousands of instructions.

Because strings are such an important (and costly) part of many C++ programs, I have devoted a whole chapter to them as a case study in optimization. Chapter 4, *Optimize String Use: A Case Study* introduces and motivates many optimization concepts within the familiar context of string handling. Chapter 6, *Optimize Dynamically Allocated Variables* is devoted to reducing the cost of dynamic memory allocation without giving up useful C++ programming idioms like strings and standard library containers.

A single call to a buffer-copying function may also consume thousands of cycles. Doing less copying is thus an obvious way to speed up your code. A lot of copying happens in association with memory allocation, so fixing one often does away with the other. Other hot spots for copying are constructors and assignment operators, and input/output. Chapter 6, *Optimize Dynamically Allocated Variables* covers this subject.

Remove Computation

Aside from allocation and function calls, the cost of a single C++ statement is generally insignificant. But execute that same code a million times in a loop, or every time a program processes an event, and suddenly it's a big deal. Most programs have one or more main event processing loops, and one or more functions that process characters. Identifying and optimizing these loops is almost always fruitful. Chapter 7, *Optimize Hot Statements* offers some advice on how to find frequently executed code. You can bet it will always be in a loop.

The literature on optimization contains a cornucopia of techniques for using individual C++ statements efficiently. Many programmers believe that knowledge of these tricks is the bread and butter of optimization. The problem with this thinking is that, unless the code is extremely hot (frequently executed), removing one or two memory accesses from it does not make a measurable difference in overall performance. Chapter 3, *Measure Performance* contains techniques to determine what parts of a program are frequently executed, before attempting to reduce the amount of computation in these places.

It is also the case that modern C++ compilers do a really outstanding job of finding these local improvements. Developers should therefore attempt not to go all OCD on a big code base changing every occurrence of i++ to ++i, unrolling all the loops, and breathlessly explaining to each colleague exactly what Duff's device is and why it's so cool. Still, I take a brief look into this cornucopia in Chapter 7, *Optimize Hot Statements*.

Use Better Data Structures

Selecting the most appropriate data structure has a profound effect on performance. This is partly because the algorithms for inserting, iterating, sorting, and retrieving entries have a runtime cost that depends on the data structure. In addition, different data structures make differing use of the memory manager. It is also partly because the data structure may have good cache locality, or not. Chapter 10, *Optimize Data Structures* explores the performance, behavior, and trade-offs among data structures provided by the C++ standard library. Chapter 9, *Optimize Searching and Sorting* discusses use of standard library algorithms to implement table data structures on top of simple vectors and C arrays.

Increase Concurrency

Most programs must wait for activities taking place in the tiresome, lumbering world of physical reality to complete. They must wait for files to be read off mechanical disks, pages to be returned from the Internet, or users' slow fingers to press mechanical key switches. Any time a program's forward progress is blocked waiting for such an event is a wasted opportunity to perform some other computation.

Modern computers have more than one processor core available to execute instructions. If work is parceled out to several processors, it can be completed sooner.

Along with concurrent execution come tools for synchronizing concurrent threads so that they can share data. These tools can be used well or poorly. Chapter 12, *Optimize Concurrency* covers some considerations in synchronizing concurrent threads of control efficiently.

Optimize Memory Management

The memory manager, the part of the C++ runtime library that manages the allocation of dynamic memory, is frequently executed code in many C++ programs. C++ has an extensive API for memory management, though most developers have never used it. Chapter 13, *Optimize Memory Management* shows some techniques for improving the performance of memory management.

Summary

This book helps the developer identify and exploit the following opportunities to improve code performance:

- *Use better compilers, and turn on the optimizer.*

- *Use optimal algorithms.*
- *Use better libraries, and use libraries better.*
- *Reduce memory allocation.*
- *Reduce copying.*
- *Remove computation.*
- *Use optimal data structures.*
- *Increase concurrency.*
- *Optimize memory management.*

As I said, the devil is in the details. Let's press on.

## CHAPTER 2

Computer Behavior Affecting Optimization

Lying, the telling of beautiful untrue things, is the proper aim of Art.

—Oscar Wilde, "The Decay of Lying," *Intentions* (1891)

The purpose of this chapter is to provide the bare minimum of background information about computer hardware to motivate the optimizations described in this book, to prevent readers going mad poring over 600-page processor handbooks. It takes a superficial look at processor architecture to extract some heuristics to guide optimization efforts. The very impatient reader might skip this chapter for now and return when other chapters refer to it, though the information here is important and useful.

Microprocessor devices in current use are incredibly diverse. They range from sub-$1 embedded devices with just a few thousand gates and clock rates below 1 MHz to desktop-class devices with billions of gates and gigahertz clocks. Mainframe computers can be the size of a large room, containing thousands of independent execution units and drawing enough electrical power to light a small city. It is tempting to believe that nothing connects this profusion of computing devices that would lead to usable generalizations. In reality, though, they have useful similarities. After all, if there were no similarities, it would not be possible to compile C++ code for the many processors for which there are compilers.

All computers in wide use execute instructions stored in memory. The instructions act upon data that is also stored in memory. The memory is divided into many small *words* of a few bits each. A few precious memory words are *registers*, which are directly named in machine instructions. Most memory words are named by a numerical *address*. A particular register in each computer contains the address of the next instruction to execute. If the memory is like a book, the *execution address* is like a finger pointing to the next word to read. An *execution unit* (also called processor, core, CPU, computer, and a bunch of other names) reads a stream of instructions from the memory and acts upon them. The instructions tell the execution unit what data to read (load, fetch) from memory, how to act upon the data, and what results to write (store, save) to memory. The computer is made up of devices that obey physical laws. It takes some nonzero amount of time to read or write each memory address, and time for an instruction to transform the data upon which it acts.

Beyond this basic outline, familiar to any first-year computer science major, the family tree of computer architectures grows in a riot of profusion. Because computer architectures are so variable, rigorous numerical rules regarding hardware behavior are hard to come by. Modern processors do so many different, interacting things to speed up instruction execution that instruction timing has become for all intents and purposes nondeterministic. Couple that with the problem that many developers don't even know precisely what processors their code will run on, and heuristics are the most you can expect.

Lies C++ Believes About Computers

Of course, a C++ program at least pretends to believe in a version of the simple model of the computer laid out in the previous section. There is memory, addressable in char-sized bytes, which is essentially infinite. A special address called nullptr exists, which is different from any valid memory address. Integer 0 converts to nullptr, though nullptr is not necessarily at address 0. There is a single conceptual execution address pointing to the source code statement that is currently being executed. Statements are executed in the order in which they are written, subject to the effects of C++ flow of control statements.

C++ knows that computers are really more complex than this simple model. It offers a few glimpses under the cover at the glittering machinery within:

- A C++ program only has to behave "as if" statements were executed in order. The C++ compiler and the computer itself may change the execution order to make the program run faster, as long as the meaning of any computation is not changed.

- As of C++11, C++ no longer believes that there is only a single execution address. The C++ standard library now comes with facilities for starting and stopping threads, and synchronizing access to memory between threads. Before C++11, programmers lied to the C++ compiler about their threads, sometimes leading to difficult-to-debug problems.

- Certain memory addresses may be device registers instead of ordinary memory. The values at these addresses may change during the interval between two consecutive reads of the location by the same thread, indicating some change in the hardware. Such locations are described to C++ as volatile. Declaring a variable volatile requires the compiler to fetch a new copy of the variable every time it is used, rather than optimizing the program by saving the value in a register and reusing it. Pointers to `volatile` memory may also be declared.

- C++11 offers a magical spell called `std::atomic<>` that causes memory to behave for just a moment as if it really was a simple linear store of bytes, wishing away all the complexities of modern microprocessors, with their multiple threads of execution, multilayer memory caches, and so on. Some developers think this is what `volatile` is for. They are mistaken.

The operating system also lies to programs and their users. In fact, the whole purpose of an operating system is to tell each program a set of very convincing lies. Among the most important lies the OS wants each program to believe are that the program is alone on the computer, that the physical memory is infinite, and that there are an infinite number of processors available for running the program's threads.

The operating system uses the computer's hardware to hide its lies, so that the C++ program really has no choice but to believe them. These lies don't generally affect the running program very much except to slow it down. However, they can complicate performance measurements.

The Truth About Computers

Only the simplest microprocessors and certain historical mainframe computers correspond directly to the C++ model. Importantly for optimization, the actual memory hardware of real computers is very slow compared to the instruction execution rate, the memory is not really accessed in bytes, the memory is not a simple linear array of identical cells, and it has a finite capacity. Real computers may have more than one instruction address. Real computers are fast, not because they execute each instruction quickly, but because they overlap execution of many instructions at the same time and contain intricate circuitry to ensure that overlapping instructions behave as if they execute one after the other.

Memory Is Slow

The main memory of a computer is very slow compared to its internal gates and registers. Pouring electrons out of the microprocessor chip into the relative vastness of a copper circuit board trace, and then pushing them down the trace to a memory chip several centimeters away, takes thousands of times as long as moving electrons across the minute distances separating transistors within the microprocessor. Main memory is so slow that a desktop processor can execute hundreds of instructions in the length of time it takes to fetch a single data word from main memory.

The implication for optimization is that *access to memory dominates other costs in a processor*, including the cost of executing instructions.

The von Neumann Bottleneck

The interface to main memory is a choke point that limits execution speed. This choke point even has a name. It's called the *von Neumann bottleneck*, after famous computer architecture pioneer and mathematician John von Neumann (1903–1957).

For example, a PC using DDR2 memory devices running at 1,000 MHz (typical of computers a few years ago, and easy to compute with) has a theoretical bandwidth of 2 billion words per second, or 500 picoseconds (ps) per word. But that doesn't mean the computer can read or write a random word of data every 500 picoseconds.

First, only sequential accesses can complete in one cycle (one-half of a tick of the 1,000 MHz clock). Access to a nonsequential location completes in somewhere between 6 and 10 cycles.

Several activities contend for access to the memory bus. The processor continually fetches memory containing the next instructions to be executed. The cache memory controller fetches data memory blocks for the cache, and flushes written cache lines. The DRAM controller also steals cycles to refresh the charge in the dynamic RAM cells of the memory device. The number of cores in a multicore processor is sufficient to guarantee that the memory bus is saturated with traffic. The actual rate at which data can be read from main memory into a particular core is more like 20–80 nanoseconds (ns) per word.

Moore's Law makes it possible to put more cores in a microprocessor each year. But it does little to make the interface to main memory faster. Thus, doubling the number of cores in the future will have a diminishing effect on performance. The cores will all be starved for access to memory. This looming limit on performance is called the *memory wall*.

Memory Is Not Accessed in Bytes

Although C++ believes every byte is separately accessible, computers often compensate for slow physical memory by fetching data in bigger chunks. The smallest processors may fetch a byte at a time from main memory. Desktop-class processors may fetch 64 bytes at once. Some supercomputers and graphics processors fetch even more.

When C++ fetches a multibyte data type like an `int`, `double`, or pointer, it may be that the bytes making up that data span two physical memory words. This is called an *unaligned memory access*. The implication for optimization is that *an unaligned access takes twice as long as if all the bytes were in the same word*, because two words must be

---

read. The C++ compiler works to align structs so that every field begins on a byte address that is a multiple of the field's size. But this creates its own problem: "holes" in the structs containing unused data. Paying attention to the size of data fields and their order in the struct can result in structs that are as compact as possible while still being aligned.

Some Memory Accesses Are Slower than Others

To further compensate for slow main memory, many computers contain *cache memory*, a kind of fast temporary storage located very close to the processor, to speed up access to the most frequently used memory words. Some computers have no cache; others have one or several levels of cache, each smaller, faster, and more expensive than the one before. When an execution unit requests bytes from a cached memory word, the bytes may be fetched rapidly without accessing main memory again. How much faster is cache memory? A rule of thumb is that each level of cache memory is about 10 times faster than the one below it in the memory hierarchy. On desktop-class processors, the time cost of a memory access can vary across five orders of magnitude depending on whether the data being accessed is in first-, second-, or third-level cache, in main memory, or on a virtual memory page on disk. This is one reason why obsessing over instruction clock cycles and other arcana is so often maddening and unhelpful; the state of the cache makes instruction execution times largely nondeterministic.

When an execution unit needs to fetch data that is not in the cache, some data that is currently in cache must be discarded to make room. The data selected to be discarded is generally the least recently used data. This matters to optimization because it means *heavily used memory locations can be accessed more quickly than less heavily used locations.*

Reading even one byte of data that is not in cache causes many nearby bytes to be cached as well (as a consequence, this also means that many bytes currently in the cache are discarded). These nearby bytes are then ready for quick access. For optimization, this is important because it means *memory in adjacent locations can be accessed more quickly (on average) than memory in distant locations.*

In C++ terms, the implication is that a block of code containing a loop may execute faster because instructions making up the loop are heavily used and close together, and thus likely to stay in cache. A block of code containing function calls or if statements that causes execution to hop around may execute more slowly because individual parts of the code are less heavily used, and not close together. Such a code block uses up more cache space than a tight loop. If the program is large and the cache is finite, some of the code must be discarded from the cache to make room for other things, slowing access the next time that code is needed. Similarly, a data structure consisting of consecutive locations, like an array or vector, may be faster to access than a data structure consisting of nodes linked by pointers, because data in consecutive locations remains in a small number of cache locations. Accessing a data structure consisting of records connected by pointers (e.g., a list or tree) may be slower because of the need to read data for each node from main memory into new cache lines.

Memory Words Have a Big End and a Little End

A single byte of data can be fetched from memory, but often what happens is that several consecutive bytes are fetched together to form a number. For instance, in Microsoft's Visual C++, four bytes fetched together form an int. Because the same memory can be accessed in two different ways, the people who design computers have to answer a question. Does the first byte—the one whose byte address is smallest—form the most significant bits of the int, or the least significant bits?

At first it seems like this couldn't possibly matter. Of course, it's important that every part of a given computer agrees on which end of the int goes at the lowest address, or chaos reigns. And sure, it's possible to *tell* the difference. If the int value 0x01234567 is stored at addresses 1000–1003, and the little end is stored first, address 1000 holds the byte 0x01 and address 1003 holds the byte 0x67, whereas if the big end is stored first, address 1000 holds 0x67 and the 0x01 is at address 1003. Computers that read the most significant bits at the first byte address are called *big-endian*. *Little-endian* computers read the least significant bits first. There are two ways to store an integer (or pointer), and no reason to choose one over the other, so different teams working on different processors for different companies may choose differently.

The problem comes when data written on disk or sent over a network by one computer must be read by a different computer. Disks and networks send a byte at a time, not a whole int at a time. So it matters which end is stored or sent first. If the sending computer and the receiving computer don't agree, the value sent as 0x01234567 is received as 0x67452301, a very different value indeed.

Endian-ness is just one of the reasons why C++ cannot specify the way bits are laid out in an int, or how setting one field in a union affects the other fields. It's one reason why programs can be written that work on one kind of computer but crash on another.

Memory Has Finite Capacity

The memory in a computer is not, in fact, infinite. To maintain the illusion of infinite memory, the operating system can use the physical memory like a cache memory, and store data that doesn't fit into physical memory as a file on disk. This scheme is called *virtual memory*. Virtual memory produces the illusion of more physical memory.

However, retrieving a block of memory from disk takes dozens of milliseconds—an eternity for a modern computer.

Making cache memory fast is expensive. There may be gigabytes of main memory in a desktop computer or smartphone, but only a few million bytes of cache. Programs and their data don't generally fit into the cache.

One effect of all this caching and virtual memory is that *due to caching, a particular function running in the context of a whole program may run slower than the same function running in a test harness* 10,000 times to measure its performance. In the context of the whole program, the function and its data are not likely to be in cache. In the context of the test, they generally are. This effect magnifies the benefit of optimizations that reduce the use of memory or disk, while leaving unchanged the benefit of optimizations that reduce code size.

A second effect of caching is that if a big program is making scattered accesses to many memory locations, there may not be sufficient cache memory to hold the data being immediately used by the program. This causes a kind of performance meltdown called *page thrashing*. When page thrashing happens in a microprocessor's internal cache, the result is reduced performance. When it happens in the operating system's virtual memory file, performance drops a thousandfold. This problem was more common when physical memory was less plentiful, but it still happens.

Instruction Execution Is Slow

Simple microprocessors of the sort embedded in coffee makers and microwave ovens are designed to execute instructions as fast as they can be fetched from memory. Desktop-class microprocessors have additional resources to process many instructions concurrently, so they are capable of executing instructions many times faster than they can be fetched from main memory, relying on a fast cache memory to feed their execution units most of the time. The significance of this to optimization is that *memory access dominates the cost of computation.*

Modern desktop-class computers execute instructions at an awesome rate *if* nothing gets in the way. They can complete an instruction every few hundred picoseconds (a picosecond is 10^{-12} seconds, a ridiculously short time). But that doesn't mean that each instruction only takes picoseconds to perform. The processor contains a "pipeline" of instructions that it is working on concurrently. Instructions work their way through the pipeline, being decoded, getting their arguments, performing their computations, and saving their results. The more powerful the processor, the more complicated this pipeline becomes, breaking instruction execution into a dozen phases so that more instructions can be concurrently processed.

If instruction A computes a value needed by instruction B, then instruction B can't do its computation until instruction A produces its result. This causes a *pipeline stall*, a brief pause in instruction execution that occurs because execution of the two instructions can't be fully overlapped. The pipeline stall is particularly long if instruction A fetches a value from memory, then performs a computation that produces a value needed by instruction B. Pipeline stalls defeat all the fancy machinery of the microprocessor, making it nearly as slow as the processor in your toaster from time to time.

Making Decisions Is Hard for Computers

Another thing that can cause a pipeline stall is when the computer needs to make a decision. After most instructions, execution continues with the instruction at the next memory address. Most of the time, this next instruction is already in cache. Consecutive instructions can be fed into the pipeline as soon as the first pipeline stage becomes available.

Transfer-of-control instructions are different. A jump or jump-to-subroutine instruction changes the execution address to an arbitrary new value. The "next" instruction cannot be read from memory and put in the pipeline until the execution address is updated, some time during processing of the jump instruction. The memory word at the new execution address is less likely to be in cache. The pipeline stalls while the execution address is updated and the new "next" instruction is loaded into the pipeline.

After a conditional branch instruction, execution continues in one of two different places: either the next instruction or else the instruction at the address that is the branch target, depending upon the result of some previous computation. The pipeline stalls until all instructions involved in the previous computation complete, and remains stalled while the next execution address is determined and the value at that address is fetched.

The significance of this for optimization is that *computation is faster than decision*.

There Are Multiple Streams of Program Execution

Any program running on a modern operating system shares the computer with other programs running at the same time, with periodic maintenance processes checking the disk or looking for Java or Flash updates, and with the various parts of the operating system that control the network interface, disks, sound devices, accelerometers, thermometers, and other peripherals. *Every program competes with other programs for the computer's resources.*

A program generally doesn't notice this too much. It just runs a little slower. An exception occurs, however, when many programs start simultaneously and all compete for the memory and disk. For performance tuning, *if a program must run at startup, or at times of peak load, performance must be measured under load.*

As of early 2016, desktop computers have up to 16 processor cores. The microprocessors used in phones and tablets have up to eight. A quick look at the Windows Task Manager, Linux's process status output, or Android's task list typically shows there are a great many more software processes than this, and most processes have multiple threads of execution. The operating system runs each thread for a short time, then switches contexts to another thread or process. To the program, it is as if one statement took a nanosecond, and the next statement took 60 milliseconds.

What does it mean to switch contexts? If the operating system is switching from one thread to another thread in the same program, it means saving the processor's registers for the thread being suspended, and loading the saved registers for the thread being resumed. The registers of a modern processor contain hundreds of bytes of data. When the new thread resumes execution, its data may not be in cache, so there is an initial period of slow execution while the new context is loaded into cache. There is thus a considerable cost to switching thread contexts.

When the operating system switches context from one program to another, the procedure is even more expensive. All dirty cache pages (ones with written data that has not reached main memory) must be flushed to physical memory. All the processor registers are saved. Then the physical-to-virtual memory page registers in the memory manager are saved. Next, the physical-to-virtual memory page registers for the new process are reloaded, and the processor registers for the new process are reloaded. Finally, execution can resume. But the cache is empty, so there is an initial period of slow performance and heavy memory contention while the cache is refilled.

When a program must wait for some event to occur, it may continue to wait even after the event occurs until the operating system makes a processor available to continue the program. This can make the program run time longer and more variable when the program runs in the context of other programs competing for the computer's resources.

The execution units of a multicore processor and their associated cache memories act more or less independently of one another to achieve better performance. However, all execution units share the same main memory. Execution units must compete for access to the hardware linking them to main memory, making the von Neumann bottleneck even more limiting in a computer with multiple execution units.

When an execution unit writes a value, the value goes first into cache memory. It eventually has to be written through the cache all the way to main memory, so that the value is visible to other execution units. But because of contention for access to main memory among the execution units, main memory may not be updated until hundreds of instructions after the execution unit changes a value.

If the computer has multiple execution units, one execution unit may thus not see the data written by another execution unit change in main memory for an extended period of time, and changes to main memory may not occur in the same order as instruction execution order. Depending upon unpredictable timing factors, an execution unit may see either the old value of a shared memory word or the updated value. Special synchronization instructions must be used to ensure that threads running in different execution units see a consistent view of memory. The significance of this to optimization is that *it's much slower to access* data shared between threads of execution than unshared data.

Calling into the Operating System Is Expensive

All but the smallest processors have hardware to enforce isolation between programs, so that program A can't read, write, or execute in physical memory belonging to program B. The same hardware protects the kernel of the operating system from being overwritten by programs. The OS kernel, on the other hand, needs to access memory belonging to every program, so the programs can make system calls into the operating system. Some operating systems also allow programs to make requests to share memory. The many ways system calls occur and shared memory is arranged are varied and arcane. The significance for optimization is that *system calls are expensive*; hundreds of times more expensive than function calls within a single thread of one program.

C++ Tells Lies Too

The biggest lie C++ tells its users is that the computer it runs on has a simple, consistent structure. In exchange for pretending to believe this lie, C++ lets developers program without having to learn the intimate details of every microprocessor device, like they would have to do to program in brutally honest assembly language.

All Statements Are Not Equally Expensive

In the peaceful, bygone days of Kernighan and Ritchie's C programming, every statement was about as expensive as every other statement. A function call might contain an arbitrarily complex computation. However, an assignment statement generally copied something that fit in a machine register into something else that fit into a machine register. Thus, the statement:

```
int i,j;

...

i = j;
```

copied 2 or 4 bytes from j to i. The declaration could be `int` or `float` or `struct big struct *`, but the assignment statement still did about the same amount of work.

This is no longer true. In C++, assigning one int to another is exactly the same amount of work as the corresponding C statement. But a statement like BigInstance i = OtherObject; can copy whole structures. More significantly, this kind of assignment invokes a constructor member function of BigInstance, which can hide arbitrarily complex machinery. A constructor is also invoked for each expression passed to a function's formal arguments, and again as the function returns a value. Arithmetic operators and comparison operators can be overloaded too, so A=B*C; may multiply *n*-dimensional matrices, and if (x<y) ... may compare two paths through a directed graph of arbitrary complexity. The importance of this to optimization is that *some statements hide large amounts of computation. The form of the statement does not tell how expensive it is.*

Developers who learned C++ first may not find this rule surprising. But for those who learned C first, their instincts can lead them disastrously astray.

Statements Are Not Executed in Order

C++ programs behave as if they were executed in order, subject to C++ flow of control statements. The weasel-words "as if" in the previous sentence are the foundation upon which many compiler optimizations, and many tricks of modern computer hardware, are built.

Under the hood, of course, the compiler can and does sometimes reorder statements to improve performance. But the compiler knows that a variable must contain an up-to-date result of any computation assigned to it before it is tested or assigned to another variable. Modern microprocessors may also choose to execute instructions out of order, but they contain logic to ensure that writes to memory happen before subsequent reads of the same location. Even the microprocessor's memory control logic may choose to delay writes to memory for optimal use of the memory bus. But the memory controller knows which writes are currently "in flight" from the execution unit through cache memory to main memory, and makes sure the in-flight value is used if the same address is subsequently read.

Concurrency complicates this picture. C++ programs are compiled without knowledge of other threads that may be running concurrently. The C++ compiler does not know which variables, if any, are shared between threads. The combined effect of the compiler reordering statements and the computer delaying writes to main memory damages the illusion that statements are executed in order when a program contains concurrent threads that share data. The developer must add explicit synchronizing code to multithreaded programs to ensure consistently predictable behavior. The *synchronizing code reduces the amount of concurrency obtainable when concurrent threads share data.*

Summary

- *Access to memory dominates other costs in a processor.*
- *An unaligned access takes twice as long as if all the bytes were in the same word.*
- *Heavily used memory locations can be accessed more quickly than less heavily used locations.*
- *Memory in adjacent locations can be accessed more quickly than memory in distant locations.*
- *Due to caching, a function running in the context of a whole program may run slower than the same function running in a test harness.*
- *It's much slower to access data shared between threads of execution than unshared data.*
- *Computation is faster than decision.*
- *Every program competes with other programs for the computer's resources.*
- *If a program must run at startup, or at times of peak load, performance must be measured under load.*
- *Every assignment, function argument initialization, and function return invokes a constructor, a function that can hide arbitrary amounts of code.*
- *Some statements hide large amounts of computation. The form of the statement does not tell how expensive it is.*
- *Synchronizing code reduces the amount of concurrency obtainable when concurrent threads share data.*

## CHAPTER 3

Measure Performance

Measure what is measurable, and make measurable what is not so.

—Galileo Galilei (1564–1642)

Measurement and experimentation are the basis of any serious attempt to improve a program's performance. This chapter introduces two software tools that measure performance: the profiler and the software timer. I discuss how to design experiments to measure performance so that their results are meaningful, rather than misleading.

The most basic and most frequently performed measurement of software performance answers the question, "How long?" How long does it take to execute a function? How long to fetch a configuration from disk? How long to start up or shut down?

These questions can be attacked (clumsily) with ridiculously simple instruments. Isaac Newton measured the gravitational constant by timing falling objects against his heartbeat. I'm sure every developer has informally timed activities by counting out loud; in the United States, we count "one-Mississippi, two-Mississippi, three-Mississippi..." to get approximate seconds. A digital wristwatch with a stopwatch function was once *de rigueur* for computer geeks, and not just for the fashion statement. In the embedded world, hardware-savvy developers have nifty instruments at their disposal, including frequency counters and oscilloscopes that can time even short routines accurately. Software vendors sell a variety of specialized tools too numerous to review here.

This chapter focuses on two tools that are widely available, generally useful, and inexpensive. The first tool, the *profiler*, is typically provided alongside the compiler by the compiler vendor. The profiler produces a tabular report of the cumulative time spent in each function called during a program run. It is the go-to instrument for software optimization because it produces a list of the hottest functions in your program.

The second tool, the *software timer*, is something developers can build, like Jedi knights constructing their own lightsaber (if you will excuse the cheesy *Star Wars* reference). If the fancy version of the compiler that has a profiler is priced out of reach, or the compiler vendor on some embedded platform doesn't offer one, the developer can still perform experiments by timing long-running activities. The software timer is also helpful for timing tasks that are not compute-bound.

A third tool, the lab notebook, is so old-school that many developers may think it has gone completely out of fashion. But a lab notebook or equivalent text file is an indispensable tool in the optimization toolkit.

The Optimizing Mindset

Before diving into measurements and experiments, I would like to offer just a little of the philosophy of optimization that I practice and that I hope to teach in this book.

Performance Must Be Measured

Your senses are usually not accurate enough to detect an incremental change in performance. Your memory is inadequate to exactly recall the results of many experiments. Book learning can mislead you, causing you to believe things that are not always true. Developers often show spectacularly poor intuition when thinking about whether or not a particular piece of code needs to be optimized. They write functions, knowing they will be used, but with little thought to how heavily or by what code. Then an inefficient bit of code finds its way into critical components, where it is called zillions of times. Experience can also deceive you. Programming languages, compilers, libraries, and processors all evolve. Functions that were once reliable hot spots can become more efficient, and vice versa. Only measurement tells you if you are winning or losing the optimization game.

The developers whose skill at optimization I respect most all approach the optimization task systematically:

- They make testable predictions, and write their predictions down.
- They keep a record of code changes.
- They make measurements with the best instruments available.
- They keep detailed notes of experimental results.

Optimizers Are Big Game Hunters

> I say we take off and nuke the whole site from orbit. It's the only way to be sure.
>
> —Ellen Ripley (Sigourney Weaver), *Aliens*, 1986

Optimizers are big game hunters. Making a program run 1% faster is not worth the risk that modifying a working program might introduce bugs. The effect of a change must be at least locally dramatic to make it worthwhile. Furthermore, a 1% speedup might be a measurement artifact masquerading as improvement. Such a speedup needs to be *proven*, with randomization, sample statistics, and confidence levels. It's too much work for too little effect. It's not a place we go in this book.

A 20% improvement is a different animal. It blows through objections about methodology. There are not a lot of statistics in this book, something for which I do not apologize. The point of this book is to help the developer find performance improvements that are dramatic enough to outweigh any question of their value. Such an improvement may still depend on factors like the operating system and compiler, so it may not have much effect on another system or at another time. But changes that are dramatic almost never bite with reduced performance when the developers port their code to a new system.

The 90/10 Rule

The fundamental rule of optimization is the 90/10 rule: *a program spends 90% of its run time in 10% of its code*. This rule is a *heuristic*; not a law of nature, but rather a useful generalization to guide thinking and planning. This rule is also sometimes called the 80/20 rule. The idea is the same. Intuitively, the 90/10 rule means that certain blocks of code are *hot spots* that are executed very frequently, while other parts of the code are hardly ever executed. These hot spots are the targets for optimization efforts.

Optimization War Story

I was introduced to the 90/10 rule in one of my first projects as a professional developer: an embedded device with a keyboard interface, which very coincidentally was called the 9010A (Figure 3-1).

Figure 3-1. The Fluke 9010A (British Computer History Museum)

There was a function that polled the keyboard to see whether the STOP key had been pressed. This function was executed frequently by every routine. Hand-optimizing the C compiler's Z80 assembly language output code for this one function (a 45-minute task) improved overall throughput by 7%, which was a big deal in this particular device.

This experience was typical of optimization efforts in general. At the beginning of the optimization process, a lot of run time was spent in one place in the program. The place was pretty obvious: a housekeeping activity done repeatedly, at each iteration of every loop. Optimizing the activity required making the painful choice to code in assembly language instead of C. But the scope of the assembly language was extremely limited, reducing the risk entailed by the choice to use assembly language.

The experience was also typical in that this one block of code was very hot. After we improved this code, another block of code took first place as the most frequently executed—but its contribution to overall run time was much smaller. It was so small, in fact, that we stopped optimizing after just this one change. We could find no other change that gave us even a 1% speedup.

A consequence of the 90/10 rule is that optimizing every routine in a program is not helpful. Optimizing a small part of your code gives you practically all the performance improvement you are going to get. Identifying the hot 10% is time well spent. Selecting code to optimize by guesswork is likely time wasted.

I would like to return to the quote by Don Knuth from the first chapter. Here is a longer version of the same quote:

> Programmers waste enormous amounts of time thinking about, or worrying about, the speed of noncritical parts of their programs, and these attempts at efficiency actually have a strong negative impact when debugging and maintenance are considered. We should forget about small efficiencies, say about 97% of the time: premature optimization is the root of all evil.
>
> —Donald Knuth, *Structured Programming with go to Statements*, ACM Computing Surveys 6 (Dec 1974): 268. CiteSeerX: 10.1.1.103.6084 (*http://bit.ly/knuth-1974*)

Dr. Knuth was not warning that optimization in general was evil, as some people have suggested. He was saying only that wasting time optimizing the noncritical 90% of a program was evil. Apparently he was aware of the 90/10 rule too.

Amdahl's Law

Amdahl's Law, coined by and named after computer engineering pioneer Gene Amdahl, describes how much overall performance will improve when a portion of the code is optimized. There are several ways to express Amdahl's Law, but with regard to optimization, it may be expressed by the equation

$$S_T = \frac{1}{(1-P) + \dfrac{P}{S_P}}$$

where S_T is the proportion of improvement in the whole program run time resulting from an optimization, P is the proportion of total original run time that was subject to optimization, and S_P is the proportion of improvement in the optimized portion P.

For example, suppose a program takes 100 seconds of run time. Through profiling (see "Profile Program Execution" on page 37), you discover that the program spends 80 seconds performing multiple calls to a single function, f. Now suppose you recode f to make it 30% faster. How much would this improve the program's overall run time?

P, the proportion of the original run time spent within function f, is 0.8. S_P is 1.3. Plugging this into Amdahl's Law yields

$$S_T = \frac{1}{(1-0.8) + \dfrac{0.8}{1.3}} = \frac{1}{0.2 + 0.62} = 1.22$$

Improving this one function by 30% improved the overall program run time by 22%. In this case, Amdahl's Law illustrates the 90/10 rule, and provides an example of how powerful even a modest performance improvement can be in the hot 10% of the code.

Let's look at a second example. Suppose again that a program takes 100 seconds of run time. Through profiling, you discover that a single function, g, consumes 10 seconds of that run time. Now suppose you recode g so that it runs 100 times faster. How much will this improve the program's overall run time?

P, the proportion of the original run time spent within function g, is 0.1. S_P is 100. Plugging this into Amdahl's Law yields

$$S_T = \frac{1}{(1-P) + \frac{0.1}{100}} = \frac{1}{0.9 + 0.001} = 1.11$$

In this case, Amdahl's Law provides a cautionary tale. Even if heroic coding or black magic reduces the run time of function g to zero, it is still in the unimportant 90%. The overall performance improvement is *still* 11%, to two decimal places. Amdahl's Law says that even a really successful optimization isn't valuable if the optimized code doesn't account for much of the overall program's run time. The lesson of Amdahl's Law is that, when your colleague comes to a meeting all excited that he knows how to make some calculation run 10 times faster, it doesn't *necessarily* mean all your performance troubles are over.

Perform Experiments

Developing software is always an experiment, in the sense that you start up the program thinking that it is going to do a particular thing, and then watch to see whether it does. Performance tuning is experimental in a more formal sense. You must start with correct code, in the sense of code that does what you expect it to do. You have to look at this code with a fresh set of eyes and ask, "Why is this code hot?" Why does this particular function, out of the many hundreds in your program, appear at the top of the profiler's naughty list? Is the function wasting time doing something redundantly? Is there a faster way to do the same computation? Is the function using expensive resources? Is the function, in fact, as efficient as it possibly could be, but just called a whole lot of times, leaving no opportunity to improve performance?

Your proposed answer to the question "Why is this code hot?" forms the hypothesis you will test. The experiment takes the form of two elapsed time measurements of the running program: one before you make a change and one after. If the second time is less than the first, your experiment *validates* the hypothesis.

Note the very special language. Experiments don't necessarily *prove* anything at all. Your modified code may have run faster or slower for a variety of reasons having nothing to do with your change. For example:

- The computer might receive an email or check for a Java update while you are measuring run time.
- A colleague might check in an improved library just before you recompile.
- Your fix may run faster because it is not correct.

Good scientists are skeptics. They are always suspicious. If the expected improvement does not appear, or appears too good to be true, a skeptic tries the experiment again, or questions her assumptions, or looks for a bug.

Good scientists are also open to new knowledge, even if it contradicts knowledge already in their heads. I learned several unexpected things about optimization in the process of writing this book. The technical reviewers learned things too. Good scientists never stop learning.

Optimization War Story

Chapter 5 contains an example function for keyword lookup. I coded several versions of the example. One was a linear search, another was a binary search. When I measured the performance of these two functions, the linear search was consistently a few percent *faster* than the binary search. This, I felt, was unreasonable. The binary search just *had* to be faster. But the timing numbers told a different story.

I was aware that someone on the Internet had reported that linear lookup was often faster because it enjoyed better cache locality than binary search, and indeed my linear search implementation should have had excellent cache locality. But this result violated both experience and long-revered book learning about search performance.

In investigating more deeply, I first realized that I had been testing a table with just a few keywords, and using sample words that would be found in the table in my test. If the table had eight entries, a linear search would examine half (four) of them on average before returning. The binary search would divide the table in half four times before it found the keyword each time it was called. The two algorithms had exactly the same average performance on small keyword sets. This reality invalidated my intuition about binary search "always" being better.

But this was not the result I intended to demonstrate! So I made the table larger, thinking there must be a size at which the binary search was faster. I also added more words to my test that were not in the table. The results were as before, with the linear search being faster. At this time, I had to put this coding task aside for a couple of days. But the result gnawed at me.

I was still sure that the binary search should be faster. I reexamined the unit tests for the two searches, eventually to discover that the linear search always returned success after the first comparison. My test case had checked for a nonzero return, rather than testing for the correct return. Sheepishly, I fixed the linear search code and test cases. Now the experiment produced the expected result that the binary search was faster.

In this case, the experimental results first rejected and later validated my hypothesis—and challenged my assumptions along the way.

Keep a Lab Notebook

Good optimizers (like all good scientists) are concerned with repeatability. This is where the lab notebook comes into use. Each timing run starts with a hypothesis, one or more small code tweaks, and an input data set, and ends up with an unremarkable integer number of milliseconds. It's not too hard to remember the previous run's time long enough to compare it with the next. As long as each code change is successful, that's enough.

Eventually, however, the developer will guess wrong and the timing of the latest run will be worse than that of the previous run. Suddenly the developer's mind will be full of questions. Was run #5 faster than run #3 even though it was slower than run #4? And just what code change produced run #3? Was the speed difference just an artifact, or was it really faster?

If each experiment run is documented, it can quickly be repeated. This makes answering such questions trivial. Otherwise, the developer must go back and rerun a previous experiment to get the timing—that is, *if* he can remember exactly what code change to make or unmake. If runs are brief and the developer's memory is excellent, then he's lucky and may waste only a little time. But it is possible to be unlucky too, and lose track of a promising line of work, or maybe repeat it unnecessarily the next day.

When I give this advice, there is always someone who says, "I can do that without paper! I can write a Perl script that would modify the FOO command of the Smart-FOO check-in tool to save the test results of each run with the change set for that run. If I save the test results in a file... If I run the test in a directory set up just *so*..."

I don't want to discourage innovation among software developers. If you're a senior manager driving uptake of best practices, go for it. I will say, however, that writing on paper is a robust, easy-to-use technology that is a thousand years down its learning curve. It will continue to work when the team updates the revision manager or test suite. It will work at the developer's next job. This old-school solution may still optimize use of the developer's time.

Measure Baseline Performance and Set Goals

For a developer working alone on her own time, the optimization process can be casual, iterating until performance "feels good enough." Developers working in teams, however, have managers and stakeholders to satisfy. Optimization efforts are guided by two numbers: a baseline measure of performance before optimization, and a performance goal. The baseline performance measurement is important not just for measuring the success of individual improvements, but also for justifying the cost of optimization efforts to stakeholders.

A performance goal is important because optimization is a process with diminishing returns. Initially there is "low-hanging fruit" that may easily be picked: individual processes or naïvely coded functions that produce big improvements when optimized. But once these easy optimization targets have been improved, more effort is required for each next turn of the optimization crank.

Many teams do not initially think to set design goals for performance or responsiveness, simply because they are not accustomed to doing so. Fortunately, poor performance is usually obvious (a user interface with long periods of unresponsiveness, a server that won't scale, excessive hosting costs for CPU time, etc.). Once a team looks at performance, numerical goals are easy to set. A whole subdiscipline of user experience (UX) design centers on how users perceive waiting time. Here is a list of commonly measured performance aspects to start you off, plus just enough UX numbers to make you dangerous:

Startup time
> The elapsed time from pressing the Enter key until the program enters its main input processing loop. Often, but not always, the developer can just measure the time elapsed between entering the `main()` procedure and entering the main loop. Operating system vendors who offer certification for programs have strict requirements for programs that run as the computer starts up, or whenever a user logs on. For instance, Microsoft demands of hardware vendors seeking certification that the Windows shell must enter its main loop less than 10 seconds after starting. This limits the number of other programs the vendor is allowed to preload and launch in the busy startup environment. Microsoft offers specialized tools to measure startup time.

Shutdown time
> The elapsed time from the user clicking the Close icon or entering a command to exit until the process actually exits. Often, but not always, you can just measure the time elapsed between the main window receiving the shutdown command and exiting `main()`. Shutdown time also includes the time needed to stop all threads and dependent processes. Operating system vendors who offer certification have strict requirements for shutdown time. Shutdown time is also impor-

tant because the time it takes to restart a service or long-running program is equal to its shutdown time plus its startup time.

Response time

The average or worst-case time needed to perform a command. For websites, both the average response time and worst-case response time contribute to users' satisfaction with the site. Response times can be categorized into coarse powers-of-10 baskets as follows:

Less than 0.1 seconds: user in direct control

If response time is less than 0.1 seconds, the users feel like they are directly controlling the user interface, and that UI changes result directly from their actions. This is the maximum delay between a user beginning to drag and the dragged object moving, or between a user clicking a field and the field being highlighted. Any longer and the user feels like he is issuing a command that the computer carries out.

0.1 to 1 seconds: user in control of command

If response time is between 0.1 and 1 seconds, the users feel as though they are in charge, but interpret the brief delay as the computer executing a command and causing a change to the UI. The users are able to tolerate this amount of delay without losing their focus on their current train of thought.

1 to 10 seconds: computer in charge

If response time is between 1 and 10 seconds, the users feel they have executed a command and have lost control to the computer while it processes the command. Users may lose focus and forget things in short-term memory that they need to complete the task; 10 seconds is about the maximum time a user can remain focused. User satisfaction with the UI drops rapidly if they encounter many waits of this duration.

More than 10 seconds: time for a coffee break

If response time is greater than 10 seconds, the users perceive that they have enough time to do some other task. If their work requires them to use the UI, they will go for coffee while the computer crunches numbers. If it's an option, the user may close the program and look elsewhere for satisfaction.

Jakob Nielsen wrote an interesting article (*http://bit.ly/powers-10*) about time scales in user experience that points to scholarly studies for the extra-curious.

Throughput

The inverse of response time. Throughput is generally expressed as the average number of operations per unit of time on some test workload. Throughput measures the same thing as response time, but is more appropriate for batch-oriented programs like databases and web services. Generally you want this number as big as possible.

It is also possible to overoptimize. For instance, in many cases, users regard a response time of under 0.1 seconds as instantaneous. In such a situation, improving response time from 0.1 seconds to 1 millisecond adds virtually no value, even though it is 100 times faster.

You Can Improve Only What You Measure

Optimizing a single function, subsystem, task, or test case is never the same as improving the performance of a whole program. Your test setup differs in many ways from the production-version program running on customer data, so the performance improvements measured in your test rarely translate into the same performance improvements in the wild. Making a single task faster may not make the whole program faster, even if the task exercises much of the program's logic.

For instance, if a database developer profiles a database performing a specific select query 1,000 times, and optimizes based on that profile, she will speed up not the whole database, but the database performing a specific select query. This speedup may well improve the performance of other select queries. It will have a less predictable effect on delete or update queries, indexing, and all the other things a database does.

Profile Program Execution

A *profiler* is a program that produces statistics about where another program spends its time. The profiler constructs a report showing how frequently each statement or function is executed, and how much time accumulates in each function.

Many compiler suites, including both Visual Studio on Windows and GCC on Linux, come with a profiler to help find hot spots. Historically, Microsoft only offered its profiler with expensive versions of Visual Studio, but Visual Studio 2015 Community Edition comes with very extensive profiler support. There are open source profilers for Windows, for earlier versions of Visual Studio.

There are several ways to implement a profiler. One method used by both Windows and Linux works as follows:

1. The programmer recompiles the program to be profiled with a special compiler flag that *instruments* every function in the program. This involves adding a couple of extra assembly language instructions to the beginning and end of each function.

2. The programmer links the instrumented program with a profiling library.

3. Any time the instrumented program runs, it creates a profiling table as a file on disk.

4. The profiler takes the profiling table as input, and produces a range of available textual or graphical reports.

Another profiling method works in this way:

1. The unmodified program is instrumented by linking it with a profiling library. The library contains a routine that interrupts program execution at a high rate and records the value of the instruction pointer.

2. Any time the instrumented program runs, it creates a profiling table as a file on disk.

3. The profiler reads the profiling table as input, and produces a range of available textual or graphical reports.

The output of the profiler may take several forms. One form is a source listing annotated with the number of times each line was executed. Another form is a list of function names along with the number of times each was invoked. Another form is the same list of functions, with the total time accumulated within each function and all functions called from within it. Still another form is a list of functions and the amount of time spent in each function, minus the time spent in called functions, in system code, or waiting for events.

The profiler instrumentation is carefully designed to be as inexpensive as possible. Its effect on overall run time is small, and typically takes the form of a few percent slowdown of every operation. The first method gives exact numbers, at the cost of higher overhead and disabling of certain optimizations. The second method gives approximate results and may miss a few infrequently called functions, but has the advantage of running over the production code.

The most important advantage of a profiler is that it directly displays a list of the hottest functions in the code. The process of optimization is reduced to making a "naughty list" of functions to investigate, inspecting each function for optimization opportunities, making a change, and rerunning the code to obtain new profiler output until no single function appears particularly hot or until you run out of ideas. Because hot spots observed by the profiler are by definition places where a lot of computation takes place, this process is generally straightforward.

My experience with profiling is that profiling a debug build of a program produces results that are just as relevant as those obtained from a release build. In some ways, the debug build is easier to profile because it includes all functions, including those that are inlined, whereas the release build hides very frequently called inlined functions.

Optimizing Pro Tip

One issue with profiling a debug build on Windows is that the debug build is linked with a debug version of the runtime library. The debug version of the memory manager functions performs many extra tests so it can better report doubly freed storage and memory leaks. The cost of these extra tests can significantly increase the cost of certain functions. There is an environment variable to tell the debugger not to use the debug memory manager: go to Control Panel→System Properties→Advanced System Settings→Environment Variables→System Variables, and add a new variable called _NO_DEBUG_HEAP with a value of 1.

Using a profiler is an excellent way to find candidates for optimization, but it isn't perfect:

- A profiler cannot tell you that there is a more efficient algorithm to solve your computing problem. Tuning a bad algorithm is just a waste of time.

- A profiler does not give crisp results on input that exercises many different tasks. For instance, a SQL database may execute very different code when doing an insert query from when doing a select query. Thus, code that is hot when loading up the database with insert queries may not be executed at all when reading data from the database with select queries. Running a test that is a mix of loading the database and querying the database makes the insert code less prominent in the profiler report, unless the profiled run performs a lot of computation.

  Therefore, to identify the hottest functions more easily, try optimizing one task at a time. It can be helpful to profile a subsystem of the full program running in a test harness, if test code is available. However, you introduce another source of uncertainty if you optimize one task at a time: it doesn't necessarily improve the performance of the entire system. Results may be less dramatic when the program is run on input that performs a mix of tasks.

- The profiler gives misleading information when a program is I/O-bound or multithreaded, because the profiler subtracts time spent in system calls or waiting on events. Removing this time is theoretically sensible because the program is not solely responsible for these waits. But the result is that the profiler tells how much work a program is doing, not how much "wall clock time" it takes to perform its work. Some profilers give a count of the number of function calls as well as the time spent within each function. A very high call count can be a clue when the profiler hides wall clock time.

The profiler is a one-trick pony; there are optimization opportunities it does not highlight, and issues in interpreting profiler output. Still, for many programs, the profiler produces results good enough that no other method is needed.

Time Long-Running Code

If a program does one task that is compute-bound, profiling will automatically show the hot spots. But if a program does a lot of different things, no function may be particularly hot in the profiler. The program may also spend time waiting for I/O or external events that slow down overall progress as measured by a wall clock. In these cases, you need to time parts of the program with a stopwatch, and then try to reduce the measured run time of parts that are slow.

A developer uses run timing to find hot spots by successively narrowing the part of a long-running task being timed until one section takes a length of time that does not make intuitive sense. After identifying the suspicious section of code, the developer times experiments on small subsystems or individual functions in a test harness.

Run timing is an effective way to test hypotheses about how to reduce the cost of a particular function.

It is hardly a stretch to realize that a computer can be programmed to act as a stopwatch. A phone or laptop is quite handy for waking you up at 6:45 on weekday mornings, or reminding you 5 minutes before your stand-up meeting at 10. Measuring the submicrosecond run times of functions in modern computers is more challenging, especially because the common Windows/PC platform has historically had trouble providing a high-resolution clock that behaved consistently across hardware models and software versions.

As a developer you must therefore be prepared to "roll your own" software stopwatch, knowing that it may change in the future. To help make this possible, I will discuss how time is measured, and what tools support measuring time on computers.

"A Little Learning" About Measuring Time

> A little learning is a dangerous thing.
>
> —Alexander Pope, "An Essay on Criticism" (*http://poetry.eserver.org/essay-on-criticism.html*), 1774

A perfect measurement would exactly capture the size, weight, or, in the case of this book, duration of a measured phenomenon every single time. Making a perfect measurement is as likely as an archer reliably hitting the exact center of the bull's-eye with every shot, splitting arrow after arrow. Such archery only happens in storybooks, and it is the same with measurement.

Real measurement experiments (like real archers) must contend with *variation*: sources of error that spoil the quest for perfection. Variation comes in two flavors: *random* and *systematic*. Random variations affect each measurement differently, like a puff of wind that causes a particular arrow to drift in flight. Systematic variations affect every measurement in a similar way, like the way an archer's stance can bias every shot so that it goes to the left of its intended destination.

Variation itself can be measured. Summary measures of variation form properties of a measurement called *precision* and *trueness*. Together these properties form the intuitive property called *accuracy*.

Precision, trueness, and accuracy

It is apparently the case that the scientists who get really excited about measurement argue endlessly about terminology. You need only look up "accuracy" on Wikipedia for a taste of how much controversy there is about what words to use for explaining agreed-upon concepts. I chose to explain terms in the context of the 1994 standard ISO 5725-1 (*http://bit.ly/iso-57251*), "Accuracy (trueness and precision) of measurement methods and results - Part 1: General principles and definitions" (1994).

A measurement is *precise* if it is free from random variation. That is, if the same phenomenon is measured repeatedly, and the measured values are close together, the measurement is precise. A series of precise measurements may still contain systematic variation. An archer who puts a grouping of shots in the same off-center area can be said to be very precise even if not very accurate. His target might look like Figure 3-2.

If I measure a phenomenon (say, the run time of a function) 10 times, and get the same result all 10 times, I may hypothesize that my measurement is precise. (As in any experiment, I should remain skeptical until I have a lot of evidence.) If I get the same result six times, a slightly different result three times, and a very different result once, the measurement is less precise.

A measurement is *true* if it is free from systematic variation. That is, if I measure the same phenomenon repeatedly, and the average of all the results clusters close to the actual quantity being measured, then I may believe the measurement is true. Individual measurements may be affected by random variation so that they are closer to or further from the actual quantity. Trueness is not a skill rewarded in archery. In Figure 3-3, the average of the four shots would be in the bull's-eye if only it were an arrow. Furthermore, all these shots have the same accuracy (distance from the bull's-eye) in ring units.

Figure 3-2. High-precision (but poor-accuracy) target shooting

The *accuracy* of a measurement is an informal concept that depends on how close each individual measurement comes to the actual quantity being measured. The distance from the actual quantity has a component of random variation and a component of systematic variation. A measurement must be both precise and true to be accurate.

Figure 3-3. The archer who fired these shots has true aim

Measuring time

The software performance measurements covered in this book are either a *duration* (the amount of time that elapses between two events) or a *rate* (the number of events per unit of time, the inverse of duration). The instrument used for measuring duration is a *clock*.

All clocks work by counting some periodic fluctuation. In some clocks, the count is divided into hours, minutes, and seconds for presentation. In other clocks, the count is presented directly as a number of ticks. But clocks (other than sundials) don't directly measure hours, minutes, and seconds. They count ticks, and it is only by comparing the ticks to a second reference clock that a clock may be calibrated to present hours, minutes, and seconds.

All sources of periodic fluctuation are subject to variations that make them imperfect clocks. Some of these variations are random, while others are systematic:

- A sundial makes use of the periodic off-plane rotation of the Earth. By definition, one full rotation is one day. The Earth makes an imperfect clock because its period is long, and because its rotation speeds up and slows down detectably (in microseconds) as the continents drift slowly across its surface. This variation is random. Tidal forces from the Moon and Sun slow the overall rate of the Earth's rotation. This variation is systematic.

- A grandfather clock counts the regular swinging of a pendulum. Gears divide the pendulum's swing down to drive hands that display the time. The period of the pendulum may be manually adjusted so that the displayed time is synchronized to the Earth's rotation. The period of a pendulum's swing depends on the weight of the pendulum and its length, so that every swing may be faster or slower than desired. This variation is systematic. Friction, air pressure, and the accumulation of dust may all affect a pendulum even if it is initially set perfectly. These are random sources of variation.

- An electric clock uses the periodic 60 Hz sine wave of its AC power supply to drive a synchronous motor. Gears divide down the fundamental oscillation and drive hands to display the time. An electric clock is not a perfect clock because the AC power is only 60 Hz (in the United States) by convention, not by some law of nature. The power company slows down the oscillation in periods of heavy use, and speeds it up again later so electric clocks will not run slow. So, a second measured by an electric clock may be longer on a hot summer afternoon than on a temperate evening (as we have always suspected). This variation is random. An electric clock made for use in the United States will run consistently slow if plugged into a 50 Hz AC outlet in Europe. In contrast to the random variation introduced by temperature, the variation caused by using a European power outlet is systematic.

- A digital wristwatch uses the induced vibration of a quartz crystal as its fundamental fluctuation. A logic circuit divides the fundamental oscillation down and drives a display. The periodic oscillation of the crystal depends on its size, on the temperature, and on the voltage applied to it. The effect of the crystal's size is a systematic variation, while variations of the temperature and voltage are random.

A tick count is an inherently unsigned quantity. There is no such thing as −5 tick events. I mention this seemingly obvious fact because, as shown later, many developers implementing timekeeping functions choose a signed representation for durations. I don't know why they do this. My teenage son would say, "It's just a thing."

Measurement resolution

The *resolution* of a measurement is the size of the units in which the measurement is presented.

An archer shooting at a target gets the same score for putting an arrow anywhere in a given ring. The bull's-eye is not an infinitesimal point, but rather a circle of a certain diameter (see Figure 3-4). A shot is either a bull's-eye or is in the first ring, second ring, and so on. The width of the ring is the resolution of an archery score.

Figure 3-4. Resolution: a hit anywhere in a circle is the same score

The useful resolution of a time measurement is limited by the duration of the underlying fluctuation. A time measurement can be one tick or two ticks, but nothing in between. The period between these ticks is the clock's useful resolution.

An observer may *perceive* events as happening between two ticks of a slow clock like a pendulum clock. This just means people have a faster (but less accurate) clock in their heads that they informally compare to the pendulum clock. An observer wanting to make measurements of imperceptible durations like milliseconds has only the clock's ticks to go on.

There is no required connection between the accuracy of a measurement and the resolution with which it is presented. If I log my daily activities, I may be able to report that it took two days to write this section of this book. The useful resolution of this measurement is in this case one day. I suppose I could convert this time to seconds, reporting instead that I took 172,800 seconds. But unless I had a stopwatch in my hand, reporting the time in seconds might give a false sense that the measurement was more accurate than it was, or a misleading impression that I did not eat or sleep for this whole period.

A measurement may be reported in units smaller than the useful resolution because the units are standard. I own an oven that displays the oven temperature in degrees Fahrenheit. The thermostat that controls the oven, however, has a useful resolution of 5°F, so that as the oven heats, the display reads 300°F, then 305, 310, 315, and so on. It makes more sense to display the temperature in familiar degree units rather than thermostat units. It just means that the least significant digit of the measurement can only assume the values 0 and 5.

The reader might be surprised and disappointed to know the useful resolutions of the many inexpensive thermometers, scales, and other measuring devices around them that have display resolutions of one unit or one-tenth of a unit.

Measuring with several clocks

> A man with a watch knows what time it is. A man with two watches is never quite sure.
>
> —Most frequently attributed to Lee Segall

When two events happen in the same place, it is easy to measure the elapsed time in timer ticks on a single clock. When two events happen at a distance from one another, it may be necessary to use two clocks. Tick counts can't be compared directly between different clocks.

Humankind has attacked this problem by synchronizing clocks to the Coordinated Universal Time reference. Coordinated Universal Time is synchronized to astronomical midnight at longitude 0, an arbitrary line that passes through a nifty plaque at the Royal Observatory in Greenwich, England (see Figure 3-5). This allows a time in ticks to be converted to a time in hours, minutes, and seconds past midnight UTC (Universal Time Coordinated, a clunky acronym negotiated between French and English horologists that favors neither French nor English spelling).

If two clocks are perfectly synchronized to UTC, the UTC time from one is directly comparable to the other. But of course, perfect synchronization is not possible. The two clocks contain independent sources of variation that will cause them to drift from UTC, and from one another.

Figure 3-5. Markings of the Prime Meridian at the Royal Observatory, Greenwich England (photo by Ævar Arnfjörð Bjarmason, license CC BY-SA 3.0)

Measuring Time with Computers

Building a clock on a computer requires a source of periodic fluctuation—preferably one with good precision and trueness—and a way for software to obtain ticks from that source. A purpose-built computer designed for telling time could easily be created. However, the most popular current computer architectures were not designed with much thought to providing good clocks. I will illustrate the problems using the PC architecture and Microsoft Windows. The problems for Linux and embedded platforms are similar.

The crystal oscillator at the heart of a PC clock circuit has a typical basic accuracy of 100 parts per million, which is 0.01%, or about 8 seconds per day. While this accuracy is only a little better than that provided by a digital wristwatch, it is more than enough for performance measurement, where very informal results accurate to a few percent are usable. The clock circuits on cheap embedded processors are less accurate, but the most serious problem is not with the source of periodic fluctuation—more difficult is the problem of getting a reliable tick count for use by programs.

Hardware evolution of tick counters

The original IBM PC did not have any hardware tick counters. It did have a time-of-day clock that the software could read. The earliest Microsoft C runtime library copied the ANSI C library, providing the function time_t time(time_t*), which returns the number of seconds since 00:00 January 1, 1970 UTC. The original version of time() returned a 32-bit signed integer, but during the run-up to Y2K, this was changed to a 64-bit signed integer.

The original IBM PC used a periodic interrupt from the AC power supply to wake the kernel to perform task switches and other kernel operations. The period of this tick was 16.67 milliseconds in North America, because the AC power is 60 Hz, and 10 milliseconds where the AC power is 50 Hz.

By Windows 98, and possibly earlier, Microsoft C provided the ANSI C function clock_t clock(), which returned a tick counter in a signed format. The constant CLOCKS_PER_SEC specified the number of ticks per second. A returned value of -1 implied that clock() was not available. clock() originally reported a tick based on the periodic AC interrupt. clock() as implemented on Windows differs from the ANSI specification, measuring elapsed wall-clock time and not CPU time. clock() was recently reimplemented in terms of GetSystemTimeAsFileTime(), and in 2015 it returned a 1-millisecond tick with 1-millisecond resolution, making it a good millisecond clock in Windows.

Starting in Windows 2000, a software tick counter based on the A/C power interrupt was made available via a call to DWORD GetTickCount(). The tick counted by GetTick Count() depends on the hardware of the PC, and may be significantly longer than 1 millisecond. GetTickCount() performs a computation to convert the tick to milliseconds to partially relieve this ambiguity. An updated version of this call, ULONGLONG GetTickCount64(), returns the same tick count in a 64-bit unsigned integer so that longer durations can be measured. Although there is no way to inspect the current interrupt period, a pair of functions reduce the period and then restore it:

```
MMRESULT timeBeginPeriod(UINT)
MMRESULT timeEndPeriod(UINT)
```

These functions act on a global variable affecting all processes and many other functions, such as Sleep(), that depend on the AC interrupt. Another call, DWORD timeGetTime(), appears to get the same tick counter by a different method.

Starting with the Pentium architecture, Intel provided a hardware register called the Time Stamp Counter (TSC). The TSC is a 64-bit register that counts ticks from the processor clock. This counter could be accessed very rapidly by the RDTSC instruction.

Starting in Windows 2000, the TSC could be read by calling the function BOOL Query PerformanceCounter(LARGE_INTEGER*), which produces a tick count with no particular resolution. The resolution can be obtained through a call to BOOL QueryPerformanceFrequency(LARGE_INTEGER*), which returns the frequency in ticks per second. LARGE_INTEGER is a struct holding 64 bits of integer in a signed format, because the version of Visual Studio at the time these calls were introduced did not have a native 64-bit signed integer type.

A problem with the initial version of QueryPerformanceCounter() was that its tick rate depended on the processor's clock. The processor clock was different for different processors and motherboards. Older PCs, notably those with processors from Advanced Micro Devices (AMD), did not have a TSC at the time. When the TSC was not available, QueryPerformanceCounter() fell back to the low-resolution tick returned by GetTickCount().

Windows 2000 also added void GetSystemTimeAsFileTime(FILETIME*), which returns the number of 100-nanosecond ticks since 00:00 January 1, 1601 UTC. FILETIME is a struct holding 64 bits of integer, this time in an unsigned format. Although the displayed resolution of the tick counter appears to be very high, some implementations use the same slow counter used by GetTickCount().

More problems with QueryPerformanceCounter() soon appeared. Some processors implemented a variable clock rate to manage power consumption. This caused the tick period to change. In multiprocessor systems using several discrete processors, the value returned by QueryPerformanceCounter() depended on which processor a thread ran on. Processors began to implement instruction reordering, so that the RDTSC instruction might be delayed, reducing the accuracy of software using the TSC.

To solve these problems, Windows Vista used a different counter, typically the Advanced Configuration and Power Interface (ACPI) power management timer, for QueryPerformanceCounter(). Using this counter solved the synchronization problem in multiprocessors, but significantly increased latency. In the meantime, Intel respecified the TSC to be the maximum, nonchanging clock frequency. Intel also added the nonreorderable RDTSCP instruction.

Since Windows 8, a reliable high-resolution hardware tick count based on the TSC has been available. void GetSystemTimePreciseAsFileTime(FILETIME*) produces a high-resolution tick with fixed frequency and submicrosecond accuracy on any current system running Windows 8 or later.

The summary of this history lesson is that PCs were never designed as clocks, so the tick counters they provide are unreliable. If the past 35 years are any guide, future processors and future operating systems may continue to frustrate any hope of getting a solid, high-resolution tick count.

The only tick counter reliably available in all generations of PC is the tick counter returned by GetTickCount(), with all its warts. The 1-millisecond tick returned by clock() is better, and ought to be available in PCs manufactured in the last 10 years or so. Limiting consideration to Windows 8 and later and new processors, the 100-nanosecond tick counter from GetSystemTimePreciseAsFileTime() is very precise. However, my experience is that millisecond accuracy is sufficient for timing experiments.

Wraparound

Wraparound is what happens when the tick counter of a clock achieves its maximum value and then increments to zero. Twelve-hour analog clocks wrap around every day at noon and again at midnight. Windows 98 hung if it ran continuously for 49 days (see Q216641 (*http://bit.ly/windows-49*)) due to wraparound of a 32-bit millisecond tick counter. The Y2K bug occurred when time expressed as a two-digit year wrapped around. The Mayan calendar wrapped around in 2012, supposedly heralding the end of the world. In January 2038, the Unix epoch (signed, 32-bit seconds since 00:00 January 1, 1970 UTC) will wrap around, possibly causing the actual end of the world for some long-lived embedded systems. The problem with wraparound is that, in the absence of additional bits to record it, the next increment of time is numerically *before* the previous time. Clocks that wrap around are good only for measuring durations that are less than the wraparound interval.

For instance, on Windows, the GetTickCount() function returns a tick count with 1-millisecond resolution in a 32-bit unsigned integer. The value returned by GetTick Count() wraps around about every 49 days. GetTickCount() may be used for timing operations that take much less than 49 days without concern. If a program calls Get TickCount() at the beginning and end of an operation, the difference between the returned values may be interpreted as the number of milliseconds elapsed between the calls. For example:

```
DWORD start = GetTickCount();
    DoBigTask();
DWORD end = GetTickCount();
cout << "Startup took " << end-start << " ms" << endl;
```

The way C++ implements unsigned arithmetic produces a correct answer even in the presence of wraparound.

GetTickCount() is less effective for remembering time since startup. Many long-lived servers can remain up for months or even years. The problem with wraparound is that, in the absence of bits to record the number of wraparounds, end-start might imply no wraparounds, or one, or more.

Starting in Vista, Microsoft added the GetTickCount64() function, which returns a 64-bit unsigned tick count with 1-millisecond display resolution. GetTickCount64()

takes millions of years to wrap around, greatly reducing the likelihood of anyone ever witnessing a problem.

Resolution is not accuracy

On Windows, the GetTickCount() function returns an unsigned 32-bit integer. If a program calls GetTickCount() at the beginning and end of an operation, the difference between the returned values may be interpreted as the number of milliseconds that elapsed between the calls. The resolution of GetTickCount() is thus 1-millisecond.

For example, the following block of code measures the relative performance of an arbitrary function called Foo() on Windows, by calling Foo() in a loop. Tick counts obtained at the start and end of the loop give a time in milliseconds for the loop:

```
DWORD start = GetTickCount();
for (unsigned i = 0; i < 1000; ++i) {
    Foo();
}
DWORD end = GetTickCount();
cout << "1000 calls to Foo() took " << end-start << "ms" << endl;
```

If Foo() performed some substantial calculation, this block of code might produce the following output:

```
1000 calls to Foo() took 16ms
```

Unfortunately, the accuracy of the call to GetTickCount() may be 10 milliseconds or 15.67 milliseconds, as documented in Microsoft's web page on GetTickCount() (*http://bit.ly/gettickcount*). That is, if you call GetTickCount() twice in a row, the difference may be 0, or 1 millisecond, or 10, 15, or 16 milliseconds. So, the fundamental precision of the measurement is 15 milliseconds, and the extra resolution is valueless. The result output from the previous code block might have been 10 ms or 20 ms or exactly 16 ms.

What is especially frustrating about GetTickCount() is that, beyond having a resolution of 1 millisecond, it is not guaranteed to be implemented in any particular way, or in the same way on two different Windows computers.

I tested the various timing functions on Windows to find out what their usable resolution was on a particular computer (an i7-based Surface 3) and operating system (Windows 8.1). The test, shown in Example 3-1, calls a timing function repeatedly and checks the difference between the values returned by consecutive calls. If the usable resolution of the tick is greater than the latency of the function call, consecutive calls will return either the same value or a value differing by the size of the fundamental tick, in units of the function's resolution. I averaged the nonzero differences just in case the operating system stole a time slice for some other task.

Example 3-1. Measuring the tick duration of GetTickCount()

```
unsigned nz_count = 0, nz_sum = 0;
ULONG last, next;
for (last = GetTickCount(); nz_count < 100; last = next) {
    next = GetTickCount();
    if (next != last) {
        nz_count += 1;
        nz_sum += (next - last);
    }
}
std::cout << "GetTickCount() mean resolution "
          << (double)nz_sum / nz_count
          << " ticks" << std::endl;
```

The results of this test are summarized in Table 3-1.

Table 3-1. Measured tick durations, i7 Surface Pro 3, Windows 8.1

Function	Tick duration
time()	1 sec
GetTickCount()	15.6 ms
GetTickCount64()	15.6 ms
timeGetTime()	15.6 ms
clock()	1.0 ms
GetSystemTimeAsFileTime()	0.9 ms
GetSystemTimePreciseAsFileTime()	~450 ns
QueryPerformanceCounter()	~450 ns

Of particular note is that GetSystemTimeAsFileTime(), which has a display resolution of 100 nanoseconds, appears to be based on the same slow 1-millisecond tick as clock(), and that GetSystemTimePreciseAsFileTime() appears to be implemented using QueryPerformanceCounter().

Modern computers have fundamental clock periods measured in hundreds of picoseconds (100 picoseconds is 10^{-10} seconds!). They execute instructions in a few nanoseconds each. But there are no accessible tick counters on the PC with picosecond or nanosecond resolution. On PCs, the fastest tick counters available have 100-nanosecond resolution, and their fundamental accuracy may be far worse than their resolution. As a consequence, it isn't possible to measure the duration of a single call to many functions. See "Overcoming Measurement Obstacles" on page 54 to find out how to overcome this problem.

Latency

Latency is the length of time that elapses between commanding an activity to start and it actually beginning. Latency is the time between dropping a penny into a well and hearing the splash (see Figure 3-6). It's the time between when the starter's gun fires, and when the runner begins to move forward.

With regard to time measurement on computers, latency occurs because starting the clock, running the experiment, and stopping the clock are operations performed serially. The measurement performed can be broken up into five phases:

1. "Starting the clock" involves a function call that gets a tick count from the operating system. This call takes a nonzero amount of time. Somewhere in the middle of the function call, the tick counter value is actually read from a processor register. This value becomes the start time. Call this interval t_1.
2. After the value of the tick counter is read, it still must be returned and assigned to a variable. These actions take time. The actual clock is ticking, but the starting tick count is not increasing. Call this interval t_2.
3. The measured experiment begins and ends. Call this interval t_3.
4. "Stopping the clock" involves another function call to get the tick count. During the part of the function call up to the point where the tick counter value is read, the timer keeps ticking even though the experiment is over. Call this interval t_4.
5. After the value of the tick counter is read, it still must be returned and assigned to a variable. Since the tick counter is read, no more error accumulates even though the clock is still ticking. This interval is t_5.

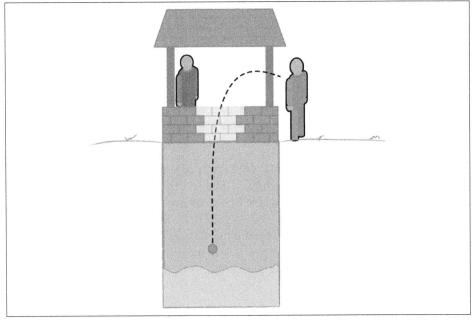

Figure 3-6. Latency: the time between throwing the penny and hearing the splash

So, while the actual duration of the measurement is t_3, the measured duration is the longer value $t_2+t_3+t_4$. The latency is thus t_2+t_4. If the latency is a significant fraction of the experiment run time, the experimenter must subtract out the latency.

Assume for instance that it takes 1 microsecond (μs) to obtain a tick count, and that the tick count is obtained by the very last instruction executed in that time. In the following pseudocode, time measurement begins on the last instruction of the first call to get_tick(), so there is no latency before the activity being measured. The latency of the call to get_tick() at the end of the test gets added to the measured duration:

```
start = get_tick() // 1uS latency before, doesn't matter
do_activity()
stop = get_tick()  // 1uS after, added onto measured interval
duration = stop-start
```

If the measured activity took 1 microsecond, the measured value will be 2 microseconds, a 100% error. If the measured activity took 1 millisecond, the measured value will be 1.001 milliseconds, a 0.1% error.

If the same function is called before and after the experiment, then $t_1=t_4$ and $t_2=t_5$. The latency is just the duration of the timer function call.

I measured the call latency of the Windows timing functions, which is just their duration. Example 3-2 presents a typical test harness for timing the GetSystemTimeAsFile Time() function.

Example 3-2. Latency of Windows timing functions

```
ULONG start = GetTickCount();
LARGE_INTEGER count;
for (counter_t i = 0; i < nCalls; ++i)
    QueryPerformanceCounter(&count);
ULONG stop = GetTickCount();
std::cout << stop - start
          << "ms for 100m QueryPerformanceCounter() calls"
          << std::endl;
```

The results of this test are summarized in Table 3-2.

Table 3-2. Latency of Windows timing functions VS 2013, i7, Win 8.1

Function	Call duration
GetSystemTimeAsFileTime()	2.8 ns
GetTickCount()	3.8 ns
GetTickCount64()	6.7 ns

Function	Call duration
QueryPerformanceCounter()	8.0 ns
clock()	13 ns
time()	15 ns
TimeGetTime()	17 ns
GetSystemTimePreciseAsFileTime()	22 ns

Among the interesting things to note here is that the latencies are all in the range of a few nanoseconds on my i7 tablet, so all these calls are reasonably efficient. This means latency won't affect measurement accuracy when function calls are timed in a loop lasting around one second. Still, the costs vary by a factor of 10, for functions that read the same low-resolution tick. GetSystemTimePreciseAsFileTime() has the highest latency, and the highest latency relative to its tick, at about 5%. Latency is a much bigger problem on slower processors.

Nondeterministic behavior

Computers are incredibly complex devices with tons of internal state, most of which is invisible to developers. Executing a function changes the state of the computer (for instance, the contents of cache memory), so that each repeated execution happens under conditions that are different from the previous one. Uncontrollable changes in internal state are thus a source of random variation in measurements.

Furthermore, the operating system schedules tasks in unpredictable ways, so that other activity on the processors and memory buses varies during a measurement run. This makes any measurement less accurate.

The operating system may even stop the code being timed to give a time slice away to another program. The tick counter continues to run during such pauses, producing a larger measured duration than if the operating system had not given a time slice to another program. This causes a somewhat larger random variation that can affect measurement.

Overcoming Measurement Obstacles

So, how bad is it really? Can we use a computer at all for timing? And what do we need to do to make it all work? This section summarizes my personal experience using the stopwatch class described in the next section to test functions for this book.

Don't sweat the small stuff

The really good news is that measurements only have to be accurate to within a couple of percent to be good enough to guide optimization. Looking at it another way, for the usual linear kinds of improvement you can expect from optimization, the measurements need only have about two significant digits—for an experiment that loops on some function for 1,000 milliseconds, about 10 milliseconds—of error. If we look at likely sources of error, as illustrated in Table 3-3, they are all well below this.

Table 3-3. Contribution of variation in 1-second Windows time measurement

Variation	Contribution %
Tick counter function latency	< 0.00001
Basic clock stability	< 0.01
Tick counter usable resolution	< 0.1

Measure relative performance

The ratio of the run time of the optimized code to the run time of the original code is called *relative performance*. Among the many good things about relative measurements is that they cancel out systematic variation, since the same variation applies to both measurements. The relative number in percentage terms is also easier to grasp intuitively than a number of milliseconds.

Improve repeatability by measuring module tests

Module tests, those staged subsystem tests using canned input data, often make good, repeatable actions for a profile run or performance measurement. Many organizations have an extensive library of module tests, and new tests can be added specifically for performance tuning.

A common concern about performance tuning goes like this: "My code is a big ball of yarn and I don't have any test cases. I have to test performance on my live input data or live database, which is always changing. I don't get consistent or repeatable results. What should I do?"

I do not have magic bullets to kill this particular beast. If I test modules or subsystems with a repeatable set of mock input data, improved performance on these tests generally translates into improved performance on live data. If I identify hot functions in a big but unrepeatable test, improving those hot functions using module test cases generally improves performance on live data. Every developer knows why they should build software systems out of loosely coupled modules. Every developer knows why they should maintain a library of good test cases. Optimization is just one more reason.

Tune performance with metrics

There is a ray of hope for the developer forced to tune performance in an unpredictable live system. Instead of measuring the value of, say, a critical response time, the developer can collect metrics, population statistics such as mean and variance, or an exponentially smoothed average of the response time. Since these statistics get their value from a large number of individual events, a durable improvement in these statistics indicates a successful code change.

Here are just a few of the issues that may arise when optimizing with metrics:

- Population statistics must be based on a large number of events to be valid. The change/test/evaluate loop is far more time-consuming with metrics than with direct measurement of a fixed input.
- Collecting metrics requires far more infrastructure than either profiling or run timing. A persistent store is usually required to hold the statistical data. Feeding this store can be expensive enough to affect performance. The system for collecting metrics must be carefully designed to make it flexible enough to support many experiments.
- Although there is a well-established methodology to verify or refute hypotheses based on statistics, the methodology requires some statistical sophistication on the part of developers to do properly.

Improve accuracy by averaging many iterations

An experiment can improve upon the accuracy of a single measurement by averaging several measurements. This is what happens when a developer times a function call in a loop or runs a program over input that causes it to call a particular function many times.

One advantage of measuring many iterations of a function call is that random variations tend to cancel out. The state of the caches tends to converge on a single value, so that each iteration is an apples-to-apples comparison. Over a long enough interval, random scheduler behavior has about the same effect on the timing of the original function and the optimized function. Although the absolute times may not be typical of the same functions in the larger program, the relative performance still measures the degree of improvement accurately.

Another advantage is that a coarser and easier-to-obtain tick counter can be used. Computers are fast enough that a single second is long enough for thousands or even millions of iterations.

Reduce nondeterministic operating system behavior by raising priority

It is possible to reduce the chance of the operating system taking slices out of a measurement run by increasing the priority of the measurement process. On Windows, the `SetPriorityClass()` function manipulates the priority of a process. The `Set ThreadPriority()` function does the same for the priority of a thread. The following code increases the priority of the current process and thread:

```
SetPriorityClass(GetCurrentProcess(), ABOVE_NORMAL_PRIORITY_CLASS);
SetThreadPriority(GetCurrentThread(), THREAD_PRIORITY_HIGHEST);
```

After the measurement, the process and thread priority should usually be restored to normal:

```
SetPriorityClass(GetCurrentProcess(), NORMAL_PRIORITY_CLASS);
SetThreadPriority(GetCurrentThread(), THREAD_PRIORITY_NORMAL);
```

Nondeterminism happens—get over it

The way I measure performance for optimization is extremely casual. It isn't informed by great knowledge of statistics. My tests run for seconds, not hours. I don't feel the need to apologize for this casual approach. These methods translate into human-visible performance improvements in overall program run time, so I must be on the right track.

If I run the same timing experiment on two different days, I get results that may differ by somewhere between 0.1% and 1%. This is no doubt due to differences in initial conditions in my PC. I have no way to control these conditions, so I don't worry. If I see larger variations, I can make the timing runs longer. As this makes my test/debug cycles longer, I don't do it unless I see a need to.

Even when I see variation of a few percent between runs, relative variation of timing measurements within a single run seems to be way below 1%. That is, I can see even relatively subtle changes by timing two variations of a function in the same test run.

I try to make timing runs on a quiet computer that isn't streaming video, running a Java update, or uncompressing a big archive. I try not to move the mouse or switch windows during a timing run. When PCs contained only one processor core, this was really important. With modern multicore processors, I don't notice much variation even if I forget to turn off Pandora.

If a timing test calls a function 10,000 times, that code and related data are going to remain in cache. If I were doing a test of worst-case absolute time for a hard real-time system, that would matter. But I am doing a relative time measurement on a system whose kernel is already nondeterministic. Furthermore, I'm testing only functions that my profiler has already identified as hot. They will thus be in cache already during production runs, so the iterated test actually represents realistic conditions.

If a modified function appears to be 1% faster, it's generally not worth modifying. Amdahl's Law will shrink its small contribution to overall run time to insignificance. An improvement of 10% has marginal value. A change of 100% is far more interesting. *Accepting only large changes in performance frees the developer from worrying about methodology.*

Create a Stopwatch Class

To time part of a program, instrument the code with a stopwatch class. The class works exactly like a mechanical stopwatch. Instantiate the stopwatch or call its `start()` member function, and the stopwatch begins to tick. Call the stopwatch's `stop()` member function or destroy the stopwatch class instance, and the stopwatch stops ticking and displays the elapsed time.

It's not hard to build a stopwatch class, and there are plenty available on the Internet. Example 3-3 shows one I have used.

Example 3-3. Stopwatch class

```
template <typename T> class basic_stopwatch : T {
    typedef typename T BaseTimer;
public:
    // create, optionally start timing an activity
    explicit basic_stopwatch(bool start);
    explicit basic_stopwatch(char const* activity = "Stopwatch",
                             bool start=true);
    basic_stopwatch(std::ostream& log,
                    char const* activity="Stopwatch",
                    bool start=true);

    // stop and destroy a stopwatch
    ~basic_stopwatch();

    // get last lap time (time of last stop)
    unsigned LapGet() const;

    // predicate: return true if the stopwatch is running
    bool IsStarted() const;

    // show accumulated time, keep running, set/return lap
    unsigned Show(char const* event="show");

    // (re)start a stopwatch, set/return lap time
    unsigned Start(char const* event_namee="start");

    // stop a running stopwatch, set/return lap time
    unsigned Stop(char const* event_name="stop");

private:    // members
    char const*     m_activity; // "activity" string
    unsigned        m_lap;      // lap time (time of last stop)
    std::ostream&   m_log;      // stream on which to log events
};
```

This code just reproduces the class definition. The member functions are inlined for maximum performance.

The class that is the value of Stopwatch's template parameter T is an even simpler kind of timer that provides operating system–dependent and C++ standard–dependent functions to access a tick counter. I wrote several versions of the TimerBase class to test different tick counter implementations. Depending on how modern the C++ compiler in use is, the class given by T can use the C++ <chrono> library or can directly obtain a tick from the operating system. Example 3-4 shows a TimerBase class that uses the C++ <chrono> library available in C++11 and later.

Example 3-4. TimerBase class using <chrono>

```
# include <chrono>
using namespace std::chrono;
class TimerBase {
public:
    // clears the timer
    TimerBase() : m_start(system_clock::time_point::min()) { }

    // clears the timer
    void Clear() {
        m_start = system_clock::time_point::min();
    }

    // returns true if the timer is running
    bool IsStarted() const {
        return (m_start.time_since_epoch() != system_clock::duration(0));
    }

    // start the timer
    void Start() {
        m_start = system_clock::now();
    }

    // get the number of milliseconds since the timer was started
    unsigned long GetMs() {
        if (IsStarted()) {
            system_clock::duration diff;
            diff = system_clock::now() - m_start;
            return (unsigned)(duration_cast<milliseconds>(diff).count());
        }
        return 0;
    }
private:
    system_clock::time_point m_start;
};
```

This class has the advantage of portability among operating systems, but it requires C++11.

Example 3-5 shows a `TimerBase` class with the same functionality that uses the `clock()` function available on both Linux and Windows.

Example 3-5. TimerBase class using clock()

```
class TimerBaseClock {
public:
    // clears the timer
    TimerBaseClock()        { m_start = -1; }

    // clears the timer
    void Clear()            { m_start = -1; }

    // returns true if the timer is running
    bool IsStarted() const  { return (m_start != -1); }

    // start the timer
    void Start()            { m_start = clock(); }

    // get the number of milliseconds since the timer was started
    unsigned long GetMs() {
        clock_t now;
        if (IsStarted()) {
            now = clock();
            clock_t dt = (now - m_start);
            return (unsigned long)(dt * 1000 / CLOCKS_PER_SEC);
        }
        return 0;
    }
private:
    clock_t m_start;
};
```

This class has the advantage of portability across C++ versions and operating systems, but the disadvantage that the `clock()` function measures somewhat different things on Linux and Windows.

Example 3-6 shows a `TimerBase` class that works for older versions of Windows and Linux. On Windows, the `gettimeofday()` function must also be explicitly provided, since it is not part of the Windows API or the C standard library.

Example 3-6. TimerBase class using gettimeofday()

```
# include <chrono>
using namespace std::chrono;
class TimerBaseChrono {
public:
```

```cpp
    // clears the timer
    TimerBaseChrono() :
        m_start(system_clock::time_point::min()) {
    }

    // clears the timer
    void Clear() {
        m_start = system_clock::time_point::min();
    }

    // returns true if the timer is running
    bool IsStarted() const {
        return (m_start != system_clock::time_point::min());
    }

    // start the timer
    void Start() {
        m_start = std::chrono::system_clock::now();
    }

    // get the number of milliseconds since the timer was started
    unsigned long GetMs() {
        if (IsStarted()) {
            system_clock::duration diff;
            diff = system_clock::now() - m_start;
            return (unsigned)
                    (duration_cast<milliseconds>(diff).count());
        }
        return 0;
    }
private:
    std::chrono::system_clock::time_point m_start;
};
```

This class is portable across C++ versions and operating systems, but it requires an implementation of the `gettimeofday()` function when used on Windows.

The simplest use of the stopwatch class makes use of the RAII (Resource Acquisition Is Initialization) idiom. The program instantiates the stopwatch class at the beginning of any set of statements enclosed by braces. When the stopwatch is instantiated, its default action is to start timing. When the stopwatch is destroyed at the closing brace, it outputs the accumulated time. The program can output the accumulated time during the program execution by calling the stopwatch's `show()` member function. This lets the developer instrument several connected regions of code with a single timer. For example:

```cpp
{
    Stopwatch sw("activity");
```

```
        DoActivity();
    }
```

This will print two lines on the standard output:

```
activity: start
activity: stop 1234mS
```

The stopwatch has no overhead while it is running. Latency at start and stop consists of the cost of the system call to get the current time, plus the cost of producing output if the show() member function is called. This latency is not significant when used to time tasks taking tens of milliseconds or more. Overhead becomes significant, and thus timing accuracy decreases, if the developer attempts to time microsecond activities.

The greatest weakness of run timing is probably the need for intuition, and thus experience, in interpreting the results. After repeated timing runs narrow the search to a particular area of interest, the developer must then inspect the code or perform experiments to identify and remove hot spots. Code inspection makes use of the developer's own experience or the heuristic rules outlined in this book. These rules have the advantage of helping you identify code that has a high runtime cost. The disadvantage is that they don't point unambiguously to a most-hot place.

Optimization Pro Tip

The developer can't always time activities that take place before main() gets control or after main() exits. If there are many classes instantiated at global scope, this may become a problem. Program time spent outside of main() can be a source of considerable overhead in large programs with many global variables. See "Remove Code from Startup and Shutdown" on page 313 for more on program startup.

Time Hot Functions in a Test Harness

Once a profiler or runtime analysis fingers a function as an optimization candidate, an easy way to work with the function is to build a test harness that calls the function many times. This allows the run time of the function to grow to a measurable value. It also evens out variations in run time caused by background tasks, context switching, and so on. The edit/compile/run cycle to time a function in isolation is faster than the more lengthy cycle of edit/compile/run followed by running the profiler and inspecting its output. Many examples in this book use this technique.

The timing test harness (Example 3-7) is just a call to the function, surrounded by a loop of, say, 10,000 iterations, surrounded in turn by an invocation of the stopwatch.

Example 3-7. Timing test harness

```
typedef unsigned counter_t;
counter_t const iterations = 10000;
    ...
{
    Stopwatch sw("function_to_be_timed()");
    for (counter_t i = 0; i < iterations; ++i) {
        result = function_to_be_timed();
    }
}
```

The number of iterations has to be guessed. The total run time should be a few hundred to a few thousand milliseconds on desktop processors if the tick counter used by Stopwatch has a useful resolution of around 10 milliseconds.

I use the type counter_t instead of unsigned or unsigned long because for some sufficiently brief functions, the variable may have to be a 64-bit unsigned long long type. It's just easier to get accustomed to using a typedef than it is to go back and retype all the type names. It's an optimization of the optimization process itself.

The outermost set of curly braces is important. It defines the scope within which sw, the instance of the Stopwatch class, exists. Because Stopwatch uses the RAII idiom, the sw constructor gets the starting tick count, and its destructor gets the final tick count and puts the results onto the standard output stream.

Estimate Code Cost to Find Hot Code

Experience has taught me that profiling and measuring run times are effective methods of finding candidates for optimization. The profiler may point to a function that is very frequently called, or that consumes a significant fraction of total processing time. It is unlikely to point to a specific C++ statement and accuse, "Colonel Mustard, in the conservatory, with the lead pipe!" There may also be times when instrumenting code for profiling is very expensive. Run timing also may implicate a large block of code without pointing to a specific problem.

The developer's next step is to estimate the cost of each statement in the identified block. This is not a precise task, like proving a theorem. Most of the value can be obtained from a cursory inspection, looking for expensive statements and structures that magnify the cost of code.

Estimate the Cost of Individual C++ Statements

As described in "Memory Is Slow" on page 17, the cost in time of memory access dominates all other instruction execution costs. On the simple microprocessors used in toasters and coffee makers, the time taken by an instruction is literally the time needed to read each byte of the instruction from memory, plus the time needed to read data needed as input to the instruction, plus the time needed to write data that is the result of the instruction. Decoding and executing the instruction itself takes a comparatively insignificant amount of time, which is hidden underneath the memory access time.

On desktop-class microprocessors, the situation is more complex. Many instructions are simultaneously in various stages of being executed. The cost of reading the stream of instructions is hidden. However, the cost of accessing the data on which the instructions operate is more difficult to hide. For this reason, the cost of reading and writing data may be used to approximate the relative cost of instruction execution across all classes of microprocessor.

To estimate how expensive a C++ statement is, a useful rule of thumb is *count the number of memory reads and writes* performed by the statement. For example, in the statement a = b + c;, where a, b, and c are integers, the values of locations b and c must be read from memory, and the sum must be written to memory at location a. This statement thus costs three memory accesses. This count doesn't depend on the microprocessor instruction set. It is the unavoidable, inevitable cost of the statement.

r = *p + a[i]; can be counted as follows: one access to read i, one to read a[i], one to read p, one to read the data to which *p points, and one to write the result in r, for a total of five accesses. The cost of function calls in memory accesses is described in "Cost of Function Calls" on page 161.

It's important to understand that this is a heuristic, a rule of thumb. In actual hardware, additional memory accesses are needed to fetch the instructions that perform the statement. However, these accesses are sequential, so they are probably very efficient. And this additional cost is proportional to the cost of accessing the data. The compiler may optimize away some of the accesses by reusing previous computations or taking advantage of static analysis of the code. The cost in units of time also depends on whether the memory accessed by the C++ statement is in cache.

But all other factors being equal, the part that matters is how many reads and writes to memory are necessary to access the data used by a statement. This heuristic is not perfect, but it's all you get unless you want to read the assembly language intermediate output of the compiler, which is tedious and usually unrewarding.

Estimate the Cost of Loops

Because each C++ statement generally performs just a handful of memory accesses, it is unlikely that a statement standing alone will be very hot unless some other factor acts on it to execute it very frequently. One such factor is when the statement appears in a loop. Then the cost of the statement is multiplied by the number of times it is executed.

If you're very lucky, you may occasionally find code that shouts out how hot it is. The profiler may finger a single function called a million times, or some hot function may contain a loop like:

```
for (int i=1; i<1000000; ++i) {
    do_something_expensive();
    if (mostly_true) {
        do_more_stuff();
        even_more();
    }
}
```

This loop is very obviously executed a million times, and is thus very hot. It's likely you'll have to do a little work to optimize it.

Estimate repeat count in nested loops

When a loop is nested inside another loop, the repeat count of the code block is the repeat count of the inner loop multiplied by the repeat count of the outer loop. For example:

```
for (int i=0; i<100; ++i) {
    for (int j=0; j<50; ++j) {
        fiddle(a[i][j]);
    }
}
```

Here, the repeat count is 100*50 = 5,000.

This particular block is extremely straightforward. There are infinite variations. For instance, in mathematics, there are important cases where code iterates over a triangular part of a matrix. And sometimes poor coding practices make it harder to discern the outline of the nested loops.

A nested loop may not be immediately obvious. If a loop invokes a function, and the function contains another loop, this inner loop is a nested loop. As we will see in "Push Loops Down into Functions to Reduce Call Overhead" on page 157, the cost of invoking the function repeatedly in the outer loop can also sometimes be eliminated.

An inner loop may be embedded within a standard library function, particularly a string-handling or character I/O function. If the repeat count is great enough, it may be worth recoding the contents of the standard library function to escape the invocation cost.

Estimate loops with variable repeat count

Not every loop provides a nice, neat count of its iterations. Many loops repeat until some condition occurs. An example is a loop that processes characters until it finds a space, or that processes digits until it finds a non-digit. The repeat count of such a loop can be estimated. Only a casual estimate is needed; say, five digits per number or six letters per word. The goal is to locate likely candidates for optimization.

Recognize implicit loops

Programs that process events (Windows UI programs, for instance) contain an implicit loop at their top level. This loop is not even visible in the program because it is hidden in the framework. If the framework is feeding events at the maximum possible rate, any code that is executed each time the event handler gets control, before the event is dispatched, or during dispatch is likely to be hot, as is code in the most frequently dispatched events.

Recognize false loops

Not every `while` or do statement is a loop at all. I have encountered code where a do statement was used to facilitate flow of control. There are other, better ways to code the simple example that follows, but with more complicated `if-then-else` logic, this idiom makes some sense. This "loop" is executed exactly once. If it reaches the `while(0)`, it exits:

```
do {
    if (!operation1())
        break;
    if (!operation2(x,y,z))
        break;
} while(0);
```

This idiom is also sometimes used to package up several statements into a C-style macro.

Other Ways to Find Hot Spots

A developer familiar with the code can choose to proceed on intuition alone, making hypotheses about areas of code that may be affecting the overall run time, and performing experiments to see whether a change in one of these areas improves overall performance.

I do not recommend this route unless you have no one to please but yourself. Instrumenting code with a profiler or timer allows developers to demonstrate to colleagues and managers that they are making progress in an optimization effort. If you go on intuition alone and do not deliver results, and sometimes even if you do deliver, your teammates will question your methods and distract you from whatever good you are doing. And they should. From their point of view, there is no way to tell if you are using your highly trained professional intuition, or just trying stuff at random.

Optimization War Story

My personal record using experience and intuition is mixed. I once reduced the unresponsive startup time of an interactive game application from an unacceptable 16 seconds to around 4 seconds. Unfortunately, I did not save a baseline measurement of the original code. My manager would only believe that I had reduced startup time from eight seconds to four, because that was what I could show him. This very evidence-minded manager then went to the trouble of instrumenting the original code with a profiler and printing the results for me. Interestingly enough, his instrumentation found pretty much the same list of functions as my intuition. However, my credibility as an optimization expert was blown because I had not pursued the task in a methodical way.

Summary

- *Performance must be measured.*
- *Make testable predictions, and write the predictions down.*
- *Make a record of code changes.*
- *If each experiment run is documented, it can quickly be repeated.*
- *A program spends 90% of its run time in 10% of its code.*
- *A measurement must be both true and precise to be accurate.*
- *Resolution is not accuracy.*
- *On Windows, the function `clock()` provides a reliable 1-millisecond clock tick. For Windows 8 and later, the function `GetSystemTimePreciseAsFileTime()` provides a submicrosecond tick.*
- *Accepting only large changes in performance frees the developer from worrying about methodology.*
- *To estimate how expensive a C++ statement is, count the number of memory reads and writes performed by the statement.*

## CHAPTER 4

Optimize String Use: A Case Study

A few can touch the magic string,
   and noisy fame is proud to win them:
Alas for those that never sing,
   but die with all their music in them!"

   —Oliver Wendell Holmes, "The Voiceless" (1858)

The C++ `std::string` class templates are among the most used features of the C++ standard library. For instance, an article in the Google Chromium developer forum (*http://bit.ly/chromium-dev*) stated that `std::string` accounted for half of all calls to the memory manager in Chromium. Any frequently executed code that manipulates strings is fertile ground for optimization. This chapter uses a discussion of optimizing string handling to illustrate recurring themes in optimization.

Why Strings Are a Problem

Strings are simple in concept, but quite subtle to implement efficiently. The particular combination of features in `std::string` interact in ways that make an efficient implementation almost impossible. Indeed, at the time this book was written, several popular compilers provided `std::string` implementations that were non-conforming in various ways.

Furthermore, the behavior of `std::string` has been changed over the years to keep up with changes in the C++ standard. This means that a conforming `std::string` implementation from a C++98 compiler may not behave the same way as a `std::string` implementation after C++11.

Strings have some behaviors that make them expensive to use, no matter the implementation. *They are dynamically allocated, they behave as values in expressions, and their implementation requires a lot of copying.*

Strings Are Dynamically Allocated

Strings are convenient because they automatically grow as needed to hold their contents. By contrast, C library functions (`strcat()`, `strcpy()`, etc.) act on fixed-size character arrays. To implement this flexibility, strings are allocated dynamically. Dynamic allocation is expensive compared to most other C++ features, so no matter what, strings are going to show up as optimization hot spots. The dynamically allocated storage is automatically released when a string variable goes out of scope or a new value is assigned to the variable. This is more convenient than having to manually release the storage, as you would with a dynamically allocated C-style character array as in the following code:

```
char* p = (char*) malloc(7);
strcpy(p, "string");
    ...
free(p);
```

The string's internal character buffer is still a fixed size, though. Any operation that makes the string longer, like appending a character or string, may cause the string to exceed the size of its internal buffer. When this happens, the operation gets a new buffer from the memory manager and copies the string into the new buffer.

`std::string` implementations do a trick to amortize the cost of reallocating storage for the character buffer as the string grows. Instead of making a request to the memory manager for the exact number of characters needed, the string implementation rounds up the request to some larger number of characters. For instance, some implementations round up the request to the next power of 2. The string then has the capacity to grow to twice its current size before needing to call the into the memory manager again. The next time an operation needs to extend the length of the string, there is room in the existing buffer, avoiding the need to allocate a new buffer. The benefit of this trick is that the cost of appending characters to a string approaches a constant asymptotically as the string grows longer. The cost of this trick is that strings carry around some unused space. If the string implements a policy of rounding up requests to a power of 2, up to half the storage in a string may be unused.

Strings Are Values

Strings behave as *values* (see "Value Objects and Entity Objects" on page 112) in assignments and expressions. Numeric constants like 2 and 3.14159 are values. You can assign a new value to a variable, but changing the variable doesn't change the value. For example:

```
int i,j;
i = 3; // i has the value 3
j = i; // j also has the value 3
i = 5; // i now has the value 5, j still has the value 3
```

Assigning one string to another works in the same way, behaving as if each string variable has a private copy of its contents:

```
std::string s1, s2;
s1 = "hot";   // s1 is "hot"
s2 = s1;      // s2 is "hot"
s1[0] = 'n'; // s2 is still "hot", s1 is "not"
```

Because strings are values, the results of string expressions are also values. If you concatenate strings, as in the statement s1 = s2 + s3 + s4;, the result of s2 + s3 is a newly allocated temporary string value. The result of concatenating s4 to this temporary string is *another* temporary string value. This value replaces the previous value of s1. Then the dynamically allocated storage for the first temporary string and the previous value of s1 are freed. This adds up to a lot of calls into the memory manager.

Strings Do a Lot of Copying

Because strings behave as values, modifying one string must not change any other strings. But strings also have mutating operations that change the contents of a string. Because of these mutating operations, each string variable must behave as if it has a private copy of its string. The simplest way to implement this behavior is to copy the string when it is constructed, assigned, or passed as an argument to a function. If strings are implemented this way, then assignment and argument passing are expensive, but mutating functions and non-const references are cheap.

There is a well-known programming idiom for things that behave as values but are expensive to copy. It is called "copy on write," and often abbreviated COW in C++ literature (see "Implement the "Copy on Write" Idiom" on page 136). In a COW string, the dynamically allocated storage can be shared between strings. A reference count lets each string know if it is using shared storage. When one string is assigned to another, only a pointer is copied, and the reference count is incremented. Any operation that changes a string's value first checks to see that there is only one pointer to that storage. If multiple strings point to the storage, any mutating operation (any operation that may change the contents of the string) allocates new storage and makes a copy of the string before making its change:

```
COWstring s1, s2;
s1 = "hot";   // s1 is "hot"
s2 = s1;      // s2 is "hot" (s1 and s2 point to the same storage)
s1[0] = 'n'; // s1 makes a new copy of its storage before
```

```
// changing anything
// s2 is still "hot", s1 is "not"
```

Copy-on-write is such a well-known idiom that developers may easily assume `std::string` is implemented that way. But *copy-on-write isn't even permitted for C++11-conforming implementations,* and is problematic in any case.

If strings are implemented using copy-on-write, then assignment and argument-passing are cheap, but non-`const` references plus any call to a mutating function requires an expensive allocate-and-copy operation if the string is shared. COW strings are also expensive in concurrent code. Every mutating function and non-`const` reference accesses the reference count. When the reference count is accessed by multiple threads, each thread must use a special instruction to get a copy of the reference count from main memory, to be sure no other thread has changed the value (see "Memory fences" on page 302).

In C++11 and later, the burden of copying is somewhat reduced by the presence of rvalue references and the move semantics (see "Implement Move Semantics" on page 137) that go with them. If a function takes an rvalue reference as argument, the string can do an inexpensive pointer copy when the actual argument is an rvalue expression, saving one copy.

First Attempt at Optimizing Strings

Suppose that profiling a large program reveals that the function `remove_ctrl()` reproduced in Example 4-1 consumes significant time in the program. This function removes control characters from a string of ASCII characters. It looks innocent enough, but the performance of the function as written is terrible, for many reasons. In fact, this function is a compact demonstration of the danger of completing a coding task without giving thought to performance.

Example 4-1. remove_ctrl(): code ready to optimize

```
std::string remove_ctrl(std::string s) {
    std::string result;
    for (int i=0; i<s.length(); ++i) {
        if (s[i] >= 0x20)
            result = result + s[i];
    }
    return result;
}
```

`remove_ctrl()` processes each character in argument string `s` in a loop. The code in the loop is what makes this function a hot spot. The `if`-condition gets a character from the string and compares it to a literal constant. This is unlikely to be the problem. The controlled statement on line 5 is another story.

As noted previously, the string concatenation operator is expensive. It calls into the memory manager to construct a new temporary string object to hold the concatenated string. If the argument to `remove_ctrl()` is typically a string of printable characters, then `remove_ctrl()` constructs a new temporary string object for nearly every character in s. For a string with 100 characters, that's 100 calls into the memory manager to create storage for the temporary string, and another 100 calls to release the storage.

In addition to the temporary strings allocated for the result of the concatenation operation, additional strings may be allocated when the string expression is assigned to `result`, depending on how strings are implemented:

- If strings are implemented using the copy-on-write idiom, then the assignment operator performs an efficient pointer copy and increments the reference count.
- If strings have a non–shared buffer implementation, then the assignment operator must copy the contents of the temporary string. If the implementation is naïve, or `result`'s buffer does not have enough capacity, then the assignment operator also allocates a new buffer to copy into. This results in 100 copy operations and as many as 100 additional allocations.
- If the compiler implements C++11-style rvalue references and move semantics, then the fact that the concatenation expression's result is an rvalue allows the compiler to call `result`'s move constructor instead of its copy constructor. The result is that the program performs an efficient pointer copy.

The concatenation operation also copies all characters previously processed into the temporary string each time it is executed. If there are n characters in the argument string, `remove_ctrl()` copies $O(n^2)$ characters. The result of all this allocation and copying is poor performance.

Since `remove_ctrl()` is a small, standalone function, it is possible to build a test harness that calls the function repeatedly to measure exactly how much performance can be improved through optimization. Building test harnesses and measuring performance is covered in Chapter 3. The code for the test harness, and other code from the book, can be downloaded from my website (*http://www.guntheroth.com*).

I wrote a timing test that repeatedly called `remove_ctrl()` with a 222-character argument string containing several control characters. On average, each call took 24.8 microseconds. This number isn't important by itself, as it depends on my PC (Intel i7 tablet), operating system (Windows 8.1), and compiler (Visual Studio 2010, 32-bit, Release build). Rather, it forms a baseline for measuring performance improvement.

In the following sections, I describe a set of optimization steps, and the resulting improvement in performance of the remove_ctrl() function.

Use Mutating String Operations to Eliminate Temporaries

I began optimizing remove_ctrl() by removing allocation and copy operations. Example 4-2 is an improved version of remove_ctrl() in which the concatenation expression in line 5 that produced so many new temporary string objects is replaced by the mutating concatenating assignment operator, +=.

Example 4-2. remove_ctrl_mutating(): mutating string operators

```
std::string remove_ctrl_mutating(std::string s) {
    std::string result;
    for (int i=0; i<s.length(); ++i) {
        if (s[i] >= 0x20)
            result += s[i];
    }
    return result;
}
```

This small change has a dramatic effect on performance. The same timing test now showed an average of only 1.72 microseconds per call, a 13x improvement. This improvement comes from eliminating all the calls to allocate temporary string objects to hold the concatenation expression result, and the associated copying and deleting of temporaries. Depending on the string implementation, allocation and copying on assignment are also eliminated.

Reduce Reallocation by Reserving Storage

The function remove_ctrl_mutating() still performs an operation that lengthens result. This means result is periodically copied into a larger internal dynamic buffer. As previously discussed, one possible implementation of std::string doubles the amount of storage allocated each time the capacity of the string's character buffer is exceeded. When std::string is implemented with this rule, reallocation might happen as many as 8 times for a 100-character string.

If we assume that strings are generally printable characters, with only occasional control characters to remove, then the length of the string argument s provides an excellent estimate of the result string's eventual length. Example 4-3 improves on remove_ctrl_mutating() by using std::string's reserve() member function to preallocate the estimated amount of storage. Not only does use of reserve() eliminate reallocation of the string buffer, but it also improves the cache locality of the data accessed by the function, so we get even more mileage out of this change.

Example 4-3. remove_ctrl_reserve(): reserving storage

```
std::string remove_ctrl_reserve(std::string s) {
    std::string result;
    result.reserve(s.length());
    for (int i=0; i<s.length(); ++i) {
        if (s[i] >= 0x20)
            result += s[i];
    }
    return result;
}
```

The removal of several allocations causes a significant improvement in performance. A test using `remove_ctrl_reserve()` consumes 1.47 microseconds per call, an improvement of 17% over `remove_ctrl_mutating()`.

Eliminate Copying of String Arguments

So far, I have been successful at optimizing `remove_ctrl()` by removing calls on the memory manager. It is thus reasonable to continue looking for allocations to remove.

When a string expression is passed into a function by value, the formal argument (in this case, `s`) is copy-constructed. This may result in a copy, depending on the string implementation:

- If strings are implemented using the copy-on-write idiom, then the compiler generates a call to the copy constructor, which performs an efficient pointer copy and increments the reference count.

- If strings have a nonshared buffer implementation, then the copy constructor must allocate a new buffer and copy the contents of the actual argument.

- If the compiler implemented C++11-style rvalue references and move semantics, then if the actual argument is an expression, it will be an rvalue, so the compiler will generate a call to the move constructor, resulting in an efficient pointer copy. If the actual argument is a variable, then the formal argument's copy constructor is called, resulting in an allocation-and-copy. Rvalue references and move semantics are described in more detail in "Implement Move Semantics" on page 137.

`remove_ctrl_ref_args()` in Example 4-4 is an improved function that never copies `s` on call. Since the function does not modify `s`, there is no reason to make a separate copy of `s`. Instead, `remove_ctrl_ref_args()` takes a `const` reference to `s` as an argument. This saves another allocation. Since allocation is expensive, it can be worthwhile eliminating even one allocation.

Example 4-4. remove_ctrl_ref_args(): argument copy eliminated

```
std::string remove_ctrl_ref_args(std::string const& s) {
    std::string result;
    result.reserve(s.length());
    for (int i=0; i<s.length(); ++i) {
        if (s[i] >= 0x20)
            result += s[i];
    }
    return result;
}
```

The result is a surprise. The timing test of `remove_ctrl_ref_args()` took 1.60 microseconds per call, 8% worse than `remove_ctrl_reserve()`.

What's going on here? Visual Studio 2010 copies string values on call, so this change should save an allocation. Either that savings isn't realized, or something else related to the change of s from string to string reference must consume that savings.

Reference variables are implemented as pointers. So, everywhere s appears in `remove_ctrl_ref_args()`, the program dereferences a pointer that it did not have to dereference in `remove_ctrl_reserve()`. I hypothesize that this extra work might be enough to account for the reduced performance.

Eliminate Pointer Dereference Using Iterators

The solution is to use iterators over the string, as in Example 4-5. String iterators are simple pointers into the character buffer. That saves two dereference operations versus the non-iterator code in the loop.

Example 4-5. remove_ctrl_ref_args_it(): iterator version of remove_ctrl_ref_args()

```
std::string remove_ctrl_ref_args_it(std::string const& s) {
    std::string result;
    result.reserve(s.length());
    for (auto it=s.begin(),end=s.end(); it != end; ++it) {
        if (*it >= 0x20)
            result += *it;
    }
    return result;
}
```

The timing test for `remove_ctrl_ref_args_it()` produced a satisfying result of 1.04 microseconds per call. It is definitely superior to the non-iterator version. But what about making s a string reference? To find out if this optimization actually improved anything, I coded an iterator version of `remove_ctrl_reserve()`. The timing test for `remove_ctrl_reserve_it()` took 1.26 microseconds per call, down from 1.47 microseconds. The string reference argument optimization definitely improved performance.

In fact, I coded iterator versions of all the remove_ctrl()-derived functions. Iterators were a definite win in all cases versus the subscripting versions (however, in "Second Attempt at Optimizing Strings" on page 80, we'll see that this is not always the case).

remove_ctrl_ref_args_it() contains one other optimization of note. The value s.end(), used to control the for loop, is cached on loop initialization. This saves another *2n* indirections, where *n* is the length of the argument string.

Eliminate Copying of Returned String Values

The original remove_ctrl() function returns its result by value. C++ copy-constructs the result into the calling context, though the compiler is permitted to *elide* (that is, simplify by removing) the copy construction if it can. If we want to be *sure* that there is no copy, we have a couple of choices. One choice that works for all versions of C++ and all string implementations is to return the string as an out parameter. This is actually what the compiler does when it elides a copy construction. An improved version of remove_ctrl_ref_args_it() appears in Example 4-6.

Example 4-6. remove_ctrl_ref_result_it(): copy of return value eliminated

```
void remove_ctrl_ref_result_it(
    std::string& result,
    std::string const& s)
{
    result.clear();
    result.reserve(s.length());
    for (auto it=s.begin(),end=s.end(); it != end; ++it) {
        if (*it >= 0x20)
            result += *it;
    }
}
```

When a program calls remove_ctrl_ref_result_it(), a reference to some string variable is passed into the formal argument result. If the string variable referenced by result is empty, then the call to reserve() allocates storage for enough characters. If the string variable has been used before—if the program called remove_ctrl_ref_result_it() in a loop—its buffer may already be big enough, in which case no new allocation takes place. When the function returns, the string variable in the caller holds the return value, with no copy required. The beautiful thing about remove_ctrl_ref_result_it() is that in many cases, it eliminates every allocation.

Measured performance of `remove_ctrl_ref_result_it()` is 1.02 microseconds per call, about 2% faster than the previous version.

`remove_ctrl_ref_result_it()` is *very* efficient, but its interface is open to misuse in a way that the original `remove_ctrl()` was not. A reference—even a `const` reference—doesn't behave exactly the same as a value. The following call will produce unintended results, returning an empty string:

```
std::string foo("this is a string");
remove_ctrl_ref_result_it(foo, foo);
```

Use Character Arrays Instead of Strings

When a program requires the ultimate in performance, it is possible to bypass the C++ standard library altogether and handcode the function using the C-style string functions, as in Example 4-7. The C-style string functions are harder to use than `std::string`, but the gain in performance can be impressive. To use the C-style string functions, the programmer must choose either to manually allocate and free character buffers, or to use static arrays dimensioned to worst-case sizes. Declaring a bunch of static arrays is problematic if memory is at all constrained. However, there is usually room to statically declare large temporary buffers in local storage (that is, on the function call stack). These buffers are reclaimed at negligible runtime cost when the function exits. Except in the most constrained embedded environments, it is no problem to declare a worst-case buffer of 1,000 or even 10,000 characters on the stack.

Example 4-7. remove_ctrl_cstrings(): coding on the bare metal

```
void remove_ctrl_cstrings(char* destp, char const* srcp, size_t size) {
    for (size_t i=0; i<size; ++i) {
        if (srcp[i] >= 0x20)
            *destp++ = srcp[i];
    }
    *destp = 0;
}
```

`remove_ctrl_cstrings()` took 0.15 microseconds per call in the timing test. This is 6 times faster than its predecessor, and an astonishing 170 times faster than the original function. One reason for the improvement is the elimination of several function calls, with a corresponding improvement in cache locality.

Excellent cache locality may, however, contribute to a simple performance measurement being misleading. In general, other operations between calls to `remove_ctrl_cstrings()` flush the cache. But when it is called in a tight loop, instructions and data stay in cache.

Another factor affecting `remove_ctrl_cstrings()` is that it has a markedly different interface to the original function. If called from many locations, changing all the calls is a significant effort, and may be one optimization too many. Nonetheless, `remove_ctrl_cstrings()` is an example of just how much performance can be gained by the developer willing to completely recode a function and change its interface.

Stop and Think

I think we might be going a bridge too far.

—Lt. General Frederick "Boy" Browning (1896–1965)

Comment to Field Marshal Montgomery on September 10, 1944, expressing his concerns about the Allied plan to capture the bridge at Arnhem. Browning's concern was prophetic, as the operation was a disaster.

As noted in the previous section, an optimization effort may arrive at a point where simplicity or safety must be traded for additional performance gains. `remove_ctrl_ref_result_it()` required a change in function signature that introduced a potential incorrect usage not possible with `remove_ctrl()`. For `remove_ctrl_cstrings()`, the cost was manually managing the temporary storage. For some teams, this may be a bridge too far.

Developers have differing opinions, sometimes very strong ones, about whether a particular performance improvement justifies the added complexity of the interface or increased need to review uses of the function. Developers who favor an optimization like returning a value in an out parameter might say that the dangerous use case isn't all that likely, and could be documented. Returning the string in an out parameter also leaves the function's return value available for useful things like error codes. Those who oppose this optimization might say there is nothing obvious to warn users away from the dangerous use case, and a subtle bug is more trouble than the optimization is worth. In the end, the team must answer the question, "How much do we need this performance improvement?"

I can offer no guidance on exactly when an optimization effort has gone too far. It depends on how important the performance improvement is. But developers should note the transition and take a moment to stop and think.

C++ offers developers a range of choices between simple and safe code that is slow and radically fast code that must be used carefully. Advocates of other languages may call this a weakness, but for optimization, it is one of the greatest strengths of C++.

Summary of First Optimization Attempt

Table 4-1 summarizes the results of the optimization effort for remove_ctrl(). These results were obtained by pursuing one simple rule: remove memory allocations and associated copy operations. The first optimization produced the most significant speedup.

Many factors affect the absolute timings, including the processor, fundamental clock rate, memory bus frequency, compiler, and optimizer. I've provided test results of both debug and release (optimized) builds to demonstrate this point. While the release build code is *much* faster than the debug code, improvement is visible in both debug and release builds.

Table 4-1. Performance summary VS 2010, i7

Function	Debug	Δ	Release	Δ	Release vs. debug
remove_ctrl()	967 µs		24.8 µs		3802%
remove_ctrl_mutating()	104 µs	834%	1.72 µs	1,341%	5923%
remove_crtl_reserve()	102 µs	142%	1.47 µs	17%	6853%
remove_ctrl_ref_args_it()	215 µs	9%	1.04 µs	21%	20559%
remove_ctrl_ref_result_it()	215 µs	0%	1.02 µs	2%	21012%
remove_ctrl_cstrings()	1 µs	9,698%	0.15 µs	601%	559%

The percentage of improvement appears far more dramatic in release builds. This is probably an effect of Amdahl's Law. In the debug build, function inlining is turned off, which increases the cost of every function call and causes the fraction of run time devoted to memory allocation to be lower.

Second Attempt at Optimizing Strings

There are other roads the developer can travel in the quest for better performance; we'll explore a few more options in this section.

Use a Better Algorithm

One option is to attempt to improve the algorithm. The original remove_ctrl() uses a simple algorithm that copies one character at a time to the result string. This unfortunate choice produces the worst possible allocation behavior. Example 4-8 improves on the original design by moving whole substrings to the result string. This change has the effect of reducing the number of allocate-and-copy operations. Another optimization introduced in remove_ctrl_block() is caching the length of the argument string to reduce the cost of the loop termination clause of the outer for loop.

Example 4-8. remove_ctrl_block(): a faster algorithm

```
std::string remove_ctrl_block(std::string s) {
    std::string result;
    for (size_t b=0, i=b, e=s.length(); b < e; b = i+1) {
        for (i=b; i<e; ++i) {
            if (s[i] < 0x20)
                break;
        }
        result = result + s.substr(b,i-b);
    }
    return result;
}
```

`remove_ctrl_block()` runs the timing test in 2.91 microseconds, about 7 times faster than the original `remove_ctrl()`.

This function in turn can be improved in the same way as before, by replacing the concatenation with a mutating assignment (`remove_ctrl_block_mutate()`, 1.27 microseconds per call), but `substr()` still constructs a temporary string. Since the function appends characters to `result`, the developer can use one of the overloads of `std::string`'s `append()` member function to copy the substring without creating a string temporary. The resulting function, `remove_ctrl_block_append()` (as shown in Example 4-9), runs the timing test in 0.65 microseconds per call. This result handily beats the best time of 1.02 microseconds per call for `remove_ctrl_ref_result_it()`, and is 36 times better than the original `remove_ctrl()`. This is a concise demonstration of the power of selecting a good algorithm.

Example 4-9. remove_ctrl_block_append(): a faster algorithm

```
std::string remove_ctrl_block_append(std::string s) {
    std::string result;
    result.reserve(s.length());
    for (size_t b=0,i=b; b < s.length(); b = i+1) {
        for (i=b; i<s.length(); ++i) {
            if (s[i] < 0x20) break;
        }
        result.append(s, b, i-b);
    }
    return result;
}
```

These results can in turn be improved by reserving storage in `result` and eliminating the argument copy (`remove_ctrl_block_args()`, 0.55 microseconds per call), and by removing the copy of the returned value (`remove_ctrl_block_ret()`, 0.51 microseconds per call).

One thing that did not improve the results, at least at first, was recoding `remove_ctrl_block()` using iterators. However, after both the argument and return value had been made reference parameters, the iterator version went suddenly from being 10 times as expensive to 20% less expensive, as shown in Table 4-2.

Table 4-2. Performance summary of second remove_ctrl algorithm

	Time per call	Δ vs. previous
`remove_ctrl()`	24.8 µs	
`remove_ctrl_block()`	2.91 µs	751%
`remove_ctrl_block_mutate()`	1.27 µs	129%
`remove_ctrl_block_append()`	0.65 µs	95%
`remove_ctrl_block_args()`	0.55 µs	27%
`remove_ctrl_block_ret()`	0.51 µs	6%
`remove_ctrl_block_ret_it()`	0.43 µs	19%

Another way to improve performance is to mutate the argument string by removing control characters from it using std::string's mutating erase() member function. Example 4-10 demonstrates this approach.

Example 4-10. remove_ctrl_erase(): mutating the string argument instead of building a result string

```
std::string remove_ctrl_erase(std::string s) {
    for (size_t i = 0; i < s.length(); )
        if (s[i] < 0x20)
            s.erase(i,1);
        else ++i;
    return s;
}
```

The advantage of this algorithm is that, since s gets shorter, there is never any reallocation, except possibly for the returned value. The performance of this function is excellent, completing the test in 0.81 microseconds per call, 30 times faster than the original remove_ctrl(). A developer arriving at this excellent result on the first attempt might be excused for declaring victory and retiring from the field of battle without any further effort. *Sometimes a different algorithm is easier to optimize or inherently more efficient.*

Use a Better Compiler

I ran the same timing tests using the Visual Studio 2013 compiler. Visual Studio 2013 implements move semantics, which should have made some of the functions considerably faster. However, the results were mixed. Running under the debugger, Visual Studio 2013 was 5%–15% percent faster than Visual Studio 2010. Running from the command line, VS2013 was 5%–20% percent slower. I tried the Visual Studio 2015 release candidate, but it was slower yet. This may have been due to changes in the container classes. A new compiler may improve performance, but it's something the developer must test, rather than taking it on faith.

Use a Better String Library

The definition of `std::string` was originally quite vague, to allow for a wide range of implementations. The demands of efficiency and predictability eventually drove clarifications to the C++ standard that eliminated most novel implementations. The behavior defined for `std::string` is thus a compromise, having evolved out of competing design considerations over a long period of time:

- Like other standard library containers, `std::string` provides iterators to access the individual characters of the string.

- Like C character strings, `std::string` provides an array-like indexing notation using `operator[]` to access its elements. `std::string` also provides a mechanism to obtain a pointer to a C-style null-terminated version of the string.

- `std::string` has a concatenation operator and value-returning functions that give it value semantics, similar to BASIC strings.

- `std::string` provides a limited set of operations that some users find constraining.

The desire to make `std::string` as efficient as C-style `char` arrays pushes the implementation toward representing the string in contiguous memory. The C++ standard requires that the iterators be random-access, and forbids copy-on-write semantics. This makes it easier to define and to reason about what actions invalidate iterators into a `std::string`, but it limits the scope for clever implementations.

Furthermore, the `std::string` implementation that comes with a commercial C++ compiler must be straightforward enough that it can be tested, to guarantee that it produces standard-conforming behavior and acceptable efficiency in every conceivable situation. The cost to the compiler vendor for making a mistake is high. This pushes implementations toward simplicity.

The standard-defined behavior of `std::string` induces some weaknesses. Inserting a single character in a million-character string causes the whole suffix of the string to be copied, and perhaps reallocated. Similarly, all the value-returning substring operations must allocate and copy their results. Some developers search for optimization opportunities by lifting one or more of the previous constraints (iterators, indexing, C-string access, value semantics, simplicity).

Adopt a richer library for std::string

Sometimes using a better library means nothing more than providing additional string functions. Here are a few of the many libraries that work with std::string:

Boost string library (http://bit.ly/boost-string)
> The Boost string library provides functions for tokenizing, formatting, and more exotic manipulations of std::string. It's a treat for those who are deeply in love with the standard library's <algorithm> header.

C++ String Toolkit Library (http://bit.ly/string-kit-lib)
> Another choice is the C++ String Toolkit Library (StrTk). StrTk is particularly good at parsing and tokenizing strings, and is compatible with std::string.

Use std::stringstream to avoid value semantics

C++ already contains several string implementations: the templatized, iterator-accessed, variable-length character strings of std::string; the simple, iterator-based std::vector<char>; and the older, C-style null-terminated character strings in fixed-size arrays.

Although C-style character strings are tricky to use well, we've already seen an experiment that showed that replacing C++'s std::string with C-style character arrays improved performance dramatically under the right conditions. Neither of these implementations is perfect for every situation.

C++ contains yet another kind of string. std::stringstream does for strings what std::ostream does for output files. The std::stringstream class encapsulates a dynamically resizable buffer (in fact, usually a std::string) in a different way, as an *entity* (see "Value Objects and Entity Objects" on page 112) to which data can be appended. std::stringstream is an example of how putting a different API on top of a similar implementation can encourage more efficient coding. Example 4-11 illustrates its use.

Example 4-11. std::stringstream: like string, but an object

```
std::stringstream s;
for (int i=0; i<10; ++i) {
    s.clear();
    s << "The square of " << i << " is " << i*i << std::endl;
    log(s.str());
}
```

This snippet shows several optimal coding techniques. Since s is modified as an entity, the long inserter expression doesn't create any temporaries that must be allocated and copied into. Another deliberate practice is that s is declared outside of the loop. In this way, the internal buffer inside s is reused. The first time through the loop the buffer may have to be reallocated several times as characters are appended, but subsequent iterations are unlikely to reallocate the buffer. By contrast, if s had been declared inside the loop, an empty buffer would have been constructed each time through the loop, and potentially reallocated as the insertion operator appended characters.

If `std::stringstream` is implemented using a `std::string`, it can never truly out-perform `std::string`. Its advantage lies in preventing some of the programming practices that lead to inefficiency.

Adopt a novel string implementation

A developer may find the whole string abstraction inadequate. One of the most important C++ features is that abstractions like strings are not built into the language, but instead provided as templates or function libraries. Alternate implementations have access to the same language features as `std::string`, so performance may be improved by a sufficiently clever implementer. Lifting one or more of the constraints listed at the beginning of this section (iterators, indexing, C-string access, simplicity) grants a custom string class access to optimizations denied to `std::string`.

Many clever string data structures have been proposed over time that promise to significantly reduce the cost of reallocating memory and copying string contents. This may be a siren song, for several reasons:

- Any pretender to the throne of `std::string` must be both more expressive and more efficient than `std::string` in a wide variety of situations. Most proposed alternative implementations don't come with good guarantees of increased general performance.

- Replacing every occurrence of `std::string` in a large program with some other string is a significant undertaking, with no assurance that it will make a difference to performance.

- While many alternative string concepts have been proposed, and several have been implemented, it will take more than a few minutes of Googling to find a string implementation as complete, well tested, and well understood as `std::string`.

Replacing `std::string` may be more practical when considering a design than when optimizing one. It may be possible for a big team with time and resources. But the payoff is uncertain enough to make this optimization perhaps a bridge too far. Still, for the brave and the desperate there is code out in the wild that might help:

`std::string_view`
> `string_view` solves some of the problems of `std::string`. It contains an unowned pointer to string data and a length, so that it represents a substring of a `std::string` or literal character string. Operations like substring and trim are more efficient than the corresponding value-returning member functions of `std::string`. `string_view` is on its way to appearing in C++14. Some compilers have it now in `std::experimental`. `string_view` has mostly the same interface as `std::string`.
>
> The problem with `string_view` is that the pointer is unowned. The programmer must ensure that the lifetime of any `string_view` is not longer than the lifetime of the `std::string` it points into.

`folly::fbstring` *(http://bit.ly/folly-lib)*
> Folly is a whole library of code used by Facebook in its own servers. It includes a very highly optimized direct replacement for `std::string` that implements a nonallocated buffer to optimize short strings. `fbstring`'s designers claim measurable performance improvements.
>
> Because of its heritage, Folly is unusually likely to be robust and complete. Folly is supported on Linux.

A Toolbox of String Classes (http://bit.ly/toolbox-strings)
> This article and code from the year 2000 describes a templatized string type with the same interface as the SGI implementation of `std::string`. It provides a fixed-maximum-size string and a variable-length string type. It is a *tour de force* of template metaprogramming magic, which may make it hard for some people to understand. For someone committed to designing a better string class, it is a viable candidate.

"C++03 Expression Templates" (http://craighenderson.co.uk/papers/exptempl/)
> This is a 2005 paper presenting some template code to solve the specific problem of concatenation. Expression templates override the + operator, to create an intermediate type that represents concatenation of two strings or a string and a string expression symbolically. Expression templates defer allocation and copying to the end of the expression performing one allocation when the expression template is assigned to a string. Expression templates are compatible with `std::string`. The existing code can improve performance significantly when a string expression is a long list of concatenated substrings. The same concept could be extended to a whole string library.

The Better String Library (http://bstring.sourceforge.net/)
> This code archive contains a general-purpose string implementation that is different from `std::string` but contains some powerful features. If many strings

are constructed from parts of other strings, `bstring` allows one string to be formed from an offset and length within another string. I worked with a proprietary implementation of this idea that was very efficient. There is a C++ wrapper class called `CBString` for the `bstring` library.

`rope<T,alloc>` *(https://www.sgi.com/tech/stl/Rope.html)*
This is a string library suitable for making insertions and deletions in very long strings. It's not compatible with `std::string`.

Boost String Algorithms (http://bit.ly/booststring)
This is a library of string algorithms to supplement the `std::string` member functions. They are built around a find-and-replace concept.

Use a Better Allocator

Inside every `std::string` is a dynamically allocated array of `char`. `std::string` is a specialization of a more general template that looks like this:

```
namespace std {
    template < class charT,
            class traits = char_traits<charT>,
            class Alloc = allocator<charT>
            > class basic_string;

    typedef basic_string<char> string;
    ...
};
```

The third template parameter, `Alloc`, defines an *allocator*, a specialized interface to the C++ memory manager. `Alloc` defaults to `std::allocator`, which calls `::opera tor new()` and `::operator delete()`, the global C++ memory allocator functions.

The behavior of `::operator new()` and `::operator delete()`, and of allocator objects, is covered in more detail in Chapter 13. For now, I'll just say that `::operator new()` and `::operator delete()` have a very complex and difficult job, allocating storage for all the many kinds of dynamic variables. They have to work for big and small objects, and for single- and multithreaded programs. Their design is a compromise to achieve such generality. Sometimes, a more specialized allocator can do a better job. Thus, `Alloc` can be specified as something other than the default to provide a specialized allocator for `std::string`.

I coded an extremely simple allocator to demonstrate what kind of performance improvement might be achievable. This allocator manages a few fixed-size blocks of memory. I created a new `typedef` for a kind of string that uses this allocator. Then I changed the original, very inefficient version of `remove_ctrl()` to use the special strings, as shown in Example 4-12.

Example 4-12. Original version of remove_ctrl() with simple fixed block allocator

```
typedef std::basic_string<
    char,
    std::char_traits<char>,
    block_allocator<char, 10>> fixed_block_string;

fixed_block_string remove_ctrl_fixed_block(std::string s) {
    fixed_block_string result;
    for (size_t i=0; i<s.length(); ++i) {
        if (s[i] >= 0x20)
            result = result + s[i];
    }
    return result;
}
```

The result was dramatic. `remove_ctrl_fixed_block()` ran the same test in 13,636 milliseconds, about 7.7 times faster than the original.

Changing allocators is not for the faint of heart. You can't assign strings based on different allocators to one another. The modified example shown here only works because `s[i]` is a char, rather than a one-character `std::string`. You can copy the contents of one string to another by converting it to a C string, for instance, by saying `result = s.c_str();`.

Changing all the occurrences of `std::string` to `fixed_block_string` has a massive effect on a code base. For this reason, if a team thinks they may fiddle with their strings, creating a project-wide `typedef` early on in the design is a good idea:

```
typedef std::string MyProjString;
```

Then experiments involving a global change can be performed in one place. This will still only work, though, if the new string has the same member functions as the one it replaces. Differently allocated `std::basic_strings` have this property.

Eliminate String Conversion

Among the complexities of the modern world is that there is more than one kind of character string. Generally, string functions only permit like kinds of string to be compared, assigned, or used as operands or arguments, so the programmer must convert from one kind of string to another. Any time conversion involves copying characters or allocating dynamic memory is an opportunity to improve performance.

The library of conversion functions themselves can be tuned. More importantly, the design of a large program can limit conversion.

Conversion from C String to std::string

One common source of wasted computer cycles is unnecessary conversion from null-terminated character strings to `std::string`. For instance:

```
std::string MyClass::Name() const {
    return "MyClass";
}
```

This function must convert the string constant `MyClass` to a `std::string`, allocating storage and copying the characters into the `std::string`. C++ does this conversion automatically because `std::string` has a constructor that takes a `char*` argument.

The conversion to `std::string` is unnecessary. `std::string` has a constructor that accepts a `char*` argument, so the conversion will happen automatically when the value returned by `Name()` is assigned to a string or passed to a function that takes a string argument. The previous function could as easily have been written as follows:

```
char const* MyClass::Name() const {
    return "MyClass";
}
```

This delays conversion of the returned value to the point where it is actually used. At the point of use, conversion is often not needed:

```
char const* p = myInstance->Name(); // no conversion
std::string s = myInstance->Name(); // conversion to std::string
std::cout << myInstance->Name();    // no conversion
```

What makes string conversion a big problem is that a big software system may have multiple layers. If one layer takes a `std::string` and the layer below it takes a `char*`, there may be code to reverse the conversion to `std::string`:

```
void HighLevelFunc(std::string s) {
    LowLevelFunc(s.c_str());
}
```

Converting Between Character Encodings

Modern C++ programs have to deal with comparing (for instance) a literal C string (ASCII, in signed bytes) to a UTF-8 (unsigned, variable bytes per character) string from a web browser, or with converting output character strings from an XML parser that produces UTF-16 word streams (with or without endian bytes) to UTF-8. The number of possible combinations is daunting.

The best way to eliminate conversions is to pick a single format for all strings, and store all strings in that format. You might want to provide specialized comparison functions between your chosen format and C-style null-terminated strings, so they don't have to be converted. I like UTF-8 because it can represent all Unicode code points, is directly comparable (for equality) with C-style strings, and is produced by most browsers.

In large and hastily written programs, you may find a string converted from an original format to a new format, and then back to its original format as it passes through layers of the software. The fix for this is to rewrite member functions at the class interfaces to take the same type of strings. Unfortunately, this task is like adding const-correctness to a C++ program. The change tends to ripple through the entire program in ways that make it difficult to control the scope of the change.

Summary

- *Strings are expensive to use because they are dynamically allocated, they behave as values in expressions, and their implementation requires a lot of copying.*

- *Treating strings as objects instead of values reduces the frequency of allocation and copying.*

- *Reserving space in a string reduces the overhead of allocation.*

- *Passing a const reference to a string into a function is almost the same as passing the value, but can be more efficient.*

- *Passing a result string out of a function as a reference reuses the actual argument's storage, which is potentially more efficient than allocating new storage.*

- *An optimization that only sometimes removes allocation overhead is still an optimization.*

- *Sometimes a different algorithm is easier to optimize or inherently more efficient.*

- *The standard library class implementations are general-purpose and simple. They are not necessarily high-performance, or optimal for any particular use.*

## CHAPTER 5

Optimize Algorithms

Time heals what reason cannot.

—Seneca the Younger (c. 4 BC–65 AD)

If a program takes hours to run, when it needs to take seconds, the only optimization likely to be successful is to select a more efficient algorithm. Most optimizations improve performance by only a constant factor. Replacing an inefficient algorithm with a better-performing one is the only sure ticket to an order-of-magnitude improvement in performance.

Design of efficient algorithms is the topic of many whole computer science textbooks and numerous doctoral dissertations. There are specialist computer scientists who devote their careers to analysis of algorithms. There's no way to cover the topic in a single short chapter. Instead, this chapter looks briefly at the time cost of algorithms, providing a guide to know when you're in trouble.

I take a look at common searching and sorting algorithms, and present a toolkit for optimizing searching and sorting in existing programs. In addition to picking an algorithm that is optimal for unknown data, there are algorithms with exceptional performance on data that is sorted or nearly sorted, or that has other special properties.

Computer scientists study important algorithms and data structures because they are examples of how to optimize code. I have collected some important optimization techniques in the hope that the reader will come to recognize places where they can be applied.

Optimization War Story

Many programming problems have simple solutions that are infeasibly slow, and more subtle published solutions that are relatively more efficient. A team's best option may be to seek an outside expert in algorithm analysis to determine whether an efficient solution to a particular problem may exist. Retaining such a consultant can be money well spent.

I once was on a team developing functional board testers (including the Fluke 9010A pictured in Chapter 2). Our board tester had a built-in RAM test for diagnosing manufacturing defects in the device under test. I once thought to examine the coverage of this test by connecting the tester to a Commodore PET computer and running the RAM test over its video memory, so that the test patterns were visible on the PET's built-in screen. I inserted faults into the RAM circuit by the crude but effective method of jabbing a screwdriver between adjacent pins of the PET's video RAM chips. We were all quite surprised to learn that faults that visibly changed the patterns written to RAM were often not detected by our test, which had been developed by some very smart engineers. Furthermore, Moore's Law was doubling the amount of RAM we needed to test every 18 months. We needed a new RAM test algorithm that was much faster than the existing test, and with demonstrably better fault coverage.

An exhaustive RAM test is infeasible, taking $O(2^n)$ accesses to memory (where n is the number of RAM addresses—see "Time Cost of Algorithms" on page 92 for more on the "big-O" notation). Published RAM test algorithms at that time were mostly infeasibly slow $O(n^2)$ or $O(n^3)$ tests developed without much thought when memory devices held only a few hundred words. Published tests that were theoretically sound required 30 accesses to each cell to achieve basic fault coverage. I had an idea for a much better test using pseudorandom sequences, but lacked the mathematical know-how to demonstrate its soundness. We had amply demonstrated that intuition alone did not guarantee success. We needed an algorithm expert.

A call to my old professors at the University of Washington led to a PhD candidate named David Jacobson who was happy to trade his research assistant stipend for a developer paycheck for a while. Our collaboration led to a best-in-class RAM test requiring only five passes through memory, several other novel functional test algorithms, and half a dozen US patents.

Time Cost of Algorithms

The *time cost* of an algorithm is an abstract mathematical function describing how rapidly the cost of the algorithm grows as a function of the size of its input. Many factors affect the run time of a program on a specific computer. As a result, run time is less than perfect as a way to talk about performance of an algorithm. Time cost abstracts away these details, leaving a simple relationship between input size and cost. Algorithms can be classified into families with similar time costs, and the families can be studied for common features. Time cost is well covered in any textbook on algorithms and data structures—I like *The Algorithm Design Manual*, Second Edition, by Steven S. Skiena (Springer-Verlag)—so this section will be brief.

The time cost is customarily written in "big-O" notation, as $O(f(n))$, where n is some significant aspect of the size of the input, and $f(n)$ is a function describing how many of some significant operations an algorithm performs to process an input of size n. The function $f(n)$ is typically simplified to show only its fastest-growing term, because for large values of n, this term dominates the value of $f(n)$.

Using searching and sorting algorithms as an example, if n is the number of items to be searched through or sorted, $f(n)$ is often the number of comparisons made between two items to put the items into sorted order.

Here is a very rough guide to the time cost of some common algorithms, and the implications of those costs to program run times:

O(1), or constant time
> The fastest possible algorithms have constant time cost. That is, they have a fixed cost that doesn't depend on the size of the input at all. A constant-time algorithm is like the Holy Grail: incredibly valuable if you find it, but you can search for your whole life without achieving your quest. *Beware, therefore, of strangers selling constant-time algorithms.* The constant of proportionality may be very high. That is, the cost may be one operation, but it may be one hellaciously long operation. In fact, it may be $O(n)$ in disguise, or worse.

O(log₂ n)
> The time cost can be less than linear. For instance, a search algorithm that can divide the input in half at each step takes $O(log_2 n)$ time. Algorithms with less than linear time cost have a cost that increases more slowly than the input does. They are thus efficient enough that there is often (but not always) no reason to look for a faster algorithm; the code implementing the algorithm simply isn't hot enough to show up on a profiler's list of expensive functions. Algorithms with $O(log_2 n)$ time cost can be invoked many times in a program's overall run without fear of making the whole program infeasibly slow. Binary search is a frequently occurring algorithm with $O(log_2 n)$ time cost.

O(n), or linear time
> If an algorithm's time cost is $O(n)$, the time taken by the algorithm is proportional to the size of its input. Such an algorithm is called a *linear-time* algorithm, or just *linear*. A time cost of $O(n)$ is typical of algorithms that scan their input from one end to the other, as to find the least or greatest value in a list. A linear-time algorithm grows more expensive at the same rate as its input. Such algo-

rithms are inexpensive enough that a program can scale to larger and larger inputs without unexpectedly great demands on computational resources. However, *multiple linear-time algorithms can combine in ways that make their overall run time O(n²) or worse*, so they may be implicated if a program's overall run time is too great for large inputs.

O(n log₂ n)

Algorithms can have a super-linear time cost. For instance, many sorting algorithms compare pairs of inputs, and divide the space to be sorted into two parts at each step. These algorithms have time cost O(*n log₂ n*). Algorithms that are O(*n log₂ n*) become relatively more costly as *n* increases, but the rate of growth is so slow that these algorithms are generally considered tractable even for large values of *n*. Still, you don't want to invoke such an algorithm needlessly during a program's run.

O(n²), O(n³), etc.

Some algorithms, including less efficient sorting algorithms, must compare each input value to every other value. These algorithms have time cost O(n^2). The cost of such algorithms grows so fast that it becomes quite worrisome for large values of *n*. There are a number of problems that have simple solutions that are O(n^2) or O(n^3), and more subtle solutions that are faster.

O(2ⁿ)

O(2^n) algorithms grow expensive so rapidly that they can be considered only for small values of *n*. Sometimes that is OK. Algorithms that require inspecting all combinations of *n* inputs are O(2^n). Scheduling and trip-planning problems like the famous Traveling Salesman problem are O(2^n). If the fundamental problem an algorithm needs to solve is O(2^n), the developer is faced with several unpalatable options: use a heuristic algorithm that doesn't guarantee an optimal solution, limit the solution to small values of *n*, or find some other way to add value that doesn't involve solving the problem at all.

Table 5-1 estimates how long algorithms of different time costs will take if each operation on the *n* input values takes a single nanosecond. A more complete version of this table can be found on page 38 of Skiena's *The Algorithm Design Manual*.

Table 5-1. Runtime cost for an algorithm taking 1 ns per operation

	$\log_2 n$	n	$n\log_2 n$	n^2	2^n
10	< 1 μs	< 1 μs	< 1 μs	< 1 μs	1 μs
20	< 1 μs	< 1 μs	< 1 μs	< 1 μs	1 μ
30	< 1 μs	< 1 μs	< 1 μs	< 1 μs	1 s

	$\log_2 n$	n	$n\log_2 n$	n^2	2^n
40	$<1\,\mu s$	$<1\,\mu s$	$<1\,\mu s$	$1.6\,\mu s$	18 min
50	$<1\,\mu s$	$<1\,\mu s$	$<1\,\mu s$	$2.5\,\mu s$	10^{13} years
100	$<1\,\mu s$	$<1\,\mu s$	$<1\,\mu s$	$10\,\mu s$	∞
1,000	$<1\,\mu s$	$1\,\mu s$	$10\,\mu s$	1 ms	∞
10,000	$<1\,\mu s$	$10\,\mu s$	$130\,\mu s$	100 ms	∞
100,000	$<1\,\mu s$	$100\,\mu s$	2 ms	10 s	∞
1,000,000	$<1\,\mu s$	1 ms $>$	20 ms	17 min	∞

Best-Case, Average, and Worst-Case Time Cost

The conventional big-O notation assumes that an algorithm has the same running time for any input. However, some algorithms are sensitive to properties of their input, running faster for some sequences of inputs than for other sequences of the same size. When considering what algorithm to use in performance-critical code, it is important to know whether the algorithm has a bad worst case. We will see some examples of this in "Time Cost of Sorting Algorithms" on page 99.

Some algorithms likewise have very fortunate best-case behavior, like a sort that takes less time if the input is already sorted or nearly sorted. When the input is likely to have useful properties like being mostly sorted, selecting an algorithm with especially good best-case performance can improve the run time of a program.

Amortized Time Cost

Amortized time cost means time cost averaged over a large number of inputs. For instance, inserting an item into a heap has $O(log_2 n)$ time cost. Building a heap one item at a time is thus $O(n\ log_2 n)$. However, building a heap by the most efficient method is $O(n)$, which means that inserting each item by this method has amortized $O(1)$ time cost. The most efficient algorithm doesn't insert items one at a time, though. It processes all the items into successively larger subheaps using a divide-and-conquer algorithm.

The significance of amortized time cost is that some individual operations are fast, while others are slow. For instance, the amortized time cost to append a character to a std::string is constant, but it involves a call to the memory manager some fraction of the time. When the string is short, the memory manager may be called nearly every time a character is appended. Only once the program has appended thousands or millions of characters does this amortized cost become small.

Other Costs

Sometimes an algorithm can be sped up by saving intermediate results. Such an algorithm thus has not only a cost in time, but also a cost in auxiliary storage. For instance, the familiar recursive algorithm for binary tree traversal runs in linear time, but also requires $log_2\ n$ auxiliary storage locations on the stack during the recursion. Algorithms that have large auxiliary space costs may not be suitable for constrained environments.

There are algorithms that run faster if they are parallelized, but have a cost in the number of processors running in parallel needed to obtain the theoretically promised speedup. Algorithms requiring more than $log_2\ n$ processors are usually not feasible on general-purpose computers, which have a small, fixed number of processors. Such algorithms may be possible using purpose-built hardware or graphics processors. I wish this book had space to cover parallel algorithm design, but alas it does not.

Toolkit to Optimize Searching and Sorting

The toolkit for optimizing searches and sorts contains just three tools:

- Replace inferior algorithms having poor average-case big-O time costs with algorithms having better average-case time costs.
- Exploit additional knowledge of the data (for instance, knowledge that the data is usually sorted or nearly sorted) to select algorithms having particularly good big-O time costs on data with these properties, and avoid algorithms with particularly poor big-O behavior on data with these properties.
- Tweak the algorithm to improve its performance by a constant factor.

I explore the application of these three tools in Chapter 9.

Efficient Search Algorithms

The time costs of the most important algorithms for searching and sorting are presented in every undergraduate computer science curriculum, and eagerly memorized by all developers early in their college education. The problem with undergraduate algorithms and data structures classes is that they are too brief. The instructor can provide in-depth coverage of just a few algorithms to teach analysis, or shallow coverage of more algorithms to provide memorable facts about time cost. The instructor is probably also teaching how to program at the same time. As a result, students exit the class proud of their new knowledge, and unaware that they have missed out on many nuances. This incompleteness of knowledge leads to optimization opportunities even when nominally optimal algorithms are in use.

Time Cost of Searching Algorithms

How fast, in big-O terms, is the fastest method to look up a table entry? Hint: binary search, at $O(log_2 n)$, is a useful benchmark, but it isn't the fastest.

Right now some readers are saying, "Wait...*WHAT*?" They weren't taught anything other than linear search and binary search. But there are many search algorithms:

- *Linear search*, at $O(n)$, is expensive, but extremely general. It can be used on an unsorted table. It requires only that keys can be compared for equality, so it works even if keys can't be put into any kind of order. If the table *is* sorted, the linear search can terminate before seeing all table elements. It's still $O(n)$, but on average about twice as fast.

  If it's OK to mutate the table, a version of linear search that moves each search result to the head of the table can perform very well in some situations. For instance, the symbol table in a programming language compiler is searched every time an identifier is used in an expression. There are so many expressions that look like i = i + 1; that this optimization can make linear search reasonably useful.

- *Binary search*, at $O(log_2 n)$, has good performance, but it's not the best possible search. Binary search requires input data that is sorted on the search key, and keys that can be compared not only for equality, but for an ordering relation such as less-than.

  Binary search is the workhorse of the searching and sorting world. It is a divide-and-conquer algorithm that repeatedly divides a sorted table in half by comparing the key to the middle element in the portion of the table being searched to determine if the key comes before or after that element.

- *Interpolation search* divides the sorted table into two parts like binary search, but uses extra knowledge about the keys to improve its partitioning guess. Interpolation search achieves a very respectable $O(log log n)$ performance when the keys are uniformly distributed. This improvement can be very noticeable if the table is large or the cost of testing a table entry is significant (like when it's on a rotating disk). However, interpolation search is not the fastest possible search.

- It is possible to find a record in average $O(1)$ time by *hashing*: converting the key to an array index in a hash table. Hashing doesn't work on just any list of key/value pairs. It requires a specially constructed table. Hash table entries need only be compared for equality. Hashing has worst-case performance of $O(n)$, and may require more hash table entries than there are records to search for. However, when the table has fixed contents (like month names or programming language keywords), these pathological cases can be eliminated.

All Searches Are Equal When n Is Small

What is the cost of searching in a table with a single entry? Does it make any difference what search algorithm is used? Table 5-2 shows the cost of searching a sorted table using the best possible versions of linear, binary, and hash-table search algorithms. The answer is that *for small tables, all methods examine the same number of entries.* For a table of 100,000 entries, however, the dominating term of the time cost function would rule, and things would look different.

Table 5-2. Table size versus average number of accesses to search

Table size	Linear	Binary	Hash
1	1	1	1
2	1	2	1
4	2	3	1
8	4	4	1
16	8	5	1
26	13	6	1
32	16	6	1

Efficient Sort Algorithms

There is an amazing menagerie of sorting algorithms. Many have been proposed only in the past 10 years or so. Many of the newer sorts are hybrids that improve best-case or worst-case performance. If you completed your computer science education prior to 2000, it is worth reviewing the literature. Wikipedia has an accessible summary of sorting algorithms. Here are just a few fun facts not always covered in algorithms classes, to prove that deeper knowledge has benefits:

- "Everyone knows" that an optimal sort runs in $O(n \ log_2 \ n)$ time, right? Wrong. Wrong twice, in fact. Only sorts that work by comparing pairs of input values have this behavior. Radix sorts (sorts that divide the input repeatedly into one of r buckets) have time cost $O(n \ log_r \ n)$, where r is the *radix*, or number of sorting buckets. This is considerably better than comparison sorts for large data sets. Furthermore, when the sorting keys are taken from certain sets, like the consecutive integers from 1 to n, flashsort can sort the data in $O(n)$ time.

- Quicksort, a frequently implemented and generally well-regarded algorithm, has poor worst-case performance of $O(n^2)$. The worst case cannot reliably be avoided, and naïve implementations often perform poorly.

- Some sorts, including insertion sort, have excellent (linear) performance if the data is almost sorted, even if they aren't all that good for random data. Other sorts (such as the naïve quicksort just mentioned) have worst-case performance on sorted data. If the data is usually sorted or almost sorted, knowledge of this additional property can be used to select a sort having good performance on sorted data.

Time Cost of Sorting Algorithms

Table 5-3 lists the time complexity of several sorts for base-case, average, and worst-case input data. While most of these sorts have the same O($n \log_2 n$) average performance, they differ in their best-case and worst-case performance, and in the amount of extra space they consume.

Table 5-3. Time cost for some sorting algorithms

Sort	Best case	Average	Worst case	Space required	Notes on best/worst case
Insertion sort	n	n^2	n^2	1	Best case is sorted or nearly sorted data
Quicksort	$n \log_2 n$	$n \log_2 n$	n^2	$log_2 n$	Worst case is sorted data and naïve (first/last) choice of pivot
Merge sort	$n \log_2 n$	$n \log_2 n$	$n \log_2 n$	1	
Tree sort	$n \log_2 n$	$n \log_2 n$	$n \log_2 n$	n	
Heapsort	$n \log_2 n$	$n \log_2 n$	$n \log_2 n$	1	
Timsort	n	$n \log_2 n$	$n \log_2 n$	n	Best case is sorted data
Introsort	$n \log_2 n$	$n \log_2 n$	$n \log_2 n$	1	

Replace Sorts Having Poor Worst-Case Performance

Quicksort is a very popular sort. Its internal overhead is quite low, and its average performance is optimal for a sort based on comparing two keys. But quicksort has a flaw. If you run quicksort on an array that is already sorted (or nearly sorted), and you use the first or last element as the pivot, its performance is very poor. Sophisticated implementations of quicksort pick a pivot at random to overcome this weakness most of the time, or spend many extra cycles to compute the median and use that as the initial pivot. It is thus naïve to assume that quicksort will always have good performance. You must either know something about the input data—specifically, that it is not already sorted—or know that the implementation of the algorithm chooses the initial pivot carefully.

If you don't know anything about the input data, mergesort, treesort, and heapsort all provide a comfortable assurance that there is no pathological case that will cause performance to balloon to unacceptable levels.

Exploit Known Properties of the Input Data

If you know that the input data is sorted or nearly sorted, the normally unacceptable insertion sort has excellent $O(n)$ performance on such data.

A relatively new hybrid sort called Timsort also has excellent $O(n)$ performance if the data is sorted or nearly sorted, and optimal $O(n \ log_2 \ n)$ performance the rest of the time. Timsort is now the standard sort in Python.

A recent sort called introsort is a hybrid of quicksort and heapsort. Introsort starts doing a quicksort, but switches to a heapsort if unfortunate input data causes quicksort's recursion depth to become too great. Introsort guarantees a reasonable $O(n \ log_2 \ n)$ worst-case time, while taking advantage of quicksort's efficient implementation to modestly reduce average-case run time. Since C++11, introsort has been the preferred implementation of `std::sort()`.

Another recently proposed sort called flashsort has excellent $O(n)$ performance for data drawn from a particular probability distribution. Flashsort is related to radix sorting; data is sorted into buckets based on percentile in the probability distribution. A simple case of flashsort occurs when the data items are uniformly distributed.

Optimization Patterns

Experienced optimizing developers don't rely exclusively on dizzying intuitive leaps to find opportunities to improve code performance. There are patterns that recur in optimized code. Developers study algorithms and data structures partly because they contain a library of ideas for improving performance.

This section gathers together a few general techniques for improving performance that are so useful that they deserve specific mention. The reader may recognize some of these patterns as the core of familiar data structures, C++ language features, or hardware innovations:

Precomputation
> Remove computation from the hot part of the program by performing it before execution arrives at the hot code—earlier in the program, at link time, compile time, or design time.

Lazy computation
> Remove computation from some code paths by performing the computation closer to the point where it is needed.

Batching
> Perform computation on several items together rather than one item at a time.

Caching

Reduce computation by saving and reusing the results of an expensive computation rather than recomputing them.

Specialization

Reduce computation by removing generality that is not used.

Taking bigger bites

Reduce the cost of a repeated operation by acting on bigger groups of input at a time.

Hinting

Reduce computation by providing a hint that might improve performance.

Optimizing the expected path

Test for inputs or events at run time in decreasing order of expected frequency.

Hashing

Compute a compact numerical summary (the hash) of a larger data structure such as a variable-length character string. The hash can stand in for the data structure in comparisons to improve performance.

Double-checking

Reduce computation by performing an inexpensive check, followed only if necessary by an expensive check.

Precomputation

Precomputation is a very general technique whose goal is to remove computation from hot code by performing it earlier, before execution arrives at the hot spot. Different variations move computation from the hot spot to a less-hot part of the code, to link time, compile time, or even design time. In general, the earlier the computation can be performed, the better.

Precomputation is only possible to the extent that the value to be computed does not depend on the context. A computation such as this can be precomputed by the compiler because it doesn't depend on anything in the program:

```
int sec_per_day = 60 * 60 * 24;
```

A related computation like this one depends on variables in the program:

```
int sec_per_weekend = (date_end - date_beginning + 1) * 60 * 60 * 24;
```

The trick with precomputation is to either realize that (`date_end - date_beginning + 1`) may have an unchanging value in the program, so it can be replaced with 2, or to factor out the part of the expression that can be precomputed.

Here are some examples of precomputation:

- The C++ compiler automatically precomputes the value of constant expressions using the compiler's built-in rules of associativity and operator precedence. The compiler precomputes the value of `sec_per_day` in the previous example with no problem.
- A template function call with particular arguments is evaluated at compile time. The compiler generates efficient code when the arguments are constants.
- The designer can observe, for example, that in the context of a particular program the concept of "weekend" is always two days, and precompute that constant as he is writing the program.

Lazy Computation

The goal of lazy computation is to delay computation to a point closer to where the computation is needed. There are several benefits to lazy computation. If the computation is not needed on all execution paths (all branches of the `if-then-else` logic) in a function, it is only performed on the paths that need the result. Examples include:

Two-part construction
Often information that is needed to construct an object is not available when the instance could be statically constructed. Instead of constructing an object all at once, the constructor contains minimal code to establish an empty object. Later, the running program calls an initialization member function to finish construction. Delaying initialization until additional data is available means the constructed object can often be an efficient, flat data structure (see "Flatten Data Structures" on page 145).

In some cases, there is a cost to check whether a lazily computed value has been computed yet. This cost is comparable to the cost of ensuring a pointer to a dynamically constructed class is valid.

Copy-on-write
Instead of copying a dynamic member variable when an object is copied, the two instances share a single copy of the dynamic variable. Copying is deferred until either instance wants to modify the variable.

Batching

The goal of batching is to collect multiple work items and process them together. Batching may be used to remove repeated function calls or other computation that would occur if the items were processed one at a time. It may also be used because there is a more efficient algorithm for processing all inputs together, to postpone computation to a time when more computational resources are available. For instance:

- Buffered output is an example of batching in which output characters are appended to a buffer until the buffer is full or the program reaches an end-of-line or end-of-file character. The entire buffer is passed to an output routine, saving the cost of calling the output routine once for each character.

- The optimal method for converting an unsorted array into a heap is an example of batching to use a more efficient algorithm. The time cost of inserting n items into a heap one by one is O($n\ log_2\ n$). The cost of building the heap all at once is O(n).

- A multithreaded task queue is an example of batching to use computing resources efficiently.

- Saving or updating in the background is an example of batching.

Caching

Caching refers to any of several methods to reduce computation by saving and reusing the result of an expensive computation, rather than recomputing the result each time it is needed. For example:

- The compiler caches the result of small repeated chunks of code, like the computation needed to dereference an array element. It sees a statement like a[i][j] = a[i][j] + c; and saves the array expression, producing code that looks more like auto p = &a[i][j]; *p = *p + c;.

- *Cache memory* refers to special circuits in computers that make frequently needed memory locations more rapidly accessible to the processor. Caching is a very important concept in the design of computer hardware. There are many levels of caching in the hardware and software of an x86 PC.

- The length of a C-style character string must be computed each time it is needed by counting the characters. std::string caches the string length rather than computing it each time it is needed.

- A thread pool is a cache of expensive-to-create threads.

- Dynamic programming is an algorithmic technique in which a computation that has a recurrence relation is sped up by computing subparts and caching the result.

Specialization

Specialization is the opposite of generalization. The goal of specialization is to eliminate parts of an expensive computation that are not required in a specific situation.

It may be possible to simplify an action or data structure by removing a feature that makes it expensive, but that is not required in a given situation in question. This can be accomplished by lifting a constraint from the problem, or adding a constraint to the implementation—making the dynamic static, bounding the unbounded, and so on. For example:

- The template function `std::swap()` has a default implementation that may copy its arguments. However, the developer can provide a specialization that is more efficient given knowledge of the internals of a data structure. (The C++11 version of `std::swap()` uses move semantics to achieve an efficient result if the argument type implements a move constructor.)

- `std::string` is dynamically resizable to hold variable-length character strings. It provides many operations to manipulate strings. If it's only necessary to compare fixed strings, a C-style array or pointer to literal string and a comparison function may have better performance.

Taking Bigger Bites

The aim of taking bigger bites is to reduce the number of iterations of a repeated operation, cutting down on the overhead of repetition. Strategies include:

- Request large blocks of input from the operating system or send large blocks of output to the operating system to reduce the overhead of calling into the kernel for small blocks or individual items. The downside of taking bigger bytes, especially when writing, is that more data may be lost if the program crashes. This can be a problem, for instance, for log files.

- Move or clear buffers by word or longword instead of byte-by-byte. This optimization only improves performance if the two ranges are aligned to the same-sized boundaries.

- Compare strings by word or longword. This only works on a big-endian machine, and not on the x86, which is little-endian (see "Memory Words Have a Big End and a Little End" on page 20). Machine architecture–dependent hacks like this one can be dangerous because they are nonportable.

- Perform more work when a thread wakes up. Check for multiple units of work to process rather than relinquishing the processor after a single unit. This saves the overhead of repeated thread wakeup.

- Instead of performing a maintenance task each time through a loop, perform it every 10th or every 100th time.

Hinting

In hinting, the cost of an operation is reduced by using a hint that, if provided, may lead to reduced computation.

For instance, one overload of the `insert()` member function of `std::map` takes an optional insertion point argument. An optimal hint can make insertion O(*1*). Otherwise, inserting in a map costs O(*log₂ n*).

Optimizing the Expected Path

In `if-then-else` code with several `else-if` arms, if the tests are laid out in random order, each time execution passes through the `if-then-else` block, about half the tests will be computed. If there is one case that happens 95% of the time, and that test is performed first, then 95% of the time only one test will be performed.

Hashing

In hashing, a large input data structure or long character string is summarized by an algorithm as an integer, called the hash. The hashes of two inputs can be efficiently compared to rule out equality of the inputs. If the hashes are different, the inputs are definitely not the same. If the hashes are equal, the inputs are probably equal. Hashing can be used with double-checking to optimize a deterministic comparison for equality. It is typical that the hash for an input is cached so that it need not be recomputed.

Double-Checking

In double-checking, an inexpensive check is used to rule out some cases, followed if necessary by an expensive check to rule out all other cases. For example:

- Double-checking is frequently used with caching. The cache is checked quickly to see if the desired value is there, and if not the value is fetched or computed by a more expensive process.

- Comparing two `std::string` instances for equality normally requires comparing them character-by-character. However, a preliminary comparison of the lengths of the two strings can quickly rule out equality.

- Double-checking may be used in hashing. The hashes of two inputs can be compared efficiently for equality; if the hashes are different, the inputs are not equal.

Only if the hashes are the same is it necessary to compare the inputs byte-by-byte.

Summary

- *Beware of strangers selling constant-time algorithms. They may be O(n).*
- *Multiple efficient algorithms can be combined in ways that make their overall run time O(n²) or worse.*
- *Binary search, at O(log₂ n), isn't the fastest search. Interpolation search is O(log log n) and hashing is constant-time.*
- *For small tables with < 4 entries, all search algorithms examine about the same number of entries.*

## CHAPTER 6

Optimize Dynamically Allocated Variables

That's where the money is.

—Bank robber Willie Sutton (1901–1980)

This quote was attributed to Sutton as the answer to a reporter's 1952 question, "Why do you rob banks?" Sutton later denied ever having said it.

Except for the use of less-than-optimal algorithms, the naïve use of dynamically allocated variables is the greatest performance killer in C++ programs. Improving a program's use of dynamically allocated variables is so often "where the money is" that *a developer can be an effective optimizer knowing nothing other than how to reduce calls into the memory manager.*

C++ features that use dynamically allocated variables, like standard library containers, smart pointers, and strings, make writing applications in C++ productive. But there is a dark side to this expressive power. When performance matters, new is not your friend.

Lest I start a panic, let me say that the goal in optimizing memory management is not to live an ascetic life free of distraction from the many useful C++ features that use dynamically allocated variables. Rather, the goal is to *remove performance-robbing, unneeded calls into the memory manager* through skillful use of these same features.

My experience is that removing even one call into the memory manager from a loop or frequently called function is enough to significantly boost performance, and there are generally opportunities to remove many more than one call.

Before talking about how to optimize the use of dynamically allocated variables, this chapter offers a review of how C++ thinks about variables. It also reviews the set of tools in the dynamic memory API.

C++ Variables Refresher

Every C++ variable (every variable of plain data type; every array, struct, or class instance) has a fixed layout in memory, the size of which is known at compile time. C++ allows a program to get the size in bytes of a variable and obtain a pointer to that variable, but does not specify the bit-by-bit layout of variables. C++ rules allow the developer to reason about the order and layout of member variables in structs. C++ also provides union types that overlay multiple variables onto the same block of memory, but what the program sees when it looks at a union is implementation-dependent.

Storage Duration of Variables

Every variable has a *storage duration*, or lifetime, that describes the period of time during which the *storage*, or memory bytes occupied by the variable, has a meaningful value. The cost to allocate memory for the variable depends on the storage duration.

The C++ syntax for declaring variables can be confusing, due to the need to maintain compatibility with C syntax while adding several new concepts. In C++, the storage duration is not directly specified, but is inferred from the variable's declaration:

Static storage duration
> Variables with *static storage duration* live in memory reserved by the compiler. Each static variable occupies a fixed amount of memory at a fixed address determined at compile time. The memory for static variables is reserved for the life of the program. Each global static variable is constructed before execution enters main() and destroyed after execution leaves main(). Static variables declared a function scope are only constructed "before the first time execution enters a function", which can be as early as when global statics are constructed, or as late as the first call to that function. C++ specifies an order of construction and destruction for global static variables so that the developer can reason exactly about their lifetimes, but the rules are so complex that they serve more as a warning than a behavior to make use of.

> Each static variable is known by a name, and may also be referred to by pointers and references. The name that refers to a static variable, as well as pointers and references to that variable, may be visible to code in the constructors and destructors of other static variables before it has a meaningful value and after its value is destroyed.

> There is no runtime cost to create the storage for static variables. However, the storage is not available for reuse. Static variables are thus appropriate for data that will be used for the whole life of the program.

Variables declared at namespace scope and variables declared `static` or `extern` have static storage duration.

Thread-local storage duration

Since C++11, a program can declare variables with *thread-local storage duration*. Before C++11, some compilers and frameworks provided similar facilities in a nonstandard manner.

Thread-local variables are constructed at thread entry and destroyed at thread exit; their lifetime is the same as the lifetime of the thread. Each thread has its own separate copy of these variables.

Thread-local variables can be more expensive to access than static variables, depending on the operating system and compiler. In some systems, the thread-local storage is allocated by the thread, so that the cost of accessing a thread-local variable is a single indirection greater than that of accessing a static variable. In others, thread-local variables must be accessed through a global table indexed by the thread ID. Although this operation can be performed in constant time, it requires a function call and some computation, making the cost of access considerably greater.

In C++11, variables declared with the `thread_local` storage class specifier keyword have thread-local storage duration.

Automatic storage duration

Variables with *automatic storage duration* exist in memory reserved by the compiler on the function call stack. Each automatic variable occupies a fixed amount of memory at a fixed offset from the stack pointer that is determined at compile time, but the absolute address of the automatic variable is not fixed until execution enters the scope of the declaration.

Automatic variables exist during the time that execution is within the scope of the surrounding code block delimited by curly braces. They are constructed at the point where they are declared, and destroyed when execution leaves the surrounding scope.

Like static variables, automatic variables are known by name. Unlike static variables, the name is visible only after the variable is constructed, and before it is destroyed. References and pointers to automatic variables may exist after the variable is destroyed, causing the chaos of undefined behavior if they are dereferenced.

Like with static variables, there is no runtime cost to allocate the storage used by automatic variables. Unlike with static variables, there is a limit to the total amount of memory that can be occupied by automatic variables at any one time. Exceeding this maximum value, via runaway recursion or very deeply nested function calls, causes a *stack overflow* and abrupt, irrevocable program termination. Automatic variables are appropriate for objects used by the code that surrounds them.

A function's formal argument variables have automatic storage duration. So do variables declared within executable blocks and not otherwise marked.

Dynamic storage duration

Variables with *dynamic* storage duration live in memory requested by the running program. The program calls into the *memory manager*, the collection of C++ runtime system functions and data structures that administers a pool of memory on behalf of the program. The program explicitly requests storage for and constructs the dynamic variable in a *new-expression* (covered in more detail in "New-Expressions Construct Dynamic Variables" on page 328), which may occur at any point in the program. The program later explicitly destroys the variable and returns the variable's memory to the memory manager in a *delete-expression* (see "Delete-Expressions Dispose of Dynamic Variables" on page 331). This can happen at any point in the program when the variable is no longer needed.

Like with automatic variables, but unlike with static variables, the address of a dynamic variable is determined at run time.

Unlike with static, thread-local, and automatic variables, the declaration syntax for arrays is extended so that the highest dimension of a dynamic array variable may be specified at run time by a (non-constant) expression. This is the only case in C++ where the size of a variable is not fixed at compile time.

A dynamic variable does not have its own name. Instead, when it's constructed, the C++ memory manager returns a pointer to the dynamic variable. The program must assign this pointer to a variable so it can return the dynamic variable to the memory manager before the last pointer to that variable is destroyed, or risk running out of the memory used for creating dynamic variables. A modern processor can exhaust gigabytes of memory in minutes if dynamic variables are not returned properly.

Unlike static and thread-local variables, the number and type of dynamic variables can change over time without any fixed limit to the amount of storage they consume. Also, unlike with static and automatic variables, there is a significant runtime cost to manage the memory used by dynamic variables.

Variables returned by *new-expressions* have dynamic storage duration.

Ownership of Variables

Another important concept of C++ variables is *ownership*. The owner of a variable determines when the variable is created and when it is destroyed. Sometimes the storage duration tells when the variable is created and destroyed, but ownership is a separate concept, and it is an important one for optimization of dynamic variables. Here are some guidelines:

Global ownership
   Variables with static storage duration are owned by the program as a whole. They are constructed before execution enters the `main()` function and destroyed after the program returns from `main()`.

Lexically scoped ownership
   Variables with automatic storage duration are owned by a lexical scope consisting of a block of code surrounded by curly braces. This may be a function body; the controlled statement block of an `if`, `while`, `for`, or `do` statement; a `try` or `catch` clause; or a compound statement delimited only by curly braces. They are constructed when execution enters the lexical scope, and destroyed when execution passes out of the lexical scope.

   The outermost lexical scope—the scope entered first and exited last—is the body of `main()`. For all intents and purposes, an automatic variable declared in `main()` has the same lifetime as a static variable.

Member ownership
   Member variables of classes and structs are owned by the class instance that contains them. They are constructed by the class constructor as an instance of the class is constructed, and destroyed as the instance is destroyed.

Ownership of dynamic variables
   Dynamic variables have no predefined owner. Rather, the *new-expression* that creates the dynamic variable returns a pointer, which must be explicitly managed by the program. The dynamic variable must be returned to the memory manager via a *delete-expression* to be destroyed before the last pointer to the dynamic variable is destroyed. The lifetime of the dynamic variable is thus completely programmable—a powerful but dangerous tool. If a dynamic variable is not returned to the memory manager through a *delete-expression* before the last pointer to it is destroyed, the memory manager loses track of that variable for the rest of the program's run time.

   Ownership of dynamic variables must be enforced by the developer and encoded into the program logic. It is not controlled by the compiler or defined by C++. Ownership of dynamic variables is important to optimization. Programs with strongly defined ownership can be made more efficient than programs where ownership is diffuse.

Value Objects and Entity Objects

Some variables get their meaning in a program from their contents. They are called *value objects*. Other variables get their meaning from the role they play in a program. These variables are called *entities* or *entity objects*.

C++ does not encode whether a particular variable behaves as a value or entity object. The developer encodes the variable's role into the program logic. C++ allows the developer to define a copy constructor and an operator==() for any class. The role of a variable determines whether the developer *should* define these operators. If the developer does not take steps to forbid operations that don't make sense, the compiler will not complain.

Entity objects may be identified by their common properties:

Entities are unique

Some objects in a program conceptually have a unique identity. The mutex that guards a specific critical region and a symbol table with many entries are examples of objects with unique identities in a program.

Entities are mutable

A program can lock or unlock a mutex, but it is still the same mutex. A program can add symbols to a symbol table, but it's still the symbol table. You can start your car and drive it to work, and it is still your car. Entities have a meaning as a whole. Changing the state of an entity doesn't change its fundamental meaning to the program.

Entities are not copyable

Entities are not copied. Their nature comes from the way they are used, not from their bits. You might copy all the bits of the system symbol table into another data structure, but it would not be the system symbol table. The program would still look for the system symbol table in the old place, and the copy would be unused. If the program sometimes modified the copy instead of the original, the symbol table would stop being valid. You might copy the bits of a mutex that guarded a critical section, but locking the copy would not produce mutual exclusion. Mutual exclusion is a property that arises from two threads agreeing to signal each other using a specific set of bits.

Entities are not comparable

The operation of comparing entities for equality does not make sense. Entities are, by their nature, individuals. A comparison must always return false.

Likewise, value objects have common properties that are the opposite of the properties of entity objects:

Values are interchangeable and comparable
> The integer 4 and the string "Hello, World!" are values. The expression 2 + 2 compares equal to the value 4, and not equal to the value 5. The value of the expression string("Hello") + string("!") compares equal to the string "Hello!", and not equal to "Hi". The meaning of a value comes from its bits, not from its use in the program.

Values are immutable
> There is no operation able to change a 4 into a 5, so that 2 + 2 = 5. You can change an integer variable that holds a 4 so that it now holds a 5. That changes the variable, which is an entity with a unique name. But that doesn't change the value 4.

Values are copyable
> Copying a value makes sense. Two string variables can have the value "foo" and the program is still correct.

Whether a variable is an entity object or a value object determines whether copying and comparison for equality make sense. Entities should not be copied or compared. Whether a class member variable is an entity or a value determines how the class copy constructor should be written. Class instances may share ownership of an entity, but cannot validly copy the entity. Understanding entities and value objects is important because variables that behave as entities are often structures with many dynamically allocated variables that would be expensive to copy if copying even made sense.

C++ Dynamic Variable API Refresher

C++ contains a robust toolkit for managing dynamic variables. Options range from automation to fine control over memory management and the construction of dynamically allocated C++ variables. Even experienced developers may have used only the most basic of these tools. We'll start with a quick look at those, before going into depth on the features that bear particularly on optimization:

Pointers and references
> Dynamic variables in C++ don't have a name. They are accessed through a C-style pointer or a reference variable. Pointers abstract hardware addresses to hide the complexity and variability of computer architectures. Not every value a pointer variable can hold corresponds to a usable memory location, but there is nothing about the bits that tell the programmer that. One specific value called nullptr in C++11 is guaranteed by the C++ standard never to point to a valid memory location. The integer 0 stood in for nullptr prior to C++11; and is con-

vertible to nullptr in C++11, however, the all-zeros bit pattern in a pointer variable is not necessarily equal to nullptr. C-style pointers that are declared without an initializer have no predefined value (for efficiency's sake). Reference variables cannot be declared without an initializer, so they always point to valid locations.[1]

New- and delete-expressions

Dynamic variables in C++ are created via a *new-expression* (see "New-Expressions Construct Dynamic Variables" on page 328). A new-expression gets the storage needed to hold the variable, constructs a variable of a specified type in the storage, and returns a typed pointer to the newly constructed variable. The new-expression for creating arrays is different from the new-expression for creating a single instance, but both return the same type of pointer.

Dynamic variables are disposed of via a *delete-expression* (see "Delete-Expressions Dispose of Dynamic Variables" on page 331). A delete-expression destroys a variable and disposes of its storage. The delete-expression for disposing of an array is different from the one for individual instances. Both operate on a pointer of the same type, however, so you can't tell from the pointer whether it points to an array or a scalar. The developer must remember the kind of new-expression used to create a dynamic variable and destroy it with a matching kind of delete-expression, or chaos reigns. Undefined behavior results if a pointer-to-array is deleted as a pointer-to-instance, or vice versa.

New-expressions and *delete-expressions* are baked into the syntax of the C++ language. Here are some brief examples of the basic kinds of *new-* and *delete-expressions* that all developers are aware of:

```
{
    int n = 100;
    char* cp;            // cp has no particular value
    Book* bp = nullptr; // bp points to invalid address

//    ...

    cp = new char[n];    // cp points to new dynamic array
    bp = new Book("Optimized C++"); // new dynamic class instance

//    ...
```

---

1 A developer might go out of her way to cast a numerical machine address to a reference for the purpose of initializing a reference variable. Although that might seem crazy, it could conceivably be useful in embedded programming, where the architecture of the target computer is fixed and known. It is more efficient to use the linker to set the address of an extern variable than to use the compiler to cast a numeric constant to a reference or pointer. My advice is, "Look away, nothing to see here."

```
        char array[sizeof(Book)];
        Book* bp2 = new(array) Book("Moby Dick"); // placement new

//      ...

        delete[] cp;   // delete dynamic array before changing pointer
        cp = new char; // cp now points to a single dynamic char

//      ...

        delete bp;     // done using class instance
        delete cp;     // done using dynamically allocated char
        bp2->~Book();  // done using placed class instance
}
// delete dynamic variables before pointer goes out of scope
```

Memory management functions

New-expressions and *delete-expressions* call memory management functions from the C++ standard library to allocate storage from and return storage to a pool that the C++ standard calls the "free store." These functions are overloads of `oper ator new()`, `operator new[]()` for arrays, `operator delete()`, and `operator delete[]()` for arrays. C++ also provides classic C-library memory management functions such as `malloc()` and `free()`, which allocate and release untyped blocks of storage.

Class constructors and destructors

C++ allows each class to define a constructor member function that is called to establish an initial value when an instance of that class is created. Another member function, the destructor, is called whenever a class instance is destroyed. Among other benefits, these special member functions provide a place to put *new-* and *delete-expressions* so that any dynamic member variables are automatically managed with the class instance that contains them.

Smart pointers

The C++ standard library provides "smart pointer" template classes that behave like the raw pointer types, except they also delete the pointed-to variables when they go out of scope. Smart pointers remember whether the allocated storage is an array or a single instance, and call the correct delete-expression for the type of the smart pointer. Smart pointers are explored further in the next section.

Allocator templates

The C++ standard library provides allocator templates, which generalize new- and *delete-expressions* for use with standard containers. Allocators are explored further in "Provide Custom Standard Library Allocators" on page 343.

Smart Pointers Automate Ownership of Dynamic Variables

Ownership of dynamic variables is not controlled by the compiler or defined by C++. A program may declare a pointer variable in one place, assign a dynamic variable to the pointer using a new-expression in another place, copy the pointer to another pointer in a third place, and destroy the dynamic variable referenced by that second pointer using a delete-expression in yet another place. However, a program that behaves in this way can be hard to test and debug because ownership of the dynamic variable is so diffuse. Ownership of dynamic variables is enforced by the developer and encoded into the program logic. When ownership is diffuse, every line of the program may potentially create a dynamic variable, add or remove references, or destroy the variable. The developer must potentially trace all execution paths to ensure the dynamic variables are always properly returned to the memory manager.

This complexity can be reduced through the use of programming idioms. One common practice is to declare a pointer variable as a private member of some class. The class constructor can set the pointer to `nullptr`, copy a pointer argument, or contain a new-expression to create a dynamic variable. Because the pointer is a private member, any change to the pointer must happen within member functions of the class. This limits the number of code lines that can affect the pointer, making coding and debugging far easier. The class destructor can contain a delete-expression for the dynamic variable. An instance of a class that behaves in this way is said to own the dynamic variable.

A simple class may be designed with the single purpose of owning a dynamic variable. In addition to constructing and destroying the dynamic variable, the class also implements `operator->()` and `operator*()`. Such a class is called a *smart pointer*, because it mostly behaves like a C-style pointer, but also destroys the dynamic object it points to when the smart pointer instance is destroyed.

C++ provides a smart pointer template class called `std::unique_ptr<T>` to maintain ownership of a dynamic variable of type `T`. `unique_ptr` compiles to code that is comparable in efficiency to handwritten code.

Automating ownership of dynamic variables

Smart pointers automate ownership of dynamic variables by coupling the lifetime of the dynamic variable to the lifetime of the smart pointer that owns it. The dynamic variable is properly destroyed and its memory is freed automatically, depending on the declaration of the pointer:

- A smart pointer instance declared with automatic storage duration deletes the dynamic variable it owns when execution passes out of the scope enclosing its declaration, whether this happens by executing a `break` or `continue` statement, returning from the function, or throwing an exception through the scope.

- A smart pointer instance declared as a class member deletes the dynamic variable it owns when the containing class is destroyed. In addition, because the rules for class destruction cause each member to be destroyed after the class destructor executes, it is not necessary to write explicit code in the destructor to delete the dynamic variable. The smart pointer is deleted by the built-in machinery of C++.

- A smart pointer instance declared with thread-local storage duration deletes the dynamic variable it owns when the thread terminates normally (but not, generally, if the thread is terminated by the operating system).

- A smart pointer instance declared with static storage duration deletes the dynamic variable it owns when the program ends.

Maintaining a single owner in general, and using `std::unique_ptr` to maintain ownership in particular, makes it significantly easier to reason about whether a dynamic variable points to valid storage, and whether it is properly returned to the memory manager when it is no longer needed. There is little cost penalty for using `unique_ptr`, so it should be the first choice for developers interested in optimization.

Shared ownership of dynamic variables is more expensive

C++ allows multiple pointers and references to a dynamic variable. Multiple pointers may refer to a dynamic variable if several data structures point to the dynamic variable, or if a pointer to the dynamic variable is passed as a function argument, so that one pointer is in the caller's scope and another pointer is in the scope of the called function. Multiple pointers to a dynamic variable exist briefly during assignment or construction of an object intended to own a dynamic variable.

During any time that multiple pointers refer to a dynamic variable, the developer must reason about which pointer is the owner. It is up to the developer not to explicitly delete the dynamic variable through a nonowning pointer, dereference any pointer after deleting the dynamic variable, or cause two owning pointers to refer to the same object so that it is deleted twice. This analysis becomes particularly important when an error or exception occurs.

Sometimes ownership of a dynamic variable *must* be shared between two or more pointers. Ownership must be shared when the lifetimes of two pointers to the variable overlap, but the lifetime of neither pointer fully contains the lifetime of the other.

When ownership must be shared, the C++ standard library template `std::shared_ptr<T>` provides a smart pointer capable of managing shared ownership. Instances of `shared_ptr` contain a pointer to the dynamic variable, and another pointer to a dynamic object containing a reference count. When a dynamic variable is assigned to a `shared_ptr`, the assignment operator constructs the reference counter object and sets the reference count to 1. When one `shared_ptr` is assigned to another, the reference count is incremented. When a `shared_ptr` is destroyed, the destructor decrements the reference counter, and deletes the dynamic variable only if the reference count is 0. Expensive atomic increment and decrement operations are performed on the reference count so that shared_ptr works in multithreaded programs. std::shared_ptr is therefore considerably more expensive than either a C-style pointer or std::unique_ptr.

It is up to the developer not to assign a C-style pointer (such as the pointer returned by a new-expression) to multiple smart pointers, but only to assign from one smart pointer to another. If the same C-style pointer is assigned to several smart pointers, the pointer will be deleted several times, resulting in what the C++ standard inscrutibly calls "undefined behavior." This sounds obvious, but because a smart pointer can be constructed from a plain old pointer, type conversion during argument passing can silently cause this to happen.

std::auto_ptr versus container classes

A pre-C++11 smart pointer called std::auto_ptr<T> can also manage unshared ownership of a dynamic variable. In many ways, auto_ptr behaves like unique_ptr. However, auto_ptr does not implement move semantics (discussed in "Implement Move Semantics" on page 137) and does not have a copy constructor.

Most standard library containers prior to C++11 copy-constructed their value type into the container's internal storage, so auto_ptr could not be used as the value type. Prior to the introduction of unique_ptr, standard library containers had to be programmed using C-style pointers, deep object copies, or shared_ptr. Each of these solutions had problems. Native C-style pointers created risks of errors or memory leaks, deep object copies were inefficient for large objects, and shared_ptr was inherently expensive. Some projects implemented special unsafe smart pointers for container classes whose copy constructor performed a move-like operation, such as using std::swap() to transfer an owned pointer to the constructor. This let many, but not all, container class member functions work as expected. It was efficient, but was unsafe and difficult to debug.

Prior to C++11, it was common practice to use std::shared_ptr for the value type in standard library container class instances. This practice produced correct and debuggable code, but at the expense of shared_ptr's inefficiency.

Dynamic Variables Have Runtime Cost

Because C++ is compiled to native machine code and directly executed by the computer, the cost of most C++ statements is at most a few memory accesses. However, the cost of allocating memory for a dynamic variable is measured in thousands of memory accesses. This cost is so high, on average, that eliminating even one call into the memory manager can noticeably improve the performance of a function, as demonstrated repeatedly in Chapter 4.

Conceptually, a function for allocating memory searches a collection of free memory blocks looking for a block able to satisfy the request. If the function finds a block the right size, it removes the block from the collection and returns it. If the function finds a block that is much bigger than the request, it can choose to split the block and return a portion. Obviously, this general description leaves room for many implementation choices.

If no free memory blocks are available to fill the request, the allocation function makes an expensive call into the operating system kernel for an additional large memory block from the system's pool of available memory. The memory returned by the kernel may or may not be cached in physical RAM (see "Memory Has Finite Capacity" on page 20), perhaps resulting in even more delay the first time it is accessed. Walking the list of free memory blocks is itself expensive. They are scattered through memory and less likely to be in cache than are memory blocks currently visible to the running program.

The collection of free memory blocks is a resource shared by all the threads of a program. Any changes to the free block collection must be thread-safe. If several threads make frequent calls to allocate or free memory, they experience contention for the memory manager as a resource, causing all but one thread to wait.

A C++ program must free allocated memory when the dynamic variable it contains is no longer needed. Conceptually, a function to free memory puts the returned memory block onto the free block collection. In real implementations, the behavior of the free function is considerably more complex. Most implementations try to coalesce a newly freed memory block with adjacent free blocks. This keeps the free memory collection from filling up with blocks too small to be useful. Calls to the memory freeing function have the same issues of reduced cache performance and contention for multithreaded access to the free blocks as do calls to allocate memory.

Reduce Use of Dynamic Variables

Dynamic variables are a robust solution to many problems. However, they are too expensive to use for solving *every* problem. Statically created variables can often do the work of dynamic variables.

Create Class Instances Statically

It is possible to create class instances dynamically. However, most class instances that are not part of containers can and generally should be created statically (that is, without using new). Sometimes class instances are created dynamically because the developer does not realize there is another option. For instance, an inexperienced

C++ developer who learned Java first might know that typical Java syntax for instantiating a class looks like this:

```
MyClass myInstance = new MyClass("hello", 123);
```

If the naïve user types the Java syntax into a C++ program, the C++ compiler encourages him to make `myInstance` a pointer, saying "cannot convert from 'MyClass *' to 'MyClass.'" The slightly more experienced developer might make `myInstance` a smart pointer to avoid having to explicitly delete the dynamically created class instance, if he is even aware that this is an issue:

```
MyClass* myInstance = new MyClass("hello", 123);
```

However, both solutions are wasteful. Instead, the class should usually be statically constructed, like this:

```
MyClass myInstance("hello", 123);
```

or:

```
MyClass anotherMC = MyClass("hello", 123); // maybe less efficient
```

If `myInstance` is declared in a block of executable code, it has automatic storage duration when declared in this way. It will be destroyed when execution leaves the block containing this declaration. If the program needs `myInstance` to persist longer than this, it can declare `myInstance` within an outer scope or a longer-lived object and pass a pointer into functions that need to use `myInstance`. The declaration can be moved to file scope if `myInstance` needs to live as long as the whole program.

Create class member variables statically

When member variables of a class are themselves class instances, these members can be constructed statically when the containing class is constructed. This saves the cost of allocating memory for the members.

Sometimes it seems like a class instance must be constructed dynamically because it is a member of another class, and some resource needed to construct the member is not available at the time the enclosing class is constructed. An alternative pattern is to make the problem class (rather than a pointer to it) a member of the containing class, and simply not to initialize the problem class fully when it is constructed. Create a member function in the problem class to initialize the variable fully once resources are available. Then insert a call to the initialization member function at the point where a dynamic instance would have been instantiated using `new`. This common pattern is called *two-part initialization*.

There is no cost to two-part initialization. The member could not be used before the point where it was constructed anyway. Any cost of checking whether the member instance was fully initialized is the same as the cost to see whether the pointer to it was `nullptr`. An additional benefit of the method described here is that an initialization member function can return error codes or other information, whereas a constructor cannot.

Two-part initialization is especially useful when a class must do something during initialization that is time-consuming, like reading a file, or that can fail, like requesting a web page from the Internet. Providing a separate initialization function makes it possible to do either of these kinds of initialization concurrently (see Chapter 12) with other program activity, and makes it easier to repeat the second kind of initialization in case of failure.

Use Static Data Structures

`std::string`, `std::vector`, `std::map`, and `std::list` are the containers most C++ developers use every day. Used carefully, they can be reasonably efficient. But they're not the only choices. `std::string` and `std::vector` reallocate their storage occasionally to grow as you add items to the container. `std::map` and `std::list` allocate a new node for every added item. Sometimes, this is too expensive. We'll explore alternatives here.

Use std::array instead of std::vector

`std::vector` allows the program to define dynamically resizable arrays of any type. If the size of the array, or the maximum size, is known at compile time, `std::array` offers a similar interface, but with a fixed-size array and no calls into the memory manager.

`std::array` is copy-constructible and offers standard library–style random-access iterators and subscripting via `operator[]`. `size()` returns the fixed size of the array.

From an optimization standpoint, `std::array` is almost indistinguishable from C-style arrays. From a programming standpoint, `std::array` has a comfortable similarity to the standard library containers.

Create large buffers on the stack

Chapter 4 demonstrated that inserting into a string can be expensive because of the need to reallocate the string's storage as it grows longer. If the developer knows the maximum possible size the string can reach, or at least its maximum reasonable size, it may be possible to use an oversized C-style array having automatic storage duration as a temporary, mutate the string in the temporary, and then copy the result.

The design pattern is to call a function to create or mutate the data, which declares a very large automatic array. The function copies the data from its argument to the local array and performs insertions, deletions, or other permutations on the static array.

Although there is a limit to the total storage you can declare on the stack, this limit is frequently very large. On desktop systems, for instance, unless the algorithm uses very deep recursion, there is room on the stack for arrays of 10,000 characters.

A cautious developer worried about overflowing the local array can check the length of the argument string or array, and default to a dynamically constructed array if the argument is too big for the local array.

Why is all this copying any faster than using a dynamic data structure like std::string? Partly, it's because mutating operations often copy the input anyway. Partly it's because copying blocks of even a few thousand bytes is inexpensive on desktop-class hardware, compared to the cost of allocating dynamic storage for intermediate results.

Create linked data structures statically

Linked data structures can be constructed as static initialized data. For instance, the tree structure shown in Figure 6-1 can be reproduced statically.

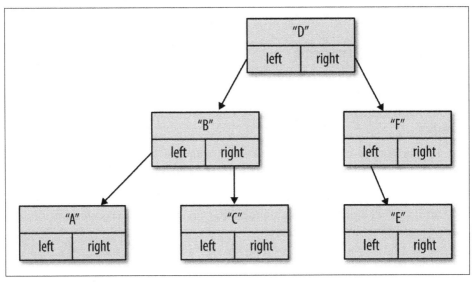

Figure 6-1. Simple tree structure

In this particular example, the tree is a binary search tree, the nodes are laid out in an array in breadth-first order, and the first element is the root:

```
struct treenode {
    char const* name;
    treenode* left;
    treenode* right;
} tree[] = {
    { "D", &tree[1], &tree[2] }
```

```
        { "B", &tree[3], &tree[4] },
        { "F", &tree[5], nullptr  },
        { "A", nullptr,  nullptr  },
        { "C", nullptr,  nullptr  },
        { "E", nullptr,  nullptr  },
    };
```

This works because the addresses of array elements are constant expressions. This notation allows any linked structure to be defined, but the initializers are not very mnemonic, so it's easy to make a typing error when building such a structure.

Another way to statically create linked structures is to initialize a variable for each element of the structure. This mechanism is very mnemonic, but has the disadvantage that forward references (like the one from fourth to first in the following code) have to be specially declared. The most natural way to declare this structure (first, second, third, fourth) would require extern declarations for all four variables. It's defined in reverse order so that most of the references are to already-declared variables:

```
struct cyclenode {
    char const* name;
    cyclenode* next;
}
extern cyclenode first; // forward reference
cyclenode fourth = { "4", &first  );
cyclenode third  = { "3", &fourth };
cyclenode second = { "2", &third  };
cyclenode first  = { "1", &second };
```

Create binary trees in an array

Most developers learn about binary trees as an example of a linked data structure, in which each node is a separate instance of a class that contains pointers to the left and right child nodes. An unfortunate consequence of defining the tree data structure in this way is that a class storing something as small as a single character requires enough storage for two pointers as well, plus any overhead imposed by the dynamic memory manager.

An alternative approach is to build a binary tree in an array. Instead of containing explicit links to child nodes, the array indexes of a node's children are computed from the index of the node. If the index of a node is i, its two children are at index $2i$ and $2i+1$. As an additional bonus, the parent of a node is at index $i/2$. Because these multiplications and divisions can be implemented as left and right shifts, the computation is inexpensive even on extremely modest embedded processors.

The nodes of a tree implemented in an array require a mechanism to determine whether their left and right children are valid nodes in the tree or if they are the equivalent of null pointers. If the tree is left-balanced, a single integer retaining the array index of the first invalid node suffices.

These properties—the ability to compute child and parent nodes, and the efficiency of representation of a left-balanced tree—make a tree-in-an-array an efficient implementation for heap data structures.

A tree-in-an-array representation may be less efficient for balanced binary trees than a linked representation. An array of up to 2*n* positions may be required to hold a balanced binary tree of *n* nodes, depending on the balancing algorithm. Further, a balancing operation requires copying nodes to different array locations, rather than merely updating pointers. On smaller processors, and for larger node sizes, the copy operation may be too expensive. But if the node size is smaller than three pointers, the tree-in-an-array representation may still be a performance win.

Use a circular buffer instead of a deque

`std::deque` and `std::list` are so often used for a FIFO (first-in-first-out) buffer that the standard library has a container adapter called `std::queue`.

A double-ended queue, or deque, may also be implemented over a circular buffer. A circular buffer is an array data structure in which the front and back of the queue are given by two array indexes, modulo the length of the array. A circular buffer has similar properties to a deque, including constant-time `push_back()` and `pop_front()`, and random-access iterators. However, a circular buffer does not require reallocation as long as the consumer keeps up with the producer. The size of the circular buffer does not determine how many inputs it can process, but instead determines how far ahead the producer can get.

The difference between a circular buffer and a list or deque is the limit to the number of items in the buffer made visible by the circular buffer. Specializing the general queue data structure by exposing this constraint to the user makes a significantly more efficient implementation possible.

Boost has a circular buffer (*http://bit.ly/b-buffer*) implemented as a standard library container. There are plenty of other implementations on the Web. A circular buffer can be designed with a static buffer whose size is given by a template parameter, with an initial size requiring a single allocation, or with a dynamically resizable buffer like `std::vector`. The performance of the circular buffer is similar to that of `std::vector`.

Use std::make_shared Instead of new

A shared pointer such as `std::shared_ptr` really contains two pointers. One points to the object referred to by the pointer. The other points to a second dynamic variable holding the reference count shared by all the `std::shared_ptrs` that refer to the object. So, a statement like:

```
std::shared_ptr<MyClass> p(new MyClass("hello", 123));
```

calls into the memory manager *twice*—once to create an instance of `MyClass`, and once again to create the hidden reference count object.

The pre-C++11 way around the expense of allocating the reference counter is to add an intrusive reference count as a base class of `MyClass` and create a custom smart pointer that uses the intrusive reference count:

```
custom_shared_ptr<RCClass> p(new RCClass("Goodbye", 999));
```

The standard writers heard our pain, and invented a template function called `std::make_shared()` that allocates a single block of storage to hold both the reference count and an instance of `MyClass`. `std::shared_ptr` also has a deleter function that knows which of the two ways the shared pointer was constructed. Now you know why `std::shared_ptr` seems so complicated internally when you step through it in the debugger.

`make_shared()` is pretty easy to use:

```
std::shared_ptr<MyClass> p = std::make_shared<MyClass>("hello", 123);
```

or the even simpler C++11-style declaration:

```
auto p = std::make_shared<MyClass>("hello", 123);
```

Don't Share Ownership Unnecessarily

Multiple `std::shared_ptr` instances can share ownership of a dynamic variable. `shared_ptr` is useful when the lifetimes of the various pointers overlap unpredictably, but it is expensive. Incrementing and decrementing the reference count in a `shared_ptr` is performed not with a simple increment instruction, but with an expensive atomic increment with a full memory fence (see "Atomic Operations on Shared Variables" on page 301) so that `shared_ptr` works in multithreaded programs.

If the lifetime of one `shared_ptr` completely encloses the lifetime of another, the expense of the second `shared_ptr` is unnecessary. The following code illustrates a common situation:

```
void fiddle(std::shared_ptr<Foo> f);
    ...
shared_ptr<Foo> myFoo = make_shared<Foo>();
    ...
fiddle(myFoo);
```

`myFoo` owns a dynamic instance of `Foo`. When the program calls `fiddle()`, the call creates a second link to the dynamic `Foo` instance, incrementing the `shared_ptr`'s reference count. When `fiddle()` returns, the `shared_ptr` argument releases its owner-ship of the dynamic `Foo` instance. The caller still owns a pointer. The minimum cost of this is an unnecessary atomic increment and decrement, each with a full memory fence. Across one function call, this extra cost is negligible. But as a programming practice, making every function argument that passes a pointer-to-Foo a `shared_ptr` across a whole program can result in significant cost.

Making the argument to `fiddle()` a plain pointer saves this cost:

```
void fiddle(Foo* f);
    ...
shared_ptr<Foo> myFoo = make_shared<Foo>();
    ...
fiddle(myFoo.get());
```

There is received wisdom that naked C-style pointers should never appear in a pro-gram except in the implementation of smart pointers, but another view is that plain pointers are fine as long as they are understood to represent nonowning pointers. In a team where developers feel really strongly that plain pointers are the devil's play-things, the same result can be accomplished with references. Making a function argu-ment a `Foo&` sends two messages—that the caller is responsible to ensure the reference remains valid for the duration of the call, and that the pointer is non-null:

```
void fiddle(Foo& f);
    ...
shared_ptr<Foo> myFoo = make_shared<Foo>();
    ...
if (myFoo)
    fiddle(*myFoo.get());
```

The dereferencing operator `*` converts the pointer-to-Foo returned by `get()` into a reference to Foo. That is to say, it generates no code at all, just a note to the compiler. References are a convention that means "unowned, non-null pointer."

Use a "Master Pointer" to Own Dynamic Variables

`std::shared_ptr` is easy. It automates management of a dynamic variable. But as pre-viously noted, shared pointers are expensive. In many cases, they are unnecessary.

Very often, a single data structure owns a dynamic variable for its whole lifetime. Ref-erences or pointers to the dynamic variable may be passed to and returned by func-tions, assigned to variables, and so on, but none of these references outlive the "master" reference.

If there is a master reference, it can be efficiently implemented using `std::unique_ptr`. A naked C-style pointer or C++ reference can be used to refer to the object during function calls. When this is done consistently, the use of naked pointers and references documents that these are "unowned" pointers.

A faction of developers become very uncomfortable with any deviation from use of `std::shared_ptr`. However, these same developers use iterators every day, not realizing perhaps that they behave as unowned pointers that can be made invalid. My experience using master pointers in several large projects is that problems leading to memory leaks or double frees do not happen in practice. When there is an obvious owner, master pointers are a big optimization win. When in doubt, `std::shared_ptr` is always available.

Reduce Reallocation of Dynamic Variables

Often the convenience of a dynamic variable is just too much to pass up. `std::string` comes to mind. But that doesn't excuse the developer from being careful. Techniques exist to reduce the number of allocations made when using standard library containers. These techniques can be generalized even to the developer's own data structures.

Preallocate Dynamic Variables to Prevent Reallocation

As data is appended to a `std::string` or `std::vector`, its dynamically allocated internal storage eventually becomes full. The next append operation causes the string or vector to allocate a larger block of storage and copy the old contents to the new storage. Both the call to the memory manager and the copy perform many memory accesses and consume many instructions. Yes, it's true that an append takes place in O(*1*) time, but the constant of proportionality (how big the constant time is in milliseconds) can be significant.

Both `string` and `vector` have a member function, `reserve(size_t n)`, that tells the string or vector to ensure there is sufficient space for at least n entries. If the size can be computed or estimated, a call to `reserve()` keeps the string or vector's internal storage from needing to be reallocated as it grows to this limit:

```
std::string errmsg;
errmsg.reserve(100); // only one allocation for all this appending
errmsg += "Error 1234: variable ";
errmsg += varname;
errmsg += " was used before set. Undefined behavior.";
```

A call to `reserve()` acts as a hint to the string or vector. Unlike with allocating a worst-case static buffer, the only penalty for too low a guess is the possibility of additional reallocations. Even an extravagant overestimate for the expected size is not a problem if the string or vector will be used briefly and then destroyed. The `shrink_to_fit()` member function of `std::string` or `std::vector` can also be used to return unused space to the memory manager after using `reserve()` to preallocate a string or vector.

The standard library hash table type `std::unordered_map` (see "std::unordered_map and std::unordered_multimap" on page 256) has a backbone array (a list of buckets) containing links to the rest of the data structure. It also has a `reserve()` member function. Unfortunately, `std::deque`, which also has a backbone array, lacks a `reserve()` member function.

Developers designing their own data structures containing a backbone array would do their users a favor by including a function like `reserve()` to preallocate this backbone.

Create Dynamic Variables Outside of Loops

The following small loop has a big problem. It appends the lines of each file in `namelist` to the `std::string` variable `config`, then extracts a small amount of data from `config`. The problem is that `config` is created each time through the loop, and each time through the loop it's reallocated as it grows longer. Then, at the end of the loop, `config` goes out of scope and is destroyed, returning its storage to the memory manager:

```
for (auto& filename : namelist) {
    std::string config;
    ReadFileXML(filename, config);
    ProcessXML(config);
}
```

One way to make this loop more efficient is to move the declaration of `config` outside the loop. Inside the loop, `config` is cleared. However, `clear()` does not free the dynamically sized buffer inside `config`. It just sets the length of the contents to zero. After the first time through the loop, `config` won't be reallocated unless a subsequent file is significantly larger than the first file:

```
std::string config;
for (auto& filename : namelist) {
    config.clear();
    ReadFileXML(filename, config);
    ProcessXML(config);
}
```

A variation on this theme is to make `config` a class member variable. This latter advice may smell to some developers like advocating the unclean practice of using global variables. And in a sense it is. However, making dynamically allocated variables long lived can have a dramatic impact on performance.

This trick works not just with `std::string`, but also with `std::vector` and any other data structure that has a dynamically resizable backbone.

Optimization War Story

I once wrote a multithreaded program in which each thread entered a class instance. These threads each logged their activities. The logging functions originally defined a local temporary string into which the log information was formatted. I discovered that when there were more than half a dozen threads, each banging away at the memory manager to create lines of logging information, contention for the memory manager became so great that performance fell precipitously. The solution was to make the temporary string that held each log line a class member that was reused for each logged line. Once the string had been used a few times, it became long enough that reallocation was never required. Replicating this single trick through a large program provided the largest performance boost of any change I made, allowing the program (a telephony server) to scale easily to 10 times as many simultaneous calls.

Eliminate Unneeded Copying

In the classical Kernighan and Ritchie (K & R) definition of C, all the entities that could be directly assigned were primitive types like char, int, float, and pointers, which fit into a single machine register. Thus, any assignment statement like a = b; was efficient, generating only one or two instructions to fetch the value of b and store it into a. In C++, assignment of basic types like char, int, or float is just as efficient.

But there are simple-looking assignment statements that are *not* efficient in C++. If a and b are instances of the class BigClass, the assignment a = b; calls a member function of BigClass called the *assignment operator*. The assignment operator *can* be as simple as copying the fields of b into a. But the point is that it *may* do absolutely anything a C++ function can do. BigClass may have dozens of fields to copy. If Big Class owns dynamic variables, these may be copied, resulting in calls to the memory manager. If BigClass owns a std::map with a million entries, or even a char array with a million characters, the cost of the assignment statement may be significant.

In C++, the initialized declaration Foo a = b; may invoke another member function called the *copy constructor* if Foo names a class. The copy constructor and assignment operator are closely related member functions that mostly do the same thing: copy the fields of one class instance to another. And like with the assignment operator, there is no upper limit to the cost of the copy constructor.

A developer scanning a hot piece of code for optimization opportunities must pay special attention to assignments and declarations, because these are places where expensive copying may lurk. In fact, copying may occur in any of the following places:

- Initialization (calls constructor)
- Assignment (calls assignment operator)
- Function arguments (each argument expression is move- or copy-constructed into its formal argument)
- Function return (calls move or copy constructor, perhaps twice)
- Inserting items into a standard library container (items are move- or copy-constructed)
- Inserting items into a vector (all items are move- or copy-constructed if the vector is reallocated)

Scott Meyers, among many others, covers the topic of copy construction extensively and well in his book *Effective C++*. The brief notes here are just an outline.

Disable Unwanted Copying in the Class Definition

Not every object in a program should be copied. For instance, objects that behave as entities (see "Value Objects and Entity Objects" on page 112) must not be copied or they lose their meaning.

Many objects that behave as entities have a considerable amount of state (a vector of 1,000 strings or a table of 1,000 symbols, for instance). A program that inadvertently copies an entity into a function meant to examine the entity's state may appear to function correctly, but the runtime cost of the copy may be considerable.

If copying a class instance is expensive or undesirable, one expedient way to avoid this expense is to forbid copying. Declaring the copy constructor and assignment operator `private` prevents them being called. Since they can't be called, no definition is even necessary; the declaration alone is enough. For example:

```
// pre-C++11 way to disable copying
class BigClass {
private:
    BigClass(BigClass const&);
    BigClass& operator=(BigClass const&);
public:
    ...
};
```

In C++11, the `delete` keyword can be appended to a declaration of the copy constructor and assignment operator to achieve the same result. It's a good idea to make deleted constructors public because the compiler provides a clearer error message in this case:

```
// C++11 way to disable copying
class BigClass {
public:
```

```
    BigClass(BigClass const&) = delete;
    BigClass& operator=(BigClass const&) = delete;
    ...
};
```

Any attempt to assign an instance of a class declared in this way—or pass it by value to a function, or return it by value, or use it as the value of a standard library container class—will result in compile errors.

Still permitted is to assign or initialize variables with pointers or references to the class, or pass and return references or pointers to the instance in functions. From an optimization standpoint, assigning, passing, or returning a pointer or reference is far more efficient, because the pointer or reference fits into a machine register.

Eliminate Copying on Function Call

I'll start this section by detailing the overhead during a function call when a C++ program evaluates the arguments. Read carefully, because the consequences for optimization are significant. When a program calls a function, each argument expression is evaluated, and each formal argument is constructed, with the value of the corresponding argument expression as its initializer.

"Constructed" means that a constructor member function of the formal argument is invoked. If the formal argument is a basic type like an int, double, or char*, the basic type's constructor is conceptual, not an actual function. The program just copies the value into the formal argument's storage.

If a formal argument is an instance of some class, however, one of the class's copy constructors is called to initialize the instance. In all but trivial cases, the copy constructor is an actual function. Code is executed to call the function, and for whatever the copy constructor does. If the argument class is a std::list with a million entries, its copy constructor calls the memory manager a million times to create new entries. If the argument is a list of maps of strings, that whole data structure may be copied, node by node. For a very large and complex argument, the copy will probably take long enough to attract the original developer's attention. But if the argument only had a few entries during testing, there's a risk that the error will remain undiscovered until the design is long entrenched and becomes an obstacle to scaling the program. Consider the following example:

```
int Sum(std::list<int> v) {
    int sum = 0;
    for (auto it : v)
        sum += *it;
    return sum;
}
```

When the function Sum() shown here is called, the actual argument is a list: for instance, int total = Sum(MyList);. The formal argument v is also a list. v is constructed by finding a constructor that takes a reference to a list. This is the copy constructor. The copy constructor for std::list makes a copy of each element of the list. If MyList is always just a few elements long, the cost, while unecessary, is bearable. But the overhead can be burdensome as MyList scales. If it has 1,000 elements, the memory manager is invoked 1,000 times. At the end of the function, the formal argument v goes out of scope, and those 1,000 elements are returned to the free list one by one.

To avoid this expense, formal arguments can be defined as types that have trivial copy constructors. To pass class instances into a function, pointers or references have trivial constructors. In the previous example, v could be a std::list<int> const&. Then, instead of copy-constructing an instance of the class, the reference is initialized with a reference to the actual argument. The reference typically is implemented as a pointer.

Passing a reference to a class instance can improve performance if copy-constructing the instance would call into the memory manager to copy its internal data, as with standard library containers, or when the class contains an array that must be copied, or has many local variables. There is some cost to accessing the instance through a reference: the pointer implementing the reference must be dereferenced each time the instance is accessed. If the function is large, and the function body uses the value of the argument many times, a point of diminishing returns may be reached where the cost of continually dereferencing the reference outweighs the cost savings by avoiding the copy. But for brief functions, passing arguments by reference is a win for all but the smallest classes.

Reference arguments don't behave exactly like value arguments. A reference argument modified within the function modifies the referenced instance, while modifying a value argument has no effect outside the function. Declaring reference arguments as const prevents accidental modification.

Reference arguments can also introduce aliases, which can cause unanticipated effects. That is, if a function signature is:

```
void func(Foo& a, Foo& b);
```

the call func(x,x); introduces an alias. If func() updates a, it will find that b also is suddenly updated.

Eliminate Copying on Function Return

When a function returns a value, the value is copy-constructed into an unnamed temporary of the type returned by the function. Copy construction is trivial for basic types like long or double, or pointers, but when variables are classes, the copy constructor is typically a real function call. The bigger and more complex the class is, the more time-consuming its copy constructor is. Here is a simple example:

```
std::vector<int> scalar_product(std::vector<int> const& v, int c) {
    std::vector<int> result;
    result.reserve(v.size());
    for (auto val : v)
        result.push_back(val * c);
    return result;
}
```

The cost of copy-constructing that already-constructed return value can be avoided in some cases by returning a reference, as discussed in the previous section. Unfortunately, that trick doesn't work if the value to be returned is computed within the function and assigned to a variable with automatic storage duration. Such a variable goes out of scope when the function returns, leaving a dangling reference to unknown bytes off the end of the stack that will almost immediately be written over. Worse still, computing a result within the function is a very common use case, so that most functions return values, not references.

As if the cost of copy-constructing into the return value wasn't bad enough, the value returned from a function is often assigned to a variable in the caller, as in `auto res = scalar_product(argarray, 10);`. So, on top of the copy constructor called inside the function, another copy constructor or assignment operator is invoked in the caller.

This double copy construction was a tremendous performance killer in early C++ programs. Fortunately, the big-brained folks who brought us the C++ standard and the many wonderful C++ compilers found a way to eliminate the extra copy constructor. This optimization is variously called *copy elision* or *return value optimization* (RVO). Developers may have heard of RVO, and may think it means they can return objects by value without worrying about the cost. This is unfortunately not the case. The conditions under which the compiler can perform RVO are very specific. The function must return a locally constructed object. The compiler must be able to determine that the same object is returned on all control paths. The object must have the same type as the declared return type of the function. To a first order of approximation, if a function is brief and has a single control path, the compiler is quite likely to do RVO. If the function is larger, or the control path is branched, it's harder for the compiler to determine that RVO is possible. Compilers also vary in the quality of their analysis.

There is a way to eliminate construction of a class instance inside the function, plus *both* copy constructions (or the equivalent copy constructor followed by assignment operator) that happen on returning from a function. It involves direct action by the developer, so the result is deterministically better than hoping the compiler does RVO in a given situation. Instead of returning a value using a `return` statement, the value can be returned as an *out parameter*, a reference argument updated to the returned value inside the function:

```
void scalar_product(
    std::vector<int> const& v,
    int c,
    vector<int>& result) {
    result.clear();
    result.reserve(v.size());
    for (auto val : v)
        result.push_back(val * c);
}
```

Here, an out parameter named `result` has been added to the function's argument list. There are several advantages to this mechanism:

- The object is already constructed when the function is called. Sometimes the object must be cleared or reinitialized, but this is unlikely ever to be more expensive than construction.

- The object updated inside the function need not be copied into an unnamed temporary in the `return` statement.

- Because the actual data is returned in an argument, the return type of the function can be `void`, or the return value can be used for status or error information.

- Because the updated object is already bound to a name in the caller, it need not be copied or assigned upon return from the function.

But wait, there's more. Many data structures (strings, vectors, hash tables) have a dynamically allocated backbone array that can often be reused if a function is called more than once in a program. Sometimes the result of the function must be saved in the caller, but this cost is never more than the cost of the copy constructor that would be called if the function returned a class instance by value.

Are there any extra runtime costs to this mechanism, such as the cost of an extra argument? Not really. What the compiler actually does with an instance-returning function is convert it to a form with an extra argument, a reference to uninitialized storage for the unnamed temporary returned by the function.

There's one place in C++ where there's no choice but to return objects by value: operator functions. Developers writing matrix math functions who want to use the readable operator syntax `A = B * C;` cannot use reference arguments, but must focus instead on carefully implementing operator functions so that they can use RVO and move semantics to maximal efficiency.

Copy Free Libraries

When a buffer, struct, or other data structure to be filled is a function argument, a reference can be passed through several layers of library calls inexpensively. I have heard libraries that implement this behavior described as "copy free" libraries. This pattern appears in many libraries of performance-critical functions. It's worth learning.

For example, the C++ standard library `istream::read()` member function has the following signature:

```
istream& read(char* s, streamsize n);
```

This function reads up to n bytes into the storage pointed to by s. The buffer s is an out parameter, so the read data doesn't have to be copied into newly allocated storage. Since s is an argument, `istream::read()` can use the returned value for something else; in this case, returning its "this" pointer as a reference.

But `istream::read()` doesn't actually fetch data from the operating system kernel itself. It calls another function. While implementations differ, it may call the C library function `fread()`, which has the following signature:

```
size_t fread(void* ptr, size_t size, size_t nmemb, FILE* stream);
```

`fread()` reads `size*nmemb` bytes of data and stores them in the storage pointed to by ptr. The ptr argument of `fread()` is the same as the s argument of `istream::read()`.

But `fread()` isn't the end of the calling chain. On Linux, `fread()` calls the standard Unix function `read()`. On Windows, `fread()` calls the `ReadFile()` function from Win32. These two functions have similar signatures:

```
ssize_t read(int fd, void *buf, size_t count);
```

```
BOOL ReadFile(HANDLE hFile, void* buf, DWORD n, DWORD* bytesread,
              OVERLAPPED* pOverlapped);
```

Both functions take a `void*` to the buffer to fill in, and a maximum number of bytes to read. Although its type has been cast from `char*` to `void*` on its way down the calling chain, the pointer refers to the same storage.

There is an alternative design aesthetic that says these structures and buffers should be returned by value. They are created in the function, so they shouldn't exist prior to the function call. The function is "simpler" with one less argument. C++ allows the developer to return structures by value, so this way must be the "natural" way in C++. With the developers of Unix, Windows, C, and C++ all behind the copy-free style, I am bewildered that there are supporters for this alternative aesthetic, which has a high cost: that of copying the structure or buffer, not once, but several times as it passes up the layers of a library. If the returned value has dynamic variables, the cost may include calling the memory manager several times to make copies. An attempt to allocate the structure once and return a pointer requires ownership of the pointer to be transferred several times. RVO and move semantics only partially address these costs, and require careful attention from the developer to implement well. From the standpoint of performance, a copy-free design is far more efficient.

Implement the "Copy on Write" Idiom

Copy on write (sometimes abbreviated COW) is a programming idiom used to copy class instances containing expensive-to-copy dynamic variables efficiently. COW is a well-known optimization with a long history. It has been used frequently over the years, especially in the implementation of C++ character string classes. CString character strings in Windows use COW. Some older implementations of std::string also use COW. However, the C++11 standard forbids its use in implementing std::string. COW is not always an optimization win, so it must be used judiciously, despite its august tradition.

Normally, if an object that owns a dynamic variable is copied, a new copy must be made of the dynamic variable. This is called a *deep copy* operation. An object that contains nonowning pointers can get by with copying the pointers, rather than the pointed-to variables. This is called a *shallow copy*.

The idea of copy on write is that two copies of an object are the same until one of them is modified. So, until one instance or the other is modified, they can share pointers to any expensive-to-copy parts. Copy on write initially performs a shallow copy operation, and delays performing the deep copy until an element of the object is mutated.

In a modern C++ implementation of COW, any class member that refers to a dynamic variable is implemented using a shared-ownership smart pointer such as std::shared_ptr. The class copy constructor copies the shared-ownership pointer, delaying the creation of a new copy of the dynamic variable until any copy wants to mutate the dynamic variable.

Any mutating operation in the class checks the reference count of the shared pointer before proceeding. If the reference count is greater than 1, indicating shared ownership, the operation makes a new copy of the object, swaps the shared pointer member with the shared pointer to the new copy, and releases the old copy, decrementing its reference count. Now the mutating operation can proceed, knowing that the dynamic variable is unshared.

It's important to construct the dynamic variable in the COW class using std::make_shared(). Otherwise, use of the shared pointer costs an extra trip to the memory manager to get the reference count object. For many dynamic variables, this is the same cost as simply copying the dynamic variable into new storage and assigning it to a (nonsharing) smart pointer. So, unless many copies are made, or mutating operators are not usually called, the COW idiom may not buy anything.

Slice Data Structures

Slicing is a programming idiom in which one variable refers to a portion of another. For instance, the experimental `string_view` type proposed for C++17 refers to a substring of another character string, containing a `char*` pointer to the beginning of the substring and a length that places the substring's end within the string being referred to.

Slices are small, easily copied objects, without the high cost of allocating storage for and copying contents into a subarray or substring. If the sliced data structure is owned by shared pointers, slices can be completely safe. But experience teaches that slices are ephemeral. They typically serve their purpose briefly and then go out of scope, before the sliced data structure can be deleted. `string_view`, for instance, uses an unowned pointer into the strings.

Implement Move Semantics

With respect to optimization, the *move semantics* added to C++11 are the biggest thing to happen to C++ in, well, ever. Move semantics solve several recurring problems from previous versions of C++. For example:

- An object is assigned to a variable, causing the internal contents of the object to be copied at significant runtime expense, after which the original object is immediately destroyed. The effort of copying is wasted, because the contents of the original object could have been reused.
- The developer wishes to assign an entity (see "Value Objects and Entity Objects" on page 112), such as an `auto_ptr` or resource handle, to a variable. The "copy" operation in the assignment is undefined on such an object because it has a unique identity.

Both these cases bite hard in dynamic containers such as `std::vector`, where the internal storage of the container must be reallocated as the number of items in the container grows. The first case makes reallocating a container more expensive than necessary. The second case prevents entities like `auto_ptr` from being stored in containers at all.

The problem arises because the copy operation performed by copy constructors and assignment operators works fine for basic types and unowned pointers, but doesn't make sense for entities. Objects with this type of member could be put in C-style arrays, but not in dynamic containers like `std::vector`.

Prior to C++11, C++ offered no standard way to efficiently move the contents of a variable to another variable, leaving nothing behind, for situations when the expense of copy was not needed.

Nonstandard Copy Semantics: A Painful Hack

When a variable behaves as an entity, making a copy is typically a one-way ticket to undefined behavior land. It is good practice to disable the copy constructor and assignment operator for such a variable. But containers like `std::vector` require contained objects to be copied when the container is reallocated, so disabling copy means you can't use that type of object in a container.

For the desperate designer wanting to put entities into standard library containers before the advent of move semantics, a workaround was to implement assignment in a nonstandard way. For instance, a kind of smart pointer could be created that implemented assignment as shown in Example 6-1.

Example 6-1. Hacky smart pointer noncopying assignment

```
hacky_ptr& hacky_ptr::operator=(hacky_ptr& rhs) {
    if (*this != rhs) {
        this->ptr_ = rhs.ptr_;
        rhs.ptr_ = nullptr;
    }
    return *this;
}
```

This assignment operator compiles and runs. A statement such as `q = p;` transfers ownership of the pointer to `q`, setting the pointer in `p` to `nullptr`. Ownership is preserved by this definition. A pointer defined in this way works in `std::vector`:

Although the signature of the assignment operator offers a subtle hint that `rhs` is modified, which is not usual for assignment, the assignment itself offers no clue to its deviant behavior (see Example 6-2).

Example 6-2. hacky_ptr use causes surprises

```
hacky_ptr p, q;
p = new Foo;
q = p;
    ...
p->foo_func(); // surprise, dereferences nullptr
```

A new developer expecting this code to work will be disappointed, possibly after a lengthy debugging session. Debasing the meaning of "copy" in this way is a coding horror, difficult to justify even when it seems necessary.

std::swap(): The Poor Man's Move Semantics

Another possible operation between two variables is "swap," in which the two variables exchange contents. Swap is well defined even when the variables are entities, because at the end of the operation, only one variable contains each entity. C++ provides the template function `std::swap()` to exchange the contents of two variables:

```
std::vector<int> a(1000000,0);
    ...
std::vector<int> b; // b is empty
std::swap(v,w);     // now b has a million entries
```

The default instantiation of `std::swap()` prior to move semantics is equivalent to this:

```
template <typename T> void std::swap(T& a, T& b) {
    T tmp = a; // make a new copy of a
    a = b;     // copy b to a, discarding a's old value
    b = tmp;   // copy temp to b, discarding b's old value
}
```

This default instantiation works only for objects for which the copy operation is defined. It is also potentially inefficient: a's original value is copied twice, and b's original value is copied once. If type `T` contains dynamically allocated members, three copies are made, and two are destroyed. This is more expensive than the conceptual copy operation, which does only one copy and one delete.

The swap operation's super power is that it can be applied recursively to the members of a class. Instead of copying objects referred to by pointers, the pointers themselves can be swapped. For classes that point to big, dynamically allocated data structures, swap is far more efficient than copy. In practice, `std::swap()` can be specialized for any desired class. Standard containers provide a `swap()` member function to swap pointers to their dynamic members. The containers also specialize `std::swap()`, producing an efficient swap that does not call into the memory manager. User-defined types may also provide a specialization for `std::swap()`.

`std::vector` is not defined to use swap to copy its contents when its backbone array grows, but a similar data structure could be defined to do so.

The problem with swap is that, while it is more efficient than copy for classes with dynamic variables that require a deep copy, it is less efficient than copy for other classes. "Swap" at least has a reasonable meaning for both owned pointers and simple types, which makes it a step in the right direction.

Shared Ownership of Entities

An entity cannot be copied. However, a shared pointer to an entity can. Thus, while it was not possible to create, for example, a `std::vector<std::mutex>` prior to move semantics, one could define a `std::vector<std::shared_ptr<std::mutex>>`. Copying a `shared_ptr` has a well-defined meaning: to make an additional reference to a unique object.

Of course, making a shared_ptr to an entity is a workaround. While it has the advantage that it uses C++ standard library tools as they were intended to be used, it is full of unnecessary complexity and runtime overhead.

The Moving Parts of Move Semantics

The standard writers realized they needed to enshrine the "move" operation as a fundamental concept in C++. Move handles transfer of ownership. It is more efficient than copy, and well defined for both values and entities. The result is called *move semantics*. I'm going to hit the highlights of move semantics here, but there are a lot of minutiae I can't cover in this brief space. I recommend very highly having a look at Scott Meyers's *Effective Modern C++*; he spends 10 out of 42 total sections on move semantics. Thomas Becker's "C++ Rvalue References Explained" (*http://bit.ly/becker-rvalue*) provides an accessible introduction to move semantics on the Web for free, but there is more to know than is covered here.

To facilitate move semantics, the C++ compiler was modified to recognize when a variable exists only as a temporary. Such an instance has no name. For example, the object returned by a function or resulting from a new-expression has no name. There can be no other references to such an object. The object is available to initialize or be assigned to a variable, or to be the argument to an expression or function call, but will be destroyed at the next sequence point. Such an unnamed value is called an *rvalue* because it is similar to the result of an expression on the right side of an assignment statement. An *lvalue*, by contrast, is a value that is named by a variable. In the statement y = 2*x + 1; the result of the expression 2*x + 1 is an rvalue; it is a temporary value with no name. The variable on the left side of the equals sign is an lvalue, and y is its name.

When an object is an rvalue, its contents can be plundered to become the value of an lvalue. All that is required is that the rvalue remain in a valid state so its destructor will behave correctly.

The C++ type system was extended so it can distinguish an rvalue from an lvalue on function call. If T is any type, the declaration T&& is an rvalue reference to T—that is, a reference to an rvalue of type T. The function overload resolution rules were extended so that when an rvalue is an actual function argument, the rvalue reference overload is preferred, and when an lvalue is an argument, the lvalue reference overload is required.

The list of special member functions was extended to include a move constructor and a move assignment operator. These functions are overloads of the copy constructor and assignment operator that take an rvalue reference. If a class implements the move constructor and move assignment operator, initializing or assigning an instance can use efficient move semantics.

Example 6-3 is a simple class containing a unique entity. The compiler autogenerates move constructors and move assignment operators for simple classes. These move operators perform a move operation for each member that defines a move operation, and a copy for other members. This is the equivalent of performing `this->member = std::move(rhs.member)` for each member.

Example 6-3. Class with move semantics

```
class Foo {
    std::unique_ptr<int> value_;
public:
    ...
    Foo(Foo&& rhs) {
        value_ = rhs.release();
    }

    Foo(Foo const& rhs) : value_(nullptr) {
        if (rhs.value_)
            value_ = std::make_unique<int*>(*rhs.value_);
    }
};
```

Actually, the compiler autogenerates the move constructor and move assignment operator only in the simple case when the program does not specify a copy constructor, assignment operator, or destructor,[2] and the move operator is not disabled in any member or base class. This rule makes sense because the presence of definitions for these special functions implies that something special (rather than memberwise move) may be required.

If move constructor and move assignment are not provided by the developer or autogenerated by the compiler, the program may still compile. What happens is that the compiler uses the less efficient copy constructor and copy assignment operator. Because the rules for autogeneration are so complex, it's good practice to explicitly declare, default declare, or disable all the special functions (default constructor, copy constructor, copy assignment operator, move constructor, move assignment operator, and destructor) together, to make the developer's intent clear.

Update Code to Use Move Semantics

Updating code to use move semantics can be done on a class-by-class basis. Here's a little checklist to help with the process:

---

[2] The copy constructor and assignment operator are autogenerated even if a destructor is defined, although this is deprecated as of C++11. The best practice is to explicitly delete the copy constructor and assignment operator if they shouldn't be defined.

- Identify a problem that could benefit from move semantics. For instance, lots of time being spent in copy constructors and memory management functions may point to heavily used classes that would benefit from the addition of a move constructor and move assignment operator.

- Update the C++ compiler (and standard library, if it doesn't come with the compiler) to a version that supports move semantics. Rerun performance tests after updating, because this compiler change may significantly improve the performance of code using standard library components like strings and vectors, changing the hot function leader board.

- Check third-party libraries to see whether there is a newer version that supports move semantics. Move semantics in the compiler buy the developer nothing at all if libraries are not also updated to use move semantics.

- Define a move constructor and move assignment operator for classes with identified performance problems.

Subtleties of Move Semantics

I won't say move semantics are a hack. This feature is too important, and the standard writers really did do a great job of making it semantically similar to copy construction. But I think it's fair to say that move semantics are *subtle*. This is one of those features of C++ that has to be used carefully, and with knowledge, to get anything out of it.

Moving instances into std::vector

It's not enough just to write a move constructor and move assignment operator if you want your object efficiently moved when it's in a `std::vector`. The developer must declare the move constructor and move assignment operator `noexcept`. This is necessary because `std::vector` provides the *strong exception safety guarantee*: that an exception occurring in a vector operation leaves the vector as it was before the operation occurred. The copy constructor doesn't alter the source object. The move constructor destroys it. Any exception in the move constructor violates the strong exception safety guarantee.

If the move constructor and move assignment operator are not declared `noexcept`, `std::vector` uses the less efficient copy operations instead. There may be no warning from the compiler that this has happened, and the code will still run correctly, if slowly.

`noexcept` is a very strong promise. Making the `noexcept` promise means not calling into the memory manager, or I/O, or any other functions that might throw an exception. Or it means swallowing all exceptions, with no way to report that the program has done so. On Windows, it means that converting structured exceptions to C++ exceptions is fraught with risk, because violating the noexcept promise means the sudden, irrevocable termination of the program. But it's the price of efficiency.

Rvalue reference arguments are lvalues

When a function takes an rvalue reference as an argument, it uses the rvalue reference to construct the formal argument. Because the formal argument has a name, it is an lvalue, even though it was constructed from an rvalue reference.

Fortunately, the developer can explicitly cast an lvalue to an rvalue reference. The standard library provides the nifty <utility> template function std::move() to do this job, as shown in Example 6-4.

Example 6-4. Explicit move

```
std::string MoveExample(std::string&& s) {
    std::string tmp(std::move(s));
//  Watch out! s is now empty.
    return tmp;
}
    ...
std::string s1 = "hello";
std::string s2 = "everyone";
std::string s3 = MoveExample(s1 + s2);
```

In Example 6-4, the call to MoveExample(s1 + s2) causes s to be constructed from an rvalue reference, meaning the actual argument is moved to s. The call to std::move(s) creates an rvalue reference to s's contents. Since this rvalue reference is the return value of the function std::move(), it has no name. The rvalue reference initializes tmp, calling std::string's move constructor. At this point, s no longer refers to the actual string argument to MoveExample(). It is probably the empty string. When tmp is returned, conceptually what happens is the value of tmp is copied to the anonymous return value, and then tmp is deleted. The value of MoveExample()'s anonymous return value is copy-constructed into s3. However, what actually happens in this case is that the compiler is able to perform RVO, so that the argument s is actually moved directly into the storage of s3. RVO is generally more efficient than moving.

Here is a move semantics–aware version of the std::swap() function template that uses std::move():

```
    template <typename T> void std::swap(T& a, T& b) {
    {
      T tmp(std::move(a));
      a = std::move(b);
```

```
        b = std::move(tmp);
    }
```

This function performs three moves and no reallocations, provided T implements move semantics. It falls back on copy otherwise.

Don't return an rvalue reference

Another subtlety of move semantics is that functions should not normally be defined as returning rvalue references. Returning an rvalue reference makes intuitive sense. In a call like x = foo(y), returning an rvalue reference would produce an efficient move of the returned value from the unnamed temporary to the assignment target x.

But in reality, returning an rvalue reference interferes with the return value optimization (see "Eliminate Copying on Function Return" on page 132), which allows the compiler to eliminate the copy from the unnamed temporary to the target by passing a reference to the target into the function in an implicit argument. Making the return value an rvalue reference produces two move operations, while making the return value a value produces a single move operation once the return value optimization is accounted for.

So, neither the actual argument to the return statement nor the declared return type of the function should be an rvalue reference if RVO is possible.

Moving bases and members

To implement move semantics for a class, you must implement move semantics for all the bases and members too, as shown in Example 6-5. Otherwise, the bases and members will be copied instead of moved.

Example 6-5. Moving bases and members

```
class Base {...};
class Derived : Base {
    ...
    std::unique_ptr<Foo> member_;
    Bar* barmember_;
};

Derived::Derived(Derived&& rhs)
  : Base(std::move(rhs)),
    member_(std::move(rhs.member_)),
    barmember_(nullptr) {

    std::swap(this->barmember_, rhs.barmember_);
}
```

Example 6-5 shows a bit of the subtlety of writing a move constructor. Assuming Base has a move constructor, it is invoked only if the lvalue rhs is cast to an rvalue reference by calling std::move(). Likewise, std::unique_ptr's move constructor is only called if rhs.member_ is cast to an rvalue reference. For barmember_, which is a plain old pointer, or for any object that does not define a move constructor, std::swap() implements a move-like operation.

std::swap() may be troublesome when implementing the move assignment operator. The problem is that this may refer to an object that already has allocated memory. std::swap() doesn't destroy the unneeded memory. It saves it into rhs, and the memory isn't reclaimed until rhs is destroyed. This is potentially a big deal if a member contains a million-character string or a million-entry table. In this case, it is better to explicitly copy the pointer barmember_, then delete it in rhs to keep the destructor of rhs from freeing it:

```
void Derived::operator=(Derived&& rhs) {
    Base::operator=(std::move(rhs));
    delete(this->barmember_);
    this->barmember_ = rhs.barmember_;
    rhs.barmember_ = nullptr;
}
```

Flatten Data Structures

A data structure can be described as *flat* if its elements are stored together in a contiguous piece of storage. Flat data structures have significant performance advantages over data structures whose parts are linked together by pointers:

- Flat data structures require fewer expensive calls into the memory manager to construct than data structures linked together by pointers. Some data structures (list, deque, map, unordered_map) create many dynamic objects, and others (vector) less so. As Chapter 10 repeatedly shows, even when similar operations have the same big-O performance, flat data structures like std::vector and std::array have a significant advantage.

- Flat data structures like array and vector take up less memory than node-based data structures like list, map, and unordered_map, due to the cost of the link pointers in the node-based structures. Compactness improves cache locality even if the total number of bytes consumed is not an issue. Flat data structures have an advantage in cache locality that makes them more efficient to traverse.

- Tricks like making vectors or maps of smart pointers that were required before the arrival of move semantics in C++11 to store uncopyable objects are no longer necessary. The significant runtime cost to allocate the smart pointers and the pointed-to objects can now be eliminated.

Summary

- *Naïve use of dynamically allocated variables is the greatest performance killer in C++ programs. When performance matters, new is not your friend.*
- *A developer can be an effective optimizer knowing nothing other than how to reduce calls into the memory manager.*
- *A program can globally change how memory is allocated by providing a definition of ::operator new() and ::operator delete().*
- *A program can globally change how memory is managed by replacing malloc() and free().*
- *Smart pointers automate ownership of dynamic variables.*
- *Shared ownership of dynamic variables is more expensive.*
- *Create class instances statically.*
- *Create class members statically and use two-part initialization if needed.*
- *Use a master pointer to own dynamic variables, and unowned pointers instead of sharing ownership.*
- *Create copy-free functions that pass data out in out parameters.*
- *Implement move semantics.*
- *Prefer flat data structures.*

## CHAPTER 7

Optimize Hot Statements

> The idea is there, locked inside, and all you have to do is remove the excess stone.
>
> —Michelangelo di Lodovico Buonarroti Simoni (1475–1564), in response to the question, "How do you create your masterpieces?"

Optimizing at the statement level can be modeled as a process of *removing instructions from the stream of execution*, in a manner similar to how Michelangelo described the process of sculpting his masterpieces. The problem with Michelangelo's advice is that it doesn't address which part of the stone is excess, and which part is the masterpiece.

The problem with optimizing at the statement level is that, aside from function calls, no C++ statement consumes more than a handful of machine instructions. Focusing on such small-scale optimizations doesn't generally produce enough improvement to make them worth the effort unless the developer can find factors that magnify the cost of the statement, making it hot enough to be worth optimizing. These factors include:

Loops

The cost of statements within a loop is multiplied by the number of times they are repeated. Loops must be identified by the developer. The profiler may point to a function containing a hot loop, but it won't say which loop in the function is hot. It may point to a function that is hot because it is called from inside one or more loops, but it won't say which call sites are hot. Since the profiler does not point directly to the loop, the developer must inspect the code to find the loop, using the profiler output as a source of clues.

Frequently called functions

The cost of the function is multiplied by the number of times the function is called. A profiler points directly to hot functions.

Idioms used throughout the program

This is a catch-all category of C++ statements and idioms for which less expensive alternatives exist. If these idioms are widely used within a program, changing to less expensive idioms may improve overall performance.

Optimizing code at the statement level can produce significant performance improvements on the smaller, simpler processors that are embedded into instruments, appliances, peripherals, and toys, because instructions are fetched directly from memory and executed one after another. However, desktop- and handset-class processors provide so much instruction-level concurrency and caching that statement-level optimization produces smaller returns than optimizing allocation or copying.

On programs designed for desktop-class computers, statement-level optimization may thus only be appropriate for frequently called library functions, or the most inner loops of programs like game graphics engines or programming language interpreters that run flat-out all the time.

An issue with optimizing at the statement level is that the effectiveness of optimizations can be compiler-dependent. Each compiler has one or more plans for how to generate code for a particular C++ statement. A coding idiom that improves performance on one compiler may produce no result on another, or may even slow down the code. A trick that improved performance when using GCC may not work with Visual C++. More critically, it means that when a team upgrades to a new compiler version, the new compiler may deoptimize their carefully tuned code. This is another reason why statement-level optimization may be less fruitful than other kinds of performance improvement efforts.

Remove Code from Loops

A loop has two parts: a block of controlled statements that are executed repeatedly, and a controlling clause that determines how many times the loop is repeated. The general comments on removing computation from C++ statements apply to the controlled statements of a loop. With loops, the controlling clause offers extra opportunities for optimization because it is, in a sense, overhead.

Consider the for loop in Example 7-1, which traverses a string, replacing space characters with asterisks.

Example 7-1. Unoptimized for loop

```
char s[] = "This string has many space (0x20) chars. ";
    ...

for (size_t i = 0; i < strlen(s); ++i)
    if (s[i] == ' ')
        s[i] = '*';
```

The test i < strlen(s) in the for loop is performed for each character in the string.[1] The call to strlen() is expensive, traversing its string argument to count its characters, turning this algorithm from $O(n)$ to $O(n^2)$. This is an example of an inner loop hidden in a library function (see "Estimate the Cost of Loops" on page 64).

Ten million iterations of this loop took 13.238 milliseconds when compiled with Visual Studio 2010, and 11.467 milliseconds with Visual Studio 2015. The VS2015 measurement is 15% faster, signaling that the two compilers are generating somewhat different code for this loop.

Cache the Loop End Value

The loop end value, the value returned by the expensive call to strlen(), can be precomputed and cached in the loop entry code to improve performance. The modified for loop looks like Example 7-2.

Example 7-2. for loop with cached end value

```
for (size_t i = 0, len = strlen(s); i < len; ++i)
    if (s[i] == ' ')
        s[i] = '*';
```

The effect of this change is dramatic, because strlen() is so costly. A test of the optimized code runs in 636 milliseconds with VS2010 and 541 milliseconds with VS2015 —nearly 20 times faster than the original. VS2015 is still outrunning VS2010, this time by 17%.

Use More Efficient Loop Statements

This is the syntax for the C++ for loop:

```
for (init-expression ; condition ; continue-expression ) controlled-statement
```

Roughly speaking, this compiles into code that looks like this:

```
    initial-expression ;
L1: if ( ! condition ) goto L2;
    controlled-statement ;
    continue-expression ;
    goto L1;
L2:
```

---

1 Some readers react, "Aagghh! Why would anyone write such code? Don't they know std::string has a constant-time length() function?" Yet this sort of code is distressingly common in programs needing optimization. I also wanted to make the example obvious, because I'm illustrating a point.

The for loop must jump twice: once if *condition* is false, and once more after evaluating the *continue-expression*. These jumps may slow down execution. C++ also has a simpler loop form called the do loop that is less widely used. Its syntax is:

```
do controlled-statement while ( condition ) ;
```

Roughly speaking, this compiles into the following code:

```
L1: controlled-statement
    if ( condition ) goto L1;
```

So, a for loop can often be simplified into a do loop that may be faster. Example 7-3 is the example string-scanning code as a do loop.

Example 7-3. for loop converted to do loop

```
size_t i = 0, len = strlen(s); // for loop init-expression
do {
    if (s[i] == ' ')
        s[i] = ' ';
    ++i;                        // for loop continue-expression
} while (i < len);              // for loop condition
```

With Visual Studio 2010, this was a performance win: it took 482 milliseconds to run the test loop, a 12% improvement. With Visual Studio 2015, however, this change performed significantly less well: 674 milliseconds on the test loop, or 25% *slower* than the for loop.

Count Down Instead of Up

A variation on caching the end value is to count down instead of up, caching the end value in the loop index variable. Many loops have one end condition that is less expensive to evaluate than the other. For instance, in the loop in Example 7-3, one end condition is a constant 0, while the other end is an expensive call to strlen(). Example 7-4 is the for loop of Example 7-1 reorganized to count down instead of up.

Example 7-4. Optimized loop counting down

```
for (int i = (int)strlen(s)-1; i >= 0; --i)
    if (s[i] == ' ')
        s[i] = '*';
```

Note that I changed the type of the induction variable i from size_t, which is unsigned, to int, which is signed. The for loop's termination clause is i >= 0. If i was unsigned, it would be, by definition, greater than or equal to zero, and the loop could not terminate. This is a very typical mistake when counting down to zero.

The same timing test measured this loop at 619 milliseconds when compiled with Visual Studio 2010, and 571 milliseconds for Visual Studio 2015. It's not clear that these results represent a significant change compared to the code in Example 7-2.

Remove Invariant Code from Loops

Example 7-2, where the loop end value is cached for efficient reuse, is an instance of the more general technique of moving *invariant* code out of a loop. Code is invariant with respect to a loop if it does not depend on the loop induction variable. For instance, in the somewhat contrived loop in Example 7-5, the assignment statement j = 100; and the subexpression j * x * x are loop-invariant.

Example 7-5. Loop with invariant code

```
int i,j,x,a[10];
    ...
for (i=0; i<10; ++i) {
    j = 100;
    a[i] = i + j * x * x;
}
```

The loop can be rewritten as shown in Example 7-6.

Example 7-6. Loop with invariant code moved out

```
int i,j,x,a[10];
    ...
j = 100;
int tmp = j * x * x;
for (i=0; i<10; ++i) {
    a[i] = i + tmp;
}
```

Modern compilers are good at finding bits of invariant code (like the ones shown here) that are computed over and over, and moving the computations out of loops to improve performance. A developer would not normally need to rewrite this loop because the compiler already finds the invariant code and rewrites the loop.

When a statement inside a loop calls a function, the compiler may not be able to determine if the value returned by the function depends on something in the loop. The function may be complex, or the function's body may be in another compilation unit and not visible to the compiler. The developer must manually identify loop-invariant function calls and remove them from loops.

Remove Unneeded Function Calls from Loops

A function call can execute an arbitrarily large number of instructions. If the function is loop-invariant, it's plainly a good idea to pull it out of the loop to improve performance. In Example 7-1, reproduced here, the call to `strlen()` is loop-invariant and can be pulled out of the loop:

```
char* s = "sample data with spaces";
    ...
for (size_t i = 0; i < strlen(s); ++i)
    if (s[i] == ' ')
        s[i] = '*'; // change ' ' to '*'
```

Example 7-7 shows what the revised loop might look like.

Example 7-7. Loop where strlen() is loop invariant

```
char* s = "sample data with spaces";
    ...
size_t end = strlen(s);
for (size_t i = 0; i < end; ++i)
    if (s[i] == ' ')
        s[i] = '*'; // change ' ' to '*'
```

In Example 7-8, the value returned by `strlen()` is not loop-invariant, because removing a space character decreases the string length. The end condition cannot be pulled out of this loop.

Example 7-8. Loop in which strlen() is not loop-invariant

```
char* s = "sample data with spaces";
size_t i;
    ...
for (i = 0; i < strlen(s); ++i)
    if (s[i] == ' ')
        strcpy(&s[i], &s[i+1]); // remove space
s[i] = '\0';
```

There is no simple rule for determining whether a function is loop-invariant in a particular situation. Example 7-8 shows that a particular function can be loop-invariant for one loop, but not invariant for another. This is a place where human judgment is a superior tool to the compiler's thorough but limited analysis. (The repeated call to `strlen()` is not the only thing less than optimal about this function. Other optimizations are left as an exercise.)

One kind of function that can always be pulled out of a loop is a *pure function*, a function whose returned value depends only on the value of its arguments, and which has no side effects. If such a function appears in a loop, and its argument is not modified

---

in the loop, the function is loop-invariant and can be pulled out of the loop. In Example 7-8, the function `strlen()` is a pure function. In the first loop, its argument s is never modified by the loop, so the call to `strlen()` is loop-invariant. In the second loop, the call to `strcpy()` modifies s, so the call `strlen(s)` is not loop-invariant.

Here is another example involving the math functions `sin()` and `cos()`, which return the mathematical sine and cosine of a value in radians. Many mathematical functions are pure functions, so this situation arises frequently in numerical calculations. In Example 7-9, a graphics rotation transformation is applied to a figure with 16 vertices. A timing test performing this transformation 100 million times took 7,502 milliseconds with VS2010 and 6,864 milliseconds with VS2015, with the latter continuing to show about a 15% speed advantage.

Example 7-9. rotate() with loop containing invariant pure functions

```
void rotate(std::vector<Point>& v, double theta) {
    for (size_t i = 0; i < v.size(); ++i) {
        double x = v[i].x_, y = v[i].y_;
        v[i].x_ = cos(theta)*x - sin(theta)*y;
        v[i].y_ = sin(theta)*x + cos(theta)*y;
    }
}
```

The functions `sin(theta)` and `cos(theta)` depend only on the function argument `theta`. They don't depend on the loop variable. They can be lifted out of the loop as shown in Example 7-10.

Example 7-10. rotate_invariant() with invariant pure functions lifted out of the loop

```
void rotate_invariant(std::vector<Point>& v, double theta) {
    double sin_theta = sin(theta);
    double cos_theta = cos(theta);
    for (size_t i = 0; i < v.size(); ++i) {
        double x = v[i].x_, y = v[i].y_;
        v[i].x_ = cos_theta*x - sin_theta*y;
        v[i].y_ = sin_theta*x + cos_theta*y;
    }
}
```

The revised function runs the test loop about 3% faster, at 7,382 milliseconds (VS2010) and 6,620 milliseconds (VS2015).

The savings are less dramatic on a PC than those made by lifting the call to `strlen()` in the previous section, because the math functions generally operate on one or two numbers held in registers and do not access memory like `strlen()` does. On a retro PC from the 1990s or an embedded processor without floating-point instructions in hardware, the savings might be more dramatic because the computation of sines and cosines is more expensive.

Sometimes, a function called within a loop does no work at all, or does work that is not necessary. Such functions can, of course, be removed. It is easy to say, "Well, *duh!* No competent developer would call a function that does no useful work!" Far harder is to remember all the places where a function is called, and check them all when the function's behavior changes during the several-year lifetime of a project.

The following is an idiom that I have encountered repeatedly in my career:

```
UsefulTool subsystem;
InputHandler input_getter;
   ...
while (input_getter.more_work_available()) {
    subsystem.initialize();
    subsystem.process_work(input_getter.get_work());
}
```

In this recurring pattern, `subsystem` is repeatedly initialized for processing work, and then asked to process the next unit of work. There may be something wrong with this code that can only be determined by inspecting `UsefulTool::initialize()`. It may be that `initialize()` need only be called before the *first* unit of work is processed, or perhaps for the first unit of work and also after an error. Often `process_work()` establishes on exit the same class invariant that `initialize()` does. Calling `initialize()` each time through the loop just repeats the same code as `process_work()`. If so, the call to `initialize()` can be lifted out of the loop:

```
UsefulTool subsystem;
InputHandler input_getter;
   ...
subsystem.initialize();
while (input_getter.more_work_available()) {
    subsystem.process_work(input_getter.get_work());
}
```

It is presumptuous to blame the developer who wrote the original code for being sloppy. Sometimes the behavior of `initialize()` changes, moving code into `process_work()`. Sometimes the project documentation is inadequate, or the schedule is rushed, or the purpose of the code of `initialize()` is unclear, and the developer was just programming defensively. But I have found several times that initialization that only needs to be done once is done every time work is processed.

If saving time is important enough, it is worth looking at each function call in a loop to see whether that work is actually needed.

Remove Hidden Function Calls from Loops

Normal function calls have a distinctive look, with a function name and list of argument expressions in parentheses. C++ code can also call functions implicitly, without this easy-to-spot syntax. This can happen when a variable of class type appears in any of the following situations:

- Declaration of a class instance (calls constructor)
- Initialization of a class instance (calls constructor)
- Assignment to a class instance (calls assignment operator)
- Arithmetic expressions involving class instances (calls operator member functions)
- Scope exit (calls destructor of class instances declared in the scope)
- Function arguments (each argument expression is copy-constructed into its formal argument)
- Function return of a class instance (calls copy constructor, perhaps twice)
- Inserting items into a standard library container (items are move- or copy-constructed)
- Inserting items into a vector (all items are move- or copy-constructed if the vector is reallocated)

These function calls are *hidden*. They don't have the familiar look of a function call with a name and argument list; they look like assignments and declarations. It's easy to miss the fact that a function is being called. I've talked about these before, in "Eliminate Unneeded Copying" on page 129.

Hidden function calls resulting from constructing a function's formal arguments can sometimes be eliminated if the function signature is changed to pass a reference or pointer to the class instead of passing the actual argument by value. The benefit of this was demonstrated for strings in "Eliminate Copying of String Arguments" on page 75, and for any object that copies data in "Eliminate Copying on Function Call" on page 131.

Hidden function calls resulting from copying out the function's return value can be removed if the function signature is changed so the class instance to be returned goes into a reference or pointer argument used as an out parameter instead. The benefit of this was demonstrated for strings in "Eliminate Copying of Returned String Values" on page 77, and for any object that copies data in "Eliminate Copying on Function Return" on page 132.

If an assignment or initialized declaration is loop-invariant, it can be lifted out of the loop. Sometimes even if the variable needs to be set for each pass through the loop, you can lift the declaration out of the loop and perform a less expensive function on each iteration of the loop. For example, `std::string` is a class that contains a dynamically allocated array of `char`. In the following code:

```
for (...) {
    std::string s("<p>");
    ...
    s += "</p>";
}
```

it is expensive to put the declaration of `s` in the `for` loop. At the closing brace of the controlled block of statements, `s`'s destructor is called. The destructor frees `s`'s dynamically allocated memory, so it must be reallocated the next time through the loop. This code can be rewritten as follows:

```
std::string s;
for (...) {
    s.clear();
    s += "<p>";
    ...
    s += "</p>";
}
```

Now `s`'s destructor is not called until later. This not only saves the cost of a function call each time through the loop but, as a side effect, the dynamic array inside `s` is reused, possibly eliminating a hidden call to the memory manager when characters are appended to `s`.

This behavior doesn't apply only to strings, or only to classes that contain dynamic memory. A class instance may contain a resource fetched from the operating system, such as a window or file handle, or may do any expensive thing inside its constructors and destructors.

Remove Expensive, Slow-Changing Calls from Loops

Some function calls are not invariant, but they might as well be. A good example is a call to get the current time of day to use in a logging application. It takes a nontrivial number of instructions to fetch the time of day from the operating system, and more time to format the time as text. Example 7-11 is a function to format the current time into a null-terminated character array.

Example 7-11. timetoa(): format the time into an array of char

```
# include <ctime>

char* timetoa(char *buf, size_t bufsz) {
    if (buf == 0 || bufsz < 9)
        return nullptr; // invalid arguments
```

```
time_t t  = std::time(nullptr); // get time from O/S
tm      tm = *std::localtime(&t); // break time into hours, minutes, seconds
size_t sz = std::strftime(buf, bufsz, "%c", &tm); // format into buffer
if (sz == 0) strcpy(buf, "XX:XX:XX"); // error
return buf;
}
```

In an experimental test loop, `timetoa()` took about 700 nanoseconds to fetch the time and format it. But this cost is significant. It is about twice as long as it takes to append two text strings to a file. In the same test loop, the statement

```
out << "Fri Jan 01 00:00:00 2016"
    << " Test log line test log line test log line\n";
```

took only 372 nanoseconds, whereas the statement

```
out << timetoa(buf, sizeof(buf))
    << " Test log line test log line test log line\n";
```

took 1,042 nanoseconds.

Logging must be as efficient as possible, or else it slows down the program being logged. This is bad if it makes the program slower, but worse if that slowdown changes the program's behavior so that bugs disappear when logging is turned on. Getting the current time dominates the cost of logging in this example.

The time of day changes very slowly compared to the instruction execution rate of a modern computer. Apparently my program could log a million lines between time ticks. Two consecutive calls to fetch the time of day are thus very likely to return the same value. If several lines are to be logged at once, it doesn't make sense to fetch the time anew for each line.

I ran another test to simulate the behavior of logging when a program requests the time once, and puts out a group of 10 lines using the same data. As expected, this test printed lines in an average of 376 nanoseconds per line.

Push Loops Down into Functions to Reduce Call Overhead

If a program iterates through a string, array, or other data structure and calls a function for each iteration, it may be possible to improve performance by a technique called *loop inversion*. A loop calling a function is inverted by putting the loop inside the function. This changes the function's interface to reference the whole data structure, rather than referencing a single entry. In this way, the cost of *n–1* function calls can be removed if the data structure contains *n* entries.

For a very simple example, imagine a library function that replaces nonprinting characters with a dot (".") character:

```
# include <ctype>
```

```
void replace_nonprinting(char& c) {
    if (!isprint(c))
        c = '.';
}
```

To replace all the nonprinting characters in a string, a program calls `replace_non`
`printing()` in a loop:

```
for (unsigned i = 0, e = str.size(); i < e; ++i)
    replace_nonprinting(str[i]);
```

If the compiler cannot inline the call to the `replace_nonprinting()` function, it will
call the function 26 times if the preceding loop is given the string "Ring the carriage
bell\x07\x07!!" to process.

The library designer might add an overload of `replace_nonprinting()` to process a
whole string:

```
void replace_nonprinting(std::string& str) {
    for (unsigned i = 0, e = str.size(); i < e; ++i)
        if (!isprint(str[i]))
            c = '.';
}
```

The loop is now inside the function, eliminating *n–1* calls to `replace_nonprint`
`ing()`.

Note that the code implementing the behavior of `replace_nonprinting()` must be
duplicated in the new overload. It doesn't work to just move the loop around. The
following version actually adds a function call to the previous total:

```
void replace_nonprinting(std::string& str) {
    for (unsigned i = 0, e = str.size(); i < e; ++i)
        replace_nonprinting(str[i]);
}
```

Do Some Actions Less Frequently

Here's a motivating question: "A program's main loop processes about 1,000 transactions per second. How frequently does it need to check for a command to terminate
the loop?"

Of course, the answer is, "It depends." In fact, it depends on two things: how fast the
program needs to respond to the termination request, and how costly it is to check
for termination.

If the program needs to terminate within 1 second to achieve its responsiveness goal,
and it takes an average of 500 ± 100 milliseconds to stop after detecting that shutdown was commanded, it is necessary to check every 400 milliseconds (1,000 – (500
+ 100) = 400 milliseconds). Checking more often would be wasteful.

The other factor is the cost to check for termination. If the loop is a Windows message loop, and the termination command arrives as the `WM_CLOSE` Windows message, there is no extra overhead for checking. The cost is built into dispatching the event. If a signal handler causes a `bool` flag to be set, the cost of checking this flag each time through the loop is tiny.

But what if the loop is on an embedded device where a key press must be polled for, and the key has to be debounced[2] for 50 milliseconds? Testing each time through the loop will add the 50-millisecond key polling cost to the cost of each transaction, dropping the transaction rate from 1,000 per second to $\frac{1}{0.051} \approx 20$ transactions per second. Ouch!

If the program instead polls only at 400-millisecond intervals, the effect on the loop is less dramatic. The math here is a bit tedious, but let's go through it. Transactions take about 1 millisecond (1,000 transactions per second). To complete a 50-millisecond poll every 400 milliseconds, the poll must be started every 350 milliseconds, or 2.5 times per 1,000 milliseconds. That results in a transaction rate of 1,000 – (2.5 * 50) = 875 transactions per second.

Example 7-12 shows code to check for such a key press.

Example 7-12. Check for events occasionally

```
void main_loop(Event evt) {
    static unsigned counter = 1;
    if ((counter % 350) == 0)
        if (poll_for_exit())
            exit_program(); // noreturn
    ++counter;

    switch (evt) {
        ...
    }
}
```

Execution enters `main_loop()` every millisecond (assuming events occur every millisecond). Every time through the loop, `counter` is incremented. When it reaches 350, the program calls `poll_for_exit()`, which takes 50 milliseconds. If the exit key is detected in `poll_for_exit()`, the code calls `exit_program()`, which takes 400–600 milliseconds to shut things down.

---

2 When a real, mechanical key is depressed, it makes a connection that is at first intermittent. Taking an instantaneous look at the connection state may show the key as not pressed when in fact it is still in that initial, intermittent phase. "Debouncing" delays reporting a key as being pressed until the connection becomes continuous; 50 milliseconds is a typical debouncing interval.

This casual polling method illustrates how to take bigger bites of computation between polling. It is, however, fraught with assumptions:

- It assumes that events happen every millisecond, and not sometimes every 2 or every 5 milliseconds, and that the event rate doesn't slow down if there is no work.
- It assumes that polling always takes exactly 50 milliseconds.
- It assumes that a debugger will never get control so that no events are processed for half a minute while the developer inspects some variables.

A more careful approach is to measure the elapsed time from event to event, and from beginning to end of `poll_for_exit()`.

A developer wishing to achieve the full 1,000 transactions per second under the constraints listed here must find some source of true concurrency to separate polling the keyboard from the main loop. This is typically implemented via interrupts, multiple cores, or a hardware keyboard scanner.

What About Everything Else?

There are many sources on the Internet of low-level optimization techniques involving loops. For instance, some sources note that `++i` is generally faster than `i++` because no intermediate value need be saved and returned. Some sources recommend loop unrolling, to reduce the total number of times the loop test and increment code is executed.

The problem with these recommendations is that they don't always make any difference at all. You may spend the time to do an experiment and observe no improvement. The recommendations may be based on conjecture not informed by experiment, or may apply only to a particular compiler at a particular date. They may come from a compiler design textbook, describing optimizations that the C++ compiler is already programmed to do. Thirty years on, modern C++ compilers are *very* good at finding code to move out of loops. In fact, the compiler is better at it than most programmers. This is why such optimizations are so often frustratingly ineffective, and thus why this section isn't longer.

Remove Code from Functions

Functions, like loops, consist of two parts: a block of code that is the body of the function, and the head of the function consisting of the argument list and return type. Like with loops, these two parts can be separately optimized.

Although the cost of executing the function's body can be arbitrarily large, the cost of calling the function, like the cost of most C++ statements, is minuscule. But when the function is called many times, that cost is multiplied and can become significant, so that reducing this cost becomes important.

Cost of Function Calls

Functions are the oldest and most important abstraction in programming. The programmer defines a function once, then calls its name from many locations in the code. For each call, the computer saves its place in the executing code, transfers control to the function body, then returns to the next statement after the function call, effectively inserting the function's body into the stream of instruction execution.

This notational convenience does not come for free. Each time a program calls a function, something like the following happens (depending of course on processor architecture and optimizer settings):

1. The executing code pushes a new frame onto the call stack to hold the function's arguments and local variables.
2. Each argument expression is evaluated and copied into the stack frame.
3. The execution address is copied into the stack frame to form the return address.
4. The executing code updates the execution address to the first statement of the function body (instead of the next statement after the function call).
5. The instructions in the function body execute.
6. The return address is copied from the stack frame into the instruction address, transferring control to the statement after the function call.
7. The stack frame is popped off the stack.

There is some good news about the cost of functions. A program with functions is generally more compact than the same program with large functions expanded inline. This improves cache and virtual memory performance. Still, all other things being equal, making frequently called functions more efficient can be an effective optimization.

Basic cost of function calls

There are a number of details that can slow down function calls in C++, and which therefore form the basis for optimization of function calls:

Function arguments
    Beyond the cost of evaluating the argument expressions, there is a cost to copy each argument value onto the stack in memory. The first few arguments may be passed efficiently in registers if they are small, but if there are many arguments, at least some are passed via the stack.

Member function calls (versus function calls)

Every member function call has an extra hidden argument: a pointer to the "this" class instance through which the member function is invoked, that must be written to memory on the call stack or saved in a register.

Call and return

These add nothing to the useful work of the program. They are pure overhead that would not exist if the function call was replaced by the function body. Indeed, many compilers attempt to put the function body inline if the function is small, and if the function definition is available at the point of the function call. If the function cannot be inlined, there are several costs.

Calling the function requires the execution address to be written to the stack frame in memory to form the return address.

Function return requires the execution address to be read from the stack and loaded into the execution pointer. At the call and again at the return, execution continues at a nonconsecutive memory address. As noted in "Making Decisions Is Hard for Computers" on page 22, the computer executes consecutive instructions very efficiently. However when execution transfers to a nonconsecutive location, there is a good chance of a pipeline stall and/or a cache miss.

Cost of virtual functions

In C++, the program can define any member function *virtual*. Derived classes can define a member function with the same signature that *overrides* the base class's virtual member function, providing a new function body to be used when the virtual function is called on an instance of the derived class, even if called from a pointer or reference to the base class's type. The program selects what function to call when it dereferences the class instance. The particular override invoked is thus determined at run time by the actual type of the class instance.

Each instance of a class with virtual member functions contains an unnamed pointer to a table, called the *vtable*, which points to the body associated with each virtual function signature visible in that class. The vtable pointer is generally made the first field of the class instance to make dereferencing it less expensive.

Since a virtual function call selects one of several function bodies, the code to call a virtual function dereferences the pointer to the class instance to get a pointer to the vtable. The code indexes into the vtable (that is, the code adds a small integer offset to the vtable, and dereferences that address) to get the virtual function's execution address. There are thus two extra nonsequential memory loads for every virtual function call, each with increased probability of a cache miss and execution pipeline stall. Another issue with virtual functions is that it is difficult for the compiler to inline them. The compiler can do so only if it has access both to the function body and to the code that constructs the instance (so it can tell which virtual function body to call).

Member function calls in derived classes

When one class is derived from another, member functions of the derived class may have to do extra work:

Virtual member functions defined in a derived class
If the most base class (the class at the root of the derivation hierarchy) has no virtual member functions, the code must add an offset to the "this" class instance pointer to get to the vtable of the derived class, then index into the vtable to get the function execution address. This code contains more instruction bytes, and the instructions are often slower because of the extra arithmetic they do. This cost is significant on small embedded processors, but on desktop-class processors instruction-level concurrency hides most of the cost of the extra arithmetic.

Member function calls defined in a derived class with multiple inheritance
The code must add an offset to the "this" class instance pointer to form the class instance pointer to a multiply inherited class. This cost is significant on small embedded processors, but on desktop-class processors instruction-level concurrency hides most of the cost of the extra arithmetic.

Virtual member function calls defined in a derived class with multiple inheritance
As for virtual member function calls in a derived class, if the most base class has no virtual member functions, the code must add an offset to the "this" class instance pointer to get to the vtable of the derived class, then index into the vtable to get the function execution address. The code must also add a potentially different offset to the "this" class instance pointer to form the class instance pointer of the derived class. This cost is significant on small embedded processors, but on desktop-class processors instruction-level concurrency hides most of the cost of the extra arithmetic.

Virtual multiple inheritance
The code must dereference a table in the class instance to determine the offset to add to the class instance pointer to form the instance pointer of a virtually multiply inherited class. There is additional overhead, as described previously, if the called function is virtual.

Cost of pointers to functions

C++ provides function pointers so that code can explicitly choose at run time which of several function bodies is executed as a result of a function call through the function pointer. These mechanisms have additional costs beyond the basic cost of function call and return:

Function pointers (pointers to free functions and static member functions)

C++ allows a program to define variables that are pointers to functions. Function pointers permit the programmer to explicitly choose any free function with a specific *signature*, consisting of its list of argument types and return type, to be called at run time when the function pointer is dereferenced. The program selects what function to call through the function pointer explicitly, by assigning a function to the function pointer.

The code must dereference a pointer to get the execution address of the function. It is also unlikely that the compiler can inline these functions.

Member function pointers

Member function pointer declarations identify both the function signature and the class in the context of which the call is interpreted. The program selects what function to call through the member function pointer explicitly, by assigning a function to the function pointer.

A member function pointer may have any of several representations. It must be general enough to call any member function under any of the complex circumstances listed previously. It is not unreasonable to assume worst-case performance for a member function pointer.

Summary of function call costs

A C-style void function call with no arguments is thus the cheapest, having no cost if it can be inlined, and only two memory accesses plus the cost of two nonlocal transfers of execution otherwise.

A virtual function call belonging to a derived class whose base class has no virtual functions, contained in a class having virtual multiple inheritance, is a worst-case scenario. Fortunately, it is extremely rare. The code must dereference a table in the class instance to determine the offset to add to the class instance pointer, form the instance pointer of the virtually multiply inherited function's instance, then dereference the instance to get the vtable, then index into the vtable to get the function execution address.

At this point, the reader may either be shocked that a function call can be so expensive, or amazed at how efficiently C++ implements very complex features. Both thoughts are appropriate. The point to understand is that there are costs to calling functions, and thus opportunities for optimization. The bad news here is that removing one nonsequential memory access is not much of an improvement unless the function is very frequently called. The good news is that a profiler will point directly to the most frequently called functions, allowing the developer to quickly home in on the best targets for attention.

Declare Brief Functions Inline

An effective way to remove function call overhead is to inline the function. To inline a function, the compiler must have access to the function definition at the point of the call to be inlined. Functions whose bodies appear inside the body of a class definition are implicitly declared inline. Functions defined outside the class definition may also be explicitly declared inline by declaring them with storage class `inline`. Additionally, the compiler may choose on its own to inline short functions when their definitions appear before their first use in a particular compilation unit. Although the C++ standard says that the `inline` keyword is only a "hint" to the compiler, compilers must be good at inlining in order to be commercially successful.

When the compiler inlines a function, it has additional opportunities to improve the code, beyond removing the call and return statements. Some arithmetic may be performed at compile time. Some branches may be eliminated because the compiler determines they cannot be taken when arguments have particular values. Inlining is thus a means of removing redundant computation to improve performance, by performing the computation at compile time.

Function inlining is probably the most powerful code optimization. In fact, the difference in performance of the "debug" versus "release" builds in Visual Studio (or the *-d* versus *-O* flags in GCC), comes mostly because by default, debug builds turn off function inlining.

Define Functions Before First Use

Defining a function (providing the function body) above the point of the first call to the function gives the compiler a chance to optimize the function call. The compiler can choose on its own to inline a function call if it has the function definition available when it compiles a call to that function. This even works with virtual functions, if the compiler can see both the function body and the code that instantiates the class variable, pointer, or reference through which the virtual function is called.

Eliminate Unused Polymorphism

In C++, virtual member functions are frequently used to implement *runtime polymorphism*. Polymorphism allows a member function to do one of several different but semantically related things, depending on the object on which the member function is called.

To implement polymorphic behavior, a base class defines a virtual member function. Any derived classes can choose to override the behavior of the base class function with behavior specialized to that derived class. The various implementations are all related by a semantic concept that must be implemented differently for each derivation.

A classic example of polymorphism is the `Draw()` function defined in a hierarchy of classes derived from `DrawableObject`, representing graphical objects to draw on the screen. When a program calls `drawObjPtr->Draw()`, the implementation of `Draw()` is selected by dereferencing the virtual function table in the instance pointed to by `drawObjPtr`. The selected implementation of `Draw()` makes a triangle when the class instance is an instance of `Triangle`, a box when it is an instance of `Rectangle`, and so forth. The program declares `DrawableObject::Draw()` `virtual`, so that the proper derived class's `Draw()` member is called. When the program must select among several implementations at run time, the virtual function table is a very fast mechanism, despite its overhead of two additional memory loads and their associated pipeline stalls.

Still, polymorphism can occasionally cause unnecessary overhead. A class may have originally been designed to facilitate a hierarchy of derived classes that is never implemented, or a function may have been declared `virtual` in the expectation of polymorphic behavior that was never implemented. In the preceding example, all the drawable objects might end up being implemented as a list of points that are connected in order, so that the base class version of `Draw()` is always used. Removing the `virtual` specifier on the `DrawableObject` declaration of `Draw()` when there are no overrides speeds up all calls to `Draw()`.

Stop and Think

There is tension between the designer's wish to say that `DrawableObject` can be the root of a set of `DrawableObject`-derived classes, and the optimizing developer's wish to improve performance because the `Draw()` member function has no overrides. Presumably the `Draw()` member function has been fingered by some experiment as being costly. If so, the designer will probably bow out. It's easy to put the `virtual` specifier back in later if needed. The wisest optimizing developers know better than to weaken the design without good reason, and don't go chasing every virtual function in a program with scalpel in hand.

Discard Unused Interfaces

In C++, virtual member functions can be used to implement *interfaces*. An interface is a declaration of a common set of functions that together describe the intended behavior of an object, and which may be implemented in different ways under different circumstances. A base class *defines* the interface by declaring a set of pure virtual functions (functions with declarations, but no function body). Because pure virtual functions have no body, C++ prevents the interface base class from being instantiated. Derived classes *implement* the interface by providing overrides (definitions) for all the pure virtual functions in the interface base class. An advantage of the interface idiom in C++ is that the derived class must implement all the functions declared in the interface, or the compiler will not allow the program to create instances of the derived class.

For example, a developer may use an interface class to isolate operating system dependencies, particularly if the design foresees implementing the program for several operating systems. A class for reading and writing files might be defined by the interface class File that follows. File is called an *abstract base class* because it cannot be instantiated:

```
// file.h - interface
class File {
public:
    virtual ~File() {}
    virtual bool Open(Path& p) = 0;
    virtual bool Close() = 0;
    virtual int GetChar() = 0;
    virtual unsigned GetErrorCode() = 0;
};
```

Somewhere else in the code, a derived class WindowsFile is defined, supplying overrides that implement these functions on the Windows operating system. The C++11 keyword override is optional, and tells the compiler that this declaration is meant to override a virtual function declaration in a base class. When override is specified, if there is no virtual function declaration in the base class, the compiler issues a warning message:

```
// Windowsfile.h - interface

# include "File.h"
class WindowsFile : public File { // C++11-style declaration
public:
    ~File() {}
    bool Open(Path& p) override;
    bool Close() override;
    int GetChar() override;
    unsigned GetErrorCode() override;
};
```

In addition to the header file, there is also a *windowsfile.cpp* file containing the implementations of the override functions for the Windows implementation:

```
// windowsfile.cpp - windows implementation
# include "WindowsFile.h"
bool WindowsFile::Open(Path& p) {
    ...
}
bool WindowsFile::Close() {
    ...
}
...
```

Sometimes a program defines an interface, but only provides a single implementation. In this case, the cost of the virtual function calls (particularly the frequently used call to `GetChar()`) may be saved by eliminating the interface, removing the `virtual` keyword from the class definition in *file.h*, and providing implementations for the `File`'s member functions.

Stop and Think

As in the previous section, there is tension between the designer's wish to clearly define an interface (which is a Good Thing) and the optimizing developer's desire to improve performance (which also matters if `GetChar()` has been flagged by the profiler as a hot function). When the program is mature, it may be easier to judge whether there will likely ever be another implementation. This knowledge can illuminate the choice to optimize or retain the original design. The optimizing developer, if she is not the architect who originally defined the interface, must be prepared for push-back when she proposes this change. She would be well advised to have performance numbers to hand to justify the change.

Select interface implementation at link time

Virtual functions permit a running program to choose among several implementations. Interfaces allow a designer to specify what functions must be coded during development to make an object useful. The problem with implementing the interface idiom using C++ virtual functions is that virtual functions provide a runtime solution with runtime cost to a design-time problem.

In the previous section, an interface called `File` was defined to isolate operating system dependency. The interface was implemented in the derived class `WindowsFile`. If the program is ported to Linux, the source code may eventually include a `LinuxFile` derivation of the `File` interface, but `WindowsFile` and `LinuxFile` can never be instantiated in the same program. Each makes low-level calls that are only implemented on one operating system. The overhead of the virtual function call is unneeded. Further, if a program reads large files, `File::GetChar()` may be hot enough to optimize.

The developer can use the linker to select among several implementations if the decision doesn't have to be made at run time. Instead of declaring a C++ interface, the header file declares (but does not implement) the member functions directly, in much the same way as if they were standard library functions:

```
// file.h - interface
class File {
public:
    File();
    bool Open(Path& p);
    bool Close();
```

```
      int GetChar();
      unsigned GetErrorCode();
};
```

A file called *windowsfile.cpp* contains the Windows implementation:

```
// windowsfile.cpp - Windows implementation
# include "File.h"

bool File::Open(Path& p) {
    ...
}

bool File::Close() {
    ...
}
...
```

A similar file called *linuxfile.cpp* contains the Linux implementation. The Visual Studio project file references *windowsfile.cpp*. The Linux makefile references *linuxfile.cpp*. The decision is implemented by the list of arguments handed to the linker. Now the call to GetChar() will be as efficient as a function call can be. (Note that there are other approaches to optimizing a call like GetChar(), including loop inversion, described in "Push Loops Down into Functions to Reduce Call Overhead" on page 157.)

Selecting the implementation at link time has the advantage of being very general. Its disadvantage is that part of the decision is in the *.cpp* files, and part is in the makefile or project file.

Select interface implementation at compile time

In the previous section, an implementation of the File abstraction was selected by the linker. This was possible because the implementation of File depended on the operating system. A particular program executable can run on only one operating system, so the decision didn't have to be made at run time.

If a different compiler is used for the two different implementations of File (say, Visual Studio for the Windows version and GCC for the Linux version), the implementation can be selected at compile time using #ifdef. The header file remains the same. This time there is a single file called *file.cpp*, and the preprocessor selects the implementation:

```
// file.cpp - implementation
# include "File.h"
# ifdef _WIN32
    bool File::Open(Path& p) {
        ...
    }
```

```
    bool File::Close() {
        ...
    }
    ...
# else // Linux
    bool File::Open(Path& p) {
        ...
    }

    bool File::Close() {
        ...
    }
    ...
# endif
```

This solution requires a preprocessor macro that can be used to select the desired implementation. Some developers like this solution because more of the decision making is visible in the *.cpp* file. Others find it messy and un-object-oriented to have both implementations in the same file.

Select Implementation at Compile Time with Templates

C++ template specializations are another means of selecting implementation at compile time. Templates allow the developer to create a family of classes with a common interface, but behavior that depends on a type parameter to the template. Template parameters may be any type—class types that provide their own set of member functions, or basic types that provide their built-in set of operators. There are thus two interfaces: the public members of the template class, and the interface defined by the operators and functions invoked on the template parameters. Interfaces defined in abstract base classes are very strict, requiring the derived class to implement all functions in the abstract base class. Interfaces defined by templates are less strict. Only functions in the parameters that are actually invoked by a particular use of a template need be defined.

This property of templates is a two-edged sword: the compiler doesn't give an error message right away if the developer forgets to implement an interface function in a particular template specialization, but the developer can also choose not to implement functions that are inconvenient if they aren't used in a given context.

From an optimization standpoint, the most important difference between polymorphic class hierarchies and template instances is that generally the whole template is available at compile time. In most use cases, C++ inlines template function calls, improving performance in several ways (as noted in "Declare Brief Functions Inline" on page 165).

Template programming provides powerful optimizations. For the developer not familiar with templates, it is worth the considerable mental effort required to learn to use this C++ feature effectively.

Eliminate Uses of the PIMPL Idiom

PIMPL, short for "Pointer to IMPLementation," is a coding idiom used as a *compilation firewall*, a mechanism to prevent a change in one header file from triggering recompilation of many source files. During the adolescence of C++ in the 1990s, use of the PIMPL idiom was justifiable because the compilation time for a large program might be measured in hours. Here's how PIMPL works.

Imagine a widely used class called `BigClass` (declared in Example 7-13) that has some inline functions and is implemented using classes `Foo`, `Bar`, and `Baz`. Normally, any change to *bigclass.h*, *foo.h*, *bar.h*, or *baz.h*, even if the change only amounted to a single character in a comment, would trigger recompilation of the many files that included *bigclass.h*.

Example 7-13. bigclass.h before implementing the PIMPL idiom

```
# include "foo.h"
# include "bar.h"
# include "baz.h"
class BigClass {
public:
    BigClass();
    void f1(int a) { ... }
    void f2(float f) { ... }
    Foo foo_;
    Bar bar_;
    Baz baz_;
};
```

To implement PIMPL, the developer defines a new class, called `Impl` in this example. *bigclass.h* is changed as follows, shown in Example 7-14.

Example 7-14. bigclass.h after implementing the PIMPL idiom

```
class Impl;
class BigClass {
public:
    BigClass();
    void f1(int a);
    char f2(float f);
    Impl* impl;
};
```

C++ permits a pointer to be declared that points to an *incomplete type*—that is, to an object for which there is no definition yet. In this case, Impl is an incomplete type. This works because all pointers are the same size, so the compiler knows how to reserve storage for the pointer. After implementing PIMPL, BigClass's externally visible definition does not depend on *foo.h*, *bar.h*, or *baz.h*. The complete definition of Impl is inside *bigclass.cpp* (Example 7-15).

Example 7-15. bigclass.cpp, containing the definition of Impl

```
# include "foo.h"
# include "bar.h"
# include "baz.h"
# include "bigclass.h"

class Impl {
    void g1(int a);
    void g2(float f);
    Foo foo_;
    Bar bar_;
    Baz baz_;
};

void Impl::g1(int a) {
  ...
}

char Impl::g2(float f) {
  ...
}

void BigClass::BigClass() {
    impl_ = new Impl;
}

void BigClass::f1(int a) {
    impl_ -> g1(a);
}

char BigClass::f2(float f) {
    return impl_ -> g2(f)
}
```

At compile time, after implementing PIMPL, changes to *foo.h*, *bar.h*, or *baz.h*, or the implementation of Impl cause *bigclass.cpp* to be recompiled, but *bigclass.h* is unchanged, limiting the scope of the recompilation.

At run time, the story is different. PIMPL adds nothing to the program except delay. Member functions of BigClass that might have been inlined now require a member function call. Furthermore, each member function now calls a member function of

Impl. Projects that use PIMPL often use it in many places, creating many layers of nested function calls. Furthermore, debugging is tedious due to the extra layers of function calls.

In 2016, there is little need to use PIMPL. Compilation times are maybe 1% of the times experienced in the 1990s. Furthermore, even in the '90s, for PIMPL to be necessary, BigClass had to *be* a big class depending on many header files. Such classes violate many rules of object-oriented programming. Breaking BigClass up to provide more focused interfaces might be just as effective as implementing PIMPL.

Eliminate Calls into DLLs

Calls into dynamic link libraries (DLLs) on Windows are made through a function pointer that is either explicitly set in the program if the DLL is loaded on demand, or implicitly set if the DLL is automatically loaded at startup. Linux has dynamic libraries too, with the same implementation.

Some DLL calls are necessary. For instance, an application may implement a third-party plug-in library. Other reasons to use DLLs are less clear-cut. For instance, one reason DLLs have been used is to provide the ability to patch bugs by replacing just a DLL. Experience has demonstrated that bug fixes are generally produced in batches, covering many areas of the program at once. This limits the chance that a single DLL will contain all the fixes, spoiling this use for DLLs.

Changing DLLs into object code libraries and linking the libraries into a single executable is another way to improve function call performance.

Use Static Member Functions Instead of Member Functions

Every call to a member function has an additional, implicit argument: a "this" pointer to the class instance whose member is being called. Class member data is accessed via an offset from the "this" pointer. Virtual member functions must dereference the "this" pointer to get the vtable pointer.

Sometimes a member function depends only on its arguments, doesn't access any member data, and doesn't call any virtual member functions. In this case, the "this" pointer serves no purpose.

Such member functions should be declared static. Static member functions don't have to evaluate an implicit "this" pointer. They can be referred to with regular function pointers instead of more expensive member function pointers (see "Cost of pointers to functions" on page 163).

Move Virtual Destructor to Base Class

The destructor of any class that will have derived classes should be declared `virtual`. This is necessary so that if a delete-expression references a pointer to the base class, both the derived class destructor and the base class destructor will be called.

There is another reason to provide some virtual function declaration in the most base class of any hierarchy: to ensure that a vtable pointer will be included in the base class.

The base class has a special position in a class hierarchy. If the base class has virtual member function declarations, the vtable pointer will be at offset zero in any class instance derived from this base class. If the base class declares member variables and doesn't declare any virtual member functions, but some derived class does declare virtual member functions, every virtual member function call will have to add an offset to the "this" pointer to obtain the address of the vtable pointer. Ensuring that at least one member function in the base class is virtual forces the vtable to appear at offset zero, which generates more efficient code.

The destructor is an excellent candidate to be that function. It must be virtual anyway if the base class will have derived classes. The destructor is called only once during the life of a class instance, so the cost of making it virtual is minimal except for very small classes that are constructed and destroyed at a high rate in the program (and rarely are these small classes used to derive subclasses).

This may seem like such a rare case that it doesn't deserve mention, but I have worked on several projects where important class hierarchies had a base class containing an intrusive reference count, transaction ID, or some such variable. This base class had little knowledge about what classes might be derived from it. Usually the first derivation in the hierarchy was an abstract base class declaring a bunch of virtual member functions. One thing the base class *did* know was that instances would eventually be destroyed.

Optimize Expressions

Below the statement level, at the level of arithmetic expressions involving basic data types (integers, floats, pointers), there is a final opportunity to optimize. If a very hot function consists of a single expression, it may be the only opportunity.

Stop and Think

Modern compilers are *very* good at optimizing expressions involving basic data types. They are so good that they range from amazing all the way up to provably optimal. But they are not very brave. They will optimize expressions only when they can *prove* that the optimization does not change the behavior of the program.

Developers are smarter than compilers, though far less meticulous. Developers can code optimizations in situations where the compiler cannot determine that an optimization is safe, because developers can reason about the *design* and the *intent* of functions defined in other code modules not visible to the compiler.

It is in these relatively rare cases that developers can do better than compilers.

Optimizing expressions can have a significant effect on smaller processors that execute instructions one at a time. On desktop-class processors with multistage pipelines, the performance improvement is detectable, but not great. This is not the place to hunt for big game in the optimization jungle. Go here only on those rare occasions when you must squeeze the final iota of performance out of some red-hot inner loop or function.

Simplify Expressions

C++ evaluates expressions in strict order by the precedence and associativity of their operators. The expression a*b+a*c is evaluated as if written ((a*b)+(a*c)) because the precedence rules in C++ make multiplication higher priority than addition. The C++ compiler never uses the distributive law to recode this expression to a more efficient form like a*(b+c). The expression a+b+c is evaluated as if written ((a+b)+c), because the + operator associates to the left. The compiler never rewrites the expression to (a+(b+c)) even though that is equivalent in the math of integers and real numbers.

The reason C++ leaves its hands off expressions is because the modular arithmetic of the C++ int type isn't exactly like the mathematics of integers, and the approximate arithmetic of the C++ float type is not exactly like real math. C++ must give the programmer power to specify his intention precisely, or the compiler will reorder expressions in ways that cause overflows of various kinds. That means the developer is responsible for writing expressions in a form that uses the fewest possible operators.

Horner's rule for evaluating polynomials exemplifies how powerful rewriting expressions to a more efficient form can be as an optimization. Although most C++ developers don't evaluate polynomials every day, we are all familiar with them.

The polynomial $y = ax^3 + bx^2 + cx + d$ could be written in C++ as:

```
y = a*x*x*x + b*x*x + c*x + d;
```

This statement performs six multiplies and three adds. Horner's rule uses a repeated application of the distributive law to rewrite this statement as:

```
y = (((a*x + b)*x) + c)*x + d;
```

The optimized statement performs three multiplies and three adds. In general, Horner's rule simplifies an expression from $n(n-1)$ multiplies to n, where n is the degree of the polynomial.

---

a / b * c: A Cautionary Tale

The reason C++ does not reorder arithmetic expressions itself is because it's dangerous. Numerical analysis is another subject that produces whole books. This is a single example of what can go wrong.

The C++ compiler will evaluate the expression a / b * c as if it was parenthesized ((a / b) * c). But there's a problem with this expression. If a, b, and c are integral types, the result of a / b is not exact. Thus, if a = 2, b = 3, and c = 10, a / b * c is 2 / 3 * 10 = 0, when we really want it to be 6. The problem is that the inexactness in a / b is multiplied by c, producing a very incorrect result. A developer with good math skills might rearrange this expression as c * a / b, which the compiler will evaluate as if parenthesized ((c * a) / b). Then 2 * 10 / 3 = 6.

Problem solved, right? Well actually, no. If you do the multiplication first, there is a danger of overflow. If a = 86,400 (the number of seconds in a day), b = 90,000 (a constant used in video sampling), and c = 1,000,000 (the number of microseconds in a second), the expression c * a overflows a 32-bit unsigned. The original expression, while having a significant error, is less wrong than the revised one.

The developer is solely responsible for knowing that the expression as written, with arguments having the expected magnitudes, will produce a correct result. The compiler cannot help with this task, which is why it leaves expressions alone.

Group Constants Together

One thing the compiler *can* do is evaluate constant expressions. Faced with an expression like

```
seconds = 24 * 60 * 60 * days;
```

or

```
seconds = days * (24 * 60 * 60);
```

the compiler can evaluate the constant part of the expression to produce something equivalent to

```
seconds = 86400 * days;
```

But if the programmer writes

```
seconds = 24 * days * 60 * 60;
```

the compiler is obliged to perform the multiplications at run time.

Always group constant expressions together with parentheses, or put them on the left side of the expression, or better yet, separate them out into the initializer of a const variable or put them in a constexpr function if your compiler supports this C++11 feature. This allows the compiler to efficiently evaluate the constant expression at compile time.

Use Less-Expensive Operators

Some arithmetic operations are less expensive to compute than others. For instance, all but the smallest processors in use today can perform a shift or addition in one internal clock cycle. A few specialized digital signal processor chips have single-cycle multipliers, but for PCs, multiplication is an iterated computation similar to the decimal multiplication procedure taught to schoolchildren. Division is a more complex iterated procedure. This hierarchy of costs provides opportunities for optimization.

For instance, the integer expression x*4 can be recoded more efficiently as x<<2. Any half-decent compiler already performs this *reduction in strength* optimization. But what if the expression is x*y or x*func()? In many cases, the compiler cannot determine that y or func() always produces a value that is a power of two. This is where the programmer's knowledge and skill beats the compiler. If one argument or the other can be modified to provide the exponent rather than the power of two value, the developer can rewrite the expression to use shift instead of multiplication.

Another possible optimization is to rewrite a multiplication into a sequence of shifts and adds. For instance, the integer expression x*9 can be rewritten as x*8+x*1, which in turn can be rewritten as (x<<3)+x. This optimization is most effective when the constant operand does not contain many set bits, because each set bit expands to a shift-and-add term. It's effective on desktop- or handset-class processors that have instruction caches and pipelined execution units, and on very small processors where long multiplication is a subroutine call. Like all optimizations, this one should be tested to be sure it improves performance on a particular processor, but it is generally a win.

Use Integer Arithmetic Instead of Floating Arithmetic

Floating-point arithmetic is expensive. Floating-point numbers have a complex internal representation with a normalized integer mantissa, a separate exponent, and two signs. The hardware that implements the floating-point unit on a PC may occupy as much as 20% of the die area. Some multicore processors share a single floating-point arithmetic unit but have multiple integer arithmetic units per core.

Integer results can be computed at least 10 times faster than equivalent floating-point results, even on processors with hardware floating-point arithmetic units, and even when results of integer division are rounded instead of truncated. On small processors where floating-point math is implemented via a function library, integer math is many times faster. And yet, it is very typical to find developers using floating point for things as simple as rounded division.

Example 7-16 is the way most code I've encountered produces a rounded quotient. It converts the integral arguments to floating point, performs the division, and rounds the result.

Example 7-16. Integer rounding with floating point

```
unsigned q = (unsigned)round((double)n / (double)d));
```

A test loop that repeats this operation 100 million times took 3,125 milliseconds on my PC.

To obtain a rounded integral quotient, it is necessary to look at the remainder from division. The value of the remainder ranges from 0 to *d–1*, where *d* is the denominator. If the remainder is greater than or equal to half the denominator, the quotient should be rounded up to the next integer. The formula for signed integers is only a bit more complex.

C++ provides a function ldiv() from the C runtime library, which produces a structure containing both the quotient and remainder. Example 7-17 is a function to round a division result using ldiv().

Example 7-17. Rounding integer division using ldiv()

```
inline unsigned div0(unsigned n, unsigned d) {
    auto r = ldiv(n, d);
    return (r.rem >= (d >> 1)) ? r.quot + 1 : r.quot;
}
```

This function isn't perfect. ldiv() expects int arguments, and complains about a signed/unsigned mismatch. It produces a correct result if both arguments are positive when regarded as ints. div0() runs the test loop in 435 milliseconds, a satisfying 6 times faster than the floating-point version.

Example 7-18 is a function to compute the rounded quotient of two unsigned arguments.

Example 7-18. Rounding integer division

```
inline unsigned div1(unsigned n, unsigned d) {
    unsigned q = n / d;
    unsigned r = n % d;
    return r >= (d >> 1) ? q + 1 : q;
}
```

div1() computes the quotient and remainder. (d >> 1) is an efficient, reduced-strength form of d/2, which is half the denominator d. If the remainder is greater than or equal to half the denominator, the quotient is rounded up. Key to the success of this function is an optimization performed by the compiler. The x86 machine instruction that divides two integers produces both a quotient and a remainder. The Visual C++ compiler is smart enough to invoke this instruction only once when this code is executed. The same test, calling this function instead of using floating-point math, took 135 milliseconds. This is a rewarding 22 times faster.

Example 7-19 is another way to round an unsigned that is even faster, though at a price.

Example 7-19. Rounding integer division

```
inline unsigned div2(unsigned n, unsigned d) {
    return (n + (d >> 1)) / d;
}
```

div2() adds half the denominator d to the numerator n before dividing. div2()'s weakness is that for large numerators, n + (d >> 1) may overflow. If the developer is aware of the general magnitude of the arguments, div2() is very fast, at 102 milliseconds in the test loop (30 times faster than the floating-point version that is so common).

Double May Be Faster than Float

On my i7 PC running Visual C++, double floating-point computations were faster than float floating-point computations. First I present the result, then I will speculate about why this may occur.

The following code iteratively computes the distance traveled by a falling body, a typical floating-point computation:

```
float d, t, a = -9.8f, v0 = 0.0f, d0 = 100.0f;
for (t = 0.0; t < 3.01f; t += 0.1f) {
    d = a*t*t + v0*t + d0;
```

Ten million iterations of this loop consumed 1,889 milliseconds.

The same routine coded to use double variables and constants looks like this:

```
double d, t, a = -9.8, v0 = 0.0, d0 = 100.0;
for (t = 0.0; t < 3.01; t += 0.1) {
    d = a*t*t + v0*t + d0;
```

Ten million iterations of this version took only 989 milliseconds, making the double version almost twice as fast.

Why does this happen? Visual C++ generates floating-point instructions that reference the old "x87 FPU coprocessor" register stack. In this scheme, all floating-point computations are performed in a single 80-bit format. Single-precision `float` and double-precision `double` values are lengthened when they are moved into the FPU registers. The conversion for `float` may take more time than the conversion for `double`.

There are many ways to compile floating-point operations. On the x86 platform, using the SSE registers allows computation to be done directly in four different sizes. A compiler that used SSE instructions might behave differently, as might a compiler for a non-x86 processor.

Replace Iterative Computations with Closed Forms

What is it about C++ and bit-twiddling? Does the rich collection of arithmetic and bit-logical operators in C++ just facilitate moving bits around, or did the need to get bits of information into and out of device registers and network packets mold C++ into the language it is today?

Many occasions arise to count the number of set bits, find the most significant bit, determine the parity of bits in a word, determine whether the bits in a word represent a power of two, and so on. Most of these problems have simple O(n) solutions involving iterating through the n bits of the word. There may be more complex iterative solutions with better performance. But for some problems, there are faster and more compact *closed-form* solutions: constant-time computations that produce a solution without the need for iteration.

For example, there is a simple iterative algorithm to determine whether an integer value is a power of two. All such values have a single bit set, so counting the number of set bits is one solution. A simple implementation of this algorithm might look like Example 7-20.

Example 7-20. Iterative test of whether an integer is a power of 2

```
inline bool is_power_2_iterative(unsigned n) {
    for (unsigned one_bits = 0; n != 0; n >>= 1)
        if ((n & 1) == 1)
            if (one_bits != 0)
                return false;
            else
                one_bits += 1;
    return true;
}
```

A test loop of this algorithm took 549 milliseconds.

This problem also has a closed-form solution. If x is the nth power of two, it has a single set bit in the nth position (counting from zero for the least significant bit). Then $x-1$ is a bitmask with set bits in positions $n-1,...,0$, and $x \& (x-1)$ equals zero. If x is not a power of two, it has some additional bits set, $x-1$ zeros out only the least significant set bit, and $x \& (x-1)$ does not equal zero.

A function to determine whether x is a power of two using the closed form looks like Example 7-21.

Example 7-21. Closed-form test of whether an integer is a power of 2

```
inline bool is_power_2_closed(unsigned n) {
    return ((n != 0) && !(n & (n - 1)));
}
```

The same test loop using this revised function runs in 238 milliseconds, 2.3 times as fast. There are even faster ways. Rick Regan has an excellent web page (*http://bit.ly/regan-10*) that explores 10 ways, with timing measurements.

Get a Copy of *Hacker's Delight*

The preceding section contains some advice on efficient bit-twiddling, but it's only a sample to get you interested. There are hundreds of little tricks to improve arithmetic performance.

There is a book that should be in the library of every developer with an interest in optimizing at the expression level: *Hacker's Delight* by Henry S. Warren, Jr. (Addison-Wesley Professional), now in its second edition. If you have the slightest interest in efficient expressions, reading *Hacker's Delight* is like opening your first Lego kit or building your first electronic circuit from discrete components. Warren also maintains a website for *Hacker's Delight* (*http://hackersdelight.org/*), with even more interesting links and discussions.

For a free taste of the *Hacker's Delight* drug, you can peruse MIT Artificial Intelligence Laboratory Memo 239, affectionately known as HAKMEM (*http://bit.ly/mit-hackmem*),[3] on the Web. HAKMEM is the conceptual ancestor of *Hacker's Delight*, chock-full of bit-twiddling hacks collected at a time when the fastest processors were 10,000 times slower than your phone.

---

3 Beeler, Michael, Gosper, R. William, and Schroeppel, Rich, "HAKMEM," Memo 239, Artificial Intelligence Laboratory, Massachusetts Institute of Technology, Cambridge, MA, 1972.

Optimize Control Flow Idioms

As noted in "Making Decisions Is Hard for Computers" on page 22, computation is faster than flow of control, due to pipeline stalls that occur in the processor when the instruction pointer must be updated to a nonconsecutive address. The C++ compiler tries hard to reduce the number of instruction pointer updates. It pays to be aware of what the compiler is doing in order to write the fastest code possible.

Use switch Instead of if-elseif-else

The flow of control in an `if-else if-else` statement is linear: evaluate the `if` condition, and if true, execute the first controlled block. Otherwise evaluate each `else if` condition, and execute the controlled block for the first one that evaluates to true. Testing a variable for each of n values, takes an `if-then-else if` sequence with n controlled blocks. If all possible cases are about equally likely, the `if-then-else if` sequence makes O(n) comparisons. When this code is executed very frequently, as for event or instruction dispatch code, the cost adds up significantly.

The `switch` statement will also test a variable for each of n values, but the form of the `switch` statement, which compares the `switch` value against a series of constants, lets the compiler perform a number of useful optimizations.

In a frequently occurring case, when the constants to be tested against are taken from a set of sequential or nearly sequential values, the `switch` statement compiles into a jump table indexed by the test value or an expression derived from the test value. The `switch` statement performs a single indexing operation and jumps to the address in the table. The cost of the comparison is O(1), no matter how many cases appear. The cases don't have to be presented in sequential order; the compiler can sort the jump table.

When the constants form a sequence with large gaps, a jump table becomes unmanageably large. The compiler may still sort the tested constants and emit code that performs a binary search. For a `switch` statement comparing against n values, the worst-case cost of this search is O($log_2 n$). In any case, the compiler never emits code for a `switch` statement that is slower than an equivalent `if-then` statement.

Sometimes a single branch of the if-elseif-else logic is very probable. In this case, the amortized performance of an `if` statement may approach a constant if the very probable case is tested first.

Use Virtual Functions Instead of switch or if

Before C++, if developers wanted to introduce polymorphic behavior in a program, they might have coded a `struct` or `union` type with a discriminator variable that told what the particular struct or union represented. The program would have been full of code that looked like this:

```
if (p->animalType == TIGER) {
    tiger_pounce(p->tiger);
}
else if (p->animalType == RABBIT) {
    rabit_hop(p->rabbit);
}
else if (...)
```

Most experienced developers know this antipattern is the poster child for object-oriented programming. But it takes a while for the object-oriented mindset to become ingrained in novice developers. I have seen lots of production C++ code containing halfway-objectified code like this:

```
Animal::move() {
    if (this->animalType == TIGER) {
        pounce();
    }
    else if (this->animalType == RABBIT) {
        hop();
    }
    else if (...)
    ...
}
```

From an optimization standpoint, the problem with this code is the use of a block of if statements to discriminate the derived type of the object. C++ classes already contain a mechanism to do this: virtual member functions, and the vtable pointer as discriminator.

A virtual function call indexes into the vtable to get the address of the virtual function body. It's a constant-time operation, always. Thus, a virtual move() member function in the base class is overridden in derived classes representing each animal with the code for pounce, hop, swim, and so on.

Use No-Cost Exception Handling

Exception handling is one of those optimizations best applied at design time. The design of an error propagation method ripples through every line of a program, so retrofitting a program for exception handling may be too expensive. That said, use of exception handling leads to programs that are faster when they execute normally, and better behaved when they fail.

Some C++ developers regard the C++ exception handling facility with suspicion. There is received wisdom that exception handling makes programs larger and slower, and that turning exception handling off via a compiler switch is thus an optimization.

The truth is more complex. It is true that if a program doesn't use exception handling, turning it off via a compiler switch will make the program smaller, and maybe a bit faster. Jeff Preshing measured the cost at between 1.4% and 4% in a blog entry (*http://bit.ly/preshing*). But it isn't clear exactly how well the resulting program will work. All the containers in the C++ standard library use new expressions that throw exceptions. Many other libraries, including stream I/O and the concurrency libraries covered in this book (see Chapter 12) throw exceptions. The `dynamic_cast` operator throws exceptions. With exception handling turned off, it isn't clear what happens when the program encounters a situation where it would throw an exception.

If the program doesn't throw exceptions, it may completely ignore error codes. In this case, the developer gets what she deserves. Otherwise, the program must patiently, carefully pass error codes up through its many layers of function calls, translating error codes from one code set to another at library boundaries and freeing resources as it goes. It must do this whether each operation succeeds or fails.

With exceptions, some of the cost of handling errors is moved from the happy path of normal program execution to the error path. In addition, the compiler automatically reclaims resources by invoking the destructors of all automatic variables on the path between the exception throw and the `try/catch` block that handles the exception. This simplifies the logic of the program's happy path, with consequent performance gains.

In the early days of C++, each stack frame contained an exception context: a pointer to the list of objects that had been constructed, and thus must be destroyed if an exception was thrown through the stack frame. This context was updated dynamically as the program executed. This was undesirable because it put runtime cost in the happy path; this may be the source of the legend of the high cost of exception handling. A newer implementation maps the objects that need to be destroyed to a range of instruction pointer values. This mechanism has no runtime cost unless an exception is thrown, so exceptions are very inexpensive. Visual Studio uses this newer no-cost mechanism for 64-bit builds, and the older mechanism for 32-bit builds. The mechanism is selectable by a compiler switch in Clang.

Don't use exception specifications

Exception specifications decorate function declarations, saying what exceptions the function may throw. A function with no exception specification may throw exceptions without penalty. A function with an exception specification may throw only the exceptions listed in the specification. If it throws any other exception, the program is unconditionally and immediately stopped by a call to `terminate()`.

There are two problems with exception specifications. One problem is that it is difficult for the developer to know what exceptions may be thrown by a called function, especially one in an unfamiliar library. This makes programs using exception specifications brittle and likely to fail suddenly.

The second problem is that exception specifications negatively affect performance. Thrown exceptions must be checked, as if every function call with an exception specification entered a new `try/catch` block.

Traditional exception specifications were deprecated as of C++11.

C++11 introduced a new exception specification called `noexcept`. Declare a function `noexcept` tells the compiler that the function cannot possibly throw any exception. If the function does throw one, `terminate()` is called just as in the `throw()` specification. The difference is that the compiler requires certain move constructors and move assignment statements to be declared `noexcept` to implement move semantics (discussed in "Implement Move Semantics" on page 137). The `noexcept` specification on these functions serves as a declaration that move semantics are more important than the strong exception safety guarantee for certain objects. It's very obscure, I know.

Summary

- *Optimizing at the statement level doesn't provide enough improvement to make it worthwhile unless there are factors that magnify the cost of the statement.*
- *The cost of statements in loops is magnified by the number of iterations of the loops.*
- *The cost of statements in functions is magnified by the number of times the functions are called.*
- *The cost of a frequently used idiom is magnified by the number of times the idiom is used.*
- *Some C++ statements (assignment, initialization, function argument evaluation) contain hidden function calls.*
- *Function calls into the operating system are expensive.*
- *An effective way to remove function call overhead is to inline the function.*
- *There is currently little need for the PIMPL idiom. Compile times today are maybe 1% of what they were when PIMPL was invented.*
- *`double` arithmetic may be faster than `float` arithmetic.*

## CHAPTER 8

Use Better Libraries

A great library is one nobody notices because it is always there, and always has what people need.

> —Vicki Myron, author of *Dewey, the Small Town Library Cat*, and librarian of the town of Spencer, Iowa

Libraries are an area of focus in the optimization process. Libraries provide the primitives from which programs are built up. Library functions and classes are often used at the bottom of nested loops, and are thus often hot. Libraries provided by the compiler or operating system command attention to see that they are used efficiently. Project-specific libraries deserve careful design to ensure that they *can* be used efficiently.

This chapter discusses issues in the use of the C++ standard library, then examines issues in the design of custom libraries that bear on optimization.

Most of *Optimized C++* is about tweaking functions to improve performance. This chapter offers instead advice for designers who need to achieve high performance in their initial design, based on my personal experience. Although I introduce this discussion in the context of library design, this section is also a checklist of how good C++ design techniques contribute to good performance.

Optimize Standard Library Use

C++ provides a compact standard library for the following general uses:

- Determining implementation-dependent behavior, like the largest and smallest values of each numeric type.

- Functions that might not best be written in C++, like `strcpy()` and `memmove()`.

- Easy to use but fussy to write and validate portable transcendental math functions like sine and cosine, log and power, random numbers, and so on.

- Portable, general data structures like strings, lists, and tables that do not depend on the operating system except for memory allocation.

- Portable, general algorithms for searching, sorting, and transforming data.

- Functions that connect to basic services of the operating system in an operating system–independent way, to perform tasks like memory allocation, threading, timekeeping, and stream I/O. This includes a library of functions inherited from the C programming language for compatibility.

Much of the C++ standard library consists of template classes and functions that produce extremely efficient code.

Philosophy of the C++ Standard Library

In keeping with its mission as a systems programming language, C++ provides a somewhat Spartan standard library. The standard library is meant to be simple, general, and fast. Philosophically, *functions and classes enter the C++ standard library either because they cannot be provided any other way, or because they promote very wide reuse across multiple operating systems.*

Advantages of the C++ approach include that C++ programs can run on hardware that provides no operating system at all, and that programmers can choose a specialist library tailored to the features of a particular operating system when that is appropriate, or use a cross-platform library when platform independence is the goal.

By contrast, some programming languages, including C# and Java, provide extensive standard libraries that include windowing user interface frameworks, web servers, socket networking, and other large subsystems. An advantage of the all-inclusive approach is that developers need only learn one set of libraries to be effective on any supported platform. But such libraries impose many requirements on the operating systems on which they can be made to run (sometimes deliberately). The libraries provided with a programming language also come to represent a least common denominator, less powerful than the native windowing system or networking capabilities of any specific operating system. They can thus be somewhat limiting to programmers accustomed to the native capabilities of a specific OS.

Issues in Use of the C++ Standard Library

While the following discussion is tailored to the C++ standard library, it applies equally to the standard Linux libraries, the POSIX library, or any other widely used cross-platform library. Usage issues include the following:

Standard library implementations have bugs

Although bugs are an inevitable part of software development, even experienced developers may not have encountered bugs in standard library code. They may thus have come to believe that the various implementations of the standard library are rock solid. I am sorry to burst this happy bubble. In writing this book, I came across several standard library bugs.

Classic "Hello, World!" programs are quite likely to work as expected. However, optimization takes the developer into the dark corners and back alleys of the standard library, where bugs are most likely to lurk. The optimizing developer must be ready for occasional disappointment when a promising optimization cannot be implemented, or when an optimization that works on one compiler produces an error message on another.

How can it happen that 30-year-old code still contains bugs, the reader may ask? For one thing, the standard library has been evolving for all that time. The definition of the library and the code that implements it has always been a work in progress. It's not 30-year-old code. The standard library is maintained separately from the compiler, which also has bugs. For GCC, the library maintainers are volunteers. For Microsoft's Visual C++, the standard library is a purchased third-party component that has its own release schedule that differs from both the Visual C++ release cycle and the C++ standard release cycle. Changing requirements of the standard, diffuse responsibility, schedule issues, and the complexity of the standard library all take their inevitable toll on quality. What is actually more interesting is that there are so *few* bugs in the standard library implementations.

Standard library implementations may not conform to the C++ standard

There is probably no such thing as a "standard-conforming implementation." In the real world, compiler vendors consider their tools to be shippable if they provide a reasonably large subset of the relevant C++ standard, including its most important features.

As for libraries, these are released on a different schedule from that of the compiler, and the compiler is released on a different schedule from that of the C++ standard. A standard library implementation may either lead or trail the standard conformance of the compiler. Different parts of the library my lead or trail to different extents. For developers interested in optimization, changes in the C++ standard, such as the change in optimal insertion points for new map entries (see "Inserting and Deleting in std::map" on page 252), mean that the behavior of some functions may surprise the user, since there is no way to document or to determine the version of the standard to which a particular library conforms.

Some libraries are limited by the compiler. For instance, a library cannot implement move semantics until the compiler supports this feature. Imperfect compiler support may lead to limitations in the standard library classes that can be shipped with the compiler. Sometimes, attempting to use a feature gives a compiler error, and it is impossible for a developer to determine whether it is the compiler or the standard library implementation that is broken.

The optimizing developer who is very familiar with the standard may thus be disappointed when an infrequently used feature turns out to be unimplemented by the compiler he is using.

Performance is not the most important thing to standard library developers

Although performance is important to C++ developers, it is not necessarily the most important factor to the developers of the standard library. Coverage is important, especially if it permits them to check a box on the latest C++ standard's list of features. Simplicity and maintainability are important, because the library is long-lived. Portability is important if the library implementation must support multiple compilers. Performance may sometimes take a back seat to any of these other important factors.

The path from the standard library function call to the related native function may be long and winding. I once traced an `fopen()` call through half a dozen layers of functions dedicated to argument translation before it arrived at the Windows `OpenFile()` call that ultimately asked the operating system to open the file. The goal appeared to have been minimizing the number of lines of code, but the many layers of function call could not have helped with performance.

Library implementations may frustrate optimization attempts

The Linux AIO library (not a standard C++ library, but very useful to the optimizing developer) was intended to provide a very efficient, asynchronous, copy-free interface for reading files. The problem was that AIO required a particular kernel version. Until a reasonably large fraction of Linux distros implemented the kernel update, AIO was coded in terms of older, slower I/O calls. The developer could write AIO calls but not get AIO performance.

Not all parts of the C++ standard library are equally useful

Some C++ features, like the elaborate exception hierarchy, vector<bool>, and standard library Allocators, were added to the standard before being wrung out in use. These features actually make coding harder instead of easier. Fortunately, the standard committee seems to have gotten over its earlier enthusiasm for untested new features. Proposed library features now gestate in the Boost library (*http://www.boost.org*) for several years before being taken up by the standard committee.

The standard library is not as efficient as the best native functions

The standard library does not provide features available on some operating systems, such as asynchronous file I/O. The optimizing developer can only go so far with the standard library. To obtain the final iota of performance, she must descend to native calls, sacrificing portability on the altar of the gods of speed.

Optimize Existing Libraries

Optimizing an existing library is like clearing a minefield. It may be possible. It may be necessary. But it is a difficult job that requires patience and attention to detail, or *boom!*

The easiest kind of library to optimize is well designed, with good separation of concerns and good test cases. Unfortunately, this kind of library is already probably optimized. The reality is that if you are asked to optimize a library, it is probably a mess of functionality squeezed into functions or classes that do too much or too little.

Making changes to a library introduces the risk that some other program relies on unintended or undocumented behavior of the existing implementation. While making a function run faster is not itself likely to cause problems, some accompanying change in behavior may be more of a problem.

Making changes to an open source library introduces potential incompatibility between your project's version and the main repository. This becomes a problem when the open source library is next revised to fix bugs or add functionality. Either your changes must manually be propagated to the changed library, or your changes are lost in the upgrade, or your modified library becomes fixed in time and does not get the advantage of changes made by other contributors. It is thus a good idea, when picking open source libraries, to be sure the community is welcoming of your changes, or that the library is very mature and stable.

Still, it's not completely hopeless. The following sections cover some rules for attacking existing libraries.

Change as Little as Possible

The best advice for library optimizers is to *change as little as possible*. Don't add or remove functionality from classes or functions, or change function signatures. These kinds of changes are almost guaranteed to break compatibility between the modified library and programs that use it.

Another reason to make the fewest changes possible is to limit the part of the library code that must be understood.

Optimization War Story

I once worked for a company that sold and supported an industrial-strength version of OpenSSH, which is based on a program developed in 1995 by Tatu Ylönen, a

---

researcher at the Helsinki University of Technology, for personal use. Being new to the open source world, I noted that the code had not been written by a highly experienced developer, and was thus not as tidy as it could have been. I made some significant changes, to make the code more easily maintained. Or so I thought at first.

Wonderful though my personal code stylings may have been, I found out they could never be deployed.

In retrospect, the reason should have been obvious. My changes made our code differ too much from the open source variant. We relied on the community for important, security-related bug fixes that were automatic on unmodified code, but time-consuming to reimplement on my heavily modified code. While I might have proposed these changes for inclusion in the open source version, the security community is extremely conservative about changes, and rightly so.

I needed to change only code that affected security improvements requested by our users, and then to the minimum extent possible. Refactoring was never even an option with this code, badly as it seemed to cry out for it.

Add Functions Rather than Change Functionality

One bright spot in the gloomy world of optimizing libraries is that new functions and classes can be added to a library in relative safety. There is of course a risk that a future version of the library will define a class or function with the same name as one of your additions, but that risk is controllable by choice of names, and sometimes reparable with macros.

Here are some reasonably safe upgrades that may improve the performance of existing libraries:

- Add functions that move loops down into the library, reflecting idioms of use in your code.
- Implement move semantics in older libraries by adding function overloads that take rvalue references. (See "Implement Move Semantics" on page 137 for more details on move semantics.)

Design Optimized Libraries

Faced with a badly designed library, there's little the optimizing developer can do. Faced with a blank screen, the optimizing developer has more latitude to use best practices and avoid pitfalls.

Some of the items in this checklist are aspirational goals. That is, this section offers no specific advice on how to achieve each goal in a particular library, but only notes that the best and most useful libraries tend to embody these virtues. If a particular library design is straying away from these aspirational goals, a review of the design is appropriate.

Code in Haste, Repent at Leisure

> Marry in haste, repent at leisure.
>
> —Samuel Johnson (1709–1784), English lexicographer, essayist, and poet

Stability of interface is a core deliverable of a library. A library designed in a rush, or a bunch of independently written functions pulled together into a library, will not match in call and return conventions, allocation behavior, or efficiency. The pressure to make a casually built library consistent will arise almost immediately. However, the time required to fix all functions in the library may prevent developers from acting to fill this need.

Designing an optimized library is like designing other C++ code, only the stakes are higher. Libraries, by definition, are meant for broad use. Any imperfections in the design, implementation, or performance of a library are shared among all its users. Casual coding practices, which can be tolerated in noncritical code, are more problematical when developing libraries. Old-school development methods, including upfront specification and design, documentation, and module tests, find their uses in development of critical code like libraries.

Optimization Pro Tip: Test Cases Are Critical

Test cases are important for any software. They help verify the correctness of the original design, and help reduce the chance that changes made during optimization will affect a program's correctness. It should not be surprising that they assume an even greater importance in library code, where the stakes are higher.

Test cases help identify dependencies and couplings during the design of a library. The functions of well-designed libraries can be tested in isolation. If many objects must be instantiated before testing a target function, it is a signal to the designer that there is too much coupling between the components of the library.

Test cases help the library designer practice use of the library. Without this practice, it's far too easy for even experienced designers to leave out important interface functions. Test cases help the library designer identify rough edges in the design at an early stage, when breaking changes to the library interface are not painful. Using the library helps the designer to identify idioms of use, so that these are encoded in the library design, resulting in more efficient function interfaces.

> Test cases make good targets for timing tests. Timing tests ensure that any proposed optimizations actually improve performance. Timing tests themselves can be added to the other test cases to ensure that changes do not rob performance.

Parsimony Is a Virtue in Library Design

For those few readers who don't use this word in their daily lives, Merriam-Webster online defines *parsimony* (*http://www.merriam-webster.com/dictionary/parsimony*) as *the quality of being careful with money or resources; economy in the use of means to an end.* Readers may know this as the KISS (keep it simple, stupid) principle. Parsimony means a library is focused on a particular task and contains the minimum amount of machinery needed to perform that task.

For instance, it is more parsimonious for a library function to accept a valid `std::istream` reference argument from which to read data than to open a file named by a filename argument; handling operating system–dependent filename semantics and I/O errors is not core to a data processing library. See "Create a Parsimonious Function Signature" on page 267 for an example of this. Accepting a pointer to a memory buffer is more parsimonious than allocating storage to return; it means the library doesn't have to handle out-of-memory exceptions. See "Copy Free Libraries" on page 134 for an example. Parsimony is the ultimate result of consistently applying good C++ development principles like the single responsibility principle and the interface-segregation principle of SOLID design.

Parsimonious libraries are simple. They contain free functions or simple classes that are complete as they stand. They can be learned and understood one piece at a time. This is the way most programmers learn the C++ standard library, a big library that is nevertheless parsimonious.

Make Memory Allocation Decisions Outside the Library

This is a specific instance of the parsimony rule. Since memory allocation is so expensive, push allocation decisions out of the library if possible. For instance, fill in a buffer given as an argument to a library function, rather than returning a buffer allocated by the library function.

Pushing allocation decisions out of library functions allows the caller to implement the optimizations described in Chapter 6, reusing memory where possible instead of allocating new storage for each call.

Pushing allocation out of the library also reduces the number of times a buffer of data may need to be copied as it is passed from function to function.

If necessary, make memory allocation decisions in derived classes, so that the base class keeps only a pointer to the allocated memory. This way, new classes can be derived that allocate memory in different ways.

Requiring memory to be allocated outside of the library affects function signatures (for instance, passing in a pointer to a buffer versus returning an allocated buffer). It is important to make this decision at the time the library is designed. Trying to change the library once functions are in use will definitely cause breaking changes.

When in Doubt, Code Libraries for Speed

In Chapter 1, I quoted Don Knuth's admonition, "Premature optimization is the root of all evil." I suggested this was too dogmatic. But in library design, this advice is especially dangerous.

Good performance is particularly important for a library class or function. The library designer cannot predict when the library may be used in a context in which performance matters. Improving performance after the fact can be difficult or impossible, especially if it involves changes to function signatures or behavior. Even a library used within a single enterprise may be invoked from many programs. If the library is widely disseminated, as with open source projects, there is no way to update or even discover all users. Any change becomes a breaking change.

Functions Are Easier to Optimize than Frameworks

There are two kinds of libraries: function libraries and frameworks. A framework is a conceptually large class that implements a complete program skeleton: a windowing application or a web server, for instance. You decorate the framework with small functions that customize it, to be your specific windowing application or your particular web server.

The second kind of library is a collection of functions and classes that are components that together can be used to implement a program: parsing URIs for a web server or drawing text on a window, for instance.

Both kinds of libraries can embody powerful functionality and enhance productivity. A given set of capabilities can be packaged either as functions (as in Windows SDK) or as a framework (as in Windows MFC, for example). However, from an optimizer's standpoint, function libraries are easier to work with than frameworks.

Functions have the advantage that they can be tested and their performance tuned in isolation. Invoking a framework turns on all its machinery at once, making it harder to isolate and test a change. Frameworks violate the separation of concerns or single responsibility rule. That makes them hard to optimize.

Functions can be used in focused ways within a larger application: a drawing subroutine here, a URI parser there. Only as much functionality as needed is linked from the library. Frameworks contain "god functions" (see "Beware of 'God Functions'" on page 199) that themselves link in many parts of the framework. This can bloat the executable with code that is not actually ever used.

Well-designed functions make few assumptions about the environment in which they run. By contrast, a framework is based on a big, general model of what the developer wants to do. Inefficiency results any time there is a mismatch between the model and the developer's actual needs.

Flatten Inheritance Hierarchies

Most abstractions require no more than three layers of class derivation: a base class with common functions, one or more derivations to implement polymorphism, and perhaps a mixin layer of multiple inheritance for really complex cases. For specific cases, a developer's judgment must prevail. However, inheritance hierarchies much deeper than this are a sign that the abstraction represented by the class hierarchy is not clearly thought out, introducing complexity that leads to lower performance.

From an optimization standpoint, the deeper the inheritance hierarchy, the greater the chance to introduce extra computation when a member function is called (see "Cost of Function Calls" on page 161). The constructors and destructors in classes with many layers of parents must traverse that whole long chain to do their jobs. Although these functions are not usually called frequently, they still pose a potential risk of introducing expensive calls into performance-critical operations.

Flatten Calling Chains

As with derived classes, *the implementations of most abstractions require no more than three nested function calls*: a free function or member function implementing strategy, calling a member function of some class, calling some public or private member function implementing the abstraction or accessing data.

If the data is being accessed in a nested abstraction implemented using a contained class instance, that may result in as much as three more layers. This analysis proceeds recursively down chains of nested abstractions. A library that is cleanly decomposed does not contain long chains of nested abstractions. These add overhead in the form of calls and returns.

Flatten Layered Designs

Sometimes one abstraction must be implemented in terms of another abstraction, creating a layered design. As noted previously, this can be carried to extremes that affect performance.

But other times, a single abstraction is reimplemented in a layered fashion. This may be done for several reasons:

- To implement a layer using the façade pattern that changes calling conventions: perhaps switching from project-specific to operating system–specific codes in arguments, switching from text-string to numeric codes in arguments, or inserting project-specific error handling
- To implement an abstraction in terms of a closely related abstraction for which library code already exists
- To implement a transition between error-returning function calls and exception-throwing function calls
- To implement the PIMPL idiom (see "Eliminate Uses of the PIMPL Idiom" on page 171)
- To call into a DLL or plug-in

The designer's judgment must rule in each situation, because there are excellent reasons for doing most of these things. However, each layer transition is an extra function call and return that saps the performance of every call. The designer must review layer transitions to see if they are necessary, or whether two or more layers can be compressed into one. Here are a few thoughts to guide code review:

- Many instances of the façade pattern in a single project may signal overdesign.
- One sign that a design is too layered is if a given layer occurs more than once, as in an error-returning layer calling an exception-handling layer, which then calls an error-returning layer.
- Nested instances of PIMPL are difficult to justify in terms of PIMPL's original purpose of providing a recompilation firewall. Most subsystems are simply not big enough to require nested PIMPLs (see "Eliminate Uses of the PIMPL Idiom" on page 171).
- Project-specific DLLs are often proposed for encapsulating bug fixes. Few projects ever realize this utility, as bug fixes tend to be released in batches that cross DLL boundaries.

Eliminating layers is a task that can be done only at design time. At design time, there is a business need for the library. Once the library is complete, no matter how flawed it is, the cost of any change must be weighed against the benefit. Experience teaches that no manager will welcome your request to spend a couple of sprints fixing up the library, unless there is a gun to their head.

Avoid Dynamic Lookup

Big programs contain big configuration profiles or long lists of registry entries. Complex data files such as audio or video streams contain optional metadata describing the data. When there are just a few metadata items, it's easy to define a struct or class to contain them. When there get to be dozens or hundreds, many designers are tempted to think of a lookup table design in which each metadata item can be looked up, given a key string. When the profiles are written in JSON or XML, the temptation grows, because there are libraries for dynamically finding items in JSON or XML files. Some programming languages, such as Objective-C, come with system libraries that work this way. However, dynamically searching a symbol table is a performance killer, for several reason:

- Dynamic lookup is inherently inefficient. Some libraries that find JSON or XML items have $O(n)$ performance with respect to the size of the file *per lookup*. Table-based lookup may be $O(log_2n)$. By contrast, fetching a data item from a struct is $O(1)$ and the constant of proportionality is tiny.

- The library designer may not know all the ways the metadata will be accessed. If an initialization profile is only read once at startup, the cost is probably insignificant. But many kinds of metadata must be read repeatedly during processing, and may change between units of work. While premature optimization may be the root of all evil, a library *interface* that searches for a key string can never be made faster than the search in the underlying key/value table without a change that breaks existing implementations. Apparently evil has more than one root!

- Once a lookup table–based design is in place, the next question that arises is one of consistency. Does the table contain all the metadata needed for a given transformation? Do command-line argument sets that must appear together actually appear? Although a table-based repository can be checked for consistency, it is an expensive runtime operation involving code and multiple expensive searches. Accessing the data in a simple struct is vastly faster than multiple table lookups.

- A struct-based repository is self-documenting in the sense that all possible metadata items are immediately visible. By contrast, a symbol table is just a big opaque bag of named values. A team using such a repository might choose to carefully document the metadata present at each stage in the program's execution. But such discipline is rare, in my experience. The alternative is to write endless code that attempts to regenerate missing metadata, never knowing whether the code will ever be called, and thus if it is correct.

Beware of 'God Functions'

A "god function" is a function implementing high-level strategy that, when used in a program, causes the linker to add many more library functions to the executable file. Increasing the size of the executable exhausts physical memory in embedded systems and increases virtual memory paging in desktop-class computers.

Many existing libraries have god functions that are expensive to use. Good libraries eliminate these functions by design. They are inevitable in libraries designed as frameworks.

Optimization War Story

This is a parable I call printf() is not your friend.

"Hello, World" is about the simplest possible C++ (or C) program:

```
# include <stdio.h>
int main(int, char**) {
    printf("Hello, World!\n");
    return 0;
}
```

How many executable bytes should this program contain? If you guessed "around 50 or 100 bytes," you're wrong by two orders of magnitude. This program was over 8 KB on an embedded controller I once programmed. And that's just code, not symbol tables, loader information, or anything else.

Here is another program that does the same thing:

```
# include <stdio.h>
int main(int, char**) {
    puts("Hello, World!");
    return 0;
}
```

This program is virtually the same, differing only in the use of puts() to output the string instead of printf(). But the second program occupies around 100 bytes. What causes the difference in size?

printf() is the culprit. printf() can print each particular type in three or four formats. It can interpret a format string to read a variable number of arguments. printf() is a big function on its own, but what really makes it big is that it pulls in standard library functions that format each basic type. On my embedded controller, it was even worse because the processor did not implement floating-point arithmetic in hardware; an extensive library of functions was used instead. printf() is in fact the poster child for the god function—a function that does so much that it sucks in huge swaths of the C runtime library.

On the other hand, `puts()` just puts one string on the standard output. It is internally quite simple, and furthermore, it doesn't cause half the standard library to be linked in.

Summary

- *Functions and classes enter the C++ standard library either because they cannot be provided any other way, or because they promote very wide reuse across multiple operating systems.*
- *Standard library implementations have bugs.*
- *There is no such thing as a "standard-conforming implementation."*
- *The standard library is not as efficient as the best native functions.*
- *When updating a library, change as little as possible.*
- *Stability of interface is a core deliverable of a library.*
- *Test cases are critical for optimizing a library.*
- *Designing a library is like designing other C++ code, only the stakes are higher.*
- *Most abstractions require no more than three layers of class derivation.*
- *The implementations of most abstractions require no more than three nested function calls.*

## CHAPTER 9

Optimize Searching and Sorting

There's a way to do it better—find it.

—Thomas A. Edison (1847–1931), American inventor and optimizer

C++ programs do a lot of searching. From programming language compilers to web browsers, from list controls to databases, many repeated activities have a search at the bottom of some inner loop. Searching comes up frequently on lists of hot functions in my experience. It is thus worthwhile to devote special attention to searching efficiently.

This chapter looks at searching in tables through the optimizer's eye. I use searching as an example of a general process that a developer can use to approach the optimization task, by breaking down an existing solution into its component algorithms and data structures, then looking at each of these for opportunities to improve performance. I also evaluate some specific search methods to demonstrate the optimization process.

Most C++ developers know that the standard library container `std::map` can be used for looking up values that are associated with an index number or alphanumeric key string. Such associations are called *key/value tables*. They create a *map* from *keys* to *values*, hence the name of the container. Developers who know `std::map` remember that its performance is good in a big-O sense. This chapter explores ways to optimize the basic map-based search.

Fewer developers know that the C++ standard library's `<algorithm>` header contains several iterator-based algorithms that can search sequence containers. These algorithms don't all have the same big-O efficiency, even under optimal conditions. The best algorithm for each situation isn't obvious, and the advice on the Internet doesn't always point to the optimal method. Searching for the best search algorithm is presented as another example of the optimization process.

Even developers who know their way around the standard library algorithms may not yet have heard that hash-table based containers have been added to C++11 (and have been available in Boost (*http://www.boost.org/*) for years). These unordered associative containers achieve excellent, average constant-time lookup efficiency, but they are not a panacea.

Key/Value Tables Using std::map and std::string

As an example, this section explores the performance of searching and sorting a very common kind of key/value table. The table's key type is a string of ASCII characters that can be initialized by a C++ string literal or held in a `std::string`.[1] This kind of table is typical of tables used to parse initialization profiles, command lines, XML files, database tables, and other applications requiring a limited set of keys. The table's value type can be as simple as an integer, or arbitrarily complex. The value type doesn't affect search performance, except that a really big value might reduce cache performance. In my experience, simple value types dominate anyway, so this table's value is a simple `unsigned`.

It's easy to build a table that maps `std::string` names to values using `std::map`. The table may be defined simply:

```
# include <string>
# include <map>
std::map<std::string, unsigned> table;
```

Developers using a C++11 compiler can use the list initializer syntax shown here to easily populate the table with entries:

```
std::map<std::string, unsigned> const table {
    { "alpha",   1 },   { "bravo",    2 },
    { "charlie", 3 },   { "delta",    4 },
    { "echo",    5 },   { "foxtrot", 6 },
    { "golf",    7 },   { "hotel",    8 },
    { "india",   9 },   { "juliet", 10 },
    { "kilo",   11 },   { "lima",    12 },
    { "mike",   13 },   { "november",14 },
    { "oscar",  15 },   { "papa",    16 },
    { "quebec", 17 },   { "romeo",   18 },
    { "sierra", 19 },   { "tango",   20 },
    { "uniform",21 },   { "victor",  22 },
    { "whiskey",23 },   { "x-ray",   24 },
```

---

1 Such a table might not meet the needs of Arabic- or Chinese-speaking developers. Meeting these needs is another subject about which whole books are written. It is my expectation that developers using wide character sets have already solved these problems. Some English-speaking developers still find them mysterious and distracting, so I am wishing that complexity away in this example.

```
            { "yankee", 25 },   { "zulu",   26 }
};
```

Otherwise, the developer must write code like the following to insert each element:

```
table["alpha"] = 1;
table["bravo"] = 2;
...
table["zulu"] = 26;
```

Values may be retrieved or tested simply:

```
unsigned val = table["echo"];
...
std::string key = "diamond";
if (table.find(key) != table.end())
    std::cout << "table contains " << key << std::endl;
```

Creating tables with `std::map` is an example of how the C++ standard library provides powerful abstractions that achieve reasonable big-O performance with minimal thought and typing effort. It's an instance of a general property of C++ mentioned in Chapter 1:

> *The mix of features in C++ provides a continuum of implementation choices ranging from hands-off automation and expressiveness on one hand, to increasingly fine control over performance on the other hand. It is this degree of choice that makes it possible to tune C++ programs to meet requirements for performance.*

Toolkit to Improve Search Performance

But what if a profiling run fingers a function containing a table lookup as one of the hottest functions in a program? For instance:

```
void HotFunction(std::string const& key) {
    ...
    auto it = table.find(key);
    if (it == table.end()) {
    //  activity when table item not found
        ...
    }
    else {
    //  activity when table item is found
        ...
    }
    ...
}
```

Can the developer do better than the simplest implementation? How do we find out?

An experienced developer's eye may of course immediately spot inefficiencies that can be tackled. He may know that an algorithm is suboptimal, or that a better data structure exists. I sometimes operate in this way, though the path is fraught with risk. It is better for the developer interested in optimization to proceed methodically:

- Measure performance of the existing implementation to obtain a baseline for comparison.
- Identify the abstract activity to be optimized.
- Decompose the activity to be optimized into its component algorithms and data structures.
- Change or replace algorithms and data structures that may not be optimal, and perform experiments to determine if the changes are effective.

If the activity being optimized is viewed as an abstraction, the optimization task is picking the abstraction's baseline implementation apart into its pieces and building up a more specialized abstraction with better performance.

I like to do this process on a whiteboard if possible, or in a text editor, or in an engineering notebook. The process is iterative. The longer you spend pulling the problem apart, the more parts you discover. *There are enough parts in most activities worth optimizing that human beings cannot reliably remember them all if they try to hold the whole thing in their heads. Paper has a better memory*, and a whiteboard or text editor is even better because it allows thoughts to be easily added and erased.

Make a Baseline Measurement

As mentioned in "Measure Baseline Performance and Set Goals" on page 35, it is important to measure the performance of the unoptimized code, to get a baseline measurement against which to test possible optimizations.

I wrote a test that looks up all 26 values in the table introduced in "Key/Value Tables Using std::map and std::string" on page 202, and also 27 values not in the table. I repeated these 53 lookups a million times to get a measurable duration. For maps of strings, this test ran for about 2,310 milliseconds.

Identify the Activity to Be Optimized

The next step is to identify the activity to be optimized, so that the activity can be decomposed into pieces that can more easily be searched for candidate optimizations.

The idea of "the activity to be optimized" is a matter of judgment on the developer's part. But there are a couple of clues. In this case, the developer can see that the baseline implementation is a `std::map` with `std::string` keys. A look at the hot code reveals a call to `std::map::find()`, a function that returns an iterator to the found entry, or to `end()`. Although `std::map` supports lookup, insertion, deletion, and iteration, the hot function is only doing a lookup. It may be necessary to look at other places in the code to see if other operations are performed on the table. Identifying where the table is constructed and destroyed is particularly interesting, because these activities may be time-consuming.

In this case, the activity to be optimized is reasonably obvious: looking up values in a key/value table implemented as a map with string keys. It is important to abstract from the baseline solution, however. The developer must not limit their investigation to only tables built from `std::map` and `std::string`.

There is a technique called "thinking backward and forward" for abstracting from a baseline implementation to a problem statement. The technique for thinking backward is to ask, "Why?" Why does the baseline implementation use a `std::map`, and not some other data structure? The answer is reasonably obvious: `std::map` facilitates looking up a value given a key. Why does the baseline implementation use `std::string`, as opposed to `int` or pointer-to-Foo? The answer is that the keys are strings of ASCII text. This analysis leads the developer to write a more abstract problem statement, *looking up values in a key/value table with text keys*. Notice the words *map* and *string* do not appear in this statement. This is a deliberate attempt to free the problem description from its baseline implementation.

Decompose the Activity to Be Optimized

The next step is to decompose the activity to be optimized into its component algorithms and data structures. The baseline solution (a map with string keys) can again be used as an example of the algorithms and data structures comprising the activity. However, the baseline solution represents one specific implementation of the activity, and the optimizing developer is seeking other possible implementations. That is why it is important to describe the algorithms and data structures in a general way that doesn't restrict thinking to the existing solution.

The activity to be optimized is *looking up values in a key/value table with text keys*. Decomposing this statement into its component algorithms and data structures and checking the result against the baseline implementation produces this list:

1. The table, a data structure containing the keys and associated values

2. The key, a data structure that contains text

3. An algorithm to compare keys

4. An algorithm to search the table data structure to see if a specific key is present, and if so get the associated value

5. An algorithm to construct the table, or insert keys into the table

How did I know I needed these parts? Mostly it came from looking at the definition of the baseline solution's data structure, `std::map`:

1. In the baseline solution, the table is a `std::map`.

2. In the baseline solution, the keys are instances of `std::string`.

3. Partly this is logic, but also `std::map`'s template definition provides a defaultable parameter for specifying a key comparison function.

4. The hot function contains a call to `std::map::find()` rather than using `operator[]`.

5. This comes from knowledge that the map must be constructed and destroyed. General knowledge about `std::map` informs me that it is implemented as a balanced binary tree. The map is thus a linked data structure that must be constructed node by node, so there must be an insertion algorithm.

The last item, the algorithm for (and thus the time cost of) building and destroying tables, is often overlooked. This cost can be significant. Even if the cost is small compared to the time consumed doing table lookups, if the table has static storage duration (see "Storage Duration of Variables" on page 108) the initialization cost may be added to all other initialization taking place at startup (see "Remove Code from Startup and Shutdown" on page 313). The program becomes unresponsive if there are too many initializations. If the table has automatic storage duration, it may be initialized multiple times during the program run, making the startup cost more significant. Luckily, there are key/value table implementations with low or no cost to create and destroy.

Change or Replace Algorithms and Data Structures

In this step, the developer can think forward, asking, "How?" How, and in what different ways, can the program look up values in a key/value table with text keys? The developer looks for algorithms in the baseline solution that are less than optimal, and looks for costly behaviors provided by the data structures that are not necessary for the particular activity being optimized, and can thus be removed or simplified. Then the developer performs experiments to see whether any changes improve performance.

The activity to be optimized offers the following opportunities:

- The table data structure may be changed or made more efficient. Some choices of table data structure constrain the choice of search and insertion algorithm. Choice of table data structure may also affect performance if the data structure contains dynamic variables that require calls to the memory manager.

- The key data structure may be changed or made more efficient.

- The comparison algorithm may be changed or made more efficient.

- The search algorithm may be changed or made more efficient, though it may be constrained by the choice of table data structure.

- The insertion algorithm, and also when and how to construct and destroy the data structure, may be changed or made more efficient.

Here are some observations that are relevant:

- `std::map` is implemented as a balanced binary tree. The search algorithm in a balanced binary tree is O($log_2 n$). The biggest performance gain would likely result if `std::map` could be replaced by a data structure that facilitates lookup at a lower time cost.

- A quick look at the definition of `std::map` shows that the operations defined on maps are inserting items into the map, looking up items in the map, deleting items from the map, and traversing the items in the map. To facilitate this dynamism, `std::map` is a node-based data structure. The consequence is that `std::map` frequently calls into the memory manager during construction, and has poor cache locality. In the activity to be optimized, items are only inserted into the table during its construction, and never deleted until the table is. A less dynamic data structure might improve performance by invoking the allocator less, and having better cache locality.

- The functionality actually needed for a key data structure is to contain the characters, and to compare two keys. `std::string` does a bunch of additional stuff beyond what is needed for a table key. Strings maintain a dynamically allocated buffer so they can be modified and be made longer or shorter, but the key/value table does not modify keys. Furthermore, looking up a literal string causes an expensive conversion to `std::string` that might not be necessary if the keys were stored differently.

- `std::string` instances are designed to act as *values*. `std::string` defines all six comparison operators so that strings can be compared for equality or put into order. `std::map` is designed to work by default with value-like key types that implement the comparison operators. A data structure that does not define its own comparison operator can be used with `std::map`, by providing a comparison function as a template argument.

- The C++11-style list initialization shown previously for maps with string keys resembles a C-style static aggregate initializer, but it is not one. The initializer invokes executable code that invokes the memory allocator to create a `std::string` from each string literal, then calls `insert()` to add each item into the map, which invokes the allocator again to allocate a new node in the map's balanced tree data structure. The advantage of this initializer is that the resulting table is `const`. However, the runtime cost is about the same as that of building up a map the pre-C++11 way, by inserting one value at a time. A data structure that could be constructed using a real C-style aggregate initializer would have zero runtime cost to construct and destroy.

Using the Optimization Process on Custom Abstractions

In the case of maps with string keys, the developer is fortunate. Many things about `std::map` can be programmed. The key type can be set. The key type's comparison algorithm can be modified. The way the map allocates nodes can be programmed. Furthermore, there are options beyond `std::map` that allow the data structure and search algorithm to be improved, all within the C++ standard library. This, in a nutshell, is why C++ can be tuned for performance so effectively. The next few sections take the reader through this process.

The deliberate process outlined here can be used to optimize non–standard library abstractions too, but it may require more work. `std::map` and `std::string` are well-defined and well-documented data structures. Excellent resources on the Web reveal what operations they support, and how they are implemented. For a custom-built abstraction, if the abstraction was designed thoughtfully, its header file tells the developer what operations are provided. Comments or well-designed code tells what algorithm is in use, and how frequently the memory manager is called.

If the code is a mess, or if the interface is poorly designed and the code is spread across many files, then I have bad news and good news. The bad news is that the optimization process outlined here offers no specific help for the developer. All I have are platitudes, like "You knew the job was dangerous when you took it," and "That's why you make the big bucks." The good news is that the more horrible the code is, the more likely it contains opportunities for optimization that will reward the developer for wading in.

Optimize Search Using std::map

The optimizing developer can improve performance by changing the data structure representing keys, and therefore the algorithm for comparing keys, while leaving the table data structure alone.

Use Fixed-Size Character Array Keys with std::map

As noted in Chapter 4, a developer may want to avoid the costs of using `std::string` keys in a really hot key/value table. Allocation dominates the cost of creating the table. The developer can cut this cost in half by using a key type that does not dynamically allocate storage. Furthermore, if the table uses `std::string` keys, and the developer wants to look up entries given by C-style string literals, as in

```
unsigned val = table["zulu"];
```

every lookup converts the char* string literal to a std::string, costing the allocation of more memory that is then immediately destroyed.

If the maximum size of a key is not too long, one solution is to make the key type some class type that contains a char array big enough to hold the biggest key. It isn't possible to use an array directly, like this:

```
std::map<char[10],unsigned> table
```

because C++ arrays don't have built-in comparison operators.

Here is the definition of a simple fixed-size character array template class called charbuf:

```
template <unsigned N=10, typename T=char> struct charbuf {
    charbuf();
    charbuf(charbuf const& cb);
    charbuf(T const* p);
    charbuf& operator=(charbuf const& rhs);
    charbuf& operator=(T const* rhs);

    bool operator==(charbuf const& that) const;
    bool operator<(charbuf const& that) const;

private:
    T data_[N];
};
```

charbuf is extremely simple. It can be initialized with or assigned a C-style null-terminated string. It can be compared to another charbuf. Because the constructor charbuf(T const*) is not explicit, it can also be compared to a null-terminated string by type conversion. Its size is fixed at compile time. It does not use dynamic memory at all.

Out of the box, C++ does not know how to compare two class instances or put them in order. The developer must define any relational operators she intends to use. The C++ standard library generally uses only operator== and operator<. The other four operators can be synthesized from these two. The operators may be defined as free functions:

```
template <unsigned N=10, typename T=char>
    bool operator<(charbuf<N,T> const& cb1, charbuf<N,T> const& cb2);
```

But it is easier and better C++ style to define an operator< inside charbuf, where it has access to charbuf's implementation.

charbuf requires the programmer to think. It can handle only strings that fit in its fixed-size internal buffer, counting the trailing zero byte. It is therefore not guaranteed to be safe, like std::string. Verifying that all potential keys fit in the charbuf is an example of pushing computation out of run time all the way to design time. It is also an example of a safety compromise that may be required to improve performance. Only an individual design team has the perspective to say whether the benefits outweigh the risks. Pundits making blanket assertions are not credible.

I ran the same test of 53 names a million times using a `std::map` with `charbuf` keys. The test ran in 1,331 milliseconds. This is about twice as fast as the version using `std::string`.

Use C-Style String Keys with std::map

Sometimes the program has access to long-lived C-style null-terminated character strings, whose `char*` pointers can be used for the keys in a `std::map`. For instance, the table may be constructed using C++ string literals. The program can avoid the cost of constructing and destroying `std::string` instances by using the `char*`s directly.

There is a problem with using `char*` as the key type, though. `std::map` puts key/value pairs into its internal data structure using an ordering relation on the key type. By default, this relation evaluates the expression `key1 < key2`. `std::string` defines an `operator<` to compare the character strings. `char*` also defines an `operator<`, but the operator compares the pointers, not the pointed-to strings.

`std::map` allows the developer to solve this problem by providing a nondefault comparison algorithm. This is an example of the fine control that C++ offers over the behavior of its standard containers. The comparison algorithm is provided by the third template parameter of `std::map`. The default value for the comparison algorithm is the function object `std::less<Key>`. `std::less` defines a member function, `bool operator()(Key const& k1, Key const& k2)`, which compares two keys by returning the result of the expression `key1 < key2`.

The program could in principle specialize `std::less` for `char*`. However, this specialization would be visible for at least the whole file, possibly causing unexpected behavior of some other part of the program.

Instead of a function object, the program can provide a C-style free function to perform the comparison, as shown in Example 9-1. The function's signature becomes the third argument to the map declaration, and the map is initialized with a pointer to the function.

Example 9-1. Map with C-style char* keys, free function as comparison function

```
bool less_free(char const* p1, char const* p2) {
    return strcmp(p1,p2)<0;
}
```

...

```
std::map<char const*,
         unsigned,
         bool(*)(char const*,char const*)> table(less_free);
```

A test using this variation ran for 1,450 milliseconds, a significant improvement over the version using `std::string` keys.

The program could also create a new function object to encapsulate the comparison. In Example 9-2, `less_for_c_strings` is the name of a class type, so it serves as the type argument, and no pointer is needed.

Example 9-2. Map with char* keys, function object as comparison function

```
struct less_for_c_strings {
    bool operator()(char const* p1, char const* p2) {
        return strcmp(p1,p2)<0;
    }
};
```

   ...

```
std::map<char const*,
         unsigned,
         less_for_c_strings> table;
```

This variation ran the test in 820 milliseconds. This is almost three times as fast as the original version, and nearly twice as fast as the `char*`-and-free-function version.

In C++11, another way to provide a `char*` comparison function for `std::map` is to define a lambda and pass it to the map constructor. Lambdas are convenient because they can be defined locally and have compact syntax. This approach is illustrated in Example 9-3.

Example 9-3. Map with char* keys, lambda as comparison function

```
auto comp = [](char const* p1, char const* p2) {
    return strcmp(p1,p2)<0;
};
std::map<char const*,
         unsigned,
         decltype(comp)> table(comp);
```

Note in this example the use of the C++11 `decltype` keyword. The third argument to the map is a type. The name `comp` is a variable, and `decltype(comp)` is the type of that variable. The type of a lambda doesn't have a name, and each lambda's type is unique, so `decltype` is the only way to get the lambda's type.

In the preceding example, the lambda behaves like a function object containing an operator(), so this mechanism has the same measured performance as the previous one, although the lambda must be passed as a constructor argument to the map.

The best time for the null-terminated string table was about three times faster than the original string version, and 55% faster than the fixed-size array version.

C++ Versus the Visual Studio Compiler

Visual Studio 2010 and Visual Studio 2015 compiled Example 9-3 correctly, but Visual Studio 2012 and 2013 produced an error message due to a reported bug in Visual Studio's standard library implementation.

It is an interesting C++ factoid that a lambda with no capture can *decay* to a function pointer. For users who really like lambda syntax, it is possible to use a lambda even on the Visual Studio 2012 and 2013 compilers. As the third constructor argument to the map, use the signature of the function pointer to which the lambda decays:

```
auto comp = [](char const* p1, char const* p2) {
    return strcmp(p1, p2)<0;
};
std::map<char const*,
         unsigned,
         bool(*)(char const*, char const*)> kvmap(comp);
```

In this case, the performance becomes that of std::map with a free function pointer, which is slower than its performance with a function object.

As the evolving C++ standard gradually teaches C++ compilers to do more and more type deduction, lambdas are going to become more interesting. As of early 2016, however, there is not much to recommend them over function objects.

Using Map's Cousin std::set When the Key Is in the Value

Some programmers find it natural to define a data structure containing both a key and other data serving as the key's value. Indeed, std::map internally declares a struct that combines the key and value as if it was defined as follows:

```
template <typename KeyType, typename ValueType> struct value_type {
    KeyType const first;
    ValueType second;
// ... constructors and assignment operators
};
```

If the program defines such a data structure, it can't be used directly in a std::map. std::map demands that the key and value be defined separately for pragmatic reasons. The key must be constant, because changing the key could make the whole map data structure invalid. Also, specifying the key lets the map know how to access it.

`std::map` has a cousin, `std::set`, that facilitates the use of data structures containing their own keys. This type uses a comparison function that, by default, compares two whole elements using `std::less`. Thus, to use `std::set` and a user-defined struct that contains its own key, the developer must specialize `std::less` for the user-defined struct, specify `operator<` for the user-defined struct, or provide a nondefault comparison object. There is nothing to recommend any of these methods over the other. It is a style preference.

I mention this now because when I describe using a sequence container for a key/value table, it will also be necessary either to define a comparison operator for the item data structure or to specify a comparison function when the search algorithm is invoked.

Optimize Search Using the <algorithm> Header

In the previous section, I explored improving performance by changing the data structure representing keys, and therefore the algorithm for comparing keys. In this section, I explore changes to the search algorithm and table data structure.

In addition to data structures like `std::string` and `std::map`, the C++ standard library provides a collection of algorithms, including algorithms for searching and sorting. Standard library algorithms take *iterators* as arguments. Iterators abstract the behavior of pointers, separating the traversal of values from the data structure that contains those values. Standard library algorithms are specified in terms of the abstract behavior of their iterator arguments, rather than in terms of some concrete data structure. Iterator-based algorithms can be applied within many kinds of data structures, as long as the iterators over these data structures have the required properties.

The standard library search algorithms take two iterators: one pointing to the beginning of the sequence of items to be searched, and one to the end (the item just past the last item) of the sequence to be searched. All take a key to be searched for, and optionally take a comparison function. The algorithms differ in what they return, and whether the comparison function must define an ordering relationship among the keys or just an equality test.

The part of the data structure to be searched can be described as the *range [first, last)*, where the square bracket to the left of *first* means that *first* is included in the interval, and the close parenthesis after *last* means that *last* is not included. The range notation sees much use in descriptions of standard library algorithms.

Some iterator-based search methods implement divide-and-conquer algorithms. These algorithms rely on a particular property of some iterators—the ability to compute the *distance*, or number of elements, between two iterators—and in this way achieve their better-than-linear big-O behavior. The distance between two iterators can always be computed by incrementing one iterator until it compares equal to the second, but this results in a time cost of O(n) to compute the distance. A special property of *random-access iterators* is that the distance can be computed in constant time.

The sequence containers that provide random-access iterators are C-style arrays, `std::string`, `std::vector`, and `std::deque`. Divide-and-conquer algorithms *can* be applied to `std::list`, but their time cost will be O(n), not O($log_2 n$), because of the higher cost to compute the distance on bidirectional iterators.

The names *string* and *map* are evocative of their function, and may lead the novice user directly to a solution using these data types. Unfortunately, not all algorithms for iterator-based search have very evocative names. They are also very general, so that choosing the right one makes a considerable difference in performance, although they have the same big-O time cost.

Key/Value Table for Search in Sequence Containers

There are several reasons to choose a sequence container implementation for a key/value table over using `std::map` or its cousin `std::set`. Sequence containers consume less memory than maps. They can also be less expensive to set up. One very useful property of standard library algorithms is that they can iterate over ordinary arrays of any type. They can thus perform efficient lookups in statically initialized arrays of structs. This eliminates all costs of setting up and destroying the tables. Furthermore, coding standards, such as MISRA C++ (*http://www.misra-cpp.com/*), forbid or limit the use of dynamically allocated data structures. It is reassuring to have an efficient solution for searching in these environments.

The examples in this section make use of the following `struct` definition:

```
struct kv { // (key,value) pairs
    char const* key;
    unsigned    value; // can be anything
};
```

A static array of these key/value pairs is defined as follows:

```
kv names[] = {// in alphabetical order
    { "alpha",   1 },  { "bravo",     2 },
    { "charlie", 3 },  { "delta",     4 },
    { "echo",    5 },  { "foxtrot",   6 },
    { "golf",    7 },  { "hotel",     8 },
    { "india",   9 },  { "juliet",   10 },
    { "kilo",   11 },  { "lima",     12 },
    { "mike",   13 },  { "november",14 },
    { "oscar",  15 },  { "papa",     16 },
    { "quebec", 17 },  { "romeo",    18 },
    { "sierra", 19 },  { "tango",    20 },
    { "uniform",21 },  { "victor",   22 },
    { "whiskey",23 },  { "x-ray",    24 },
```

```
        { "yankee", 25 },   { "zulu",    26 }
};
```

The initializer for the names array is a static aggregate initializer. The C++ compiler creates initialized data for C-style structs at compile time. There is zero runtime cost to create such arrays.

The various algorithms are evaluated by searching in this small table for each of its 26 keys, and for 27 invalid strings chosen to fall between the values in the table. The 53 searches are then repeated a million times. This is the same test performed for std::map-based containers in the previous section.

Standard library container classes provide member functions begin() and end() so the program can obtain an iterator range to search. C-style arrays are more primitive, and offer no such functions. However, a little template magic provides typesafe template functions for this purpose. Since they take an array type as an argument, the array does not decay to a pointer as it normally would:

```
//  get size and begin/end from a C-style array
template <typename T, int N> size_t size(T (&a)[N]) {
    return N;
}
template <typename T, int N> T* begin(T (&a)[N]) {
    return &a[0];
}
template <typename T, int N> T* end(T (&a)[N]) {
    return &a[N];
}
```

In C++11, more sophisticated definitions for begin() and end() using the same template magic can be found in the namespace std in the <iterator> header. This header is included any time a standard library container class header is included. Visual Studio 2010 provides these definitions in anticipation of the standard. Unfortunately, size() is not scheduled for standardization until C++14, and it does not appear in Visual Studio 2010, though a simple equivalent is easy enough to provide.

std::find(): Obvious Name, O(n) Time Cost

The standard library <algorithm> header defines a template function find() as follows:

```
template <class It, class T> It find(It first, It last, const T& key)
```

The find() algorithm is a simple linear search. Linear search is the most general kind of search. It doesn't require the searched data to be ordered in any way. It only requires the keys to be comparable for equality.

find() returns an iterator to the first entry in a sequence container that compares equal to key. The iterator arguments first and last delimit the range to be searched, with `last` pointing to the first element after the end of the data to be searched. The types of `first` and `last`, given by the template parameter `It`, depend on the kind of data structure to be traversed by `find()`. An example is given in Example 9-4.

Example 9-4. Linear search using std::find()

```
kv* result=std::find(std::begin(names), std::end(names), key);
```

In this invocation, `names` is the name of the array to be searched. `key` is a value to be compared to each kv entry. To do the comparison, a specific function comparing keys must be defined in the scope where `find()` is instantiated. This function tells `std::find()` everything it needs to know to do the comparison. C++ allows the equality operator `bool operator==(v1,v2)` to be overloaded for values of arbitrary pairs of types. If `key` is a pointer to `char`, the required function is:

```
bool operator==(kv const& n1, char const* key) {
    return strcmp(n1.key, key) == 0;
}
```

A timing experiment using `std::find()` and a set of keys both in and not in the sample 26-element table took 1,425 milliseconds.

A variation of `find()` called `find_if()` takes the comparison function as a fourth argument. Instead of defining `operator==()` in the scope of `find()`, the developer can write it as a lambda. The lambda takes a single argument, the table element being compared against. So, the lambda must capture the key value from the environment.

std::binary_search(): Does Not Return Values

Binary search is a divide-and-conquer strategy that is so generally useful that the C++ standard library provides several different algorithms that use it. But for some reason, the evocative name `binary_search` was used for an algorithm that is not particularly useful for looking up values.

The standard library algorithm `binary_search()` returns a `bool` indicating whether a key is in a sorted table. Strangely enough, there is no related function to return the matching table element. Thus, neither of the two most obvious names, `find` and `binary_search`, provide the solution we are seeking.

If the program just wants to know if an item is in the table, instead of finding its value, `std::binary_search()` performed the timing test in 972 milliseconds.

Binary Search Using std::equal_range()

If the sequence container is sorted, the developer can piece together an efficient searching function from the bits and pieces provided by the C++ standard library.

Unfortunately, these pieces have names that don't evoke the obvious notion of a binary search.

The C++ standard library's `<algorithm>` header contains the template function `std::equal_range()`, defined as:

```
template <class ForwardIt, class T>
    std::pair<ForwardIt,ForwardIt>
        equal_range(ForwardIt first, ForwardIt last, const T& value);
```

`equal_range()` returns a pair of iterators delimiting a subsequence of the sorted sequence [`first, last`) that contains entries equal to `value`. If no entries are equal to `value`, `equal_range()` returns a pair of iterators that point to the same value, indicating an empty range. If the returned iterators are unequal, there is at least one entry that matched `key`. By construction, in the example problem there can be no more than one match, and the first iterator points to it. Example 9-5 sets `result` to the matching table entry, or to the end of the table.

Example 9-5. Binary search using std::equal_range()

```
auto res = std::equal_range(std::begin(names),
                            std::end(names),
                            key);
kv* result = (res.first == res.second)
           ? std::end(names)
           : res.first;
```

An experiment to test the performance of `equal_range()` on the sample table ran for 1,810 milliseconds. This is actually worse than the linear search for the same-sized table, which is pretty shocking. However, we'll see that `equal_range()` was not the best choice for a binary search function.

Binary Search Using std::lower_bound()

Although `equal_range()` promises O(*log₂ n*) time cost, it actually contains more machinery than is necessary for table lookup. A possible implementation of `equal_range()` might look like this:

```
template <class It, class T>
    std::pair<It,It>
        equal_range(It first, It last, const T& value) {
    return std::make_pair(std::lower_bound(first, last, value),
                          std::upper_bound(first, last, value));
}
```

`upper_bound()` makes a second divide-and-conquer pass through the table to find the end of the returned range, because `equal_range()` is general enough to work with sorted sequences containing more than one value with the same key. But by construction, in the example table the range will always contain either one entry or none. The search can be performed using lower_bound() and one additional comparison, as shown in Example 9-6.

Example 9-6. Binary search using std::lower_bound()

```
kv* result = std::lower_bound(std::begin(names),
                              std::end(names),
                              key);
if (result != std::end(names) && key < *result.key)
    result = std::end(names);
```

In this example, std::lower_bound() returns an iterator to the first entry in the table whose key is not less than key. This iterator points to the end of the table if all the entries are less than key. It may point to an entry that is greater than key. The final if statement sets result to the end of the table if either of these conditions is true. Otherwise, result points to the entry whose key is equal to key.

A version of the experiment using this search took 973 milliseconds, which is a satisfying 86% faster than std::equal_range(). This is to be expected because it is doing about half the work.

A search using std::lower_bound has performance that is competitive with the best implementation using std::map, and has the additional advantage of zero cost to construct or destroy the static table. The function std::binary_search() also runs the experiment in 973 milliseconds, albeit with only the Boolean result. It seems as if this is as far as we can go using the C++ standard library algorithms.

Handcoded Binary Search

It is possible to handcode a binary search taking the same arguments as the standard library functions. The standard library algorithms all use a single ordering function, operator<(), so that only the minimum interface need be provided. Because these functions eventually have to determine if a key matches an entry, they do an extra comparison at the end, noting that a == b can be defined as !(a < b) && !(b < a).

The original table occupies a range of consecutive values denoted as *[start, end)*. At each step in the search, the function (shown in Example 9-7) computes the midpoint of the range and compares key against the entry at the midpoint. This effectively partitions the range into two halves, *[start, mid+1)* and *[mid+1, stop)*.

Example 9-7. Handcoded binary search using "<" for comparison

```
kv* find_binary_lessthan(kv* start, kv* end, char const* key) {
    kv* stop = end;
    while (start < stop) {
```

```
        auto mid = start + (stop-start)/2;
        if (*mid < key) {// search right half [mid+1,stop)
            start = mid + 1;
        }
        else {// search left half [start,mid)
            stop = mid;
        }
    }
    return (start == end || key < *start) ? end : start;
}
```

A timing run for this binary search took 968 milliseconds. This is approximately the same as the earlier version based on `std::lower_bound()`.

Handcoded Binary Search using strcmp()

It is possible to peel the onion yet further, noting that `operator<()` is defined in terms of `strcmp()`. Like `operator<()`, `strcmp()` compares two keys. But `strcmp()` produces more information: an `int` result that is less than, equal to, or greater than zero, as the first key is less than, equal to, or greater than the second key. The resulting code, as shown in Example 9-8, looks like what you might write in C.

During each iteration of the `while` loop, the sequence to search is given by the interval *[start,stop)*. At each step `mid` is set to the midpoint of the sequence to be searched. The value returned by `strcmp()` divides the sequence into *three* parts instead of two: *[start,mid)*, *[mid,mid+1)*, and *[mid+1,stop)*. If `mid->key` is greater than `key`, we know that key must be in the left part of the sequence, before `mid`. If `mid->key` is less than `key`, `key` must be in the right part of the sequence beginning with `mid+1`. Otherwise, `mid->key` equals `key`, and the loop terminates. The `if`/`else` logic does the more frequently occurring comparisons first to improve performance.

Example 9-8. Handcoded binary search using strcmp()

```
kv* find_binary_3(kv* start, kv* end, char const* key) {
    auto stop = end;
    while (start < stop) {
        auto mid = start + (stop-start)/2;
        auto rc = strcmp(mid->key, key);
        if (rc > 0) {
            stop = mid;
        }
        else if (rc < 0) {
            start = mid + 1;
        }
        else {
            return mid;
        }
    }
```

```
     return end;
}
```

A timing run for this version of the binary search took 771 milliseconds. This is nearly 26% faster than the best standard library–based search.

Optimize Search in Hashed Key/Value Tables

The previous section examined changes to the algorithm for a particular table data structure that was very efficient to set up. In this section, I examine another table data structure and algorithm: that of hash tables.

The idea of a hash table is that the key, whatever its type, can be fed to a *hash function* that reduces the key to an integer *hash*. The hash in turn becomes an array index that leads directly to a table entry. If the table entry then matches the key, the search is a success. If the hash always leads directly to the table entry, the hash table allows access in constant time. The only cost is the cost of producing the hash. Like linear search, hashing does not assume any ordering relationship among the keys, but requires only a means to compare keys for equality.

The complicated part of implementing a hash table is finding an efficient hash function. A 10-letter string contains many more bits than a 32-bit integer. More than one string can thus hash to the same table index. Some mechanism must be provided to resolve such *collisions*. Each entry in the hash table might be the head of a list of entries that hash to that index. Alternately, adjacent indexes might be searched for the matching entry until an empty index is found.

Another problem is that the hash function may not produce a particular index for any of the valid keys in the table, leaving an unused location in the hash table. This makes a hash table potentially larger than a sorted array of the same entries.

A poor hash function or an unlucky set of keys can cause many keys to hash to the same index. Then the performance of the hash table degrades to $O(n)$, making it no better than a linear search.

A good hash function produces array indexes that are not highly correlated to the bits of the key. Random number generators and cryptographic encoders are good for this goal. But if the hash function is costly to compute, there may be no advantage over a binary search unless the table is very large.

Hunting better hash functions has been a pastime of computer scientists for many years. A Q&A on Stack Exchange (*http://bit.ly/se-hash*) provides performance data and reference links for several popular hash functions. The developer tuning hash table code should be aware that these waters have been heavily fished. There are no big performance improvements to be found here.

C++ defines a standard hash function object called `std::hash`. `std::hash` is a template with specializations for integers, floating-point data, pointers, and `std::string`. The unspecialized definition of `std::hash`, which is also used for pointers, converts the hashed type to a `size_t`, and then randomizes the bits of this value.

Hashing with a std::unordered_map

In C++11, the standard header `<unordered_map>` provides a hash table. Visual Studio 2010 anticipated the standard and provided this header as well. `std::unordered_map` can't be used with the handcoded static table used in previous examples, though. The entries must be inserted into the hash table, adding cost at startup. The code for creating a hash table using `std::unordered_map` and inserting entries is shown in Example 9-9.

Example 9-9. Initializing a hash table

```
std::unordered_map<std::string, unsigned> table;
for (auto it = names; it != names+namesize; ++it)
    table[it->key] = it->value;
```

The default hash function used by `std::unordered_map` is the template function object `std::hash`. This template has a specialization for `std::string`, so no hash function need be explicitly provided.

After entries are installed in the table, a lookup can be performed:

```
auto it = table.find(key);
```

`it` is an iterator to the table that points either to a valid entry or to `table.end()`.

`std::unordered_map` with `std::string` keys uses all the default values of the map's template to achieve simplicity and reasonable performance. An experiment to measure the performance of `std::unordered_map` took 1,725 milliseconds, not counting time to construct the table. This is 56% faster than `std::map` with string keys, but hardly a world-beating result. Given the hype about hashing being a performance win, this result was surprising and disappointing.

Hashing with Fixed Character Array Keys

A version of the simple fixed character array template class `charbuf` from section "Use Fixed-Size Character Array Keys with std::map" on page 208 can be used with hash tables. The following template extends `charbuf` with a means to hash the character string and an `operator==` for comparing keys if there is a collision:

```
template <unsigned N=10, typename T=char> struct charbuf {
    charbuf();
    charbuf(charbuf const& cb);
```

```
    charbuf(T const* p);
    charbuf& operator=(charbuf const& rhs);
    charbuf& operator=(T const* rhs);

    operator size_t() const;

    bool operator==(charbuf const& that) const;
    bool operator<(charbuf const& that) const;
private:
    T data_[N];
};
```

The hash function is `operator size_t()`. This is a little unintuitive, and also a little unclean. It happens that the default specialization for `std::hash()` casts the argument to a `size_t`. For pointers, this normally just casts the bits of the pointer, but with a `charbuf&` what happens is that `charbuf::operator size_t()` is called, returning the hash as a `size_t`. Of course, with `operator size_t()` hijacked for this use, it isn't available to return the size of a `charbuf`. The expression `sizeof(charbuf)` will return very misleading data. The declaration of a hash table using `charbuf` looks like this:

```
std::unordered_map<charbuf<>, unsigned> table;
```

Performance of this hash table was disappointing. It ran the test of 53 keywords in 2,277 milliseconds, worse even than the hash table or a map with `std::string`.

Hashing with Null-Terminated String Keys

These things must be done caaaaarefully, or it hurts the spell.

—The Wicked Witch of the West (Margaret Hamilton), *The Wizard of Oz*, 1939,
musing about how to remove the ruby slippers from Dorothy's feet

If the hash table can be initialized with long-lived null-terminated strings, such as C++ string literals, a hash-based key/value table can be constructed with pointers to these strings. There is performance gold to be mined by making `std::unordered_map` work with `char*` keys. But it isn't trivial.

The full definition of `std::unordered_map` is:

```
template<
    typename Key,
    typename Value,
    typename Hash = std::hash<Key>,
    typename KeyEqual = std::equal_to<Key>,
    typename Allocator = std::allocator<std::pair<const Key, Value>>
> class unordered_map;
```

`Hash` is a function object or function pointer type declaration for the function that hashes a `Key`. `KeyEqual` is a function object or function pointer type declaration for the function that compares two instances of Key for equality to resolve hash collisions.

When Key is a pointer, Hash is well defined. The program compiles without errors. It may even appear to run. (My initial tests ran, producing an excellent test run time and a false sense of accomplishment.) But the program is not correct. What happens is that std::hash produces a hash of the pointer values, rather than a hash of the pointed-to strings. If, for instance, a test program loads the table from an array of strings, then tests that each string can be found, the pointers to the test keys are the same as the pointers to the keys that initialized the table, and it appears to work. Test the table with a duplicate string taken from user input, however, and the test claims that the string is not in the table because the pointer to the test string is not the same as the pointer to the key that initialized the table.

This problem can be solved by providing a nondefault hash function in place of the default value for the third argument to the template. Just as for a map, this hash function can be a function object, lambda declaration, or free function pointer:

```
struct hash_c_string {
    void hash_combine(size_t& seed, T const& v) {
        seed ^= v + 0x9e3779b9 + (seed << 6) + (seed >> 2);
    }

    std::size_t operator() (char const* p) const {
        size_t hash = 0;
        for (; *p; ++p)
            hash_combine(hash, *p);
        return hash;
    }
};

// this solution is incomplete -- see below
std::unordered_map<char const*, unsigned, hash_c_string> table;
```

I have taken the hash function from Boost. It is in standard library implementations if they conform to C++14 or later. Alas, Visual Studio 2010 did not provide this function.

Careful testing reveals that this declaration is still not correct, although it compiles without error and produces a program that may work for some small tables. The problem is with KeyEqual, the fourth argument of the std::unordered_map template. The default value of this argument is std::equal_to, a function object that applies operator== to its two operands. operator== is defined for pointers, but it compares the pointers for their order in the computer's memory space, rather than the pointed-to strings.

The solution, of course, is another nondefault function object for the KeyEqual template parameter. The complete solution is shown in Example 9-10.

Example 9-10. std::unordered_map with null-terminated string keys

```
struct hash_c_string {
    void hash_combine(size_t& seed, T const& v) {
        seed ^= v + 0x9e3779b9 + (seed << 6) + (seed >> 2);
    }

    std::size_t operator() (char const* p) const {
        size_t hash = 0;
        for (; *p; ++p)
            hash_combine(hash, *p);
        return hash;
    }
};

struct comp_c_string {
    bool operator()(char const* p1, char const* p2) const {
        return strcmp(p1,p2) == 0;
    }
};

std::unordered_map<
    char const*,
    unsigned,
    hash_c_string,
    comp_c_string
> table;
```

This version of the key/value table, using `std::unordered_map` and `char*` keys, ran the test in 993 milliseconds. This is 73% faster than the hash table based on `std::string`. But it's a paultry 9% faster than the best implementation based on `std::map` and `char*` keys. And it is slower than the binary-search algorithm on a simple static array of key/value entries using `std::lower_bound`. This is *not* what years of hype led me to expect. (In "std::unordered_map and std::unordered_multi-map" on page 256, we'll see that larger hash tables have a greater advantage over binary search–based search algorithms.)

Hashing with a Custom Hash Table

A hash function for use with unknown keys must be very general. If the keys are known in advance, as they are in the example table, a very simple hash function may suffice.

A hash that creates a table in which there are no collisions for a given set of keys is called a *perfect hash*. A hash that creates a table with no unused spaces is called a *minimal hash*. The Holy Grail of hash functions is a *minimal perfect hash*, creating a table with no collisions and no empty spaces. Perfect hashes for reasonably short sets of keywords are easy to create, and perfect minimal hashes are only a little more difficult. The first letter (or first couple of letters), the sum of the letters, and the length of the key are all example hash functions that might be tried.

In the example table for this section, the 26 valid entries each begin with a different letter and they are sorted, so a hash based on the first letter is a perfect minimal hash. It doesn't matter what invalid keys hash to. They are compared against the valid key at their hash, and the comparison fails.

Example 9-11 shows a very simple custom hash table implemented to resemble std::unordered_map.

Example 9-11. Minimal perfect hash table based on the example table

```
unsigned hash(char const* key) {
    if (key[0] < 'a' || key[0] > 'z')
        return 0;
    return (key[0]-'a');
}

kv* find_hash(kv* first, kv* last, char const* key) {
    unsigned i = hash(key);
    return strcmp(first[i].key, key) ? last : first + i;
}
```

hash() maps the first letter of key to one of the 26 table entries, hence the mod 26. This is defensive programming to prevent accessing undefined storage in case the key was something like "@#$%".

An experiment to test find_hash() ran in 253 milliseconds. This result is stunning.

Although the simple hash function that worked for the sample table was particularly fortunate, the table was not contrived to achieve this result. There is often a simple function that is a minimal perfect hash. There are papers on the Internet discussing various methods to automatically generate perfect minimal hash functions for small keyword sets. The GNU Project (among others) has built a command-line tool called gperf (*http://www.gnu.org/software/gperf/*) for producing a perfect hash function that is often also minimal.

Stepanov's Abstraction Penalty

The experiment I used for searches looked up all 26 valid table entries and 27 invalid table entries. This creates a kind of average performance. Linear search looked relatively better on tests consisting only of keys in the table, because linear search terminates as soon as it finds a matching entry. Binary searches make about the same number of comparisons whether they find the key in the table or not.

Table 9-1 summarizes the results of the search experiments.

Table 9-1. *Summary of search performance experiments*

	VS2010 release, i7, 1m iterations	% improvement vs. previous	% improvement vs. category
map<string>	2,307 ms		
map<char*> free function	1,453 ms	59%	59%
map<char*> function object	820 ms	77%	181%
map<char*> lambda	820 ms	0%	181%
std::find()	1,425 ms		
std::equal_range()	1,806 ms		
std::lower_bound	973 ms	53%	86%
find_binary_3way()	771 ms	26%	134%
std::unordered_map()	509 ms		
find_hash()	195 ms	161%	161%

As expected, binary search was faster than linear search, and hashing was faster than binary search.

The C++ standard library provides a bunch of ready-to-use, debugged algorithms and data structures that are useful in many situations. The standard defines their worst-case time cost in big-O terms to demonstrate that they are widely applicable.

But there is a cost for using the extremely powerful and general-purpose machinery of the standard library. Even when a standard library algorithm with good performance exists, it is often not competitive with the best handcoded algorithm. This may be due to weaknesses in the template code or weaknesses in the compiler design, or just because the standard library code has to work for very general situations (like using only operator<() and not strcmp()). This cost may persuade the developer to code really important searches by hand.

The gap in performance between standard algorithms and good, handcoded algorithms is called Stepanov's Abstraction Penalty, after Alexander Stepanov, who designed the original standard library algorithms and container classes, at a time when no compiler existed that could compile them. Stepanov's Abstraction Penalty is the inevitable cost of providing a universal solution versus a custom-coded one. *Stepanov's Abstraction Penalty is a toll for using highly productive tools like the C++ standard library algorithms.* It's not a bad thing, but it's a thing developers need to keep in mind when they need to go really fast.

Optimize Sorting with the C++ Standard Library

A sequence container must be sorted before it can be searched efficiently using a divide-and-conquer algorithm. The C++ standard library provides two standard algorithms, `std::sort()` and `std::stable_sort()`, that can sort sequence containers efficiently.

Although the standard does not specify which sorting algorithm is used, it was written so that `std::sort` could be implemented using some variation of quicksort, and `std::stable_sort` could be implemented using merge sort. C++03 requires `std::sort` to have average performance that is $O(n \ log_2 \ n)$. Implementations conforming to C++03 generally implemented `std::sort` using quicksort, usually with some median-picking trick to reduce the chance of quicksort's $O(n^2)$ worst-case. C++11 requires the worst-case performance to be $O(n \ log_2 \ n)$. Implementations conforming to C++11 are generally hybrid sorts such as Timsort or introsort.

`std::stable_sort` is usually a variant of merge sort. The standard's peculiar wording is that `std::stable_sort` runs in $O(n \ log_2 \ n)$ time if sufficient additional memory can be allocated, but otherwise runs in $O(n \ (log_2 \ n)^2)$ time. A typical implementation is to use merge sort if the recursion depth is not too great, and heapsort if it is.

The value of a stable sort is that a program can sort a range of records by each of several criteria (like first name, and then last name) and get records sorted by the second criterion, then by the first criterion within the second (like last name, and then first name within last name). Only stable sorts provide this property. This additional property justifies having two sorts.

Table 9-2 reports the results of an experiment in which I sorted 100,000 randomly generated key/value records stored in a `std::vector`. An interesting result is that `std::stable_sort()` actually performed better than `std::sort()`. I also tested sorting an already-sorted table. I examine sorting in different data structures in Chapter 10.

Table 9-2. Summary of sort performance experiments

std::vector, 100k items, VS2010 release, i7	Time
`std::sort()` vector	18.61 ms
`std::sort()` sorted vector	3.77 ms
`std::stable_sort()`	16.08 ms
`std::stable_sort()` sorted	5.01 ms

The sequence container `std::list` provides only bidirectional iterators. On a list, therefore, `std::sort()` would run in $O(n^2)$ time. `std::list` provides a `sort()` member function that is $O(n \ log_2 \ n)$.

The ordered associative containers maintain their data in sorted order, so it isn't necessary to sort them. The unordered associative containers maintain their data in a particular order that is not meaningful to users. They cannot be sorted.

The C++ standard library `<algorithm>` header contains pieces of the various sort algorithms, from which more complicated sorts can be built up for input data that has additional special properties:

- `std::heap_sort` converts a range having the heap property into a sorted range. `heap_sort` is not a stable sort.
- `std::partition` performs the basic action of a quicksort.
- `std::merge` performs the basic action of a merge sort.
- The `insert` member of the various sequence containers performs the basic action of an insertion sort.

Summary

- *The mix of features in C++ provides a continuum of implementation choices ranging from hands-off automation and expressiveness on the one hand, to fine control over performance on the other hand. It is this degree of choice that makes it possible to tune C++ programs to meet requirements for performance.*
- *There are enough parts in most activities worth optimizing that human beings cannot reliably remember them all. Paper has a better memory.*
- *In a test of searching a table with 26 keys, `std::unordered_map` with string keys was only 52% faster than `std::map` with string keys. Given the hype about hashing being a performance win, this result was surprising.*
- *Stepanov's Abstraction Penalty is a toll for using highly productive tools like the C++ standard library algorithms.*

## CHAPTER 10

Optimize Data Structures

A thing of beauty is a joy forever

— John Keats (1818)

If you have never stopped to marvel at the container classes of the C++ standard library (formerly the Standard Template Library, or STL), perhaps you should do so now. At the time it was introduced into the draft C++ standard in 1994, *Stepanov's Standard Template Library was the first reusable library of efficient containers and algorithms.* Prior to the STL, every project developed its own linked list and binary tree implementations, possibly adapting source code from other users. C has no equivalent. Standard library containers have allowed many programmers to forget their algorithms and data structures classes and choose exclusively from the standard library's menu of prebuilt containers for the past 20 years.

Get to Know the Standard Library Containers

There are many things to like about the C++ standard library containers, such as uniform naming and a consistent notion of iterators for traversing the containers. But for optimization purposes, some properties are especially important. These include:

- Big-O performance guarantees for the cost of insertion and deletion
- Amortized constant-time cost of appending to sequence containers
- Ability to finely control the dynamic memory allocated by the container

The C++ standard library containers seem almost similar enough that they can be substituted for one another, notwithstanding their obviously different implementations. But this is an illusion. The standard library containers are old enough to vote. Like other parts of C++, standard library containers have evolved independently of one another. The interfaces are only partially overlapping. Big-O performance of the same operation differs by container. Most importantly, the semantics of some member functions differ from container to container, even when they have the same name. The developer must know each container class in detail to understand how to use them optimally.

Sequence Containers

The *sequence containers* `std::string`, `std::vector`, `std::deque`, `std::list`, and `std::forward_list` keep items in the order in which they are inserted. Therefore, each container has a front and a back. All sequence containers have means to insert items. All but `std::forward_list` have constant-time member functions to push items onto the back. However, only `std::deque`, `std::list`, and `std::forward_list` can efficiently push items onto the front.

The items in `std::string`, `std::vector`, and `std::deque` are numbered from 0 to *size–1*, and can be retrieved efficiently by subscripting. `std::list` and `std::for ward_list` are different, having no subscripting operator.

`std::string`, `std::vector`, and `std::deque` are built on an array-like internal backbone. When an item is inserted, any item following it must be bumped up to the next location in the array, which makes the cost of inserting anywhere but at the end $O(n)$, where *n* is the number of items. When items are inserted, these internal arrays may be reallocated, which invalidates all iterators and pointers. By contrast, `std::list` and `std::forward_list` invalidate iterators and pointers only to list elements that are removed. Two `std::list` or `std::forward_list` instances can even be spliced together or merged without invalidating iterators. Insertion in the middle of a `std::list` or `std::forward_list` takes constant time, assuming that an iterator already points to the insertion point

Associative Containers

Associative containers all store inserted items based on some ordering property of the items, rather than on the order of insertion. All associative containers provide efficient, sub-linear-time access to the items they contain.

Maps and sets present different interfaces. Maps store a separately defined key and value, and thus provide an efficient mapping from key to value. Sets store unique, ordered values, and provide efficient tests for the presence of a value. "Multimaps" differ from maps (and similarly "multisets" differ from sets) only in that they permit insertion of multiple items that compare as equal.

In implementation terms, there are four *ordered associative containers*: `std::map`, `std::multimap`, `std::set`, and `std::multiset`. The ordered associative containers require that an ordering relationship like operator<() be defined on the keys (std::map) or items themselves (std::set). The ordered associative containers are implemented as balanced binary trees. It is not necessary to sort an ordered associative container. Iterating through them produces items in order by their ordering relationship. Inserting or removing items takes amortized O($log_2 n$) time, where n is the number of items in the container.

Although it is possible for maps and sets to have different implementations, in practice all four associative containers are implemented as separate façades over the same balanced binary tree data structure. This was true of the compilers I used. I therefore do not present separate timing results for multimaps, sets, and multisets.

Since the introduction of C++11, there are also four *unordered associative containers*: std::unordered_map, std::unordered_multimap, std::unordered_set, and std::unordered_multiset. These containers appear in Visual C++ as early as 2010. The unordered associative containers require only an equality relationship to be defined on the keys (std::unordered_map) or items (std::unordered_set). Unordered associative containers are implemented as hash tables. Iterating through an unordered associative container produces the items in no defined order. Inserting or removing items takes constant time on average, although worst-case time is O(n).

Associative containers make obvious choices for lookup tables. The developer can also store items that have an ordering relation in a sequence container, sort the container, and do relatively efficient O($log_2 n$) searches.

Experimenting with the Standard Library Containers

I built several types of containers with 100,000 elements, and measured performance for insertion, deletion, and visiting each element. In the sequence containers, I also measured the cost of sorting. These are common building blocks for the infinite uses to which data structures may be applied.

This number of elements is enough that the amortized cost of insertion approaches the asymptotic behavior specified for the container—100,000 elements is enough to exercise the cache memory pretty thoroughly. It isn't a small container by any means, nor is it so impractically large that it would be rare.

That said, *big-O performance does not tell the full story. I found that some containers were many times faster than others*, even when an operation had O(*1*) asymptotic cost on both containers being compared.

I also found that unordered maps, with their O(*1*) search cost, were faster than maps, but not by the wide margin I had expected. And the cost in memory to obtain that performance was significant.

Most types of container provide several ways in which items can be inserted. I discovered that certain ways of inserting were 10% or 15% faster than others, and often with no clear reason why.

The cost of inserting 100,000 elements into a container comes in two parts: the cost of allocating storage, and the cost of copy constructing the elements into the storage. The cost of allocating storage is fixed for items of a specific size, while the cost of copy-construction is not bounded, depending on the whim of the programmer. In the case of a very expensive item copy constructor, the copying cost will come to dominate the cost of building the container. In this case, all containers will perform approximately the same when tested for insertions.

Most types of container also provide several ways to iterate through items. Again, I found certain ways to be significantly faster than others, with no obvious reason for the differences. Interestingly, there was less difference than I expected in the cost to iterate in the various container types.

I tested the cost of sorting the sequence containers to see how they might fare if substituted for associative containers in applications that search tables. Some containers sort their elements as part of inserting them; other containers cannot be sorted at all.

The results reported here are significant enough to be interesting, but are probably fragile. As implementations evolve over time, the fastest method may change. For instance, while `stable_sort()` consistently outperformed `sort()`. I suspect this would not have been the case when `stable_sort()` was added to the algorithms library.

Element data type

For the items in the sequence containers, I used a key/value structure. The associative containers create a very similar structure built out of `std::pair`:

```
struct kvstruct {
    char key[9];
    unsigned value; //  could be anything at all
    kvstruct(unsigned k) : value(k)
    {
        if (strcpy_s(key, stringify(k)))
            DebugBreak();
    }
    bool operator<(kvstruct const& that)  const {
        return strcmp(this->key, that.key) < 0;
    }
    bool operator==(kvstruct const& that) const {
        return strcmp(this->key, that.key) == 0;
    }
};
```

The copy constructor for this class is generated by the compiler, but it is nontrivial, having to bit-copy the contents of one kvstruct to another. As before, my goal was to make copying and comparison at least a little expensive to simulate real-world data structures.

The keys themselves were C-style null-terminated character strings comprised of seven-digit numbers. The keys were drawn from a uniform random distribution using C++'s <random> header. The same number was stored as an unsigned integer as the item's value field. Duplicate keys were eliminated, to produce an initial vector of 100,000 distinct values in no particular order.

A note on designing the experiment

Some containers are very inexpensive to insert into or traverse, even with 100,000 items. To get the test to run for a measurable amount of time, I had to repeat the insertion or traversal 1,000 times. But this presented a problem. Each time I inserted items into a container, I had also to clear out the container by deleting the items, which affected the total run time. For instance, the following code measures the cost of assigning one vector to another. It inevitably and inextricably combines the cost of constructing a new copy of random_vector and then deleting it:

```
{   Stopwatch sw("assign vector to vector + delete x 1000");
    std::vector<kvstruct> test_container;
    for (unsigned j = 0; j < 1000; ++j) {
        test_container = random_vector;
        std::vector<kvstruct>().swap(test_container);
    }
}
```

To obtain separate costs for the assignment and the deletion, I constructed a more complex version of this code to accumulate separately the time taken to create the new copy and to delete it:

```
{   Stopwatch sw("assign vector to vector", false);
    Stopwatch::tick_t ticks;
    Stopwatch::tick_t assign_x_1000 = 0;
    Stopwatch::tick_t delete_x_1000 = 0;
    std::vector<kvstruct> test_container;
    for (unsigned j = 0; j < 1000; ++j) {
        sw.Start("");
        test_container = random_vector;
        ticks = sw.Show("");
        assign_x_1000 += ticks;
        std::vector<kvstruct>().swap(test_container);
        delete_x_1000 += sw.Stop("") - ticks;
    }
    std::cout << "    assign vector to vector x 1000: "
              << Stopwatch::GetMs(assign_x_1000)
              << "ms" << std::endl;
```

```
        std::cout << "    vector delete x 1000: "
                  << Stopwatch::GetMs(delete_x_1000)
                  << "ms" << std::endl;
    }
```

The first statement in the loop, `sw.Start("");`, starts the stopwatch without printing anything. The next statement, `test_container = random_vector;`, consumes time copying the vector. The third statement, `ticks = sw.Show("");`, sets `ticks` to the elapsed time so far.

What value is in `ticks`? The source of ticks in the `Stopwatch` instance `sw` has a 1-millisecond tick. The time taken by the assignment is far less than 1 millisecond, so mostly the value in `ticks` is 0. But not always. The clock is independent of this code, ticking steadily somewhere in the hardware. So occasionally, a situation arises where, for instance, the stopwatch started during the 987th microsecond of a 1-millisecond tick, and by the time the assignment statement completed, the tick had occurred. In this case, `ticks` will equal 1. If the assignment takes 500 microseconds, this will happen about half the time. If the assignment takes 10 microseconds, it will happen about 1% of the time. Given enough repetitions of the loop, an accurate aggregate time emerges.

`ticks` is accumulated in `assign_x_1000`, the variable that counts the time taken by the assignment. Then, the statement `std::vector().swap(test_container);` deletes the contents of the vector `test_container`. Finally, `delete_x_1000 += sw.Stop("")` `- ticks;` gets another tick count that is either zero or one, subtracts the tick count from the end of the assignment, and accumulates the difference in `delete_x_1000`. The measured cost of deleting the vector 1,000 times is 111 milliseconds, or 0.111 milliseconds per deletion.

Armed now with the cost of deleting a container with 100,000 entries, the remaining code can be tackled with arithmetic. The following code is another loop that fills a container 1,000 times, which also must include the cost of deleting the container:

```
    {   Stopwatch sw("vector iterator insert() + delete x 1000");
        std::vector<kvstruct> test_container;
        for (unsigned j = 0; j < 1000; ++j) {
            test_container.insert(
                test_container.begin(),
                random_vector.begin(),
                random_vector.end());
            std::vector<kvstruct>().swap(test_container);
        }
    }
```

A particular test run of the preceding code took 696 milliseconds to fill the container and delete the container 1,000 times. If the cost of deleting the vector 1,000 times, as

measured earlier, is 111 milliseconds, the cost of a single call to insert() is
$\frac{696 - 111}{1000} = 0.585$ milliseconds.

Modern C++ Coding Note

There is a little-remarked standard library in C++ for generating random numbers, called <random>. Once I discovered this library, it became one of my favorite tools for generating random search keys. For instance, Example 10-1 shows the code I used to generate the random strings for my container tests.

Example 10-1. Creating a vector of unique kvstruct instances

```
# include <random>

// build count-element vector containing unique random strings
void build_rnd_vector(std::vector<kvstruct>& v, unsigned count){
    std::default_random_engine e;
    std::uniform_int_distribution<unsigned> d(count, 10*count-1);
    auto randomizer = std::bind(d,e);
    std::set<unsigned> unique;
    v.clear();
    while (v.size() < count) {
        unsigned rv = randomizer();
        if (unique.insert(rv).second == true) { // item inserted
            kvstruct keyvalue(rv);
            v.push_back(keyvalue);
        }
    }
}
```

The first line of build_rnd_vector() constructs a random number *generator*, basically a source of randomness. The second line creates a random number *distribution*, an object that transforms sequences of random numbers from the generator into sequences of numbers that follow some probability distribution. In this case, the distribution is uniform, which means each value is equally likely to occur, with minimum value count and maximum value 10*count-1. So, if count is 100,000, the values provided by the distribution will range from 100,000 to 999,999. That is, they will all be six digits long. The third line creates an object that applies the generator as an argument to the distribution, so that calling the object's operator() generates a random number.

The generators are all documented and have known properties. There is even a generator called std::random_device that produces values from a source of true randomness, if one is available.

Distributions provide the power in this library. For instance, here are a few useful distributions:

```
std::uniform_int_distribution<unsigned> die(1, 6);
```
The distribution of a fair, six-sided die, which produces numbers from 1 to 6 with equal probability. Dice with 4, 20, or 100 sides can be simulated by varying the second argument.

```
std::binomial_distribution<unsigned> coin(1, 0.5);
```
The distribution of a fair coin toss, which produces values of 0 or 1 with equal probability. A biased coin could be simulated by adjusting the second argument away from 0.5.

```
std::normal_distribution<double> iq(100.0, 15.0);
```
The distribution of assessed intelligence in the human population, returning values of type `double` such that about two-thirds of the results are between 85.0 and 115.0.

For more refined statistical tastes, there are Poisson and exponential distributions for building event simulations (also known as test drivers), and several population-based distributions.

std::vector and std::string

A sort of "product sheet" for these data structures would say:

- Sequence container
- Insert time: from back aggregate O(1), from elsewhere O(n)
- Index time: by position, in O(1)
- Sort in O($n \log_2 n$)
- Search in O($\log_2 n$) if sorted, else O(n)
- Iterators and references invalidated when the internal array is reallocated
- Iterators produce items front-to-back or back-to-front
- Reasonable control over allocated capacity independent of size

Historically, `std::string` was permitted novel implementations, but C++11 locked down the definition. Visual Studio's implementation might as well be a derived class of `std::vector` with specialized member functions for string handling. Comments about `std::vector` apply equally to Visual Studio's `std::string`.

`std::vector` is a dynamically resizable array (see Figure 10-1). Array items are instances of the template type parameter `T` that are copy-constructed into the vector. Although the item copy constructors may allocate memory for members, the only calls `std::vector` makes to the memory manager are to reallocate its internal buffer as items are added. This flat structure makes `std::vector` unusually efficient. Bjarne

Stroustrup, creator of C++, recommends `std::vector` as the go-to container class unless there is a specific reason why another container is needed. I'll show why in this section.

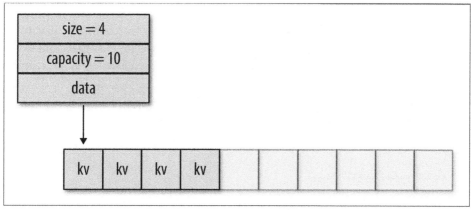

Figure 10-1. std::vector possible implementation

Many operations on `std::vector` are efficient in big-O terms, running in constant time. Among these operations are pushing a new item onto the end of the vector, and obtaining a reference to the ith element. Because of the vector's simple internal structure, these operations are quite fast in absolute terms as well. Iterators over `std::vector` are random-access iterators, which means computing the distance between two iterators in the same vector can be done in constant time. This property makes divide-and-conquer searches and sorts of `std::vector` efficient.

Performance Consequences of Reallocation

`std::vector` has a *size*, which describes how many elements are currently in the vector, and a *capacity*, which describes how big the internal buffer that holds its elements is. When *size == capacity*, any further insertions trigger an expensive expansion: reallocating the internal buffer, copying the vector elements to the new storage, and invalidating all iterators and references to the old buffer. When reallocation becomes necessary, the capacity of the new buffer is set to some multiple of the new size. The effect of this is that the cost of insertion is constant in the aggregate, though some insertions are expensive while others are not.

One secret of efficient `std::vector` use is that capacity can be reserved ahead of need by a call to `void reserve(size_t n)`, thus preventing unnecessary reallocate-and-copy cycles.

Another secret of `std::vector`'s efficiency is that it doesn't automatically return memory to the memory manager if items are removed. If a program pushes a million items onto a vector and then removes them, the vector continues to hold onto a million items' worth of storage. Developers must keep this fact in mind when std::vector is used in constrained environments.

Several member functions of std::vector affect its capacity, but the standard is cagey about making any guarantees. void clear() sets the *size* of the container to zero, but is not guaranteed to reallocate the internal buffer to reduce its capacity. In C++11, and anticipated in Visual Studio 2010, void shrink_to_fit() is a hint to the vector to reduce its capacity to match its current size, but reallocation is not mandatory.

To ensure the release of memory from a vector in all versions of C++, use the following trick:

```
std::vector<Foo> x;
    ...
vector<Foo>().swap(x);
```

This statement constructs a temporary, empty vector, swaps its contents with the contents of vector x, then deletes the temporary, so that the memory manager reclaims all memory formerly belonging to x.

Inserting and Deleting in std::vector

There are several ways to fill a vector with data. I explored the cost to construct a vector of 100,000 kvstruct instances, determining that there are definitely faster and slower methods.

The fastest way to fill up a vector is to assign it:

```
std::vector<kvstruct> test_container, random_vector;
    ...
test_container = random_vector;
```

Assignment is very efficient because it knows the size of the vector it is copying, and needs to call the memory manager only once to create the assigned vector's internal buffer. A test of the previous statement copied a 100,000-entry vector in 0.445 milliseconds.

If the data is in another container, std::vector::insert() will copy it into a vector:

```
std::vector<kvstruct> test_container, random_vector;
    ...
test_container.insert(
        test_container.end(),
        random_vector.begin(),
        random_vector.end());
```

A test of this statement copied a 100,000-entry vector in 0.696 milliseconds.

The member function `std::vector::push_back()` can efficiently (that is, in constant time) put a new item onto the end of a vector. Since the items are in another vector, there are three ways to get at them:

- The code can use a vector iterator:

```
std::vector<kvstruct> test_container, random_vector;
    ...
for (auto it=random_vector.begin(); it!=random_vector.end(); ++it)
    test_container.push_back(*it);
```

- The `std::vector::at()` member function can be used:

```
std::vector<kvstruct> test_container, random_vector;
    ...
for (unsigned i = 0; i < nelts; ++i)
    test_container.push_back(random_vector.at(i));
```

- The code can use a vector subscript directly:

```
std::vector<kvstruct> test_container, random_vector;
    ...
for (unsigned i = 0; i < nelts; ++i)
    test_container.push_back(random_vector[i]);
```

The three methods produced similar times of 2.26, 2.05, and 1.99 milliseconds, respectively, in my tests. However, this is six times the amount of time taken by the simple assignment statement.

The reason this code is slower is that it inserts items into the vector one at a time. The vector doesn't know how many items will be inserted, so it makes its internal buffer bigger incrementally. Several times during this loop, the vector's internal buffer is reallocated, and all the items are copied to the new buffer. `std::vector` guarantees that in the aggregate, `push_back()` happens in constant time, but that doesn't mean it has no cost.

The developer can use extra knowledge to make this loop more efficient, by pre-allocating a buffer big enough to hold the whole copy. The iterator variant of this code looks like this:

```
std::vector<kvstruct> test_container, random_vector;
    ...
test_container.reserve(nelts);
for (auto it=random_vector.begin(); it != random_vector.end(); ++it)
    test_container.push_back(*it);
```

The resulting loop runs in a respectable 0.674 milliseconds.

There are still more ways to insert items into a vector. Another variant of the `insert()` member function can be used:

```
std::vector<kvstruct> test_container, random_vector;
    ...
for (auto it=random_vector.begin(); it != random_vector.end(); ++it)
    test_container.insert(test_container.end(), *it);
```

This ought to be exactly as expensive as push_back(), but it isn't (in Visual Studio 2010). All three variants (iterator, at(), and subscript) run in about 2.7 milliseconds. Reserving space in advance reduces this to 1.45 milliseconds, but this is not competitive with any of the previous results.

Finally, we come to std::vector's super-weakness: inserting at the front. std::vector does not provide a push_front() member, because the time cost is O(*n*). Inserting at the front is inefficient because every item in the vector must be copied to make room for the new entry. And it is, indeed, inefficient. The following loop:

```
std::vector<kvstruct> test_container, random_vector;
    ...
for (auto it=random_vector.begin(); it != random_vector.end(); ++it)
    test_container.insert(test_container.begin(), *it);
```

takes 8,065 milliseconds. That's a comma there, not a decimal point. This loop takes almost *three thousand times as long* as inserting at the back.

So, to fill up a vector efficiently, try assignment, insert() with iterators from another container, push_back(), and insert() at the back of the vector, in that order.

Iterating in std::vector

Vectors are inexpensive to traverse, visiting each element. But as with insertion, the time cost of the available methods differs significantly.

There are three ways to iterate through a vector: with an iterator, with the at() member function, or by subscripting. If the controlled action of the loop is expensive, the difference in cost of the various traversal methods becomes insignificant. However, developers often perform only a simple, fast action on the data in each element. In this example, the loop sums the contents, which takes a negligible amount of time (it also keeps the compiler from optimizing away the whole loop as a no-op):

```
std::vector<kvstruct> test_container;
    ...
unsigned sum = 0;
for (auto it=test_container.begin(); it!=test_container.end(); ++it)
    sum += it->value;

std::vector<kvstruct> test_container;
    ...
unsigned sum = 0;
for (unsigned i = 0; i < nelts; ++i)
    sum += test_container.at(i).value;
```

```
std::vector<kvstruct> test_container;
    ...
unsigned sum = 0;
for (unsigned i = 0; i < nelts; ++i)
    sum += test_container[i].value;
```

It is reasonable for the developer to expect these loops to be nearly equivalent in cost, but in fact they are not. The iterator version takes 0.236 milliseconds. The `at()` version is slightly better, at 0.230 milliseconds, but as with insertion, the subscript version is more efficient, taking just 0.129 milliseconds. The subscripting version is 83% faster in Visual Studio 2010.

Sorting std::vector

You can sort a vector efficiently prior to using a binary search to look up items. The C++ standard library has two sorting algorithms, `std::sort()` and `std::sta ble_sort()`. Both algorithms run in O(n log_2 n) time if the container's iterators are random-access iterators, as `std::vector`'s are. Both algorithms run somewhat faster on data that is already sorted. Sorting is accomplished by a brief program fragment:

```
std::vector<kvstruct> sorted_container, random_vector;
    ...
sorted_container = random_vector;
std::sort(sorted_container.begin(), sorted_container.end());
```

The results are summarized in Table 10-1.

Table 10-1. Cost of sorting a vector of 100,000 items

std::vector	VS2010 release, i7, 100k items
std::sort() vector	18.61 ms
std::sort() sorted vector	3.77 ms
std::stable_sort()	16.08 ms
std::stable_sort() sorted	5.01 ms

Lookup with std::vector

The following program fragment looks for every key from `random_vector` in `sorted_container`:

```
std::vector<kvstruct> sorted_container, random_vector;
    ...
for (auto it=random_vector.begin(); it!=random_vector.end(); ++it) {
    kp = std::lower_bound(
                sorted_container.begin(),
                sorted_container.end(),
                *it);
    if (kp != sorted_container.end() && *it < *kp)
```

```
        kp = sorted_container.end();
    }
```

This program looked up 100,000 keys in the sorted vector in 28.92 milliseconds.

std::deque

The "product sheet" for deque looks like this:

- Sequence container
- Insert time: from back or front O(*1*), from elsewhere O(*n*)
- Index time: by position, in O(*1*)
- Sort in O(*n log₂ n*)
- Search in O(*log₂ n*) if sorted, else O(*n*)
- Iterators and references invalidated when the internal array is reallocated
- Iterators produce items front-to-back or back-to-front

`std::deque` is a specialized container for creating first-in, first-out queues (FIFO). Insertion and deletion at either end is constant-time. Subscripting is also constant-time. The iterators are random-access like those of `std::vector`, so `std::deque` can be sorted in O(*n log₂ n*) time.

Because `std::deque` makes the same performance guarantees (in big-O terms) as `std::vector`, and has constant-time insertion at both ends, it's tempting to wonder what the big deal is about `std::vector`. However, the constant of proportionality of all these operations is greater for deques than for vectors. Measured performance of common operations involving deques is 3 to 10 times slower than corresponding operations in vectors. Iterating, sorting, and lookup are relative bright spots for deques, being only about 30% slower than for vectors.

`std::deque` is typically implemented as an array of arrays (Figure 10-2). The two indirections needed to get to an item in the deque reduces cache locality, and the cost of more frequent calls to the memory manager is greater than with `std::vector`.

Pushing an item onto either end of a deque may cause at most two calls to the allocator: one to add another block of items, and, less frequently, another to extend the deque backbone. This allocation behavior is more complex, and thus harder to reason about, than the allocation behavior of vectors. `std::deque` does not offer any equivalent to `std::vector`'s `reserve()` member function to preallocate its internal data structures. The deque may seem like an obvious container with which to implement a FIFO queue. There is even a container adapter template called `std::queue`, for which deque is the default implementation. However, there is no guarantee that the allocation performance will be very good in this use.

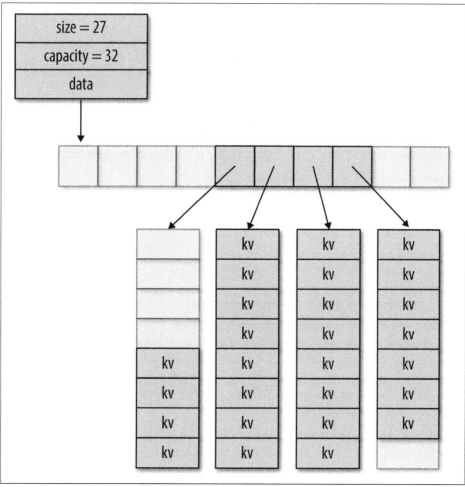

Figure 10-2. std::deque possible implementation after a few insertions and deletions

Inserting and Deleting in std::deque

`std::deque` provides the same interface for insertion as does `std::vector`, plus the member `push_front()`.

Here is an assignment of one deque to another. This operation took 5.70 milliseconds:

```
std::deque<kvstruct> test_container;
std::vector<kvstruct> random_vector;
   ...
test_container = random_vector;
```

Insertion into a deque using a pair of iterators looks like this. This operation took 5.28 milliseconds:

```
std::deque<kvstruct> test_container;
std::vector<kvstruct> random_vector;

    ...
test_container.insert(
        test_container.end(),
        random_vector.begin(),
        random_vector.end());
```

Here are three ways to copy items from a vector to a deque using push_back():

```
std::deque<kvstruct> test_container;
std::vector<kvstruct> random_vector;

    ...
for (auto it=random_vector.begin(); it!=random_vector.end(); ++it)
    test_container.push_back(*it);

for (unsigned i = 0; i < nelts; ++i)
    test_container.push_back(random_vector.at(i));

for (unsigned i = 0; i < nelts; ++i)
    test_container.push_back(random_vector[i]);
```

A developer could be excused for guessing that these three loops would cost pretty much the same. Maybe at() should be a tiny bit slower due to the extra checking it does. Indeed, the iterator version at 4.33 milliseconds was 15% faster than the subscript version at 5.01 milliseconds, with the at() version in between at 4.76 milliseconds. This is not a tremendous difference; maybe not the big game for which an optimization effort would normally want to hunt.

Results were similar for the three variants of prepending using push_front(). The iterator version took 5.19 milliseconds and the subscripting version 5.55 milliseconds —a difference of only 7%, bordering on the unrepeatable. However, the push_front() results were 20% slower than for push_back().

Inserting at the back and at the front was about twice as expensive as push_back() or push_front(), respectively.

Now take a look at the performance of std::vector versus std::deque. A vector performs an assignment 13 times faster for the same number of entries. A vector is 22 times faster at deletion, 9 times faster at iterator-based insertion, twice as fast at push_back(), and 3 times as fast when inserting at the end.

Optimization War Story

When I began performance-testing deque, I found a surprise: Operations on std::deque were a thousand times slower than equivalent std::vector operations. At first I told myself, "It is what it is. Deque must simply be an awful choice for a data

---

structure." It was only when I ran a "final" set of tests for the tables in this book that my foolishness was revealed.

My normal practice in development was to run the test programs in the debugger, because there's a big fat button for that on the IDE. I was aware that debug runs are linked to a C++ runtime library with extra debug checking. But I had never seen this make more than a slight difference in performance. For the tables in the book, it was my practice to make a final run outside the debugger, because I got more consistent timings that way. That's how I found that for `std::deque`, running under the debugger is monstrously expensive due to diagnostic code added to memory allocation routines. This was an exception to my general experience that measuring relative performance in debug builds produced similar results to measuring relative performance in release builds. It is possible to control whether the debug heap or normal heap is ued in debugging. See "Optimizing Pro Tip" on page 39.

Iterating in std::deque

Iterating through the elements of a deque took 0.828 milliseconds for the subscript-based version and 0.450 milliseconds for the iterator-based code. Interestingly, the iterator-based traversal is much faster for the deque, while the subscript-based code was faster for the vector. But the fastest deque traversal method is twice as expensive as the fastest vector traversal method, continuing the trend set previously.

Sorting std::deque

`std::sort()` processed 100,000 deque entries in 24.82 milliseconds, which is 33% more than for the vector. As for the vector, `std::stable_sort()` was faster at 17.76 milliseconds, and the time was within 10% of the time for the vector. In both cases, the presorted vector was faster to re-sort.

Lookup with std::deque

It took 35 milliseconds to look up all 100,000 keys in a sorted deque. Lookup was only about 20% more expensive for the deque than for the vector.

std::list

The "product sheet" for this data structure says:

- Sequence container
- Insert time: O(*1*) at any position
- Sort in O(*n log₂ n*)
- Search in O(*n*)

- Iterators and references never invalidated except for removed items
- Iterators visit list items front-to-back or back-to-front

`std::list` shares many properties with `std::vector` and `std::deque`. Like with vector and deque, items can be pushed onto the back of a list in constant time. Like with a deque (but unlike a vector), items can be pushed onto the front of a list in constant time. Furthermore, unlike either a vector or deque, items can also be inserted into the middle of a list in constant time, given an iterator to the insertion point. Like a deque and a vector, a list can be efficiently sorted. But unlike with vectors and deques, there is no efficient way to search a list. `std::find()`, which takes O(*n*) time, is as good as you can do.

The received wisdom is that `std::list` is too inefficient to be useful, but I did not find that when I tested its performance. While `std::list` is maybe 10 times as expensive to copy or create as `std::vector`, it is quite competitive with `std::deque`. Pushing incrementally onto the tail of a list is less than twice as expensive as for a vector. Traversing and sorting a list are only 30% more expensive than the same operations on a vector. For most of the operations I tested, `std::list` was less expensive than `std::deque`.

The same received wisdom holds that `std::list`, with its forward and reverse links and constant-time `size()` method, is more expensive than necessary for the features it provides. This thinking led eventually to the inclusion of `std::forward_list` in C++11. However, a little performance testing shows that `std::list` is almost identical to `std::forward_list` in the cost of its operations, at least on PC hardware.

Because `std::list` has no backbone array that must be reallocated, iterators and references to list items are never invalidated by insertion. They become invalid only if the items they point to are deleted.

One place `std::list` shines is that lists can be spliced (in O(*1*) time) and merged without copying list items. Even operations like splice and sort don't invalidate `std::list` iterators. Insertion into the middle of a list is constant-time, *provided the program already knows where to insert*. So, an application that creates lists of items and then shuffles them around *might* be more efficient using `std::list` than `std::vector`.

`std::list` interacts with the memory manager in a very simple and predictable way. Each list item is separately allocated when needed. There is no unused capacity hiding in a list (see Figure 10-3).

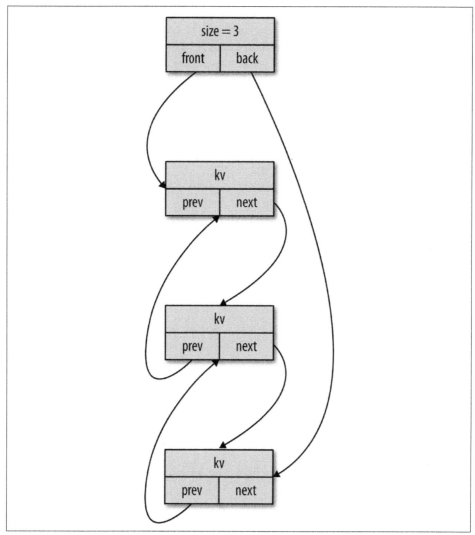

Figure 10-3. std::list possible implementation after a few insertions and deletions

The storage allocated for each list item is the same size. This helps sophisticated memory managers operate efficiently, and with less risk of fragmenting memory. It is also possible to define a simple custom allocator for std::list that exploits this property to operate efficiently (see "A Fixed-Block Allocator" on page 352).

Inserting and Deleting in std::list

The algorithms for copying one list to another by insert(), push_back(), and push_front() are identical to the listings for a vector and deque, except for the data structure declaration at the beginning. The very simple structure of std::list does not offer the compiler much chance to improve the code during compilation. Timings for all these mechanisms are thus consistent for lists, as illustrated in Table 10-2.

Table 10-2. Summary of performance experiments on std::list

std::list, 100k items, VS2010 release, i7	Time	List versus vector
Assign	5.10 ms	1046%
Delete	2.49 ms	2141%
`insert(end())`	3.69 ms	533%
Iterator `push_back()`	4.26 ms	88%
`at() push_back()`	4.50 ms	120%
Subscript `push_back()`	4.63 ms	132%
Iterator `push_front()`	4.77 ms	
`at() push_front()`	4.82 ms	
Subscript `push_front()`	4.99 ms	
Iterator insert at back	4.75 ms	75%
`at()` insert at back	4.84 ms	77%
Subscript insert at back	4.88 ms	75%
Iterator insert at front	4.84 ms	
`at()` insert at front	5.02 ms	
Subscript insert at front	5.04 ms	

Inserting at the end of a list was the fastest way to construct a list; for some reason, even faster than `operator=()`.

Iterating in std::list

There is no subscripting operator for lists. The only option to traverse the list uses iterators.

Iterating through the list of 100,000 items took 0.326 milliseconds. This was only 38% more expensive than traversing a vector.

Sorting std::list

The iterators over std::list are bidirectional iterators, less powerful than the random-access iterators over std::vector. A particular property of these iterators is that the cost to find the *distance*, or number of items between two bidirectional iterators, is $O(n)$. Thus, std::sort() has $O(n^2)$ performance on std::list. The compiler will still compile a call to std::sort() on a list, but the performance will be far worse than a developer might expect.

Fortunately, std::list has a built-in sort that is more efficient, at O($n \log_2 n$). Sorting the list using std::list's built in sort() took 23.2 milliseconds, only 25% longer than sorting the equivalent vector.

Lookup with std::list

Because std::list provides only bidirectional iterators, the binary-search algorithms are all O(n) for lists. Searching with std::find() is also O(n), where n is the number of entries in the list. This makes std::list a poor candidate to replace associative containers.

std::forward_list

The "product sheet" for std::forward_list says:

- Sequence container
- Insert time: O(1) at any position
- Sort in O($n \log_2 n$)
- Search in O(n)
- Iterators and references never invalidated except for removed items
- Iterators visit list items front-to-back

std::forward_list is a sequence container stripped down to its bare essentials. It contains a single pointer to the head node of the list. It was designed deliberately to make its implementation equivalent to a handcoded, singly linked list. There is no back() or rbegin() member function.

std::forward_list interacts with the memory manager in a very simple and predictable way. Each forward list item is separately allocated when needed. There is no unused capacity hiding in a forward list (see Figure 10-4). The storage allocated for each forward list item is the same size. This helps sophisticated memory managers operate efficiently, and with less risk of fragmenting memory. It is also possible to define a simple custom allocator for std::forward_list that exploits this property to operate efficiently (see "A Fixed-Block Allocator" on page 352).

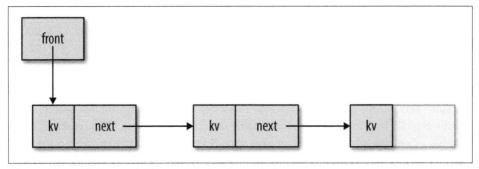

Figure 10-4. std::forward_list possible implementation

A forward list differs from a list by offering only forward iterators, as the name suggests. A forward list can be traversed with the usual loop:

```
std::forward_list<kvstruct> flist;
// ...
unsigned sum = 0;
for (auto it = flist.begin(); it != flist.end(); ++it)
    sum += it->value;
```

Insertion, however, requires a different approach. Instead of an `insert()` method, `std::forward_list` has `insert_after()`. There is also a function called `before_begin()` to get an iterator to before the first list element (there is no other way to insert before the first element because the elements only have pointers to the next element):

```
std::forward_list<kvstruct> flist;
std::vector<kvstruct> vect;
// ...
auto place = flist.before_begin();
for (auto it = vvect.begin(); it != vect.end(); ++it)
    place = flist.insert_after(place, *it);
```

`std::forward_list` wasn't significantly faster than `std::list` on my PC. The things that made `std::list` slow (allocation per item, poor cache locality) were just as big a problem for `std::forward_list`. `std::forward_list` may be useful on smaller processors with tighter memory constraints, but for desktop- and handset-class processors, there is little to recommend it.

Inserting and Deleting in std::forward_list

`std::forward_list` has constant-time insertion at any position, provided there is an iterator pointing to just before that position. Inserting 100,000 entries into a forward list took 4.24 milliseconds, about the same as for `std::list`.

`std::forward_list` has a `push_front()` member function. Inserting 100,000 entries in this way took 4.16 milliseconds, again about the same as for `std::list`.

Iterating in std::forward_list

There is no subscripting operator for `std::forward_list`. The only option to traverse the list uses iterators.

Iterating through the forward list of 100,000 items took 0.343 milliseconds. This was only 45% more expensive than traversing a vector.

Sorting std::forward_list

Like `std::list`, `std::forward_list` has a built-in sort that runs in $O(n \log_2 n)$. The performance of the sort was similar to that of `std::list`, sorting 100,000 entries in 23.3 milliseconds.

Lookup in std::forward_list

Because `std::forward_list` provides only forward iterators, the binary-search algorithms are $O(n)$ for forward lists. Searching with the far simpler `std::find()` is also $O(n)$, where n is the number of entries in the forward list. This makes the forward list a poor candidate to replace associative containers.

std::map and std::multimap

The "product sheet" for these data structures says:

- Ordered associative container
- Insert time: $O(\log_2 n)$
- Index time: by key $O(\log_2 n)$
- Iterators and references never invalidated except for removed items
- Iterators produce items in sorted or reverse-sorted order

`std::map` maps instances of a key type to corresponding instances of some value type. `std::map` is a node-based data structures, like `std::list`. However, a map orders its nodes according to the value of a key. Internally, a map is implemented as a balanced binary tree with additional links to facilitate iterator-based traversal (see Figure 10-5).

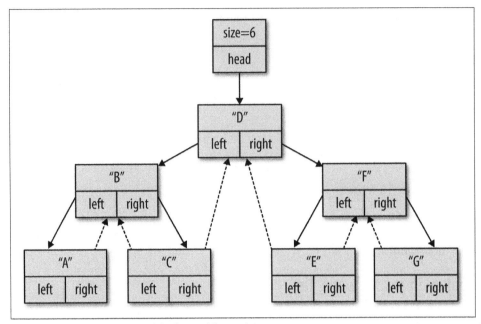

Figure 10-5. std::map simplified possible implementation

Although `std::map` is implemented using a tree, it is not a tree. There is no way to inspect the links, perform a breadth-first traversal, or do other tree-ish things on a map.

`std::map`'s interaction with the memory manager is simple and predictable. Each map item is separately allocated when needed. `std::map` has no backbone array that might be reallocated, so iterators and references to map items are never invalidated by insertion. They become invalid only if the items to which they point are deleted.

The storage allocated for each list item is the same size. This helps sophisticated memory managers operate efficiently, and with less risk of fragmenting memory. It is also possible to define a simple custom allocator for `std::map` that exploits this property to operate efficiently (see "A Fixed-Block Allocator" on page 352).

Inserting and Deleting in std::map

Inserting 100,000 random entries from a vector iterator into a `std::map` took 33.8 milliseconds.

Inserting into a map is normally O($log_2 n$) due to the need to traverse the map's internal tree looking for the insert point. This cost is high enough that `std::map` provides a version of `insert()` that takes an extra map iterator serving as a hint that inserting at this point might be more efficient. If the hint is optimal, insertion time goes to amortized O(*1*).

There is good news and bad news about the insertion hint. The good news is that the insert-with-hint can never be more expensive than an ordinary insert. The bad news is that the optimum value recommended for the insertion hint changed for C++11. Before C++11, the optimum value for the insertion hint was the position *before* the new item—that is, if items are inserted in sorted order, the position of the previous insertion. Since C++11, the optimal insertion hint is the position *after* the new item; that is, if items are inserted in sorted order, the position hint should be end(). To make the previously inserted item the optimal position, the program should iterate through the sorted input in reverse, as shown in Example 10-2.

Example 10-2. Insert from sorted vector using C++11-style hint

```
ContainerT test_container;
std::vector<kvstruct> sorted_vector;
    ...
std::stable_sort(sorted_vector.begin(), sorted_vector.end());
auto hint = test_container.end();
for (auto it = sorted_vector.rbegin(); it != sorted_vector.rend(); ++it)
    hint = test_container.insert(hint, value_type(it->key, it->value));
```

As my experience with both GCC and Visual Studio 2010 showed, the standard library implementation may either anticipate or trail the latest standard. As a result, a program optimized using the pre-C++11-style hint might slow down when moved to a newer compiler, even if the compiler does not fully conform to C++11.

I ran an insertion test using three hints: end(), an iterator to the predecessor node as specified for standard libraries prior to C++11, and an iterator to the successor node as specified for C++11. Table 10-3 shows the results. To perform this test, the input also had to be sorted.

Table 10-3. Performance of insert-with-hint into a std::map

Experiment	Time/call
Sorted vector insert()	18.0 ms
Sorted vector insert() end hint	9.11 ms
Sorted vector insert() pre-C++11 hint	14.4 ms
Sorted vector insert() C++11 hint	8.56 ms

It appears that Visual Studio 2010 implements the C++11-style hint. But either hint performed better than no hint at all, and better than the no-hint version of insert() and unsorted input.

Optimizing the check-and-update idiom

In a commonly occurring idiom, a program checks to see whether some key is in the map, then performs an action depending on the result. A performance optimization is possible when the action involves inserting or updating the value corresponding to the searched-for key.

The key to understanding the optimization is that map::find() and map::insert() both cost O(log_2 n) because of the need to check for the presence of the key and later to find the insertion point. Both of these operations traverse the same set of nodes in the map's binary tree data structure:

```
iterator it = table.find(key); // O(log n)
if (it != table.end()) {
    // key found path
    it->second = value;
}
else {
    // key not found path
    it = table.insert(key, value); // O(log n)
}
```

If the program captures the result of the first search, it can use that as a hint to insert(), making the insert run in O(1). There are two ways to improve this idiom, depending on the needs of the program. If all you need is to know whether the key was initially found, you can use a version of insert() that returns a pair containing an iterator to the found or inserted entry, and a bool that is true if the entry was found and false if it was inserted. This solution works if the program knows how to initialize the entry before finding out whether it is present or not, or if the value is inexpensive to update:

```
std::pair<value_t, bool> result = table.insert(key, value);
if (result.second) {
    // key found path
}
else {
    // key not found path
}
```

The second method involves finding the key or the insertion point through a call to lower_bound() for a C++98-style hint, or upper_bound() for a C++11-style hint. lower_bound() returns an iterator to the smallest entry in the map whose key is less than the search key, or to end(). This iterator is the insertion hint if the key must be inserted, and it points to the key if an existing entry must be updated. This method makes no assumptions about the entry to be inserted:

```
iterator it = table.lower_bound(key);
if (it == table.end() || key < it->first) {
    // key not found path
    table.insert(it, key, value);
```

```
    }
    else {
        // key found path
        it->second = value;
    }
```

Iterating in std::map

Iterating through the 100,000-item map took 1.34 milliseconds, about 10 times longer than iterating through a vector.

Sorting std::map

Maps are inherently sorted. Iterating through a map produces entries in order by their key and the search predicate in use. Note that it isn't possible to re-sort a map by another sorting predicate without copying all elements to another map.

Lookup with std::map

Looking up all 100,000 entries in the map took 42.3 milliseconds. By contrast, it took 28.9 milliseconds to look up all 100,000 entries in a sorted vector and 35.1 milliseconds for a sorted deque, using `std::lower_bound()`. Table 10-4 summarizes the performance of a vector and a map when used as a lookup table.

Table 10-4. Insertion and lookup time for vector versus map

	Insert+sort	Lookup
Vector	19.1 ms	28.9 ms
Map	33.8 ms	42.3 ms

For a 100,000-element table that is constructed all at once and then searched repeatedly, a vector-based implementation will be faster. If the table will change frequently, with insertions or deletions, re-sorting the vector-based table will consume any advantage it may have had in search time.

std::set and std::multiset

The "product sheet" for these data structures says:

- Ordered associative container
- Insert time: O($log_2 n$)
- Index time: by key O($log_2 n$)
- Iterators and references never invalidated except for removed items

- Iterators produce items in sorted or reverse-sorted order

I did not performance-test `std::set`. On Windows, `std::set` and `std::multiset` use the same data structure as `std::map` (see Figure 10-6), so the performance characteristics are the same as for a map. Although a set could in principle be implemented using a different data structure, there's no reason why it should be.

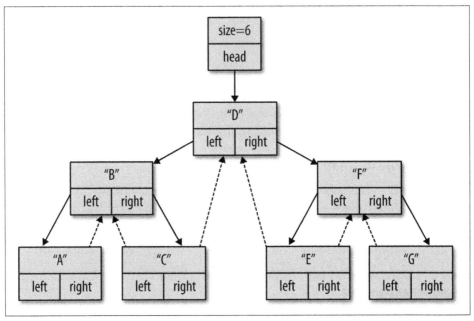

Figure 10-6. std::set simplified possible implementation

One difference between `std::map` and `std::set` is that the items returned by lookup are `const`. This is less of a problem than it seems. If you really want to use the set abstraction, fields in the value data type that don't participate in the ordering relationship can be declared `mutable`, specifying that they don't participate in the ordering relationship. Of course, the compiler believes the developer unconditionally, so it's important not to change members that participate in the ordering relation, or the set data structure will become invalid.

std::unordered_map and std::unordered_multimap

The "product sheet" for these data structures says:

- Unordered associative container
- Insert time: O(*1*) average, O(*n*) worst case
- Index time: by key O(*1*) average, O(*n*) worst case

- Iterators invalidated on rehash, references invalidated only for removed items
- Capacity can be increased or decreased independent of size

`std::unordered_map` maps instances of a key type to corresponding instances of some value type. In this way it is similar to `std::map`. However, the mapping is accomplished differently. `std::unordered_map` is implemented as a hash table. Keys are converted to an integer hash, which is used as an array index to find the value in amortized average constant time.

The C++ standard constrains the implementation of `std::unordered_map`, just as it does for `std::string`. So, while there are several ways in which a hash table might be implemented, only a design with a dynamically allocated backbone array of *buckets* pointing to linked lists of dynamically allocated nodes is likely to comply with the standard's definitions.

An unordered map is expensive to construct. It contains dynamically allocated nodes for each table entry, plus a dynamically resizable bucket array that is periodically real-located as the table grows (Figure 10-7). It thus consumes a considerable amount of memory to achieve an improvement in search performance. Iterators are invalidated every time the bucket array is reallocated. However, references point to the nodes; they are invalidated only on deletion.

Hash tables like `std::unordered_map` have several parameters to adjust in pursuit of optimal performance. This is either a strength or a weakness, depending on the developer's point of view.

The number of entries in the unordered map is its *size*. The computed ratio *size / buckets* is called the *load factor*. A load factor greater than 1.0 implies that some buckets have a chain of multiple entries, reducing lookup performance for these keys (in other words, the hash is not *perfect*). In real hash tables, collisions among the keys cause entries to appear in chains even when the load factor is less than 1.0. A load factor less than 1.0 implies that there are unused buckets consuming space in the unordered map's backbone array (in other words, the hash is not *minimal*). When the load factor is less than 1.0, the value *1 – load factor* is a lower bound on the number of empty buckets, but since hash functions can be imperfect, the amount of unused space is generally higher.

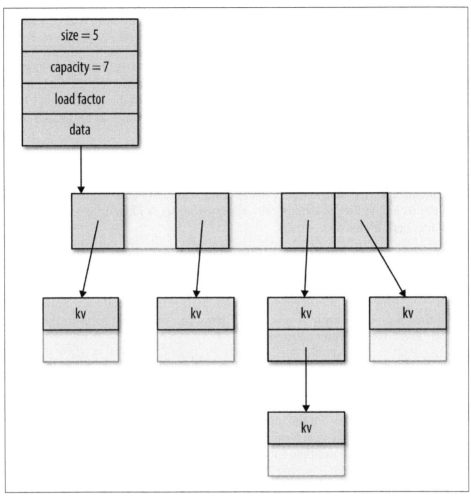

Figure 10-7. std::unordered_map possible implementation

The load factor is a dependent variable in `std::unordered_map`. A program can observe its value, but cannot directly set it or predict its value after a reallocation. When a new entry is inserted in the unordered map, if the load factor exceeds a *maximum load factor* that may be specified by the program, the bucket array is reallocated and all the entries are rehashed to buckets in the new array. Since the number of buckets is always increased by a factor greater than 1, the cost of insertion is amortized O(*1*). Insertion and lookup performance decline significantly when the maximum load factor is greater than 1.0, which is the default. Performance can be improved modestly by reducing the maximum load factor below 1.0.

The initial number of buckets in an unordered map can be specified as a constructor argument. The container will not be reallocated until its size exceeds *buckets * load* *factor*. The program can increase the number of buckets in an unordered map by calling its rehash() member function. rehash(size_t n) sets the bucket count to be at least n, reallocates the bucket array, and rebuilds the table, moving all entries to their appropriate buckets in the new array. If n is less than the current number of buckets, rehash() may or may not decrease the size of the table and rehash.

A call to reserve(size_t n) can reserve space sufficient to hold n entries before reallocation. This is equivalent to a call to rehash(ceil(n/max_load_factor())).

A call to the unordered map's clear() member function erases all the entries and returns all storage to the memory manager. This is a stronger promise than the one provided for vector or string's clear() member function.

Unlike other C++ standard library containers, std::unordered_map exposes the structure of its implementation by providing an interface for iterating through the buckets as well as for iterating through the entries in a single bucket. Inspecting the length of the chains in each bucket can help reveal any issues with the hash function. I used this interface for inspecting the quality of the hash functions, as seen in Example 10-3.

Example 10-3. Snooping on std::unordered_map behavior

```
template<typename T> void hash_stats(T const& table) {
    unsigned zeros = 0;
    unsigned ones  = 0;
    unsigned many  = 0;
    unsigned many_sigma = 0;
    for (unsigned i = 0; i < table.bucket_count(); ++i) {
        unsigned how_many_this_bucket = 0;
        for (auto it = table.begin(i); it != table.end(i); ++it) {
            how_many_this_bucket += 1;
        }
        switch(how_many_this_bucket) {
        case 0:
            zeros += 1;
            break;
        case 1:
            ones  += 1;
            break;
        default:
            many += 1;
            many_sigma += how_many_this_bucket;
            break;
        }
    }
    std::cout << "unordered_map with " << table.size()
              << " entries" << std::endl
              << "    " << table.bucket_count() << " buckets"
              << " load factor " << table.load_factor()
```

```
              << ", max load factor "
              << table.max_load_factor() << std::endl;
    if (ones > 0 && many > 0)
        std::cout << "     " << zeros << " empty buckets, "
                  << ones << " buckets with one entry, "
                  << many << " buckets with multiple entries, "
                  << std::endl;
    if (many > 0)
        std::cout << "     average length of multi-entry chain "
        << ((float) many_sigma) / many << std::endl;
}
```

I discovered, using a hash function from the Boost project, that 15% of my entries collided, and that the automatic allocation produced a table with a load factor of 0.38, meaning that 62% of the backbone array was unused. The hash functions I tried performed far worse than I expected.

Inserting and Deleting in std::unordered_map

Like `std::map`, `std::unordered_map` provides two insertion methods, with and without an insertion hint. But unlike a map, an unordered map does not use the insertion hint. It is provided for interface compatibility only, and it carries a slight performance penalty even though it accomplishes nothing.

The insertion test took 15.5 milliseconds. Insertion performance can be improved somewhat by preallocating sufficient buckets to prevent rehashing, through a call to `reserve()`. The improvement in performance was only 4% on my test, improving insertion time to 14.9 milliseconds.

Reallocation can be deferred by setting the maximum load factor very high. I tested to see whether performance improved when I did this and then rehashed after all items were inserted. This turned out to be a disastrous deoptimization for the version of `unordered_map` in Visual Studio 2010's standard library. Apparently items are inserted onto the end of the collision chain in Visual Studio's implementation, so the cost of each insertion went from constant to $O(n)$. It is possible that a more sophisticated implementation would not have this weakness.

Iterating in std::unordered_map

Example 10-4 contains code to iterate through a `std::unordered_map`.

Example 10-4. Iterating through the entries in an unordered map

```
for (auto it = test_container.begin();
        it != test_container.end();
     ++it) {
```

```
    sum += it->second;
}
```

An unordered map cannot be sorted, and iterating through an unordered map produces items in an opaque order, as the container's name implies. Iterating through the unordered map was relatively efficient at 0.34 milliseconds. This was only 2.8 times slower than the same traversal of a `std:vector`.

Lookup with std::unordered_map

Lookup is the *raison d'être* of `std::unordered_map`. I compared the lookup performance of a 100,000-entry key/value table based on an unordered map versus a sorted table based on a vector and searched with `std::lower_bound()`.

`std::unordered_map` performed my lookup test of 100,000 queries in 10.4 milliseconds. As seen in Table 10-5, this is 3 times faster than `std::map`, and 1.7 times faster than for a sorted `std::vector` using `std::lower_bound()`. Yes, this is faster—much faster. But hash tables are held in such reverence that I expected a truly astonishing, order-of-magnitude performance increase. This is not what I saw.

Table 10-5. Insertion and lookup time for vector, map, and unordered_map

	Insert+sort	Lookup
Map	33.8 ms	42.3 ms
Vector	19.1 ms	28.9 ms
Unordered map	15.5 ms	10.4 ms

Compared to `std::map`, the unordered map is somewhat faster to build and much faster to search. The downside of the unordered map is the amount of storage it uses. In a constrained environment, it may be necessary to use the more compact table based on `std::vector`. Otherwise, the unordered map is an unambiguous performance win.

Other Data Structures

The standard library containers, helpful as they are, are not the final word in data structures. The Boost (*http://www.boost.org/*) library alone contains a number of data structures in imitation of the standard library containers. Boost provides the following libraries containing alternative containers:

`boost::circular_buffer` (*http://bit.ly/circ-buffer*)
    Similar in many respects to `std::deque`, but more efficient.

Boost.Container *(http://bit.ly/boost-cont)*

Variations on standard library containers such as a stable vector (a vector in which reallocation doesn't invalidate iterators), a map/multimap/set/multiset implemented as a container adapter for `std::vector`, a static vector with variable length up to a fixed maximum, and a vector with optimized behavior when the vector has only a few elements.

dynamic_bitset *(http://bit.ly/b-bitset)*

Looks like a vector of bits.

Fusion (http://bit.ly/b-fusion)

Containers and iterators on tuples.

Boost Graph Library (BGL) (http://bit.ly/b-graphlib)

Algorithms and data structures for graph traversal.

boost.heap *(http://bit.ly/b-heap/)*

A priority queue with better performance and more nuanced behavior than the simple `std::priority_queue` container adapter.

Boost.Intrusive (http://bit.ly/b-intrusive)

Provides intrusive containers (containers that rely on node types that explicitly contain links). The point of intrusive containers is to improve performance in very hot code. This library contains singly and doubly linked lists, associative containers, unordered associative containers, and a variety of explicit balanced tree implementations. `make_shared`, along with move semantics and the `emplace()` member functions added to most containers, reduces the need for intrusive containers.

boost.lockfree (http://bit.ly/b-lockfree)

Lock-free and wait-free queue and stack.

Boost.MultiIndex (http://bit.ly/b-multi)

Containers that have multiple indices with different behaviors.

And there are doubtless other container classes buried in Boost.

Another significant contribution comes from games company Electronic Arts, who open-sourced their version of the standard library container classes, called EASTL *(http://bit.ly/ea-stl)*. Electronic Arts's take on the standard library container classes includes:

- A simpler and more sensible `Allocator` definition
- Stronger guarantees on some containers, including a guarantee that containers don't call into the memory manager until the program puts items into them
- More programmability of `std::deque`

- A bunch of containers similar to the ones provided by Boost

Summary

- *Stepanov's Standard Template Library was the first reusable library of efficient containers and algorithms.*
- *Big-O performance of container classes does not tell the full story. Some containers are many times faster than others.*
- *std::vector is the fastest container at insert, delete, iterate, and sort operations.*
- *Lookup using std::lower_bound in a sorted std::vector can be competitive with std::map.*
- *std::deque is only slightly faster than std::list.*
- *std::forward_list is no faster than std::list.*
- *The hash table std::unordered_map is faster than std::map, but not by the order-of-magnitude difference that its reputation suggests.*
- *The Internet is a rich source of containers imitating the standard library containers.*

## CHAPTER 11

Optimize I/O

A program is a spell cast over a computer, turning input into error messages.

—Anonymous

This chapter treats efficient use of the C++ streaming I/O functions for the commonly occurring example of reading and writing text data. Reading and writing data are activities so commonplace that developers don't even notice them—yet these activities are time-consuming.

The rotation of a disk platter is as ponderous and slow to today's ultra-fast computer chips as the rotation of the Earth is to us. The read heads have inertia that must be overcome to move their bulk from track to track. These physical properties fiercely resist attempts at improving hardware performance. In the internetworked world of limited data rates and busy servers, response latency may be measured in seconds rather than milliseconds. Even the speed of light becomes a significant factor when streaming data from distant computers.

Another problem with I/O is that there is a lot of code between the user's program and the spinning platters of the disk or the network interface card. The cost of all this code must be managed to make I/O as efficient as possible.

A Recipe for Reading Files

There are a number of formulas on the Web for reading and writing files (*http://bit.ly/ read-cpp*), and even some that claim to be fast. They range in performance over a whole order of magnitude in my tests. Readers who are already smart enough not to use an unvetted recipe from the Internet (such as the legendarily dangerous and incorrect recipes for making explosives or cooking meth) might be wise to add to that list recipes for reading a file in C++.

Optimization War Story

My sister-in-law Marcia liked to bake pies, but she was never satisfied with the recipes she could find for pie crust. She could not get her crusts to come out as light and flaky as the best pie crusts she had tasted. Although Marcia was not a software developer, she was a pretty good optimizer, so this is what she did.

She collected a number of recipes for pie crust, all of which claimed to be "the best pie crust ever." She noted that all of them had ingredients in common: flour, salt, water, shortening. Then she looked at the differences. Some used butter or lard instead of vegetable shortening. Some called specifically for cold ingredients or to cool the dough before rolling it out. Some added a little sugar, a tablespoon of vinegar, or an egg. Marcia took the distinctive advice from several recipes and performed tasty experiments over several months. As a result of her patient experimentation, she settled upon a combination of the advice from several recipes. The resulting pie crusts were amazing.

As with my sister-in-law's optimization effort, I discovered that there are several techniques for improving the performance of file-reading functions. Many of these techniques can be combined. I also discovered some techniques that had little value.

Example 11-1 is a simple function to read a text file into a string. I have encountered code like this over and over, often as a prelude to parsing the string as an XML or JSON block.

Example 11-1. Original file_reader() function

```
std::string file_reader(char const* fname) {
    std::ifstream f;
    f.open(fname);
    if (!f) {
        std::cout << "Can't open " << fname
                  << " for reading" << std::endl;
        return "";
    }

    std::stringstream s;
    std::copy(std::istreambuf_iterator<char>(f.rdbuf()),
            std::istreambuf_iterator<char>(),
            std::ostreambuf_iterator<char>(s) );
    return s.str();
}
```

The `fname` argument contains a filename. If the file cannot be opened, `file_reader()` prints an error message to standard output, and returns the empty string. Otherwise, `std::copy()` copies f's streambuf into `std::stringstream` s's streambuf.

Create a Parsimonious Function Signature

From a library design standpoint, `file_reader()` could be improved (see "Parsimony Is a Virtue in Library Design" on page 194). It does several different things: it opens a file; it performs error handling (in the form of reporting failure to open the file); it reads the open, valid stream into a string. As a library function, this combination of responsibilities makes `file_reader()` hard to use. For instance, if the client program implements exception handling, or wants to use a Windows resource for error message strings, or even just wants to print to `std::cerr`, `file_reader()` can't be used. `file_reader()` also creates new memory and returns it, a pattern that potentially causes multiple copies to be made as the returned value is passed up a calling chain (see "Copy Free Libraries" on page 134). When the file cannot be opened, `file_reader()` returns the empty string. It also returns the empty string if the file is readable, but doesn't contain any characters. It would be nice to get an error indication so these cases could be distinguished.

Example 11-2 is an updated version of `file_reader()` that separates the concerns of opening files and reading streams, and has a signature that users won't immediately want to change.

Example 11-2. stream_read_streambuf_stringstream(), now with parsimony!

```
void stream_read_streambuf_stringstream(
    std::istream& f,
    std::string& result) {
    std::stringstream s;
    std::copy(std::istreambuf_iterator<char>(f.rdbuf()),
              std::istreambuf_iterator<char>(),
              std::ostreambuf_iterator<char>(s) );
    std::swap(result, s.str());
}
```

The last line of `stream_read_streambuf_stringstream()` exchanges the dynamic storage of `result` with that of `s.str()`. I might instead have assigned `s.str()` to `result`, but that would have caused an allocation and copy unless the compiler and string library implementation both provided move semantics. `std::swap()` is specialized for many standard library classes to call a `swap()` member function. The member function in turn swaps pointers, which is far less expensive than an allocate-and-copy operation.

As a bonus for being parsimonious, f becomes a std::istream, rather than a std::ifstream. This function could work on other kinds of streams too, like std::stringstream, for instance. The function is also shorter and easier to read, containing just one conceptual nugget of computation.

stream_read_streambuf_stringstream() may be called with this client code:

```
std::string s;
std::ifstream f;
f.open(fname);
if (!f) {
    std::cerr << "Can't open " << fname
              << " for reading" << std::endl;
}
else {
    stream_read_streambuf_stringstream(f, s);
}
```

Notice that the client is now responsible for opening the file and for reporting errors in a manner appropriate to the client, while the stream-reading "magic" is still in stream_read_streambuf_stringstream()—only this version of the function isn't very magical.

I performed an experiment that read a 10,000-line file 100 times. This experiment exercises much of the machinery in C++ standard I/O. Because of the repetition, the operating system almost certainly caches the file contents. In real-world conditions, which are difficult to simulate in a test loop, this function probably takes longer than the measured 1,548 milliseconds in both Visual Studio 2010 and 2015.

Because this program reads the disk, and because there is only one disk on my computer, the test run was more sensitive to other disk activity on the PC than other tests I have run. I had to close nonessential programs and stop nonessential services. Even then, I had to make several test runs and report the smallest number I got.

stream_read_streambuf_stringstream() makes use of standard library idioms, but isn't particularly efficient. It uses character iterators to copy a single character at a time. It is reasonable to hypothesize that each character fetched operates a substantial amount of machinery in std::istream, and perhaps even in the host operating system's file I/O API. It is equally reasonable to imagine that a std::string in the std::stringstream is extended by one character at a time, resulting in a significant number of calls into the memory allocator.

There are several variations of the copy-the-stream-iterator idea. Example 11-3 uses std::string::assign() to copy an iterator from the input stream into a std::string.

Example 11-3. Another copy-the-stream-iterator file reader

```
void stream_read_streambuf_string(
    std::istream& f,
    std::string& result) {
    result.assign(std::istreambuf_iterator<char>(f.rdbuf()),
                  std::istreambuf_iterator<char>());
}
```

This code ran my test in 1,510 milliseconds when compiled with Visual Studio 2010, and 1,787 milliseconds using Visual Studio 2015.

Shorten Calling Chains

Example 11-4 is another character-at-a-time variation. std::istream has an opera tor<<() that takes a streambuf as an argument. Perhaps operator<<() bypasses the istream API to call directly into the streambuf.

Example 11-4. Append stream to a stringstream, a character at a time

```
void stream_read_streambuf(std::istream& f, std::string& result) {
    std::stringstream s;
    s << f.rdbuf();
    std::swap(result, s.str());
}
```

This code ran my test in 1,294 milliseconds on Visual Studio 2010 and 1,181 milliseconds on Visual Studio 2015—17% and 51% faster, respectively, than stream_read_streambuf_string(). It is my hypothesis that the underlying code just runs a smaller amount of machinery.

Reduce Reallocation

stream_read_streambuf_string() contains seeds of hope for optimization. Although there is no obvious way to optimize the iterate-the-streambuf idiom, the std::string into which the file is being read can be preallocated by a call to reserve() to prevent costly reallocation as the string grows longer, character by character. Example 11-5 tests whether this idea improves performance.

Example 11-5. stream_read_string_reserve(): Preallocating storage for the result

```
void stream_read_string_reserve(std::istream& f,
                                std::string& result)
{
    f.seekg(0,std::istream::end);
    std::streamoff len = f.tellg();
    f.seekg(0);
```

```
    if (len > 0)
        result.reserve(static_cast<std::string::size_type>(len));

    result.assign(std::istreambuf_iterator<char>(f.rdbuf()),
                  std::istreambuf_iterator<char>());
}
```

stream_read_string_reserve() finds how long the stream is by positioning its
stream pointer at the end of the stream, reading the offset, and then resetting the
stream pointer to the beginning. istream::tellg() actually returns a small struct
that gives the position, including an offset for a partially read UTF-8 multibyte character. Fortunately, this struct implements a conversion to a signed integral type. The
type must be signed because tellg() can fail, returning an offset of -1 if, for instance,
the stream has not been opened, or if there has been an error, or if end-of-file has
been reached. If tellg() returns an offset instead of -1, that value can be used as a
hint to std::string::reserve() to preallocate sufficient storage for the whole file, in
a manner similar to remove_ctrl_reserve() in Example 4-3.

stream_read_string_reserve() tests the hypothesis that the cost of seeking the file
pointer twice is less than the cost of the allocations eliminated by the call to
reserve(). This is not a foregone conclusion. If seeking to the end of the file causes
all the disk sectors in the file to be read, there is a substantial cost. On the other hand,
having read these disk sectors, the operating system may have them in cache, reducing other costs. Maybe it depends on the file size. C++ might be able to seek the file
pointer to end-of-file without reading anything but the directory entry for the file, or
there may be an operating system–dependent function for doing this (perhaps more
than one).

When the conjectures start piling up like this, the experienced optimizer recognizes
that the cost of finding the answers to all these questions is high, and the benefit
unknown. An experiment will quickly tell if the C++ idiom of seeking to end-of-file
to get the file size is helpful. On Windows, stream_read_string_reserve() performed no better on the test than stream_read_streambuf_string(). However, this
may only mean that the degree of improvement was not noticeable compared to
other inefficiencies in this method of reading the file.

Spoiler alert: the technique of finding the length of the stream and preallocating storage is a useful tool. It is good library design to factor out reusable tools into their own
functions. A function stream_size() implementing this technique is in
Example 11-6.

Example 11-6. stream_size(): compute length of a stream

```
std::streamoff stream_size(std::istream& f) {
    std::istream::pos_type current_pos = f.tellg();
    if (-1 == current_pos)
        return -1;
    f.seekg(0,std::istream::end);
    std::istream::pos_type end_pos = f.tellg();
    f.seekg(current_pos);
    return end_pos - current_pos;
}
```

A stream-reading function may be called with the stream already partially consumed.
stream_size() accounts for this possibility by saving the current position, seeking to
the end of the stream, and computing the difference between the current position and
the end. The stream pointer is restored to the saved position before the function ends.
This is actually more correct than the simplified computation done in
stream_read_string_reserve(). It's another example of how good library design
makes functions more flexible and general.

Example 11-7 is a version of stream_read_string() with the file size estimation performed outside the function. This allows the developer to provide an estimate when
called on streams that cannot determine their size. It defaults to the behavior of
stream_read_string() when no estimate is available.

Example 11-7. stream_read_string_2(): general-purpose version of stream_read_string()

```
void stream_read_string_2(std::istream& f,
                          std::string& result,
                          std::streamoff len = 0)
{
    if (len > 0)
        result.reserve(static_cast<std::string::size_type>(len));

    result.assign(std::istreambuf_iterator<char>(f.rdbuf()),
                  std::istreambuf_iterator<char>());
}
```

stream_read_string_2() ran the test in 1,566 milliseconds on VS2010 and 1,766
milliseconds on VS2015. The cost of the extra function call to stream_size(), while
presumably nonzero, was not observable in my test. On the other hand,
stream_read_string_2() was not observably faster than stream_read_string().
Did this technique fail? We'll see later.

Take Bigger Bites—Use a Bigger Input Buffer

C++ streams contain a class derived from `std::streambuf` that improves performance in the case of file reading by reading data from the underlying operating system in bigger chunks. The data goes into a buffer inside the streambuf, from which it is extracted byte-by-byte by the iterator-based input methods discussed previously. Some articles on the Internet suggest that increasing the size of this input buffer will improve performance. Example 11-8 is a simple way to do this.

Example 11-8. Increasing the size of std::streambuf's internal buffer

```
std::ifstream in8k;
in8k.open(filename);
char buf[8192];
in8k.rdbuf()->pubsetbuf(buf, sizeof(buf));
```

Many Internet-dwellers report having difficulty using `pubsetbuf()`. It must be called after the stream is opened and before any characters are read from the stream. The call fails if any status bits (`failbit`, `eofbit`) are set in the stream. The buffer must remain valid until the stream is closed. I obtained a small but measurable 20–50 millisecond improvement in test run time on most of the input functions in this section by setting a larger buffer in the streambuf. Values over 8 KB had little additional effect on run time. This was rather disappointing, because back in the day, increasing the size of a similar buffer in the C `FILE` struct produced a dramatic improvement on code I had written. This demonstrates again how prior experience can lead the optimizing developer astray. This improvement amounts to around 5% on the 1,500-millisecond test run times observed so far, but might be a bigger component if the overall run time can be reduced.

Take Bigger Bites—Read a Line at a Time

In the introduction to this section, I noted that the files to be read were often text files. For a text file divided into lines, it is a reasonable hypothesis that a function that reads lines might reduce the number of function calls, hopefully using a line-oriented or buffer-filling interface internally. In addition, if the result string is updated less frequently, there should be less copying and reallocation. Indeed, there is a function called `getline()` in the standard library, and Example 11-9 can be used to test this hypothesis.

Example 11-9. stream_read_getline() reads the file a line at a time

```
void stream_read_getline(std::istream& f, std::string& result) {
    std::string line;
    result.clear();
```

```
    while (getline(f, line))
        (result += line) += "\n";
}
```

`stream_read_getline()` appends to `result`. `result` must be cleared at the start because there is nothing requiring that it be empty when passed into the function. `clear()` does not return the string's dynamic buffer to the memory manager. It just sets the length of the string to zero. Depending how the string argument was used before the call, it might already have a substantial dynamic buffer, reducing the burden of allocation.

Testing `stream_read_getline()` validates these hypotheses: it takes only 1,284 milliseconds on VS2010 and 1,440 milliseconds on VS2015 to complete 100 iterations of reading a 10,000-line file.

Although `result` might happen already to be long enough to prevent reallocation, it's a good plan to reserve space, just in case. The same mechanism used in `stream_read_string_2()` can be added to `stream_read_getline()`, producing the function in Example 11-10.

Example 11-10. stream_read_getline_2(): line at a time, plus preallocation of result variable

```
void stream_read_getline_2(std::ifstream& f,
                           std::string& result,
                           std::streamoff len = 0)
{
    std::string line;
    result.clear();

    if (len > 0)
        result.reserve(static_cast<std::string::size_type>(len));

    while (getline(f, line))
        (result += line) += "\n";
}
```

This optimization yielded a just-measurable 3% performance improvement versus `stream_read_getline()`. This improvement can be combined with a bigger streambuf to get test run times of 1,193 (VS2010) and 1,404 (VS2015) milliseconds.

Another way to approach taking bigger bites is by using the `std::streambuf` member function `sgetn()`, which retrieves an arbitrary amount of data into a buffer argument to the call. For files of reasonable size, the entire file can be retrieved in a single big gulp. The `stream_read_sgetn()` function in Example 11-11 illustrates this approach.

Example 11-11. stream_read_sgetn()

```
bool stream_read_sgetn(std::istream& f, std::string& result) {
    std::streamoff len = stream_size(f);
    if (len == -1)
        return false;

    result.resize (static_cast<std::string::size_type>(len));

    f.rdbuf()->sgetn(&result[0], len);
    return true;
}
```

In `stream_read_sgetn()`, `sgetn()` copies data directly into the `result` string, which must be made big enough to hold the data. The size of the stream must therefore be determined before the call to `sgetn()`. It is not optional, like in the `stream_read_string_2()` function in Example 11-7. The size is determined by a call to `stream_size()`.

As previously noted, `stream_size()` can fail. It would be nice to get a failure indication out of `stream_read_sgetn()`. Fortunately, since this library function uses the copy-free idiom (see "Copy Free Libraries" on page 134), its return value is available for a success/fail indication.

`stream_read_sgetn()` is fast. It completed the test in 307 (VS2010) and 148 (VS2015) milliseconds, over 4 times faster than `stream_read_streambuf()`. When combined with a bigger rdbuf, test run time shrank to 244 (VS2010) and 134 (VS2015) milliseconds. The modest improvement from a bigger rdbuf makes a bigger contribution when the overall time is shorter.

Shorten Calling Chains Again

`std::istream` provides a `read()` member function that copies characters directly into a buffer. This function mimics the low-level `read()` function in Linux and `Read File()` on Windows. If `std::istream::read()` is wired directly to this low-level functionality, bypassing the buffering and other baggage of C++ stream I/O, it should be more efficient. Furthermore, if the entire file can be read at once, it may produce a very efficient call. Example 11-12 implements this functionality.

Example 11-12. stream_read_string() uses read() into a string's storage

```
bool stream_read_string(std::istream& f, std::string& result) {
    std::streamoff len = stream_size(f);
    if (len == -1)
        return false;

    result.resize (static_cast<std::string::size_type>(len));
```

```
    f.read(&result[0], result.length());
    return true;
}
```

`stream_read_string()`, running the test in 267 (VS2010) and 144 (VS2015) milliseconds, is about 25% faster than `stream_read_sgetn()` and 5 times faster than `file_reader()`.

A problem with `stream_read_sgetn()` and `stream_read_string()` is that they assume the pointer `&s[0]` points to a contiguous block of storage. Prior to C++11, the C++ standard did not *require* the characters of a string to be stored contiguously, though all standard library implementations of which I am aware were coded this way. The C++11 standard contains clear language in section 21.4.1 saying that string storage is contiguous.

I tested a function that dynamically allocated a character array into which data was read and then copied into a string using `assign()`. This function would be usable even if a novel string implementation violated the contiguous storage rule:

```
bool stream_read_array(std::istream& f, std::string& result) {
    std::streamoff len = stream_size(f);
    if (len == -1)
        return false;

    std::unique_ptr<char> data(new char[static_cast<size_t>(len)]);

    f.read(data.get(), static_cast<std::streamsize>(len));
    result.assign(data.get(), static_cast<std::string::size_type>(len));
    return true;
}
```

This function performed my test in 307 (VS2010) and 186 (VS2015) milliseconds, only a little slower than `stream_read_string()`.

Things That Didn't Help

I found some seriously complex advice to construct a custom streambuf to improve performance. Example 11-13 is one such function found in the wild.

Example 11-13. Kids, don't try this at home

```
// from: http://stackoverflow.com/questions/8736862
class custombuf : public std::streambuf
{
public:
    custombuf(std::string& target): target_(target) {
        this->setp(this->buffer_, this->buffer_ + bufsize - 1);
    }
```

```
private:
    std::string& target_;
    enum { bufsize = 8192 };
    char buffer_[bufsize];
    int overflow(int c) {
        if (!traits_type::eq_int_type(c, traits_type::eof())) {
            *this->pptr() = traits_type::to_char_type(c);
            this->pbump(1);
        }
        this->target_.append(this->pbase(),
                            this->pptr() - this->pbase());
        this->setp(this->buffer_, this->buffer_ + bufsize - 1);
        return traits_type::not_eof(c);
    }
    int sync() { this->overflow(traits_type::eof()); return 0; }
};

std::string stream_read_custombuf(std::istream& f) {
    std::string data;
    custombuf sbuf(data);
    std::ostream(&sbuf) << f.rdbuf() << std::flush;
    return data;
}
```

The problem with this code sample is that it's an attempt to optimize an inefficient algorithm. As observed previously (in `stream_read_streambuf()`), inserting a streambuf on an ostream wasn't particularly fast. Performance, at 1,312 (VS2010) and 1,182 (VS2015) milliseconds, was no better than that of `stream_read_streambuf()`. Any improvement was probably due to using an 8 KB buffer in the custom streambuf, which can be done with just a couple of lines of code.

Writing Files

To test my file-reading functions, I had to create files. This let me test file-writing functions. My first file-writing attempt looked like Example 11-14.

Example 11-14. stream_write_line()

```
void stream_write_line(std::ostream& f, std::string const& line) {
    f << line << std::endl;
}
```

This function, called 10,000 times to produce a file and iterated 100 times to produce timing data, took 1,972 (VS2010) and 2,110 (VS2015) milliseconds.

`stream_write_line()` pushes out each line with a `std::endl`. Something I didn't know about endl is that it flushes the output. Without the `std::endl`, writing should

---

be faster, because `std::ofstream` only pushes a few big blocks of data out to the operating system. Example 11-15 tests this hypothesis.

Example 11-15. stream_write_line_noflush() is faster

```
void stream_write_line_noflush(std::ostream& f,
                               std::string const& line)
{
    f << line << "\n";
}
```

Of course, either `stream_write_line_noflush()` must be finished with an
`f.flush()`, or the stream must be closed, so that the last buffer full of data goes out.
`stream_write_line_noflush()` produced my file in 367 (VS2010) and 302 (VS2015)
milliseconds, about 5 times faster than `stream_write_line()`.

I also called `stream_write_line_noflush()` with the entire file in a single string. As
expected, this was much faster, completing the test loop in 132 (VS2010) and 137
(VS2015) milliseconds. This was about 1.7 times faster than putting out the file line-
by-line.

Reading from std::cin and Writing to std::cout

When reading from the standard input, it is worth knowing that `std::cin` is tied to
`std::cout`. Requesting input from `std::cin` flushes `std::cout` first, so that interactive console programs display their prompts. A call to `istream::tie()` will produce a
pointer to a tied stream, if any exist. A call to `istream::tie(nullptr)` breaks an
existing tie. Flushing is quite costly, as shown in the previous section.

Another thing to know about `std::cin` and `std::cout` is that the C++ streams are
conceptually connected to the C `FILE*` objects `stdin` and `stdout`. This permits a program to use both C++ and C I/O statements and have interleaving of the output or
input make some kind of sense. The way `std::cout` is connected to `stdout` is
implementation-defined. Most standard library implementations forward `std::cout`
directly to `stdout` by default. `stdout` is line-buffered by default, a mode not present
in C++ iostreams. When `stdout` sees a newline, it flushes its buffer.

Performance improves if the connections are severed. Calling the static member
function `std::ios_base::sync_with_stdio(false)` breaks this connection, improving performance at the expense of unpredictable interleaving if a program uses both
C and C++ I/O functions.

I did not test how significant the performance difference was.

Summary

- Code for "fast" file I/O on the Internet is not necessarily fast, no matter what the site tries to sell you.

- Increasing the size of the `rdbuf` produces a few percent performance improvement on reading files.

- The best read times I could obtain used the `std::streambuf::sgetn()` function to fill a string buffer preallocated to the size of the file.

- `std::endl` flushes the output. It's expensive if you are not doing console output.

- `std::cout` is tied to `std::cin` and `stdout`. Breaking these ties can improve performance.

## CHAPTER 12

Optimize Concurrency

It's tough to make predictions, especially about the future.

—Yogi Berra (1925–2015), baseball legend and inadvertent humorist

This quip appeared in English-language physics and economics journals prior to becoming a "Yogi-ism." It is also attributed as a Danish proverb. It seems unlikely, though, that Berra misappropriated it from any of these sources.

All but the smallest modern computers process multiple execution streams concurrently. They contain multiple CPU cores, graphics processors with hundreds of simple cores, audio processors, disk controllers, network cards, and even keyboards with separate computing power and memory. Like it or not, developers live in a concurrent world, and must understand how to program concurrent activities.

Software practices for concurrency evolved in a world of single-core processors. Since 2005, the advent of multicore microprocessors providing true (versus time-sliced) concurrency has altered the development landscape, informing best practices with new rules. These rules may be unfamiliar even to developers experienced with concurrency issues that arise in single-processor systems.

If the future direction of processor development leads to commercial devices with dozens or hundreds of cores, programming best practices will continue to change. Several competing tools promoting fine-grained concurrency have arrived that anticipate this future. However, general-purpose hardware with many cores has yet to become mainstream,[1] standards of practice have not yet solidified in the developer community, and clear leaders among fine-grained concurrency solutions have yet to

---

[1] Yes, yes, I *have* heard of GPUs. When millions of developers are programming directly on GPUs, they will be mainstream. That time has yet to arrive.

emerge. This future is by no means certain. It is with some sadness that I leave this very interesting topic for others to cover.

Concurrency can be provided to programs by a variety of mechanisms. Some of them live outside of C++, in the operating system or on the hardware. C++ code appears to run normally as a single program or a group of programs communicating via I/O. Still, these approaches to concurrency have some bearing on the design of C++ programs.

The C++ standard library directly supports a shared-memory thread model of concurrency. Many developers are more familiar with the concurrency features of their operating system, or with the C-language calls of the POSIX Threads (pthreads) library. It is also my experience that developers are far less familiar with the concurrency features of C++, and concurrency in general, than they are with other areas of C++ programming. For this reason, I provide more extensive notes on how these C++ features may be used than I do for other features covered in this book.

Concurrency support in the C++ standard library is a work in progress. While the standard has made tremendous strides in providing foundational concepts and capabilities, many capabilities are still working their way through standardization and will not arrive until C++17 or later.

This chapter discusses several techniques to improve performance of thread-based concurrent programs. The discussion assumes that readers are already basically familiar with thread-level concurrency and synchronization primitives, and are looking for ways to optimize their threaded programs. Providing "basic familiarity" with thread-level concurrency would be the topic of yet another book.

Concurrency Refresher

Concurrency is the simultaneous (or apparently simultaneous) execution of multiple threads of control. The goal of concurrency is not a reduction in the number of instructions executed or data words accessed per se. It is rather an increase in utilization of computing resources that reduces run time as measured on a wall clock.

Concurrency improves performance by permitting some program activities to move forward while other activities wait for an event to occur or a resource to become available. This allows computing resources to be utilized more of the time. The more activities that proceed concurrently, the more resources are used and the more activities wait for events and resources, in a positive feedback loop that increases overall utilization of computing and I/O resources up to some saturation point, hopefully near 100% utilization. The result is a reduction of wall-clock time versus what would happen if each task was performed to completion before the next task started, with the computer idling while awaiting events.

From the standpoint of optimization, the challenge of concurrency is to find enough independent tasks to fully utilize available computing resources, even if some tasks must wait on external events or availability of resources.

C++ offers a modest library for shared-memory thread-based concurrency. This is by no means the only way that C++ programs can implement a system of cooperating programs. Other kinds of concurrency also have an impact on C++ programs, and are thus worth at least a brief look.

This section examines the C++ memory model and the basic toolkit for using shared memory in multithreaded programs. In my opinion, it's the gnarliest topic in C++. It's gnarly because our sad little monkey brains are single-threaded. They can reason naturally about just one cause-and-effect stream at a time.

A Walk Through the Concurrency Zoo

Concurrency can be provided to programs by the computer hardware, by operating systems, by function libraries, and by the features of C++ itself. This section describes a number of concurrency features and their impact on C++.

The fact that certain concurrency features are built into C++ while others are provided by library code or the operating system must not be read as an endorsement of one concurrency model over others. Some facilities are built in because they have to be. There is no other way to provide them. The most notable forms of concurrency include:

Time slicing
>   This is a function of the scheduler in the operating system. In time slicing, an operating system maintains a list of currently executing programs and system tasks, and allocates chunks of time to each program. Any time a program is waiting for an event or resource, the program is taken off the operating system's runnable list, making its share of the processor available for the other programs.
>
>   An operating system is processor- and hardware-dependent. It makes use of a timer and periodic interrupts to mediate the scheduling of processes. C++ remains unaware that it is being time sliced.

Virtualization
>   In one typical kind of virtualization, a lightweight operating system called a *hypervisor* allocates chunks of processor time to a *guest virtual machine*. The guest virtual machine (VM) contains a filesystem image and a memory image, which is typically an operating system running one or more programs. When a hypervisor runs a guest virtual machine, certain processor instructions and accesses to certain regions of memory cause a trap into the hypervisor, allowing the hypervisor to emulate I/O devices and other hardware resources. In another type of virtualization, a conventional operating system hosts the guest virtual

machines, using the operating system's I/O facilities to more efficiently emulate I/O when the host and guest virtual machines run the same operating system.

Some advantages of virtualization include:

- Guest virtual machines are packaged as disk files when they aren't running. The guest VM can be checkpointed and saved, loaded and resumed, and copied and run on multiple computer hosts.

- Multiple guest virtual machines can be run concurrently, resources permitting. Each guest VM is isolated from the others by the hypervisor, in cooperation with the computer's virtual memory protection hardware. This allows hardware to be commoditized and rented by the hour.

- Guest virtual machines can be configured to use a portion of the resources (physical memory, processor cores) of a host computer. Computing resources can be tailored to fit the requirements of the programs running on each guest VM, providing consistent levels of performance and preventing unintended interactions among multiple VMs running concurrently on the same hardware.

As with traditional time slicing, C++ remains unaware that it is running within a guest VM under a hypervisor. C++ programs may be indirectly aware that they have constrained resources. Virtualization is relevant to C++ program design because it makes it both possible to limit the computational resources consumed by a program and necessary for the program to know what resources are actually available.

Containerization

Containerization is similar to virtualization in that containers hold a filesystem image and a memory image containing a checkpointed program state. They differ in that the container host is an operating system, so that I/O and system resources can be provided directly instead of emulated less efficiently by the hypervisor.

Containerization has the same advantages as virtualization (packaging, configuration, and isolation) plus containers can run somewhat more efficiently.

Containerization is not visible to C++ programs running within a container. It is relevant to C++ programs for the same reason as virtualization.

Symmetric multiprocessing

A symmetric multiprocessor is a computer containing several execution units that execute the same machine code and have access to the same physical memory. Modern multicore processors are symmetric multiprocessors. The currently executing programs and system tasks can be run on any available execution unit, though the choice of execution unit may have consequences on performance.

A symmetric multiprocessor executes multiple threads of control with true hardware concurrency. If there are n execution units, the total run time of a compute-bound program can be reduced by a factor of as much as $1/n$. These hardware threads stand in contrast to software threads, discussed later, which may or may not run on distinct hardware threads, and thus may or may not reduce total run time.

Simultaneous multithreading

Some processors are designed so that each hardware core has two (or more) register sets and executes two or more corresponding streams of instructions. When one stream stalls (as for an access to main memory), instructions from the other stream can execute. A processor core having this feature acts like two (or more) cores, so that a "four-core processor" really can host eight hardware threads. This is important, as we'll see in "Create as Many Runnable Threads as Cores" on page 308, because the most efficient use of software threads matches the number of software threads to the number of hardware threads.

Multiple processes

Processes are concurrent streams of execution that have their own protected virtual memory space. Processes communicate using pipes, queues, network I/O, or some other unshared mechanism.[2] Processes synchronize using synchronization primitives or by *pending* on input (that is, blocking until the input becomes available).

The principal advantage of processes is that the operating system isolates one process from another. If one process crashes, the others remain alive, although they may have nothing to do.

The greatest weakness of processes is that they have a lot of state: virtual memory tables, multiple execution unit contexts, plus the contexts of all suspended threads. They are slower to start, stop, and switch between than threads.

C++ doesn't experience processes directly. Generally, a C++ program is represented by an operating system process. There are no tools in C++ to manipulate processes because not all operating systems even possess a process concept. On small processors, programs may be time sliced but not protected from one another, so that they act more like threads.

Distributed processing

Distributed processing is distribution of an activity onto a collection of processors that are not necessarily the same, and that communicate over links that are

---

2 Some operating systems permit designated blocks of memory to be shared between processes. These mechanisms for sharing memory among processes are arcane and operating system–dependent, and are not covered here.

typically slow compared to the processor. A cluster of cloud instances communicating via TCP/IP links is an example of distributed processing. An example of distributed processing on a single PC is offloading drivers to processors running on disk drives and network cards. Another example is offloading graphics tasks to the many kinds of specialized processors in a graphics processing unit (GPU). GPUs have traditionally been provided on video cards, but the latest silicon stylings from several manufacturers put GPUs onto the microprocessor die.

In a typical distributed processing setup, data flows through a pipeline or network of processes, where each process performs some transformation on the input, pushing the transformed data to the next stage in the pipeline. This model, which is as old as Unix command-line pipelines, allows relatively heavyweight processes to run efficiently. Processes in a pipeline are long-lived, avoiding startup costs. Processes can continuously transform units of work, so they use whole time slices, subject to availability of input. Most importantly, processes do not share memory or synchronize with each other, so they run at full speed.

Although C++ contains no process concept, distributed processing is relevant to C++ development because it influences the design and structure of programs. Sharing memory does not scale beyond a few threads. Some treatments of concurrency advocate abandoning shared memory altogether. Distributed processing systems often decompose naturally into subsystems, producing modular, understandable, reconfigurable architectures.

Threads

Threads are concurrent streams of execution within a process that share the same memory. Threads synchronize using synchronization primitives and communicate using shared memory locations.

Their strength, in comparison to processes, is that threads consume fewer resources and are faster to create and faster to switch between.

Threads have several weaknesses, however. Since all threads in a process share the same memory space, a thread writing to invalid memory locations can overwrite data structures in other threads, causing them to crash or behave unpredictably. Further, access to shared memory is many times slower than access to unshared memory and must be synchronized between threads, or the contents are difficult to interpret.

Most operating systems support threads with an operating system–dependent library. Up until recently, C++ developers with experience in concurrency used a native thread library or the POSIX Thread (pthread) library, which provides a cross-platform solution with basic services.

Tasks

A task is a unit of execution that can be invoked asynchronously in the context of a separate thread. In task-based concurrency, the tasks and the threads are separately and explicitly managed, so that a task is assigned to a thread for execution. By contrast, in thread-based concurrency, the thread and the executable code running on the thread are managed as a unit.

Task-based concurrency is built atop threads, so tasks share the strengths and weaknesses of threads.

An additional advantage of task-based concurrency is that the number of active software threads can be matched to the number of hardware threads so that threads execute efficiently. The program can prioritize and queue tasks for execution. By contrast, in a thread-based system, the operating system prioritizes threads in an opaque and operating system–dependent manner.

The cost of tasks' extra flexibility is greater application complexity. The program must implement some means of prioritizing or sequencing tasks. The program must also manage a pool of threads upon which to run tasks.

Interleaved Execution

Astronomers have a funny way of thinking about the universe. Hydrogen makes up 73% of the visible matter in the universe. Helium makes up 25%. Everything else makes up less than 2%. Astronomers can describe most features of the observable universe as if it consisted exclusively of hydrogen and helium. They call all the other elements—the ones that make up planets, processors, and people—"metals," as if they had no separate identity, and pretty much ignore them.

Concurrent programs can similarly be abstracted into loads, stores, and branches, and the branches mostly ignored, as if all the complexity of programming was irrelevant. Discussions of concurrency (including the ones in this book) often feature simple program fragments consisting mostly of sequences of assignment statements to illustrate concurrency concepts.

Concurrent execution of two threads of control can be modeled as interleaving the simple load and store statements of the two threads. If thread 1 and thread 2 each consist of a single statement, the possible interleavings are "12" and "21". If each thread has two statements, there are several potential interleavings: "1122", "1212", "2112", "1221", "2121", "2211". In real programs, a very large number of interleavings are possible.

In the days of single-core processors, concurrency was implemented by time slicing in the operating system. Race conditions were relatively infrequent because many statements from one thread executed before the operating system gave control to the other thread. The interleavings observed in practice were "1111...11112222....2222".

With today's multicore processors, interleavings of individual statements are possible, so race conditions are more frequently visible. Developers who wrote concurrent programs in the single-processor past may have a sense of complacency about their skill that is no longer warranted.

Sequential Consistency

As noted in Chapter 2, C++ believes in a simple, intuitive model of the computer. This model includes the requirement that programs are *sequentially consistent*. That is, programs behave as if statements are executed in the order in which they are written, subject to C++ flow of control statements. Obvious as this requirement seems, those weasel-words "as if" in the previous sentence permit many compiler optimizations and innovative microprocessor designs.

For instance, the program fragment in Example 12-1 is sequentially consistent even if y is set to 0 before x is, or x is set to 1 after y is set to 1, or even if x is set to 1 after the comparison y == 1 in the if statement, as long as the assignment x = 1 happens before assert(x == 1)—that is, before the value is used.

Example 12-1. Sequential consistency means "as if" executed in order

```
int x = 0, y = 0;
x = 1;
y = 1;
if (y == 1) {
    assert(x == 1);
```

The reader may well ask, "Why would the compiler *want* to reorder statements?" In fact, there are many reasons, all of them about the dark magic of optimal code generation in compilers, of which I dare not speak. And it's not just the compiler moving things around; modern microprocessors reorder loads and stores too (see "There Are Multiple Streams of Program Execution" on page 22).

The combined effect of compiler optimizations, out-of-order execution, caching, and write buffering can be modeled using the common metaphor of loads and stores breaking loose from their places in the program listing and moving up and down the page to a point before or after their intended position. This metaphor captures all these effects without having to explain or understand details of compiler optimizations and hardware behavior in a specific processor.

In a particular compiler/hardware combination, not all possible movements of loads and stores actually happen. Moving loads and stores of shared variables thus illustrates a worst-case scenario. But trying to reason about a specific hardware architecture when it has three levels of cache and behavior that depends on which cache line each variable is on is insanely difficult. It is also not fruitful, because most programs must run on more than one hardware device over their lifetime.

What matters is that a program remains sequentially consistent when use of a variable is moved up or down with respect to other statements, so long as it doesn't move past an update of that variable. Likewise, the program remains sequentially consistent when updates of a variable are moved up or down, so long as they don't move past a use.

Races

Concurrency creates a problem for C++, which provides no way to tell when two functions may run concurrently and what variables are shared. Code-moving optimizations that are perfectly reasonable when considering one function at a time may cause problems when two functions run concurrently.

If thread 1 consists of the statement x = 0 and thread 2 the statement x = 100, the outcome of the program depends on a *race* between the two threads. A race occurs when the result of the concurrent execution of these statements depends on which interleaving occurs in a given run of the program. The interleaving "12" produces the result x == 100, and the interleaving "21" produces x == 0. The result of this program, or any program containing a race, is *nondeterministic*—that is, unpredictable.

The C++ standard memory model says programs behave as if they were sequentially consistent, as long as they do not contain races. *If a program contains races, sequential consistency may be violated.*

Example 12-2 is a multithreaded version of Example 12-1, this time with more meaningful variable names.

Example 12-2. Sequential consistency of multiple threads

```
// thread 1, running in core 1
shared_result_x = 1;
shared_flag_y = 1;
    ...
// thread 2, running in core 2
while (shared_flag_y != 1)
    /* busy-wait for shared_flag_y to be set to 1 */ ;
assert(shared_result_x == 1);
```

shared_result_x is a result computed in thread 1 to be used by thread 2. shared_flag_y is a flag set by thread 1 that tells thread 2 that the result is ready to use. If the compiler or processor reorders the two statements in thread 1 so that shared_flag_y is set before shared_result_x, thread 2 may (but not necessarily must) exit its while loop after seeing the new value of shared_flag_y, and asserts because it still sees the old value of `shared_result_x`. Each thread is sequentially consistent, but the interaction of the two threads is a race.

Sequential consistency of variables shared between threads is guaranteed by some languages that don't have that pesky "as if" in their definition. It is provided in others because shared variables are explicitly declared; the compiler doesn't move them around and generates special code to ensure that the hardware doesn't move them either. A concurrent C++ program must explicitly force a particular interleaving to preserve sequential consistency.

Synchronization

Synchronization is the forced ordering of the interleaving of statements in multiple threads. Synchronization allows developers to reason about the order in which things happen in a multithreaded program. Without synchronization, the order in which things happen is unpredictable, making it hard to coordinate actions between threads.

Synchronization primitives are programming constructs whose purpose is to achieve synchronization by forcing a particular interleaving of concurrent programs. All synchronization primitives work by causing one thread to wait for, or *pend* on, another thread. By enforcing a specific execution order, synchronization primitives prevent races.

A variety of synchronization primitives have been proposed and implemented in the past 50 years of programming. Microsoft Windows has a rich set of synchronization primitives, including events on which threads can *pend*, two kinds of mutexes, a very general semaphore, and Unix-style signals. Linux has its own rich but distinct set.

It is important to understand that synchronization primitives exist as concepts only. There is no authoritative voice that says exactly what a semaphore is, or exactly how a monitor should be implemented. What Windows calls a semaphore can be hard to recognize from Dijkstra's original description.[3] Furthermore, the whole menagerie of proposed synchronization primitives can be synthesized out of a sufficiently rich set of pieces, in the same way that any Boolean function can be synthesized in hardware from NAND and NOR gates. Different implementations on different operating systems should thus be expected.

Classical synchronization primitives interact with the operating system to move threads between active and pending states. This implementation is appropriate for computers with only one relatively slow execution unit. However, the latency of start-

---

3 Edsger W. Dijkstra, "Cooperating Sequential Processes (EWD-123)," (*http://bit.ly/ewd-123*) E.W. Dijkstra Archive, Center for American History, University of Texas at Austin (September 1965).

ing and stopping threads using the operating system can be significant. When there are multiple processors executing streams of instructions in a truly concurrent fashion, synchronization by busy-waiting on shared variables can produce very short wait times. Synchronization library designers may also take a hybrid approach.

Atomicity

An operation on a shared variable (particularly a class instance having multiple members) is *atomic* if no thread can ever see an update performed by another thread in a half-completed state. If update operations are not atomic, some interleavings of two threads' code allow one thread to access the shared variable when it is in an inconsistent, half-updated state due to an update operation in progress on another thread. Viewed another way, atomicity is a promise that these undesirable interleavings cannot occur.

Atomicity by mutual exclusion

Traditionally, atomicity is provided via mutual exclusion. Each thread wishing to access a shared variable must *acquire* a mutex before accessing the shared variable, and *release* the mutex when the operation is complete. The part of the program bounded by acquiring and releasing the mutex is called a *critical section*. If one thread has acquired a mutex, all other threads pend when they try to acquire the mutex. Thus, only one thread at a time can perform operations on the shared data. This thread is said to *hold* the mutex. The mutex *serializes* the threads so that critical sections execute one after the other.

Loads and stores of shared variables must happen within a critical section, where only one thread is running, or a race with unpredictable results may occur. But as discussed in "Sequential Consistency" on page 286, the compiler and processor both move loads and stores. A mechanism called a *memory fence* prevents loads and stores of shared variables from leaking out of a critical section. In the processor, special instructions tell it not to move loads and stores past the memory fence. In the compiler, the memory fence is conceptual. The optimizer does not move loads past function calls, because any function call might contain a critical section.

The memory fence at the top of a critical section must prevent loads of shared variables from leaking out the top of the critical section. This memory fence is said to have *acquire semantics*, because it happens when the thread acquires a mutex. Similarly, the memory fence at the bottom of a critical section must prevent stores of shared variables from leaking out the bottom. This memory fence is said to have *release semantics*, because it happens when the thread releases a mutex.

In the days of single-core processors, memory fences were unnecessary. Compilers did not reorder loads and stores across function calls, and the operating system synchronized memory almost accidentally when it switched threads. But in the multicore world, programmers must contend with this new issue. Developers who use synchronization primitives provided by the C++ standard library or the native synchronization library of their operating system don't need to worry about memory fences, but programmers implementing synchronization primitives or lock-free data structures must take a keen interest.

Atomic hardware operations

Implementing atomicity by mutual exclusion has costs that make it a troublesome tool to wield:

- Since only one thread can hold a mutex, operations on shared variables cannot run concurrently. The more time a critical section consumes, the more time the critical section takes away from concurrent execution. The more threads that operate on the shared variable, the more time the critical section takes away from concurrent execution.

- When a thread releases a mutex, another thread pending on the mutex can acquire it. But the mutex may not guarantee *which* other thread acquires it, because providing such a guarantee is expensive. If many threads are pending on the mutex, some threads may never acquire it; the computations performed by those threads do not move forward. This situation is called *starvation*.

- If a thread holds one mutex and needs to acquire a second mutex, a situation can arise where the thread can never move forward because another thread holds the second mutex and wishes to acquire the first mutex. This situation is called *deadlock*, or, more colorfully, *the deadly embrace*. A thread can deadlock itself by trying to lock the same mutex twice. Any number of threads can deadlock because of a cyclic dependency on mutexes among the threads. There is no known way to guarantee that a program that attempts to acquire multiple mutexes is deadlock-free, although there are deadlock avoidance strategies.

For simple variables like integers and pointers, certain operations can be performed atomically on some computers because the operations are performed by single machine instructions. These special atomic instructions contain memory fences that ensure the instruction is not interrupted halfway through execution.

Atomic instructions form the basis for implementing mutexes and other synchronization primitives. Surprisingly sophisticated thread-safe data structures can be implemented using only the operations that can be done atomically by the hardware. This is called *lock-free programming* because code that works in this way does not have to wait to acquire a mutex.

Lock-free programs scale to larger numbers of concurrent threads, but they are not a cure-all. Threads are still serialized by atomic operations, even those performed by a single instruction. However, the duration of the critical section is an order of magnitude smaller than that of even the most efficient mutex.

C++ Concurrency Facilities Refresher

As of C++14, concurrency support in the C++ standard library is somewhat Spartan, compared to the rich facilities in popular operating systems. This is partly because the C++ facilities must contain only behavior implementable on all operating systems. It is also partly because C++ concurrency is still a work in progress, with substantial improvements scheduled for C++17. The advantage of using C++ concurrency features, versus native calls into the operating system, is that the C++ facilities are defined to behave in a consistent way across platforms.

The concurrency facilities of the C++ standard library fit together like a set of stacking blocks, building concurrency up from the operating system's very C-ish threading library to a fully C++ threading solution that can pass arbitrary argument lists, return values, throw exceptions, and be stored in containers.

Threads

The `<thread>` header file provides the `std::thread` template class, which allows a program to create thread objects as thin wrappers around the operating system's own threading facilities. `std::thread`'s constructor takes a *callable object* (a function pointer, function object, lambda, or `bind` expression) as an argument, and executes it in the context of a new software thread. C++ uses variadic template argument forwarding magic to call functions with arbitrary argument lists, whereas the underlying operating system thread invocation typically takes a pointer to a void function with one `void*` argument.

`std::thread` is an RAII (resource acquisition is initialization) class for managing operating system threads. It provides a `get()` member function, which returns an operating system's native thread handle. This allows a program access to the operating system's generally richer set of functions that act on threads.

Example 12-3 shows a simple example of `std::thread` use.

Example 12-3. Starting a few simple threads

```
void f1(int n) {
    std::cout << "thread " << n << std::endl;
 }

void thread_example() {
    std::thread t1;          // thread variable, not a thread
    t1 = std::thread(f1, 1); // assign thread to a thread variable
    t1.join();               // wait for thread to complete
```

```
    std::thread t2(f1, 2);
    std::thread t3(std::move(t2));
    std::thread t4([]() { return; });// works with lambdas too
    t4.detach();
    t3.join();
}
```

Thread t1 is initially empty. Threads cannot be copied because they each contain a unique handle to the underlying resource, but the move assignment operator allows an empty thread to be assigned an rvalue. t1 can own any thread that executes a function taking an integer argument. A function pointer to f1 and an integer argument are provided to the constructor. The second argument is forwarded to the callable object (f1), which is started in std::thread's constructor.

Thread t2 is started with the same function but a different second argument. Thread t3 is an example of the move constructor in action. After the move constructor, t3 is running the thread started as t2, and t2 is empty. Thread t4 shows that threads can be started with lambdas as their callable object.

The operating system thread represented by a std::thread has to be disposed of before the std::thread is destroyed. The thread can be joined, as in t3.join(), which means the current thread waits for the thread being joined to end. The operating system thread can also be dissociated from the std::thread object, as in t4.detach(). In this case, the thread continues to execute, but isn't visible to the thread that started it any longer. A detached thread ends when its callable object returns. If the callable object does not return, the thread is a resource leak, continuing to consume resources until the full program ends. If neither join() nor detach() is called before the std::thread is destroyed, its destructor calls terminate(), abruptly stopping the whole program.

Although it is possible to work directly with std::thread, it may be more productive to think of std::thread as a building block of more sophisticated facilities. Any value returned by the function object is ignored. Any exception thrown by the function object causes immediate, unconditional program termination via a call to terminate(). These limitations make naked calls to std::thread fragile, almost as if the standard writers wanted to discourage their use.

Promises and Futures

The C++ std::promise and std::future template classes are, respectively, the sending and receiving ends of a message from one thread to another. Promises and futures allow threads to asynchronously produce values and throw exceptions. The promise and future share a dynamically allocated variable called the *shared state* that can hold either a value of a defined type, or an exception of any type encapsulated in a standard wrapper. A thread of execution can pend on a future, so the future also acts as a synchronization device.

Promises and futures may be used simply to implement an asynchronous function call and return. However, the promise and future are far more general than that simple use. They can implement a graph of dynamically changing communication points among threads. That said, they provide no structuring mechanism, so completely wild and crazy communication graphs may be difficult to debug.

The C++ <future> header file contains the functionality of promises and futures. An instance of the std::promise template allows a thread to set the shared state to either a value of a specified type or an exception. The sending thread does not wait for the shared state to be read; it can continue immediately.

A promise's shared state is not *ready* until either a value or an exception is set. The shared state is meant to be set exactly once. Otherwise:

- If the thread attempts to set a value or exception more than once, the shared state is instead set to the exception std::future_error with an error code of promise_already_satisfied, and the shared state becomes *ready* releasing any futures waiting on the promise.

- If the thread never sets a value or exception, when the promise is destroyed, the destructor sets the shared state to the exception std::future_error with error code broken_promise, and the shared state becomes *ready*, releasing any futures waiting on the promise. To get this useful error indication, the promise must be destroyed in the thread's callable object.

std::future allows a thread to receive the value or exception saved in the shared state of a promise. A future is a synchronization primitive; the receiving thread pends in the call to the future's get() member function until the corresponding promise is made *ready* by a call to set the value or exception.

A future is not *valid* until it is constructed or assigned from a promise. The receiving thread cannot pend on a future until it is valid. The future must be constructed from a promise before the sending thread is executed. Otherwise, the receiving thread may try to pend on the future before it is *valid*.

Promises and futures can't be copied. They are entities that represent a specific communication rendezvous. They can be constructed and move-constructed, and a promise can be assigned to a future. Ideally, the promise is created in the sending thread and the future is created in the receiving thread. There is an idiom in which a promise is created in the sending thread, then passed as an rvalue reference using std::move(promise) to the receiving thread so its contents are moved into a promise belonging to the receiving thread. std::async() performs this strange magic for the developer. It is also possible to pass a promise by reference to the sending thread. Example 12-4 shows how to control thread interaction using promises and futures.

Example 12-4. Promises, futures, and threads

```
void promise_future_example() {
    auto meaning = [](std::promise<int>& prom) {
        prom.set_value(42); // compute the meaning of life
    };

    std::promise<int> prom;
    std::thread(meaning, std::ref(prom)).detach();

    std::future<int> result = prom.get_future();
    std::cout << "the meaning of life: " << result.get() << "\n";
}
```

In Example 12-4, the promise prom is created before the std::thread is invoked. This isn't perfect as written, because it doesn't test for a broken promise. It is necessary though, because if prom is not constructed before the thread starts, there is no way to guarantee that the future result will be *valid* before the call to result.get().

The program then constructs an anonymous std::thread. Its arguments are the lambda meaning, which is the callable object to be executed, and prom, the promise that is an argument to meaning. Note that since prom is a reference argument, it must be wrapped in std::ref() so the argument-forwarding magic will work correctly. The call to detach() dissociates the running thread from the anonymous std::thread, which is destroyed.

Now two things are happening: the operating system is getting ready to execute meaning, and the program is creating the future result. The program may execute prom.get_future() before the thread begins to run. This is why prom was created before the thread was constructed—so that the future would be *valid* and the program could pend, awaiting the thread.

The program pends in result.get(), waiting for the thread to set the shared state in prom. The thread calls prom.set_value(42), making the shared state *ready* and releasing the program. The program finishes by outputting "the meaning of life: 42".

There is nothing magical about futures. A developer who wanted to design a thread that first returned an int and then returned a std::string could make two promises. The receiving program would create two matching futures.

Making the future *ready* signals that the computation is complete. Because a program can pend on a future, it isn't necessary for the program to pend on thread termination. This will be important in "Asynchronous Tasks" on page 295, when we discuss std::async(), and in "Implement a Task Queue and Thread Pool" on page 309, where we discuss thread pools, because it is more efficient to reuse threads than it is to destroy and re-create them.

Asynchronous Tasks

The C++ standard library task template class wraps a callable object in a try block and saves the returned value or thrown exception in a promise. Tasks permit callable objects to be called asynchronously by threads.

Task-based concurrency in the C++ standard library is only half-formed. C++11 provides the async() template function that packages a callable object as a task and invokes it on a reusable thread. async() is a bit of a "god function" (see "Beware of 'God Functions'" on page 199), hiding many juicy details of thread pools and task queues.

Tasks are represented in the C++ standard library <future> header file. The std::packaged_task template class wraps any *callable* object (which can be a function pointer, function object, lambda, or bind expression) so that it can be called asynchronously. The packaged task is itself a callable object that can be the callable argument to a std::thread. The great advantage of tasks versus other callable objects is that a task can return a value or throw an exception without abruptly terminating the program. The task's return value or thrown exception is stored in a shared state that can be accessed through a std::future object.

Example 12-5 is a simplified version of Example 12-4 that uses a packaged_task.

Example 12-5. packaged_task and thread

```
void promise_future_example_2() {
    auto meaning = std::packaged_task<int(int)>(
                        [](int n) { return n; });
    auto result  = meaning.get_future();
    auto t       = std::thread(std::move(meaning), 42);

    std::cout << "the meaning of life: " << result.get() << "\n";
    t.join();
}
```

The packaged_task meaning contains both a callable object and a std::promise. This solves the problem of getting the promise destructor called in the context of the thread. Notice that the lambda in meaning simply returns; the machinery of setting the promise is all comfortably hidden.

In this example, I joined the thread instead of detaching it. Although it isn't completely obvious from this example, both main program and thread can continue running concurrently after the main program gets the future's value.

The <async> library provides a facility based on tasks. A template function std::async() executes a *callable* object argument, and the callable object may be executed in the context of a new thread. However, std::async() returns a std::future, capable of holding either a return value or an exception thrown by the callable object called by std::async(). Furthermore, an implementation may choose to allocate std::async() threads out of a thread pool for improved efficiency. This is illustrated in Example 12-6.

Example 12-6. tasks and async()

```
void promise_future_example_3() {
    auto meaning = [](int n) { return n; };
    auto result = std::async(std::move(meaning), 42);
    std::cout << "the meaning of life: " << result.get() << "\n";
}
```

The lambda defined as meaning and the lambda's argument are passed to std::async(). Type deduction is used to determine the template parameters of std::async(). std::async() returns a future able to retrieve an int result or an exception, which is moved into result. The call to result.get() pends until the thread invoked by std::async() fulfills its promise by returning its int argument. Thread termination is managed within std::async(), which may keep the thread in a thread pool.

The example code need not explicitly manage thread termination. std::async() may use a thread pool maintained by the C++ runtime system to recycle the thread if this is cheaper than destroying and re-creating threads as needed. Explicit thread pools may be added in C++17.

Mutexes

C++ provides several mutex templates to provide mutual exclusion for critical sections. The mutex template definition is simple enough to be specialized for particular operating system–dependent native mutex classes.

The <mutex> header file contains four mutex templates:

std::mutex
> A simple, relatively efficient mutex. On Windows, this class tries a busy-wait first, and falls back to operating system calls if it cannot obtain the mutex quickly.

`std::recursive_mutex`

> A mutex that allows a thread that already holds the mutex to acquire it again, as in a nested function call. This class may be less efficient due to the need to count how many times it is acquired.

`std::timed_mutex`

> A mutex that permits a timed attempt to acquire the mutex. The requirement for timed attempts generally requires intervention from the operating system, which significantly increases the latency of this type of mutex in comparison to `std::mutex`.

`std::recursive_timed_mutex`

> A mutex that is both timed and recursive, with mustard, ketchup, and secret sauce. This type of mutex is tasty, but expensive.

My experience is that recursive and timed mutexes may be warnings of a design that can be simplified. The scope of a recursive lock is difficult to reason about, so it is deadlock-bait. The expense of these mutexes should be tolerated only when necessary, and they should be avoided when designing new code.

C++14 added the `<shared_mutex>` header file containing support for *shared mutexes*, also known as *reader/writer mutexes*. A single thread can lock a shared mutex in an exclusive mode, in order to atomically update a data structure. Multiple threads can lock a shared mutex in a shared mode to atomically read a data structure, but it is locked against exclusive access until all readers have released the mutex. The shared mutex may allow more threads to access the data structure without waiting, provided most accesses are for reading. These shared mutexes are available:

`std::shared_timed_mutex`

> A shared mutex that supports timed and untimed attempts to acquire the mutex.

`std::shared_mutex`

> A simpler shared mutex, scheduled for inclusion in C++17.

It is my experience that reader/writer mutexes lead to starvation of the writer thread unless reads are infrequent, in which case the value of the reader/writer optimization is negligible. As with recursive mutexes, developers must make a strong case for using this more complex mutex, and should usually choose a simpler, more predictable mutex.

Locks

In C++, the word *lock* refers to an RAII class that acquires and releases a mutex in a structured manner. Use of the word can be confusing because mutexes are also sometimes referred to as locks. Acquiring a mutex is also called *locking* the mutex, and releasing the mutex is also called *unlocking* the mutex. In C++, the mutex member function to acquire a mutex is named lock(). I have been using mutexes for over 20 years, and I still have to concentrate to keep these concepts straight.

The C++ standard library provides a simple lock to acquire one mutex, and a more general lock to acquire multiple mutexes. The general lock implements a deadlock avoidance algorithm.

The <mutex> header file contains two lock templates:

std::lock_guard
> A simple RAII lock. During the class's construction, the program waits for the lock to be acquired, and it releases the lock on destruction of the lock_guard. Pre-standard implementations of this class were often called scope_guard.

std::unique_lock
> A general-purpose mutex ownership class that offers RAII locking, deferred locking, timed locking attempts, transfer of mutex ownership, and use with condition variables.

A lock for shared mutexes was added in C++14, in the <shared_mutex> header file:

std::shared_lock
> A mutex ownership class for shared (reader/writer) mutexes. It offers all the sophisticated features of std::unique_lock, plus control of shared mutexes.
>
> A single thread can lock a shared mutex in an exclusive mode, to atomically update a data structure. Multiple threads can lock a shared mutex in a shared mode to atomically read a data structure, but it is locked against exclusive access until all readers have released the mutex.

Condition Variables

Condition variables allow C++ programs to implement the *monitor* concept proposed by famous computer scientists C.A.R. Hoare and Per Brinch-Hansen and widely deployed in Java as synchronized classes.[4]

A monitor shares a data structure among multiple threads. When a thread successfully enters the monitor, it owns a mutex that allows it to update the shared data structure. A thread may leave the monitor after updating the shared data structure, giving up its exclusive access. It may also pend on a condition variable, temporarily giving up exclusive access until a specific change occurs.

---

4 See C.A.R Hoare, "Monitors: An Operating System Structuring Concept," *ACM Communications* 17 (Oct 1974): 549–557.

A monitor may have one or more *condition variables*. Each condition variable summarizes a conceptual change-of-state event in the data structure. When a thread running inside the monitor updates the data structure, it must notify any condition variables affected by the update that the event they represent has occurred.

C++ provides two implementations of condition variables in the <condition_vari able> header file. They differ in the generality of the lock argument they accept:

std::condition_variable
> The most efficient condition variable, this requires the use of std::unique_lock to lock the mutex.

std::condition_variable_any
> A condition variable that can use any BasicLockable lock; that is, any lock offering lock() and unlock() member functions. This condition variable may be less efficient than std::condition_variable.

When a thread is released by a condition variable, the thread must verify that the data structure is in the expected state. This is because some operating systems may spuriously notify the condition variable. (My experience is that it may also happen due to programmer error.) Example 12-7 is an extended example of using condition variables to implement a multithreaded producer/consumer.

Example 12-7. Simple producer and consumer using condition variables

```
void cv_example() {
    std::mutex m;
    std::condition_variable cv;
    bool terminate = false;
    int shared_data = 0;
    int counter = 0;

    auto consumer = [&]() {
        std::unique_lock<std::mutex> lk(m);
        do {
            while (!(terminate || shared_data != 0))
                cv.wait(lk);
            if (terminate)
                break;
            std::cout << "consuming " << shared_data << std::endl;
            shared_data = 0;
            cv.notify_one();
        } while (true);
    };

    auto producer = [&]() {
        std::unique_lock<std::mutex> lk(m);
        for (counter = 1; true; ++counter) {
            cv.wait(lk,[&]() {return terminate || shared_data == 0;});
```

```
            if (terminate)
                break;
            shared_data = counter;
            std::cout << "producing " << shared_data << std::endl;
            cv.notify_one();
        }
    };

    auto p = std::thread(producer);
    auto c = std::thread(consumer);
    std::this_thread::sleep_for(std::chrono::milliseconds(1000));
    {
        std::lock_guard<std::mutex> l(m);
        terminate = true;
    }
    std::cout << "total items consumed " << counter << std::endl;
    cv.notify_all();
    p.join();
    c.join();
    exit(0);
}
```

The producer thread in Example 12-7 "produces" by setting a single integer called shared_data to a nonzero value. The consumer "consumes" shared_data by setting it back to zero. The main program thread launches the producer and consumer, then takes a 1,000-millisecond nap. When the main thread wakes up, it locks mutex m to briefly enter the monitor, then sets a flag called terminate, which causes both producer and consumer threads to exit. The main program notifies the condition variable that the state of terminate has changed, joins the two threads, and exits.

consumer enters the monitor by locking the mutex m. The consumer is a single loop that pends on a condition variable named cv. While it is pending on cv, consumer is not in the monitor; mutex m is available. When there is something to consume, cv is notified. The consumer wakes up, relocks the mutex m, and returns from its call to cv.wait(), conceptually reentering the monitor.

Example 12-7 uses a single condition variable, which has the meaning "the data structure has been updated." The particular update consumer normally waits for is shared_data != 0, but it also needs to wake up on terminate == true. This is an economical use of synchronization primitives, in contrast to the array of signals in the Windows WaitForMultipleObjects() function. A similar example could have been coded using one condition variable to wake the consumer and another to wake the producer.

The consumer invokes cv.wait() in a loop, checking each time it wakes to see whether the proper condition exists. This is because some implementations can spuriously wake threads waiting on a condition variable accidentally, when it isn't appropriate. If the condition is met, the `while` loop exits. If the condition that woke `consumer` was `terminate == true`, `consumer` exits its outer loop and returns. Otherwise, the condition was `shared_data != 0`. `consumer` prints a message, then indicates it has consumed the data by setting `shared_data` to zero and notifying `cv` that the shared data has changed. At this point, `consumer` is still inside the monitor, holding a lock on mutex `m`, but it continues the loop, entering `cv.wait()` again, unlocking the mutex and conceptually exiting the monitor.

The producer is similar. It pends until it can lock mutex `m`, then enters an outer loop that causes it to continue until it sees `terminate == true`. The producer waits on `cv` looking for a change in state. In this example, `producer` uses a version of `wait()` that takes a predicate argument, causing it to loop until the predicate is false. The predicate is thus the condition implied by notifying the condition variable. This second form is syntactic sugar, hiding the `while` loop. Initially, `shared_data` is already zero, so the producer doesn't wait on `cv`. It updates `shared_data`, then notifies `cv`, then loops back and enters `cv.wait()`, releasing the mutex and conceptually exiting the monitor.

Atomic Operations on Shared Variables

The C++ standard library `<atomic>` header file provides low-level tools for building multithreaded synchronization primitives: memory fences and atomic load and store.

`std::atomic` provides a standard mechanism to update an arbitrary data structure, so long as it is copy constructable or move constructable. Any specialization of `std::atomic` must provide the following functions for any type `T`:

`load()`
> `std::atomic<T>` provides the member function `T load(memory_order)`, which copies the `T` object out of the `std::atomic<T>` atomically.

`store()`
> `std::atomic<T>` provides the member function `void store(T, memory_order)`, which copies a `T` object into the `std::atomic<T>` atomically.

`is_lock_free()`
> `is_lock_free()` returns `bool true` if all operations defined on this type are implemented without the use of mutual exclusion, as by a single read-modify-write machine instruction.

Specializations of `std::atomic` are provided for integral and pointer types. Where the processor supports it, these specializations synchronize memory without invoking the operating system's synchronization primitives. The specializations provide a number of operations that can be implemented atomically on modern hardware.

The performance of std::atomic depends on the processor for which code is being compiled:

- Intel-architecture PCs have a variety of read-modify-write instructions, and the cost of the atomic access depends on the memory fence, with some fences having no cost at all.

- On single-core processors with read-modify-write instructions, std::atomic may generate no extra code at all.

- On processors that do not have atomic read-modify-write instructions, std::atomic may be implemented using expensive mutual exclusion.

Memory fences

Most std::atomic member functions take an optional memory_order argument that selects a memory fence around the operation. If the memory_order argument is not provided, the default is memory_order_acq_rel. This provides a full fence that is always safe, but can be expensive. More refined fences can be selected, but this should be done only by knowledgeable users.

Memory fences synchronize main memory with the cache of multiple hardware threads. In general, a memory fence is executed on each of two threads to synchronize one thread with the other. C++ allows the following memory fences:

memory_order_acquire

    memory_order_acquire may be casually thought to mean "acquire all work done by other threads." It ensures that subsequent loads are not moved before the current load or any previous loads. It does this, paradoxically, by waiting for store operations currently in flight between the processor and main memory to complete. Without the fence, if a store is in flight when this thread does a load to the same address, the thread gets old information, as if the load had moved up inside the program.

    memory_order_acquire may be less expensive than the default full fence. It would be appropriate, for instance, to use memory_order_acquire when atomically reading the flag in the while loop of a busy-wait.

memory_order_release

    memory_order_release may casually be thought to mean "release all work done by this thread to this point." It ensures that previous loads and stores done by this thread are not moved past the current store. It does this by waiting for store operations currently in flight within this thread to complete.

`memory_order_release` may be less expensive than the default full fence. It would be appropriate, for instance, when setting the flag at the end of a home-built mutex.

`memory_order_acq_rel`

This combines the two previous guarantees, creating a full fence.

`memory_order_consume`

`memory_order_consume` is a potentially weaker (and faster) form of `memory_order_acquire` that requires only that the current load take place before other operations that are data-dependent on it. For instance, when a load of a pointer is marked `memory_order_consume`, subsequent operations that dereference this pointer won't be moved before it.

`memory_order_relaxed`

With this value, all reorderings are OK.

As currently implemented on most processors, memory fences are a blunt tool. The memory fence blocks forward progress until *all* writes in flight have completed. In reality, only writes to shared locations need be completed, but neither C++ nor x86-compatible processors have the means to identify this more restrictive set of locations, especially as the set varies from one thread to the next.

Stop and Think

Multicore x86 processors released to date have a helpful memory model. All loads have acquire semantics, and all stores have release semantics. That is, the x86 architecture imposes a strong ordering on memory access. It was probably necessary to forgo a more aggressive memory model in the x86 to maintain compatibility with a host of legacy programs whose concurrency features were not in fact correctly implemented. PowerPC, ARM, and Itanium processors all have weaker ordering (and higher performance).

What this means is that developers who write concurrent C++ programs using Visual C++ on the x86 can currently get away with multithreaded murder—but if they recompile the same program on an ARM or PowerPC processor, they may be surprised by new threading bugs in their supposedly debugged and working code.

Atomic access is no panacea. The memory fence is quite expensive. To find out just how expensive, I performed an experiment, timing an atomic store operation versus a simple store. Example 12-8 times a simple atomic store (with default full fence) performed in a loop.

Example 12-8. Atomic store test

```
typedef unsigned long long counter_t;
std::atomic<counter_t> x;
for (counter_t i = 0, iterations = 10'000'000 * multiplier;
     i < iterations; ++i)
   x = i;
```

The test took 15,318 milliseconds on my PC. The non-atomic version of this test, reproduced in Example 12-9, took 992 milliseconds—about 14 times faster. In an example with more writes in flight, the difference might be even more dramatic.

Example 12-9. Non-atomic store test

```
typedef unsigned long long counter_t;
counter_t x;
for (counter_t i = 0, iterations = 10'000'000 * multiplier;
     i < iterations; ++i)
   x = i;
```

If `std::atomic` were implemented with an operating system mutex, as it might be on some small processors, the difference in performance might be several orders of magnitude. `std::atomic` must thus be used with some knowledge of the target hardware.

If you're wondering what the single quotes are doing in the numeric constant, the ability to put group-separators in a numeric constant is one of several small but wonderful additions in C++14. Some people may find the C++14 changes small and fussy. I find them very helpful.

On Deck: Future C++ Concurrency Features

The developer community shows a tremendous interest in concurrency, driven no doubt by the availability and the need to make use of rapidly growing computer resources. Many developers became experienced with thread-based concurrency using either native calls or the C-style functions of the POSIX Threads (pthreads) library. Some of these developers built C++-style wrappers around the native calls. The best of these efforts have emerged in public, gathering user communities and cross-pollinating one another. Many proposals for new C++ concurrency features are now working their way through the standardization process. C++17 is likely to have far more extensive concurrency support—but nothing is certain about the future except that it is coming.

This is just a sample of what may arrive by C++17:

Cooperative multithreading

In cooperative multithreading, two or more software threads pass execution among themselves via explicit statements so that only one thread is actually running at a time. Coroutines are an example of cooperative multithreading.

Cooperative multithreading has a few key advantages:

- Each thread can maintain its context when not actively executing.
- Since only one thread is running at a time, variables are not shared. Mutual exclusion is not necessary.

Coroutines appear to be coming in C++17, and are available right now in Boost (*http://www.boost.org/doc/libs/1_59_0/libs/coroutine/doc/html/index.html*). A bunch of building blocks for various innovative concurrency schemes are listed in a recent proposal (*http://bit.ly/doc-n4399*) from the C++ Concurrency TR working group.

SIMD instructions

SIMD is an acronym for *single instruction multiple data*. In processors supporting SIMD, certain instructions operate on a vector of registers. The processor performs the same action simultaneously on each register in the vector, reducing overhead versus scalar operations.

The C++ compiler does not normally generate SIMD instructions because their behavior is complex and not well matched to the way C++ describes programs. Compiler-dependent pragmas or inline assembly features allow SIMD instructions to be inserted into functions, which are then provided in libraries for specialized tasks like digital signal processing or computer graphics. SIMD programming is thus both processor- and compiler-dependent. Among the many web references regarding SIMD instructions is a Stack Exchange Q&A (*http://bit.ly/simd-c-lib*) that contains lots of references about using SIMD in C++.

Optimize Threaded C++ Programs

TANSTAAFL: There ain't no such thing as a free lunch.

—First used in print in the article "Economics in Eight Words" in the *El Paso Herald-Post* on June 27, 1938. Many geeky people recognize the quote from Robert A. Heinlein's 1966 novel *The Moon Is a Harsh Mistress.*

Desktop-class microprocessors in widespread use as of early 2016 have a few cores with highly pipelined execution units and multiple levels of cache memory. Their architectures are appropriate for high-performance execution of a few threads of control. Executing many threads requires frequent, expensive context switches.

This architecture must be held in mind when designing concurrent programs. Attempting to force-fit a data-parallel, fine-grained model of concurrency onto current desktop processor designs can produce programs that use concurrency ineffi-ciently.

In the bright future of personal hover-cars and cities in the clouds, programming lan-guages will automatically parallelize programs in an effective way. Until then, it's up to individual developers to find tasks that can be done concurrently. Although oppor-tunities for concurrency are as diverse as are programs, there are some reliable places to look for threadable code. I've listed a few of these in the following sections.

The threading behavior of a program may be wired deeply into its structure. It can thus be more difficult to modify threading behavior than to optimize allocation or function calls. That said, there are some design practices for concurrent programs that optimize performance. Some of these practices have evolved only in the past few years, so they may not be familiar even to experienced users.

Prefer std::async to std::thread

From a performance standpoint, a significant problem with std::thread is that each invocation starts a new software thread. Starting a thread has both direct and indirect costs that make this operation very expensive:

- The direct cost includes calling into the operating system to allocate space for the thread in the operating system's tables, allocate memory for the thread's stack, initialize the thread's register set, and schedule the thread to run. If the thread gets a new scheduling quantum, there is a delay before it begins to run. If it gets the rest of the invoking thread's scheduling quantum, there is a delay while stor-ing the invoking thread's registers.

- An indirect cost of creating threads is an increase in the amount of memory used. Each thread must reserve storage for its own stack of called functions. If large numbers of threads are started and stopped frequently, this can cause thrashing in the cache as threads executing on the computer compete for access to a limited cache.

- Another indirect cost is incurred when the number of software threads exceeds the number of hardware threads. All threads then begin to slow down as they must be scheduled by the operating system.

I measured the cost of starting and stopping a thread by running the program frag-ment in Example 12-10 in a loop. The void function within the thread returns imme-diately. This is the briefest possible function. The call to join() causes the main program to wait until the thread finishes, causing thread invocations to be laid end-to-end with no overlap. This would be bad concurrency design if it didn't have a spe-cific goal of measuring the cost of starting threads.

Example 12-10. Starting and stopping std::thread

```
std::thread t;
t = std::thread([]() { return; });
t.join();
```

In fact, this test probably underrepresents the cost of thread invocation, because the threads don't write anything into the cache. But the results are still significant: 10,000 thread invocations took around 1,350 milliseconds, or about 135 microseconds per thread start and stop, on Windows. This is many thousands of times the cost of executing the lambda. `std::thread` is a fabulously expensive way to perform a brief computation, even if it could be done concurrently.

There is no escaping this cost because it is a latency. It is the time it takes before the call to `std::thread`'s constructor returns and the time before the call to `join()` ends. Even if the program detaches the threads instead of waiting to join them, the test still consumes over 700 milliseconds.

A useful optimization in concurrent programming is to reuse threads instead of creating new threads for each use. A thread can pend on some condition variable until needed, be released, and then execute a callable object. While some of the costs of switching threads (saving and restoring registers and flushing and refilling the cache) are the same, other costs, like allocating memory for the thread and scheduling it in the operating system, are eliminated or reduced.

The template function `std::async()` runs a callable object in the context of a thread, but the implementation is allowed to reuse threads. The standard hints that `std::async()` may be implemented using a thread pool. On Windows, `std::async()` is significantly faster. I ran the code fragment in Example 12-11 in a loop to measure the improvement.

Example 12-11. starting and stopping with async()

```
std::async(std::launch::async, []() { return; });
```

`std::async()` returns a `std::future`, which in this case is an unnamed temporary. The program calls the destructor of this unnamed `std::future` as soon as `std::async()` returns. The destructor waits for the future to become *ready*, so it can throw any exception that might occur. No explicit `join()` or `detach()` call is required. Example 12-11, like Example 12-10, lays the thread executions out end-to-end.

The improvement was dramatic: 10,000 invocations of the simple lambda took only 86 milliseconds, about 14 times faster than if a new thread was started each time.

Create as Many Runnable Threads as Cores

Older treatises on concurrency advise creating as many threads as are convenient, in a manner similar to creating dynamic variables. This thinking reflects an antique world where threads competed for the attention of a single processor. In the modern world of multicore processors, this advice is too simplistic.

The optimizing developer may distinguish two kinds of threads, with different behavior:

Runnable threads compute continuously
> A runnable thread consumes 100% of the computing resources of the core upon which it runs. If there are *n* cores, scheduling a runnable thread on each core can reduce wall clock run time almost to *1/n*. However, once a thread is running on each available core, scheduling additional threads produces no further improvement in run time. Instead, the threads simply chop up the available hardware pie into smaller and smaller slices. In fact, there is a limit to how finely access can be sliced, beyond which a time slice is all starting and stopping, with no time in the middle for computation. As the number of runnable threads increases, overall performance drops off and can ultimately approach zero.

Waitable threads wait for an external event, then compute briefly
> A waitable thread consumes just a few percent of the computational resources available on a core. Scheduling multiple waitable threads on a core uses a greater fraction of the available resources if execution of the waitable threads is interleaved so that the computation on one waitable thread happens during the wait on another waitable thread. This reduces wall clock run time up to a saturation point at which all computational resources are in use.

In the single-core past, there was no benefit from scheduling computations as runnable threads. All performance gains came from interleaving waitable threads with other threads. This is no longer the case when there are multiple cores.

C++ provides a function called `std::thread::hardware_concurrency()` that returns the number of available cores. This function accounts for cores allocated to other virtual machines by hypervisors, and cores that behave as two or more logical cores due to simultaneous multithreading. It allows a program to scale to hardware containing more (or fewer) cores as time passes.

To test the effect of multiple threads on performance, I wrote a function, `time waster()` (Example 12-12), that repeatedly performs a time-consuming computation. The computation takes 3,087 milliseconds if all the iterations are performed in a single loop in the main program.

Example 12-12. An iterated waste of computer time

```
void timewaster(unsigned iterations) {
    for (counter_t i = 0; i < iterations; ++i)
        fibonacci(n);
}
```

I then wrote a function to create threads that each ran `timewaster()`, dividing the number of iterations performed by the number of threads (Example 12-13). I used this function to test performance as I varied the number of threads.

Example 12-13. A multithreaded time waster

```
void multithreaded_timewaster(
        unsigned iterations,
        unsigned threads)
{
    std::vector<std::thread> t;
    t.reserve(threads);
    for (unsigned i = 0; i < threads; ++i)
        t.push_back(std::thread(timewaster, iterations/threads));
    for (unsigned i = 0; i < threads; ++i)
        t[i].join();
}
```

Some observations:

- `std::thread::hardware_concurrency()` returns 4 on my hardware. As expected, the fastest time, 1,870 milliseconds, came by running four threads.

- Somewhat surprisingly, the best time was closer to half (not a quarter) of the single-thread time.

- Although the general trend was for experiments with more than four threads to take longer, there was considerable variation from run to run, so that the result was not reliable.

There is, of course, a practical obstacle to limiting the number of threads launched by a program. In a big program with multiple developers, or with third-party libraries, it may be hard to know how many threads have been launched elsewhere in the program. Threads are created at need, anywhere in the program. Although the operating system serves as a container that knows all the threads that are running, this knowledge is not made explicit in C++.

Implement a Task Queue and Thread Pool

The solution to the problem of not knowing how many threads are running is to make threading explicit: provide a *thread pool*, a data structure that contains a fixed number of long-lived threads, and a *task queue*, a data structure that contains a list of computations to perform, which are serviced by the threads in the thread pool.

In *task-oriented programming*, the program is written as a collection of runnable task objects that are executed by threads from the thread pool. When a thread becomes available, it fetches a task from the task queue. When the thread finishes the task, it does not terminate; it either runs the next task or blocks, pending the arrival of a new task to be executed.

There are several advantages to task-oriented programs:

- Task-oriented programs can efficiently handle I/O completion events from non-blocking I/O calls, achieving high processor utilization.
- Having a thread pool and task queue eliminates the overhead of starting threads for short-lived tasks.
- Task-oriented programming centralizes asynchronous processing in one set of data structures, so that it is easy to limit the number of threads in use.

A disadvantage of task-oriented programs is a problem called *inversion of control*. Instead of the flow of control being specified by the program, it becomes implicit in the order of event messages received. This can make task-oriented programs difficult to reason about or debug, though my personal experience is that this confusion rarely occurs in practice.

Standard thread pools and task queues are coming to C++, probably in C++17. They are available today in the Boost library and Intel's Threading Building Blocks (*http://www.threadingbuildingblocks.org/*).

Perform I/O in a Separate Thread

The physical realities of spinning disks and distant network connections create delay between the time a program requests data and the time the data becomes available. I/O is thus a perfect place to look for concurrency. It is also typical of I/O that a program must transform the data before it can be written, or after it is read. For instance, a file of XML data may be read from the Internet. Then the data is parsed to extract information interesting to the program. Because the data is not usable until after it has been transformed, the whole process, including reading and parsing, becomes an obvious candidate to move into a separate thread.

Program Without Synchronization

Synchronization and mutual exclusion slow down multithreaded programs. Getting rid of this synchronization can improve performance. There are three easy ways to program without explicit synchronization, and one hard way:

Event-oriented programming

In event-oriented programming, the program is written as a collection of event-handling functions that are invoked from a framework. The underlying framework dispatches each event from an event queue to the handler function registered for that event. Event-oriented programming is similar in many ways to task-oriented programming. The framework in an event-oriented program acts like the task scheduler, and the event handlers are similar to tasks. The important difference is that in an event-oriented program, the framework is single-threaded, and the event-handling functions are not concurrent.

There are several advantages to event-oriented programs:

- Because the underlying framework is single-threaded, no synchronization is required.

- Event-oriented programs can efficiently handle I/O completion events from nonblocking I/O calls. An event-oriented program achieves the same high processor utilization as a multithreaded program does.

As with task-oriented programs, the chief disadvantage of event-oriented programs is a problem called *inversion of control*, where the flow of control becomes implicit in the order of event messages received. This can make event-oriented programs difficult to reason about or debug.

Coroutines

Coroutines are executable objects that explicitly hand off execution from one object to another, but remember their execution pointers so they can resume if called again. Like event-oriented programs, coroutines are not truly multithreaded, so no synchronization is required unless they are controlled by multiple threads.

Two kinds of coroutines can be distinguished. The first kind has its own stack, and can relinquish control to another coroutine at any point in execution. The second kind borrows the stack of another thread, and can relinquish control only at its top level.

Coroutines may arrive by C++17.

Message passing

In a message-passing program, threads of control take input from one or more sources, transform it, and put it on one or more output sinks. The connected outputs and inputs form a graph with well-defined entry and exit nodes. The items read and written by the thread implementing each stage of a message-passing program may be implemented as network datagrams, character I/O streams, or data structures in explicit queues.

Unix command-line pipelines and web services are examples of message-passing programming. The components of a distributed processing system are message-passing programs.

Among the advantages of message-passing programs are:

- Synchronization of the output of each stage to the input of the next stage is implicit. It is either handled by the operating system when the stages communicate with datagrams, or provided within a queue connecting the stages. The concurrency of the system happens outside the stages, so stages can usually be considered to be single-threaded code that may block on input and output actions.

- Because the outputs of one stage are each connected to a single input of the next stage, issues of starvation and fairness occur less frequently.

- Synchronization occurs less frequently, on larger units of data. This increases the fraction of time that multiple threads can run concurrently.

- Because pipeline stages do not share variables, they don't slow down for mutexes and memory fences.

- Larger units of work can be passed between pipeline stages, so that each stage uses whole time slices instead of stopping and starting for mutual exclusion. This improves processor utilization.

Disadvantages of message-passing programs include:

- Messages are not inherently object-oriented. The C++ developer must write code to marshal input messages into member function calls.

- Error recovery can be an issue when a pipeline stage crashes.

- Not every problem has an obvious solution as a pipeline of independent programs passing messages.

Stop and Think

This book discusses the C++ facilities for sharing variables and synchronizing threads, because these facilities must be baked into the C++ language to function efficiently. Message-passing programs use libraries outside of C++, so this book only spends a few words on them. That doesn't mean message passing is unimportant.

A large and vocal design community thinks explicit synchronization and shared variables are a bad idea: complex, race-prone, and unscalable. These developers think the only scalable way to program concurrently is with pipelines.

> The highly concurrent architectures of GPUs don't even provide shared memory, so for these processors a message-passing program design is required.

Lock-free programming

> Hic Sunt Dracones (English translation: Here Be Dragons)
>
> —Inscription on the Hunt-Lenox Globe (c. 1503–07), implying dangerous unknown shores

Lock-free programming refers to programming practices that permit multithreaded updates to data structures without the need for mutual exclusion. In a lock-free program, expensive mutexes are replaced by atomic operations synchronized by the hardware. Lock-free data structures can perform significantly better than conventional containers guarded by a mutex, especially when many threads access the same container.

Lock-free array, queue, and hash-table container classes in C++ have been released publically. Boost has lock-free stack and queue containers (*http://bit.ly/b-lock-free*), but they have been tested only on the GCC and Clang compilers. Intel's Threading Building Blocks (*http://www.threadingbuildingblocks.org/*) has lock-free array, queue, and hash-map containers. These containers are not identical to the equivalent C++ standard library containers due to the requirements of lock-free programming.

Lock-free data structures are insanely difficult to reason about. Even well-known experts argue about the correctness of published algorithms. For this reason, I recommend sticking to widely published and well-supported code rather than attempting to build lock-free data structures on your own.

Remove Code from Startup and Shutdown

A program can launch as many threads as needed to perform tasks concurrently or make use of multiple CPU cores. One part of the program, however, is quite difficult to run concurrently: the code executed before main() gets control, and after main() exits.

Before main() starts, all variables with static storage duration ("Storage Duration of Variables" on page 108) are initialized. For plain-old-data types, this initialization has zero cost. The linker points the variables at the initialization data. But for variables of class type and static storage duration, the initialization process calls each variable's constructor serially, in a single thread, in a particular order defined by the standard.

It is easy to forget that variables such as strings, which are initialized with static string constants, actually execute code during initialization. Likewise, constructors that contain function calls or non-`const` expressions in their initializer lists also are executed at run time, even if the constructor body is empty.

These costs, which may each be small when considered in isolation, can add up dramatically, causing large programs to be unresponsive for several seconds after startup.

Optimization War Story

Google's Chrome browser is a massive program, developed by hundreds of people over a period of years. The number of tables that must be initialized in Chrome is mind-boggling. To ensure that startup performance does not degrade (further), the Chromium project administrators added a rule to the review procedure requiring approval for every static variable initialized with executable code.

Make Synchronization More Efficient

Synchronization is the overhead cost of shared-memory concurrency. Reducing this overhead cost is an important pathway to optimal performance.

The received wisdom is that synchronization primitives such as mutexes are expensive. The truth, of course, is complicated. On both Windows and Linux, for instance, the mutex upon which `std::mutex` is based is a hybrid design that busy-waits on an atomic variable for a short period of time, then pends on an operating system signal if it cannot rapidly acquire the mutex. The cost of the "happy path," where no other thread holds the mutex, is low. The cost when the thread must pend on the signal is measured in milliseconds. The important cost of a mutex is the cost of waiting for another thread to release it, not the cost of calling `lock()`.

Multithreaded programs most frequently run into trouble when there are many threads contending to acquire the same mutex. When contention is low, holding the mutex usually doesn't slow other threads down. When contention is high, any contended mutex causes threads to run one at a time, spoiling the developer's attempt to execute the parts of a program concurrently.

Concurrent C++ programs are significantly more complex than single-threaded ones. It is harder to create examples or test cases that produce meaningful results, so I must fall back on heuristics in this section.

Reduce the Scope of Critical Sections

A critical section is a region of code bounded by acquiring a mutex and releasing that mutex. During execution of a critical section, no other thread can access shared variables controlled by that mutex. And that's the problem in a nutshell. If the critical section does anything *but* access shared variables, other threads have to wait for no good reason.

To illustrate this problem, look again at Example 12-7. The two lambdas producer and consumer are run concurrently in two threads. Both threads immediately attempt to enter the monitor controlled by mutex m. Both threads remain in the monitor except when they are in cv.wait(). producer sets the shared variable shared_data to the next value in sequence. consumer clears shared_data. But producer and consumer each do one other thing; they log one line of text to cout.

As written, cv_example can produce somewhere between 35 and 45 updates to shared_data in 1,000 milliseconds, on my i7 system compiled with Visual Studio 2015 in release mode. It may not immediately be obvious whether this is a lot or a little. But if I comment out the two output statements, cv_example can produce 1.25 *million* updates. Putting characters on the console performs a lot of behind-the-scenes magic, so this isn't too surprising in retrospect.

There are two lessons here. Lesson number one is that the monitor concept, where code is always in the monitor except while waiting on a condition variable, can be difficult to use efficiently. Lesson number two is that *performing I/O in a critical section does not lead to optimal performance.*

Limit the Number of Concurrent Threads

As mentioned in "Create as Many Runnable Threads as Cores" on page 308, *the number of runnable threads should be less than or equal to the number of processor cores* to eliminate the overhead of context switching. To provide a second reason why, I first have to explain how mutexes are implemented.

The mutex class provided by Windows, Linux, and most other modern operating systems is a hybrid design optimized for multicore processors. A thread t_1 attempting to acquire a mutex that is not locked acquires the mutex immediately. If t_1 attempts to acquire a mutex that is held by another thread, t_2, t_1 first busy-waits for a limited amount of time. If t_2 releases the mutex before the busy-wait times out, t_1 acquires the mutex and continues to run, efficiently using its whole time slice. If t_2 does not release the mutex in time, t_1 pends on an operating system event, giving up its time slice. t_1 goes on the operating system's "pending" list.

If there are more threads than cores, only some threads are assigned to cores and actually progress at any instant of time. The remaining threads wait on the operating system's "runnable" queue, and are eventually given a time slice. The operating system wakes on a periodic interrupt to make decisions about what to run. This interrupt is slow compared to the rate at which individual instructions are executed. A thread on the "runnable" queue may thus wait many milliseconds before the operating system allocates it a core on which to run.

If t_2 holds the mutex but is waiting on the operating system's "runnable" queue instead of actually executing, it cannot release the mutex. When t_1 attempts to acquire the mutex, its busy-wait times out, and t_1 pends on an operating system event, which means t_1 gives up its time slice and its core and goes on the operating system's "pending" list. Eventually t_2 gets a core to run on and releases the mutex, signaling the event on which t_1 is pending. The operating system notes that the event has occurred, and moves t_1 to the "runnable" queue. But the operating system does not necessarily allocate a core to run t_1 immediately.[5] The operating system runs the threads currently assigned to cores for their full time slices, unless they block on an event. The operating system doesn't allocate a core to the newly runnable t_1 until some other thread exhausts its time slice, which may take many milliseconds.

It is this slow path the developer attempts to eliminate by limiting the number of active threads. Avoiding the slow path means that instead of hundreds of interlocked operations per second, threads t_1 and t_2 can perform millions of interlocked operations per second.

The ideal number of threads contending for a brief critical section is two. When there are only two threads, there are no issues of fairness or starvation, and no chance of the thundering herd problem described in the following section.

Avoid the Thundering Herd

A phenomenon called the *thundering herd* occurs when many threads are pending on an event, such as the availability of work, that only one thread can service. When the event occurs, all the threads become runnable, but only a few of them can run immediately because there are only a few cores. One of these takes the work item. The operating system moves the rest to the runnable queue, and eventually runs each one. Each thread discovers that the signaled event has already been serviced, and pends again on the event, spending time on logistics without making progress.

Avoiding the thundering herd may be as easy as limiting the number of threads created to service the event. Two threads may be better than one, but 100 threads is probably *not* better (see "Limit the Number of Concurrent Threads" on page 315). Limiting the number of threads may be easier for software designs that implement work queues than for designs that associate a thread with each work item.

---

5 I'm skipping over a lot of arcane details here. Windows fiddles thread priorities to give the newly runnable thread a turn sooner. Other operating systems do other things in hopes of reducing the duration of critical sections. The takeaway should be that once the operating system gets involved in a critical section, it's going to be a long wait.

Avoid Lock Convoys

A *lock convoy* occurs when many threads synchronize, pending on a resource or critical section. This causes additional congestion because they all attempt to proceed at once and are made to progress one at a time, as if in a convoy.

In a simple case, a thundering herd occurs over and over. There are enough threads contending for a mutex that many threads pend on the mutex's operating system signal. When the thread holding the mutex releases it, the event is signaled, and all the pending threads become runnable. The first thread to get the processor locks the mutex again. All the remaining threads eventually get the processor, check the mutex, see it is still locked, and go back to pending. The overall effect is that the operating system spends a lot of time restarting threads, but most threads don't progress. Worse yet, all the threads are still synchronized. They will all wake at once when the next thread releases the mutex, and repeat the cycle.

In a more complex case, a thundering herd of threads all attempt to acquire a second mutex or perform some action, like reading a file, that is bottlenecked by the physical properties of the device. Since threads are synchronized, they all attempt to access the second resource at about the same time. Performance is degraded because the threads request the same resource at the same time, causing serialization. If they had not been synchronized, they might all have progressed.

Lock convoys are visible as systems that usually run well, but occasionally seem to become unresponsive for a few seconds at a time.

Reducing the number of threads or scheduling threads to start at different times may relieve the lock convoy, though there is always a risk that it will simply emerge in another place. Sometimes it is best simply to acknowledge that certain groups of tasks can't be performed concurrently because they share some hardware device or other bottleneck.

Reduce Contention

Threads in a multithreaded program may contend over resources. At any point where two or more threads need the same resource, mutual exclusion causes a thread to pend, losing concurrency. There are several techniques to address the problem of contention:

Be aware that memory and I/O are resources
> Not every developer realizes that the memory manager is a resource. The memory manager must serialize access in multithreaded systems, or its data structures will get corrupted. A large number of threads all attempting to allocate dynamic variables (`std::string` is a particular offender) at once may experience performance that falls off a cliff suddenly as the number of threads increases.

File I/O is a resource. The disk drive can only be in one place at a time. Attempting to do I/O on multiple files simultaneously can cause performance to fall off suddenly.

Network I/O is also a resource. The Ethernet connector is a narrow pipe through which bits squirt. It is possible for modern processors to saturate even gigabit Ethernet cables. Saturating a WiFi connection is easy.

When there is a performance problem, it is time to take a step back and ask, "What is the whole program doing right now?" Logging that is no problem most of the time may be slowing the whole system down if something else is also banging away at the disk or network interface. That dynamic data structure may not scale to many threads.

Duplicate resources

Instead of multiple threads contending for a resource such as a shared map or hash table, sometimes it is possible to duplicate the table so that each thread has an unshared copy, eliminating contention. Although maintaining two copies of a data structure is more work, it may still result in reduced wall clock time versus a shared data structure.

Even hardware resources like disk drives and network interface cards can be duplicated to improve throughput.

Partition resources

Instead of multiple threads contending for a single data structure, sometimes it is possible to partition the data structure so that each thread only accesses the portion of the data that it works with.

Fine-grained locking

Instead of locking an entire data structure with a single mutex, multiple mutexes can be used. For example, in a hash table, one mutex can lock the hash table backbone against modification (such as inserting and deleting entries), and another mutex can lock the entries against modification. Reader/writer locks may be a good choice here. To access a hash table entry, a thread takes a read lock on the backbone, and either a read or write lock on the entry. To insert or delete an entry, the thread takes a write lock on the backbone.

Lock-free data structures

Use of a lock-free data structure such as a hash table relieves the need for mutual exclusion. This is the ultimate extent to which fine-grained locking can be taken.

Resource scheduling

Some resources, such as a hard drive, are not susceptible to duplication or partitioning. But it is still possible to schedule disk activity so that it doesn't all happen at once, or so that accesses to adjacent parts of the disk are performed together.

The operating system may schedule reads and writes at a fine-grained level, but the program can sequence operations like reading configuration files so that they don't all happen at the same time.

Don't Busy-Wait on a Single-Core System

C++ concurrency features allow developers to implement high-performance synchronization primitives that do busy-waits. But busy-waiting is not always a good idea.

In a single-core processor, the only way to synchronize threads is to invoke the operating system's synchronization primitives. A busy-wait is laughably ineffective. In fact, busy-waiting causes the thread to waste its whole time slice, because a thread holding a mutex cannot run to complete its critical section until the waiting thread gives up the processor.

Don't Wait Forever

What happens to a thread that waits unconditionally for an event? If the program runs properly, perhaps nothing. But what if the user attempts to stop the program? The user interface shuts down, but the program doesn't stop, because there are threads still running. If main() tries to join the waiting thread, it hangs. If the waiting thread is detached, main() may exit. Then what happens is dependent on how the thread is waiting. If it's waiting for a flag to be set, it waits forever. If it's waiting on an operating system event, it waits forever. If it's waiting on a C++ object, then it very much depends whether some nonblocked thread deletes the object. That might cause the waiting thread to terminate. Or not.

Waiting forever is the enemy of error recovery. It is the difference between a program that mostly works but sometimes is flaky, and a program that has solid, dependable behavior that is reassuring to users.

Rolling Your Own Mutex May Be Ineffective

It is not difficult to code a simple class that acts as a mutex, busy-waiting until another thread updates an atomic variable. Such a class may even be faster than the system-provided mutex when contention is low and critical sections are brief. However, the mutexes that come with an operating system often know secrets about the operating system and the way it schedules tasks that improve their performance or avoid priority inversion issues on that particular operating system.

The design of robust mutexes is informed by the design of the operating system they must run on. Rolling your own is not a broad pathway to optimization.

Limit Producer Output Queue Length

In a producer/consumer program, any time the producer is faster than the consumer, data builds up in the queue between producer and consumer. Some of the many problems with this situation include:

- The producer contends for the processor, memory allocator, and other resources, further slowing the consumer and exacerbating the problem.
- The producer will eventually consume all system memory resources, causing the entire program to terminate unexpectedly.
- If the program is designed to recover from exceptions, it may need to process all queued data before restarting, which increases the time to recover.

This situation is especially likely in situations where a program sometimes takes input from a streaming source with a maximum rate that limits how often the producer runs, and sometimes takes input from a fixed source like a file, where the producer can run continuously.

The solution is to limit the queue size and block the producer when the queue is full. The queue only needs to be big enough to smooth any variation in the consumer's performance. Frequently only a few entries are necessary. Any extra queue entries only cause the producer to run further and further ahead, increasing resource consumption without contributing to concurrency.

Concurrency Libraries

There are a number of well-regarded concurrency libraries. The developer looking to implement a message-passing style of concurrency would be well advised to take up one of these tools. Threading Building Blocks in particular offers some features for concurrency that are not yet in the C++ standard. Options include:

Boost.Thread (http://bit.ly/b-thread) and Boost.Coroutine (http://bit.ly/b-coroutine)
Boost's Thread library is an anticipation of the C++17 standard library thread library. Some parts are still very experimental. Boost.Coroutine is also experimental.

POSIX Threads
POSIX Threads (pthreads) is a cross-platform library of threads and synchronization primitives—possibly the oldest and most widely used library for concurrency. Pthreads is a C-style function library that provides traditional capabilities. It is extensively documented, widely available on Linux distributions, and also available for Windows (*http://sourceware.org/pthreads-win32/*).

Threading Building Blocks (TBB) (http://www.threadingbuildingblocks.org/)
TBB is an ambitious, well-documented C++ threading API with a template flavor. It provides parallel for loops, tasks and thread pools, concurrent containers, data-flow message-passing classes, and synchronization primitives. TBB was developed by Intel to promote effective use of multicore microprocessors. It is now open source, has extensive documentation including at least one good book (*Intel Threading Building Blocks* by James Reinders, also from O'Reilly), and runs on both Windows and Linux.

0mq (http://zeromq.org/) (also spelled ZeroMQ)
0mq is a communication library for connecting message-passing programs. It supports a variety of communication paradigms and strives for efficiency and parsimony. My personal experience with this library has been very positive. 0mq is open source, well documented, and actively supported. There is also a reimagining of 0mq called nanomsg (*http://www.nanomsg.org*) that is said to address some issues in 0mq.

Message Passing Interface (MPI) (http://computing.llnl.gov/tutorials/mpi/)
MPI is an API specification for message passing in a distributed network of computers. Implementations have the flavor of a C-style function library. MPI has its origin at California's Lawrence Livermore National Laboratory, a place long associated with supercomputer clusters and with the kind of high-energy physics that goes boom. MPI is well documented in an old-fashioned 1980s DoD style. Implementations exist for both Linux and Windows, including one from Boost (*http://bit.ly/b-mpi*), but they don't always cover the full specification.

OpenMP (http://openmp.org)
OpenMP is an API for "multi-platform shared-memory parallel programming in C/C++ and Fortran." In use, a developer decorates a C++ program with pragmas that define its parallel behavior. OpenMP provides a fine-grained model of concurrency with an emphasis on numerical computation, and is evolving toward programming of GPUs. OpenMP is available on Linux using both GCC and Clang, and on Windows using Visual C++.

C++ AMP (http://bit.ly/cpp-accel)
C++ AMP is an open specification of a C++ library designed to perform parallel data computations on GPU devices. The version from Microsoft resolves to DirectX 11 calls.

Summary

- *A multithreaded C++ program is sequentially consistent if it contains no races.*
- *A large and vocal design community thinks explicit synchronization and shared variables are a bad idea.*
- *Performing I/O in a critical section does not lead to optimal performance.*
- *The number of runnable threads should be less than or equal to the number of processor cores.*
- *The ideal number of threads contending for a brief critical section is two.*

## CHAPTER 13

Optimize Memory Management

Efficiency is doing better what is already being done.

—Peter F. Drucker (1909–2005), American management consultant

The *memory manager* is the set of functions and data structures of the C++ runtime system that oversees allocation of memory to dynamic variables. The memory manager must meet many demands. Meeting these demands efficiently is an open research challenge. In many C++ programs, the memory manager's functions are quite hot. If its performance could be improved, it would have a global effect on the program. For all these reasons, the memory manager is a natural target for optimization efforts.

In my opinion, there are other places to look for performance improvement first, that are more likely to be fruitful than fiddling with the memory manager. Memory managers, being very hot code, are usually well wrung out right out of the box. Memory management is at best an aspect of an aspect of overall program run time. Amdahl's Law limits how much overall improvement the developer can obtain, even if the cost of memory management could be driven to zero. In large programs in one study, performance improvement from optimizing memory management ranged from negligible to about 30%.

The C++ memory manager is highly customizable, with a substantial API. Although many programmers never have to use this API, it provides many ways to optimize performance. Several high-performance memory managers exist that can be plugged into C++ by replacing the C functions `malloc()` and `free()`. In addition, the developer can substitute specialized memory managers for hot classes and standard library containers.

C++ Memory Management API Refresher

The C++ toolkit for managing dynamic variables was introduced in "C++ Dynamic Variable API Refresher" on page 113. This toolkit contains an interface to the memory manager consisting of *new-* and *delete-expressions*, memory management functions, and standard library allocator template classes.

The Life Cycle of Dynamic Variables

A dynamic variable goes through five distinct life stages. The most common variation of the *new-expression* performs the *allocate* and *place* stages. After the *use* stage, a *delete-expression* performs the *destroy* and *free* stages. C++ provides facilities to manage each of these stages separately:

Allocate

The program asks the memory manager to return a pointer to a contiguous region of memory containing at least a specified number of untyped memory bytes. Allocation can fail if memory is not available. The C library function `malloc()` and the various overloads of the C++ `operator new()` function manage the allocate phase.

Place

The program establishes the initial value of the dynamic variable, placing the value into the allocated memory. If the variable is a class instance, one of its constructors is called. If the variable is a simple type, it is optionally initialized. Placement can fail if the constructor throws an exception, requiring allocated storage to be returned to the memory manager. *New-expressions* participates in this phase.

Use

The program reads values from the dynamic variable, calls member functions of the dynamic variable, and writes values to the dynamic variable.

Destroy

If the variable is a class instance, the program calls its destructor to perform a final operation on the dynamic variable. Destruction is an opportunity for the dynamic variable to return any system resources it holds, complete any cleanup, say any last words, and make ready to go into the good night. Destruction can fail if the destructor throws an exception that is not handled in the destructor body. If this happens, the program unconditionally terminates. *Delete-expressions* manage this phase. It is possible to destroy a variable without freeing its storage by calling its destructor explicitly.

Free

The program returns the storage formerly belonging to the destroyed dynamic variable to the memory manager. The C-library `free()` function and the various overloads of the C++ `operator delete()` function perform the free phase.

Memory Management Functions Allocate and Free Memory

C++ provides a collection of memory management functions, rather than C's simple `malloc()` and `free()`. These functions provide the rich behavior of *new-expressions* described in "New-Expressions Construct Dynamic Variables" on page 328. Overloads of `operator new()` allocate storage for single instances of any type. Overloads of `operator new[]()` allocate storage for arrays of any type. When both array- and non-array functions operate in the same way, I describe them together as `operator new()`, with the understanding that there is an equivalent `operator new[]()`.

operator new() implements allocation

A *new-expression* calls one of several versions of `operator new()` to obtain memory for a dynamic variable, or `operator new[]()` to obtain memory for a dynamic array. C++ provides default implementations of these operators. It also implicitly declares them, so they can be called by the program without having to include the <new> header. The program can override the defaults with its own implementation if desired.

`operator new()` is important to examine for optimization purposes because the default memory manager is expensive. In some situations, the program can allocate memory very efficiently by providing a specialized implementation.

C++ defines several overloads of `operator new()`.

`void* ::operator new(size_t)`

By default, memory is allocated for all dynamically allocated variables by calling this overload of `operator new()`, with an argument specifying the minimum number of bytes to allocate. The standard library implementation of this overload throws a `std::bad_alloc` exception if there is not enough memory to fulfill the request.

The standard library implementations of all other `operator new()` overloads call this one. A program can globally change how memory is allocated by providing a definition of `::operator new(size_t)` in any compilation unit.

Although it is not required by the C++ standard, the standard library version of this overload is usually implemented using a call to `malloc()`.

```
void* ::operator new[](size_t)
```
Arrays are allocated with a call to this overload. The standard library implementation calls `::operator new(size_t)`.

```
void* ::operator new(size_t, const std::nothrow_tag&)
```
A *new-expression* like `Foo* p = new(std::nothrow) Foo(123);` calls the non-
throwing overload of `operator new()`. If no memory is available, this version
returns `nullptr` instead of throwing a `std::bad_alloc` exception. The standard
library implementation calls `operator new(size_t)` and catches any exceptions
it may throw.

```
void* ::operator new[](size_t, const std::nothrow_tag&)
```
This is the array version of the non-throwing `operator new()`.

A *new-expression* can invoke an `operator new()` with an arbitrary signature provided
the first argument is of type `size_t`. All of these `operator new()` overloads are called
placement `operator new()`. The *new-expression* matches the types of the arguments
in the placement parameters with available `operator new()` function signatures to
determine which function is used.

Two overloads of placement `operator new()` are provided by the standard library
and implicitly declared. These do not allocate memory (the first life stage of a
dynamic variable) but contain an extra argument that accepts a pointer to memory
that the program has already allocated. They are:

```
void* ::operator new(size_t, void*)
```
This is placement `operator new()` for variables. It accepts a pointer to memory
as its second argument and simply returns that pointer.

```
void* ::operator new[](size_t, void*)
```
This is the array version of placement `operator new()`. It accepts a pointer to
memory as its second argument and returns that pointer.

These two placement `operator new()` overloads are called by the *placement new-
expression* `new(p)` *type*, where p is a pointer to valid storage. The standard says these
overloads can't be replaced by developer code. If they were replaced, and the replacement did anything other than return its pointer argument, much of the standard
library would stop working. This is important to know, because some C++ compilers
don't enforce the prohibition against replacing these overloads, which means they *can*
be replaced—for instance, with code that prints out diagnostics.

Aside from the two placement `operator new()` overloads listed here, other placement `operator new()` overloads have no defined meaning in C++ and are available
to the developer for any use.

operator delete() frees allocated memory

A delete-expression invokes `operator delete()` to return memory for a dynamic variable to the runtime system, and `operator delete[]()` to return memory for a dynamic array.

The `new` operators and `delete` operators work together to allocate and free memory. If a program defines an `operator new()` that allocates memory from a special memory pool or in a special way, it must define a matching `operator delete()` in the same scope to return memory to the pool from which it was allocated, or behavior is undefined.

Memory management functions from the C library

C++ provides the C-library functions `malloc()`, `calloc()`, and `realloc()` to allocate memory, and the `free()` function to return memory that is no longer needed. These functions are provided for compatibility with C programs.

`void* malloc(size_t size)` implements the allocate phase of a dynamic variable's lifetime, returning a pointer to storage sufficient to hold `size` bytes, or `nullptr` if no storage is available.

`void free(void* p)` implements the free phase, returning the storage pointed to by `p` to the memory manager.

`void* calloc(size_t count, size_t size)` implements the allocate phase of a dynamic array. It performs a simple computation to convert a number `count` of array elements, each of size `size` bytes, to a number of bytes, and then returns the value of a call to `malloc()`.

`void* realloc(void* p, size_t size)` changes the size of a block of memory, moving the block to new storage if needed. The contents of the old block are copied to the new block, up to the minimum of the new and old sizes. `realloc()` must be used very carefully. Sometimes it moves the pointed-to block and deletes the old block. If it does this, pointers to the old block become invalid. Sometimes it reuses the existing block, which happens to be bigger than the requested size.

According to the C++ standard, `malloc()` and `free()` act upon a region of memory called the "heap," while overloads of `operator new()` and `operator delete()` operate on a region of memory called the "free store." The careful language of the standard preserves the option for library developers to implement the two sets of functions differently. That said, the requirements for memory management are similar in the C and C++ worlds. It just isn't sensible for a compiler to have two parallel but different implementations. In all standard library implementations of which I am aware, `operator new()` calls `malloc()` to actually allocate storage. A program can globally change how memory is managed by replacing `malloc()` and `free()`.

New-Expressions Construct Dynamic Variables

A C++ program requests creation of a dynamic variable or array using a *new-expression*. A *new-expression* contains the keyword new followed by a type, a pointer to which is returned by the *new-expression*. The *new-expression* can also contain an initializer to set the initial value of the variable or each array element. A *new-expression* returns a typed pointer to a fully initialized C++ variable or array, rather than the simple void pointer to uninitialized storage returned by C++ operator new() or C's memory management functions .

The syntax of the *new-expression*, in all its glory, looks like this:

```
::optional new (placement-params)optional (type) initializeroptional
```

or:

```
::optional new (placement-params)optional type initializeroptional
```

The difference between these two lines is in the optional parentheses around *type*, which are sometimes needed to help the compiler distinguish the end of the `placement-params` from the beginning of a complicated *type*, or the end of the *type* from the beginning of the `initializer`. cppreference (*http://en.cppreference.com/w/cpp/language/new*), among other sources, has vastly more information on all the syntactic wrinkles of *new-expressions*.

When *type* declares an array, the highest (that is, leftmost)[1] array dimension may be described by a non-constant expression, allowing the size of the array to be specified at run time. This is the only place in C++ where a declaration may have a variable size.

A *new-expression* returns an rvalue pointer to the dynamic variable or the first element of the dynamic array. (The fact that this pointer is an rvalue is important; see "Implement Move Semantics" on page 137 for details.)

All versions of the *new-expression* do a lot more than just call an operator new() function to allocate storage. If the call to operator new() is successful, the non-array version constructs a *type* object. If the constructor throws an exception, its members and bases are destroyed, and the allocated memory is returned by a call to the operator delete() whose signature corresponds to the operator new() function used to allocate the memory. If no operator delete() matches, the memory is not returned to the memory manager, potentially causing a memory leak. The *new-expression* returns the pointer, rethrows the caught exception, or returns nullptr in the case of the non-throwing *new-expression*.

---

1 In C++, an *n*-dimensional array is an array of *n–1*-dimensional arrays. Thus, the leftmost dimension is the highest dimension.

The array *new-expression* works in the same way, but with the added complexity that any of several constructors might throw an exception, requiring the array *new-expression* to destroy all successfully constructed instances and return the memory to the free store before returning or rethrowing the exception.

Why are there two kinds of *new-expression*, one for arrays and one for instances? The array *new-expression* may allocate space to store the number of array elements, as well as the space allocated for the array itself. That way, the array delete-expression need not provide this value. This extra overhead is not necessary for single instances. This C++ behavior was designed at a time when memory was far more precious than it is today.

Non-throwing new

If `placement-params` consists of the tag `std::nothrow`, the *new-expression* does not throw `std::bad_alloc`. Instead, it returns `nullptr` without attempting to construct an object.

Historically, there was a time when many C++ compilers did not properly implement exception handling. Code written for these old compilers, or ported from C, needed an allocation function that returned null when it ran out of memory.

Some industries—notably the aerospace and automotive industries—have imposed coding standards that prohibit the throwing of exceptions. This causes a problem because *new-expressions* are otherwise defined to throw on error; hence the need for a non-throwing *new-expression*.

There is received wisdom that exception handling is slow, and that therefore a non-throwing *new-expression* should be faster. However, modern C++ compilers implement an exception handling mechanism with very low runtime cost unless an exception is thrown, so the truth of this received wisdom may be compiler-dependent. See "Use No-Cost Exception Handling" on page 183 for a more extensive discussion of the cost of exception handling.

Placement new performs placement without allocation

If `placement-params` is a pointer to existing valid storage, the *new-expression* does not call the memory manager, but simply places *type* at the location indicated by the pointer, which must point to sufficient storage to hold *type*. Placement new is used like this:

```
char mem[1000];
class Foo {...};
Foo* foo_p = new (mem) Foo(123);
```

This example places an instance of class Foo on top of the array mem. Placement new calls a class constructor to perform initialization for class instances. For a basic type, placement new performs initialization instead of construction.

Since placement new does not allocate storage, there is no corresponding placement delete. The instance of Foo placed on top of mem by placement new is not automatically destroyed when mem goes out of scope. It is up to the developer to properly destroy instances created with placement new by explicitly calling the class's destructor. In fact, if an instance of Foo is placed into storage declared to be an instance of Bar, Bar's destructor is called, with undefined and typically disastrous results. Placement new should thus be used on memory returned by operator new(), or on memory occupied by an array of char or some other basic type.

Placement new is used in the Allocator template parameter of standard library containers, which must place class instances on previously allocated but unused memory. See "Provide Custom Standard Library Allocators" on page 343 for details.

Custom placement new, the half-formed hinterland of allocation

If placement-params is anything other than std::nothrow or a single pointer, the *new-expression* is called *custom placement new*. C++ does not impose any meaning on the custom *placement new-expression*. It is available for the developer's use to allocate storage in an unspecified way. The custom *placement new-expression* searches for an overload of operator new() or operator new[]() whose first argument matches size_t, and whose subsequent arguments match the types of the expression list. If the constructor for the dynamic object throws an exception, the *placement new-expression* searches for an overload of operator delete() or operator delete[]() whose first parameter is void*, and whose subsequent arguments match the types of the expression list.

Placement new is useful if the program needs to establish more than one mechanism to create dynamic variables, or to pass arguments for memory manager diagnostics.

An issue with custom placement new is that there is no way to specify a matching "custom *placement delete-expression*." Thus, while the various placement overloads of operator delete() are invoked when the object constructor throws an exception in the *new-expression*, *delete-expressions* cannot call these overloads. This creates a conundrum for the developer, since the standard says behavior is undefined if the operator delete() does not match the operator new() that allocated the dynamic variable. The matching placement operator delete() must be declared, because it is called in a *new-expression* if the object constructor throws an exception. There's just no way to call it from a *delete-expression*. However, the standard committee is working to address this issue in a future version of the C++ standard.

The simplest solution is to note that if the fancy placement `operator new()` is compatible with an ordinary `operator delete()`, the behavior, while undefined, is predictably OK. Another solution is to note that *delete-expressions* aren't so complicated or magical that they cannot be coded as free functions if needed.

Class-specific operator new() gives fine control of allocation

The *new-expression* looks up `operator new()` in the scope of the type being created. A class can thus provide implementations of these operators to get fine control over allocation for just that class. If a class does not define a class-specific `operator new()`, the global one is used. To use the global `operator new()` instead of a class-specific version, the programmer specifies the global scope operator `::` in the *new-expression*, as in

```
Foo* foo_p = ::new Foo(123);
```

A class-specific `operator new()` is invoked only to allocate instances of the class that defines that function. Member functions of the class that contain *new-expressions* involving other classes use the `operator new()` defined for that other class, if any, or the global `operator new()` by default.

A class-specific `operator new()` can be efficient because it allocates objects of a single size. Thus, the first free block is always usable. If the class is not used in multiple threads, the class-specific `operator new()` can dispense with the overhead of making its internal data structures thread-safe.

The class-specific `operator new()` is defined to be a static member function. This makes sense, because `operator new()` allocates storage for every instance.

If a class implements a custom `operator new()`, it must implement a corresponding `operator delete()` or else the global `operator delete()` called, with undefined and usually unwanted results.

Delete-Expressions Dispose of Dynamic Variables

A program returns the memory used by a dynamic variable to the memory manager using a *delete-expression*. The delete-expression handles the last two phases of the dynamic variable life cycle: destroying the variable and freeing the memory it formerly occupied. The delete-expression contains the keyword `delete` followed by an expression that produces a pointer to the variable to be deleted. The syntax of the delete-expression looks like this:

```
::optional delete expression
```

or:

```
::optional delete [] expression
```

The first form of the delete-expression deletes a dynamic variable created with a *new-expression*. The second form deletes a dynamic array created with a *new[]-expression*. Separate *delete-expressions* exist for ordinary variables and for arrays because arrays may be created in a different manner from ordinary variables. Most implementations allocate extra storage for a count of the number of array elements allocated, so that the right number of destructors are called. Using the wrong version of the delete-expression for the dynamic variable results in the destructive chaos that the C++ standard calls "undefined behavior."

Explicit Destructor Calls Destroy Dynamic Variables

It is possible to perform just the destruction of a dynamic variable without freeing its storage by calling the destructor explicitly instead of using a delete-expression. The destructor's name is just the class name with a tilde ("~") in front:

```
foo_p->~Foo();
```

Explicit destructor calls occur in the same places as placement new; in standard library `Allocator` templates where destruction and freeing happen separately.

There is no explicit constructor call… Or is there?

The C++ standard, section 13.1, says "Constructors have no name," so the program cannot directly invoke a constructor. The constructor is invoked by means of a *new-expression*. The standard is fussy about constructors because the memory occupied by a class instance is uninitialized storage before the constructor, and an instance after the constructor. It's hard to explain this magical transformation.

This isn't much of a hardship. If a program desires to invoke a constructor explicitly on an already constructed class instance, the placement new syntax is simple enough:

```
class Blah {
public:
    Blah() {...}
    ...
};

Blah* b = new char[sizeof(Blah)];
Blah myBlah;
  ...
new (b) Blah;
new (&myBlah) Blah;
```

Of course, the linker knows perfectly well that the name of `Blah`'s constructor is `Blah::Blah()`. In Visual C++, the statement

```
b->Blah::Blah();
```

compiles successfully, and invokes Blah's constructor. This is a coding horror, making *Optimized C++* one of the first C++ books in the Gothic tradition. The Linux C++ compiler GCC is a little more standard-compliant, offering an error message. The constructor is meant to be invoked via placement new.

High-Performance Memory Managers

By default, all requests for storage pass through ::operator new(), and released storage passes through ::operator delete(). These functions form C++'s default memory manager. The default C++ memory manager must meet many demands:

- It must perform efficiently, because it is likely to be hot.
- It must work correctly in multithreaded programs. Access to data structures in the default memory manager must be serialized.
- It must allocate many same-sized objects (like list nodes) efficiently.
- It must allocate many differently sized objects (like strings) efficiently.
- It must allocate very big data structures (I/O buffers, arrays of a million ints), as well as small data structures (like a single pointer).
- To be maximally efficient, it must be aware of alignment boundaries for pointers, cache lines, and virtual memory pages, at least for larger allocated memory blocks.
- Its runtime performance must not degrade over time.
- It must efficiently reuse memory returned to it.

Meeting the many demands of a C++ memory manager is an open and evolving challenge spawning ongoing academic research, with compiler vendors in uneven pursuit of the state of the art. In some situations, a memory manager may not need to meet all these demands. Both these facts provide opportunities for developers to optimize.

The version of ::operator new() shipped with most C++ compilers is a thin wrapper around the C function malloc(). In the early days of C++, these malloc() implementations were designed to meet the relatively simple needs of C programs for a few dynamic buffers, rather than the preceding long list of requirements of C++ programs. Replacing a simple, vendor-provided malloc() with a sophisticated memory manager was so successful an optimization that developers could build a reputation as wizards on the basis of this one simple spell.

A variety of more-or-less self-contained memory manager libraries have been written that claim a substantial performance advantage over the default memory manager. If a program heavily uses dynamic variables including strings and standard containers, it's tempting to view these malloc() replacements as a silver bullet, improving performance everywhere for the price of a single linker change, and without all that tedious profiling. But while state-of-the-art memory managers have outstanding performance, there are reasons not to brag prematurely about the benefits of such changes:

- Although state-of-the-art memory managers have demonstrated significant performance improvements over a naïve `malloc()` implementation, the particular baseline competitor is often not clearly specified, and may be an unrealistic straw man. I have heard a rumor that both Windows and Linux have recently raised their game with state-of-the-art memory managers. Thus, for Linux since 3.7 and Windows since Windows 7, there may be little performance boost from changing memory managers.

- A faster memory manager will help performance only to the extent that allocating and freeing dynamic variables dominates the program's run time. Even if a program allocates a zillion-node data structure, if this structure is long-lived, improving allocation has limited benefit due to Amdahl's Law (see "Amdahl's Law" on page 31). While the memory manager code itself may be 3 to 10 times faster than the default, *studied whole-program performance improvements range from negligible improvement to 30% in several large open-source programs.*

- Reducing the number of calls into the memory manager by means described in Chapter 6 provides a performance boost no matter how fast the allocator is, and can be targeted to hot code using the profiler.

- State-of-the-art memory managers may pay for improved performance by consuming significant amounts of memory for various caches and free-block pools. Constrained environments may not have this additional memory to spend.

For older operating systems and embedded development, here are some `malloc()` replacements generally regarded as high-performing:

Hoard (http://www.hoard.org/)
> Hoard is a commercialized version of a multiprocessor memory allocator from the University of Texas. It claims 3–7× improvement over `malloc()`. Hoard requires a license for commercial use.

mtmalloc (http://bit.ly/mtmalloc)
> mtmalloc is a `malloc()` replacement for highly multithreaded workloads in Solaris. It uses a fast-fit allocator.

ptmalloc (glibc malloc) (http://bit.ly/1VFcqux)
> ptmalloc is the `malloc()` provided with Linux 3.7 and later. It has per-thread arenas to reduce contention in multithreaded programs.

TCMalloc (http://bit.ly/tcmalloc) (the Thread-Caching `malloc()`)

TCMalloc (located in the *gperftools* package), is Google's `malloc()` replacement. It has a specialized small-object allocator and carefully designed spinlocks for managing large blocks. According to the designers, it is better behaved than *glibc*'s `malloc()`. tcmalloc is only tested on Linux.

For small embedded projects, it is not an impossible task to implement your own memory manager. Searching the Web for "fast-fit memory allocation" provides a bunch of links to start from. I implemented a fast-fit memory manager for an embedded project with good results. That said, the design of fully general multithreaded memory managers is another topic that would fill a whole book by itself. The people who write memory managers are specialists. The more sophisticated the program and its operating environment are, the less likely it is that a roll-your-own solution will be performant and bug-free.

Provide Class-Specific Memory Managers

Even a state-of-the-art `malloc()` is exactly the kind of compromise that creates optimization opportunities. `operator new()` can also be overridden at the class level (see "Class-specific operator new() gives fine control of allocation" on page 331). When code that dynamically creates instances of a class is hot, a class-specific memory manager can improve performance.

If a class implements `operator new()`, this function is called instead of the global `operator new()` when requesting memory for instances of the class. A class-specific `operator new()` can take advantage of extra knowledge not available to the default version. *All allocation requests for instances of a particular class request the same number of bytes. Memory managers for same-sized requests are particularly easy to write, and run efficiently* for a variety of reasons:

- Fixed-block memory managers efficiently reuse returned memory. They do not experience fragmentation, because all requests are the same size.

- Fixed-block memory managers can be implemented with low or no memory overhead.

- Fixed-block memory managers can provide a guaranteed upper bound on the amount of memory consumed.

- The functions of a fixed-block memory manager that allocate and free memory are internally simple enough that they can efficiently be inlined. The functions of the default C++ memory manager cannot be inlined. They must be function calls so they can be replaced by a developer-defined override. The C memory management functions `malloc()` and `free()` must be ordinary functions for the same reason.

- Fixed-block memory managers have good cache behavior. The last node freed can be the next node allocated.

Many developers have never seen a class-specific memory manager. I suspect this is because they have several moving parts that have to be written and strung together, so the learning curve is steep. Even in a big program, only a few classes may be hot enough to benefit from this optimization. It's not something that needs to be done many times in a given program.

Fixed-Size-Block Memory Manager

Example 13-1 defines a simple fixed-size-block memory manager that allocates blocks from a single, statically declared chunk of storage called the *arena*. Fixed-size-block memory managers of this kind are most frequently found in embedded projects, as an alternative to allocating from the free store. fixed_block_memory_man ager is internally very simple: just a singly linked list of free memory blocks. This simple design will be used for several purposes in this chapter. It's worth taking a look at it in detail.

Example 13-1. Fixed-size-block memory manager

```
template <class Arena> struct fixed_block_memory_manager {
    template <int N>
        fixed_block_memory_manager(char(&a)[N]);
    fixed_block_memory_manager(fixed_block_memory_manager&)
        = delete;
    ~fixed_block_memory_manager() = default;
    void operator=(fixed_block_memory_manager&) = delete;

    void*  allocate(size_t);
    size_t block_size() const;
    size_t capacity() const;
    void   clear();
    void   deallocate(void*);
    bool   empty() const;

private:
    struct free_block {
        free_block* next;
    };
    free_block* free_ptr_;
    size_t      block_size_;
    Arena       arena_;
};

# include "block_mgr.inl"
```

The constructor, defined in Example 13-2, accepts a C-style array of char as its argument. This array forms the arena from which blocks of memory will be allocated. The constructor is a template function that allows the array size to be captured as a template parameter.

Example 13-2. fixed_block_memory_manager constructor definition

```
template <class Arena>
    template <int N>
        inline fixed_block_memory_manager<Arena>
        ::fixed_block_memory_manager(char(&a)[N]) :
            arena_(a), free_ptr_(nullptr), block_size_(0) {
            /* empty */
        }
```

Modern C++ Coding Note

To keep template class definitions tidy, it is possible to define template class member functions outside the template class definition. I keep my member function definitions in a file with the suffix *.inl*, for "*inline* definitions." When the function definition appears outside the template class, however, a more verbose syntax is required to help the compiler connect the definition with the declaration in the template class body. The first line of the previous example, template <class Arena>, declares the template parameter of the class. The second line, template <int N>, applies to the constructor function itself, which is a template function. When the member function definition appears outside the template class body, the inline keyword must be explicitly provided, as inline linkage is assumed only when the definition appears inside the class.

The allocate() member function in Example 13-3 pops a block off the free list, if any blocks are available, and returns it. If the free list is empty, allocate() attempts to get a new list of free blocks from the arena manager, which I will describe in a moment. If the arena manager has no more memory to allocate, it returns nullptr and allocate() throws std::bad_alloc.

Example 13-3. fixed_block_memory_manager's definition of allocate()

```
template <class Arena>
    inline void* fixed_block_memory_manager<Arena>
                ::allocate(size_t size) {
    if (empty()) {
        free_ptr_ = reinterpret_cast<free_block*>
                    (arena_.allocate(size));
        block_size_ = size;
        if (empty())
```

```
        throw std::bad_alloc();
    }
    if (size != block_size_)
        throw std::bad_alloc();
    auto p = free_ptr_;
    free_ptr_ = free_ptr_->next;
    return p;
}
```

The `deallocate()` member function is very simple. It pushes a block onto the free list:

```
template <class Arena>
    inline void fixed_block_memory_manager<Arena>
                ::deallocate(void* p) {
    if (p == nullptr)
        return;
    auto fp = reinterpret_cast<free_block*>(p);
    fp->next = free_ptr_;
    free_ptr_ = fp;
}
```

Here are the remaining member function definitions. Copying and assignment of the memory manager are disabled in the class definition using the C++11 syntax:

```
template <class Arena>
    inline size_t fixed_block_memory_manager<Arena>
                ::capacity() const {
    return arena_.capacity();
}

template <class Arena>
    inline void fixed_block_memory_manager<Arena>::clear() {
    free_ptr_ = nullptr;
    arena_.clear();
}
```

Block Arena

The only complexity in `fixed_block_memory_manager` arises from how the initial free list is created. This complexity is factored into a separate template class. The implementation presented here is called `fixed_arena_controller`, and is defined in Example 13-4. As used here, *arena* means an enclosed space in which some activity takes place. `block_arena` is a fixed pool of memory that can be allocated by `block_manager`.

Example 13-4. Block arena for fixed-block memory manager

```
struct fixed_arena_controller {
    template <int N>
```

```
      fixed_arena_controller(char(&a)[N]);
    fixed_arena_controller(fixed_arena_controller&) = delete;
  ~fixed_arena_controller() = default;
  void operator=(fixed_arena_controller&) = delete;

  void*  allocate(size_t);
  size_t block_size() const;
  size_t capacity() const;
  void   clear();
  bool   empty() const;

private:
  void*  arena_;
  size_t arena_size_;
  size_t block_size_;
};
```

The purpose of the class `fixed_arena_controller` is to create a list of memory blocks. All the memory blocks are the same size. The size is set the first time `allocate()` is called. Each memory block must be big enough to hold the requested number of bytes, but it must also be big enough to hold a pointer that is used when the block is on the free list.

The constructor template function accepts the arena array from `fixed_block_memory_manager`, saving the size of the array and a pointer to its start:

```
template <int N>
    inline fixed_arena_controller
            ::fixed_arena_controller(char (&a)[N]) :
    arena_(a), arena_size_(N), block_size_(0) { /*empty*/
}
```

The `allocate()` member function is where the action takes place. It is called by the `allocate()` member function of `fixed_block_memory_manager` when the free list is empty, which happens when the first allocation request occurs.

`fixed_arena_controller` has a single block of memory to allocate. If that block is used up, `allocate()` is called again and must return an error indication, which in this case is `nullptr`. Different kinds of arena controllers might break up big blocks of memory obtained, for instance, by a call to `::operator new()`. For a different arena controller, calling `allocate()` more than once might be OK.

The first time it is called, `allocate()` sets the block size and capacity in blocks. Actually creating the free list is an exercise in reinterpreting untyped memory bytes into typed pointers. The `char` array is interpreted as a set of blocks laid end-to-end. The first bytes of each block are a pointer to the next block. The pointer in the last block is set to `nullptr`.

`fixed_arena_controller` has no control over the size of the arena array. There may be a few unused bytes at the end that are never allocated. The code for setting the free-block pointers is not pretty. It has to continually reinterpret one kind of pointer as another, stepping outside of C++'s type system into the realm of implementation-defined behavior. This is true of memory managers in general, and is unavoidable.

The allocation and deallocation code for `fixed_arena_controller` is simple, overlaying a list of free nodes over the storage provided to the constructor and returning a pointer to the first element of the list. The code looks like this:

```
inline void* fixed_arena_controller
            ::allocate(size_t size) {
    if (!empty())
        return nullptr;     // arena already allocated

    block_size_ = std::max(size, sizeof(void*));
    size_t count = capacity();

    if (count == 0)
        return nullptr;     // arena not big enough for even one item

    char* p;
    for (p = (char*)arena_; count > 1; --count, p += size) {
        *reinterpret_cast<char**>(p) = p + size;
    }
    *reinterpret_cast<char**>(p) = nullptr;
    return arena_;
}
```

Here is the rest of `fixed_arena_controller`:

```
inline size_t fixed_arena_controller::block_size() const {
    return block_size_;
}

inline size_t fixed_arena_controller::capacity() const {
    return block_size_ ? (arena_size_ / block_size_) : 0;
}

inline void fixed_arena_controller::clear() {
    block_size_ = 0;
}

inline bool fixed_arena_controller::empty() const {
    return block_size_ == 0;
}
```

Adding a Class-Specific operator new()

Example 13-5 is a very simple class with a class-specific `operator new()` and `operator delete()`. It also contains the static member `mgr_`, which is the fixed-block

---

memory manager described in "Fixed-Size-Block Memory Manager" on page 336. `operator new()` and `operator delete()` are inline functions that forward requests to the `allocate()` and `deallocate()` member functions of `mgr_`.

Example 13-5. Class with class-specific operator new

```
class MemMgrTester {
    int contents_;
public:
    MemMgrTester(int c) : contents_(c) {}

    static void* operator new(size_t s) {
        return mgr_.allocate(s);
    }
    static void  operator delete(void* p) {
        mgr_.deallocate(p);
    }
    static fixed_block_memory_manager<fixed_arena_controller> mgr_;
};
```

`mgr_` is declared public so I could reinitialize the free list to facilitate writing performance tests via a call to `mrg_.clear()`. If `mgr_` is initialized once at program startup and never needs to be reinitialized, it could as well be a private member.

A memory manager that can be reset like this is called a *pool* memory manager, and the arena it controls is called a *memory pool*. A pool memory manager can be useful in cases where a data structure is constructed, used, and then destroyed. If the entire memory pool can be reinitialized quickly, the program can dispense with freeing the data structure node-by-node.

`mgr_` is declared as a static member of the class `BlockTester`. Somewhere in the program, static members must also be defined. The definition looks like Example 13-6. This code defines a memory arena and then `mgr_`, whose constructor takes the arena as an argument.

Example 13-6. Initializing the memory manager

```
char arena[4004];
fixed_block_memory_manager<fixed_arena_controller>
    MemMgrTester::mgr_(arena);
```

The example code just shown does not define a class-specific `operator new[]()` to allocate storage for arrays. The fixed-block memory manager would not work for arrays, which by definition may have different numbers of elements. If the program tries to allocate an array of `MemMgrTester`, the *new-expression* uses the global `operator new[]()` because a class-specific one is not defined. Individual instances are allocated with the fixed-block memory manager, and arrays use `malloc()`.

Performance of the Fixed-Block Memory Manager

The fixed-block memory manager is very efficient. The allocate and free methods have a fixed cost, and the code can be inlined. But how much faster are they than `malloc()`?

I performed two experiments to test the performance of a class-specific `operator new()`. In the first test, I allocated a million `BlockTester` instances. Allocating with the class-specific `operator new()` and my fixed-block memory manager took 4 milliseconds. Allocating with the global `operator new()`, which uses `malloc()`, took 64 milliseconds. The fixed-block memory manager was 15 times faster than `malloc()` in the test. This result probably overstates the performance improvement that might be achieved in an actual program, though. Amdahl's Law implies that the more computation occurs in between allocations, the smaller the performance gain from speeding up allocation will be.

In the second experiment, I created an array of 100 pointers to `BlockTest`. I created a million `BlockTester` instances, assigning each to an array position at random and deleting any instance already there. Using the fixed-block memory manager, the test took 25 milliseconds. It took 107 milliseconds using the default global memory manager. The fixed-block memory manager was 3.3 times faster.

Variations on the Fixed-Block Memory Manager

The basic structure of the fixed-block memory manager is extremely simple. Variations (any of which you may find if you spend time searching for memory managers on the Internet) can be tried to see if any of them better suit the program being optimized:

- Instead of starting with a fixed arena, memory can be allocated using `malloc()` when the free list is empty. Freed memory blocks are cached on the free list for rapid reuse.

- The arena can be created by a call to `malloc()` or `::new` instead of being fixed. If necessary, a chain of arena blocks can be maintained so that there is no limit on how many small blocks may be allocated. The fixed-block memory manager still retains its advantages of speed and compactness even if it occasionally calls `malloc()`.

- If instances of the class are used for a while and then all discarded, the fixed-block memory manager can be used as a memory pool. In a memory pool, allocation proceeds as normal, but memory is not freed at all. When the program is done with instances of the class, they are all collected at once by reinitializing the static arena, or returning the dynamically allocated arena to the system memory manager. Even if they are all reclaimed at once, allocated blocks must still be deleted by a call to the destructor. Many pool allocators on the Internet forget this tiny but important detail.

A general memory manager can be designed that serves each different request size from a different arena, and returns each different request size to a different free list. If all request sizes are rounded to the next-higher power of two, the result is a "fast-fit" memory manager. Typically, the fast-fit memory manager allocates only objects up to a particular maximum size, sending larger requests to the default memory manager. The code for a fast-fit allocator is too big to reproduce in this book, but it's available on the Web.

Boost has a fixed-block memory manager, called Pool (*http://www.boost.org/doc/libs/ release/libs/pool/*).

Non-Thread Safe Memory Managers Are Efficient

The fixed-block memory manager owes some of its efficiency to not being thread safe. Non-thread safe memory managers are efficient for two reasons. First, they don't require synchronization mechanisms to serialize critical regions. Synchronization is expensive because a very slow memory fence (see "Atomicity by mutual exclusion" on page 289 and "Memory fences" on page 302) is at the heart of every synchronization primitive. Even if only one thread calls the memory manager (which is typical), these expensive instructions slow things down.

Second, non-thread safe memory managers are efficient because they never pend on synchronization primitives. When a program has several threads calling into the memory manager, the threads experience contention for the memory manager as a resource. The more threads there are in the system, the greater the contention is, and the more access to the allocator serializes the activity of the threads.

When a class implements a class-specific memory manager, even if the program as a whole is multithreaded, if a given class is only used in one thread it never has to wait. By contrast, calls into the default memory manager experience contention in multithreaded programs even for objects only used in one thread.

Non-thread safe memory managers are also far easier to write than thread-safe ones, since minimizing the critical section so the memory manager runs efficiently can be complex.

Provide Custom Standard Library Allocators

The container classes of the C++ standard library make heavy use of dynamic memory. They are a natural place to look for optimization opportunities, including custom memory managers like the ones described in "Fixed-Size-Block Memory Manager" on page 336.

But there is a problem. The variables dynamically allocated in a `std::list<T>` are not of the user-provided type `T`. They are of some invisible type, like `listitem<T>`, that contains the previous and next list item pointers as well as the payload type `T`. The dynamically allocated variables in a `std::map<K,V>` are of another hidden type, like `treenode<std::pair<const K, V>>`. These class templates are buried in compiler-provided header files. It isn't possible[2] to modify these classes to add a class-specific `operator new()` and `operator delete()`. And besides, templates are generic. The developer only wants to change the memory manager for certain instances of the generic template in a specific program, not for all instances in all programs. Fortunately, the C++ standard provides a mechanism to define the memory manager used by each container. Standard library containers take an `Allocator` argument that allows the same ability to customize memory management as does a class-specific `operator new()`.

`Allocator` is a template class that manages memory. At its root, an allocator does three things: it retrieves storage from a memory manager, returns storage to a memory manager, and copy-constructs itself from a related allocator. That ought to be simple, but it is not. Allocators have a long, painful history, covered in "Additional Definitions for C++98 Allocator" on page 347. Allocators are regarded by some influential developers as among the most broken parts of C++. Still, if the code is hot enough, and the container is one of the more tractable node-based containers (`std::list`, `std::forward_list`, `std::map`, `std::multimap`, `std::set`, or `std::multiset`), a performance improvement may be available through implementing a custom allocator.

Allocator implementations range from the simple to the mind-numbingly complex. The default allocator, `std::allocator<T>`, is a thin wrapper around `::operator new()`. The developer can provide a nondefault allocator with different behavior.

There are two basic kinds of allocator. The simplest kind is *stateless*—that is, an allocator type with no non-static state. `std::allocator<T>`, the default allocator for standard library containers, is stateless. Stateless allocators have desirable properties:

- A stateless allocator can be default-constructed. There is no need to create an explicit instance of a stateless allocator to pass into the constructor of the container class. `std::list<myClass, myAlloc> my_list;` constructs a list of `myClass` instances allocated with the stateless allocator `myAlloc`.

- A stateless allocator does not take up any space in container instances. Most standard library container classes inherit from their allocator, taking advantage of the empty base class optimization to produce a zero-byte base class.

---

2 Oh, you did *not* just think, "Oh sure you can. You just go into */usr/include* and ..." That is so *unclean!* Brrrrr.

- Two instances of a stateless allocator `my_allocator<T>` are indistinguishable. That means an object allocated by one stateless allocator can be freed by another. This in turn makes operations like `std::list`'s `splice()` member function possible. It is *sometimes, but not always* also the case that two stateless allocators for different types, like `AllocX<T>` and `AllocX<U>`, can be equal. This is true, for instance, of `std::allocator`.

  Equality also means that move assignment and `std::swap()` can happen efficiently. If the two allocators are not equal, the contents of one container must be deep-copied, using the allocator of the target container.

  Note that while equality may happen to be true even of instances of completely unrelated allocator types, like `AllocX<T>` and `AllocY<U>`, this property is not valuable. The type of the container includes the type of the allocator. You can't splice a `std::list<T,AllocX>` to a `std::list<T,AllocY>` any more than you can splice a `std::list<int>` to a `std::list<string>`.

Of course, the primary disadvantage of a stateless allocator is the same as its primary advantage. All instances of a stateless allocator by their nature get memory from the same memory manager. It's a global resource, a dependency on a global variable.

An allocator with internal state is more complex to create and to use, for the following reasons:

- In most cases, an allocator with local state can't be default-constructed. The allocator must be constructed, then passed to the container's constructor:

  ```
  char arena[10000];
  MyAlloc<Foo> alloc(arena);
  std::list<Foo, MyAlloc<Foo>> foolist(alloc);
  ```

- The allocator state must be stored in every variable, increasing its size. This is very painful for containers that create a lot of nodes, like `std::list` and `std::map`, but these are exactly the containers programmers most desire to customize.

- Two allocators of the same type may not compare equal because they have differing internal state, making some operations on containers using that allocator type impossible and others painfully inefficient.

Allocators with state have the critical advantage, however, that it is easier to create multiple kinds of memory arenas for different purposes when all requests don't have to go through a single global memory manager.

For a developer writing custom allocators to improve performance, the choice between allocators with or without local state comes down to how many classes the developer intends to fiddle with. If just one class is hot enough to optimize, a stateless allocator is simpler. If the developer wants to optimize more than one or two classes, then allocators with local state will be more flexible. However, such a developer may have trouble pointing to a profiling run to prove the necessity. Writing custom allocators for many containers may not optimize return on investment of the developer's time.

Minimal C++11 Allocator

If the developer is lucky enough to have a compiler and standard library that fully conform to C++11, he can provide a *minimal allocator* that requires only a few definitions. Example 13-7 is one that does approximately what `std::allocator` does.

Example 13-7. Minimal C++11 allocator

```
template <typename T> struct my_allocator {
    using value_type = T;

    my_allocator() = default;

    template <class U> my_allocator(const my_allocator<U>&) {}

    T* allocate(std::size_t n, void const* = 0) {
        return reinterpret_cast<T*>(::operator new(n*sizeof(T)));
    }

    void deallocate(T* ptr, size_t) {
        ::operator delete(ptr);
    }
};

template <typename T, typename U>
    inline bool operator==(const my_allocator<T>&,
                           const my_allocator<U>&) {
    return true;
}

template <typename T, typename U>
    inline bool operator!=(const my_allocator<T>& a,
                           const my_allocator<U>& b) {
    return !(a == b);
}
```

The minimal allocator contains these few functions:

`allocator()`

> This is the default constructor. If the allocator has a default constructor, the developer does not need to explicitly create an instance to pass into the container's constructor. The default constructor is typically empty in stateless constructors, and is typically not present at all in allocators with non-static state.

```
template <typename U> allocator(U&)
```
This copy constructor makes it possible to convert an `allocator<T>` into a related allocator for a private class such as `allocator<treenode<T>>`. This is important because in most containers, no nodes of type T are ever allocated.

The copy constructor is typically empty in stateless allocators, but must copy or clone the state in allocators with non-static state.

```
T* allocate(size_type n, const void* hint = 0)
```
This function allocates storage sufficient to hold n bytes and returns a pointer to it, or throws `std::bad_alloc`. `hint` is meant to help the allocator in an unspecified way related to "locality." I've never seen an implementation that used `hint`.

```
void deallocate(T* p, size_t n)
```
This function releases storage previously returned by `allocate()`, pointed to by p and occupying n bytes, to the memory manager. n must be the same as the argument to `allocate()` that allocated the storage pointed to by p.

```
bool operator==(allocator const& a) const
bool operator!=(allocator const& a) const
```
These functions test two allocator instances of the same type for equality. *If the instances compare equal, then objects allocated from one instance may safely be freed on another.* That means the two instances allocate objects from the same storage area.

The implication of equality is large. It means, for instance, that `std::list` items can be spliced from one list to another if and only if the two lists have the same type of allocator and the two allocator instances compare equal. The allocator type is part of the container instance type, so if the allocators are different types, it doesn't matter if they secretly share the same storage.

Stateless allocators return `true` unconditionally when tested for equality. Allocators with non-static state must compare their state to determine equality, or simply return `false`.

Additional Definitions for C++98 Allocator

C++11 takes significant pains to make allocators easier to write, at the cost of making container classes more complex. The developer who must write an allocator for a pre-C++11 standard library container will find out why.

Allocators weren't originally meant for (or at least not only meant for) managing memory. The allocator concept evolved in the 1980s, when microprocessors and developers were straining to break out of the confines of a 16-bit address space. PCs of the day formed an address from a segment register plus an offset. Each program was compiled for a *memory model*, which described the default way in which pointers worked. There were a bunch of memory models. Some were efficient, but limited the amount of memory a program or its data could occupy. Other memory models allowed more memory, but were slower. The C compilers of the day were extended with additional type modifiers so that individual pointers could be declared *near* or *far*, based on how much memory the developer wanted to access with them.

Allocators as originally imagined were meant to unmuddle this memory model mess. But by the time allocators arrived in C++, hardware makers had already heard the collective screaming of thousands of C developers, and implemented a uniform memory model with no segment registers. Furthermore, the allocator solution was unworkably inefficient using the compilers of the day.

Prior to C++11, every allocator contained all the functions in the minimal allocator, plus all of the following:

`value_type`
> The type of the object to be allocated.

`size_type`
> An integral type big enough to hold the maximum number of bytes that can be allocated by this allocator.
>
> For allocators used as parameters to standard library container templates, this definition must be `typedef size_t size_type;`.

`difference_type`
> An integral type big enough to hold the maximum difference between two pointers.
>
> For allocators used as parameters to standard library container templates, this definition must be `typedef ptrdiff_t difference_type;`.

`pointer`
`const_pointer`
> The type of a pointer to (`const`) T.
>
> For allocators used as parameters to standard library container templates, these definitions must be:
>
> ```
> typedef T* pointer;
> typedef T const* const_pointer;
> ```
>
> For other allocators, `pointer` might be a pointer-like class that implements `operator*()` to dereference the pointer.

```
reference
const_reference
```
    The type of a reference to (const) T.

    For allocators used as parameters to standard library container templates, the
    definitions must be:

```
typedef T& reference;
typedef T const& const_reference;
```

```
pointer address(reference)
const_pointer address(const_reference)
```
    Functions that produce a pointer to (const) T, given a reference to (const) T.

    For allocators used as parameters to standard library container templates, these
    definitions are required to be:

```
pointer address(reference r) { return &r; }
const_pointer address(const_reference r) { return &r; }
```
    These functions were meant to abstract memory models. Unfortunately, they
    have been hamstrung for compatibility with the standard library containers,
    which need pointer to actually *be* a T* so like magic line random-access iterators
    and binary search work efficiently.

Even though these definitions have fixed values for allocators used by standard
library containers, the definitions are required, as the container code in C++98 uses
them. For instance:

```
typedef size_type allocator::size_type;
```

Some developers derive their allocator templates from std::allocator, to get these
definitions without writing them. But this practice is controversial. std::allocator
might change someday, after all. It changed a lot in the early years, and it changed
again for C++11, so these fears are well founded. Another approach is to simply factor out the most unchanging of these definitions, as in

```
template <typename T> struct std_allocator_defs {
    typedef T value_type;
    typedef T* pointer;
    typedef const T* const_pointer;
    typedef T& reference;
    typedef const T& const_reference;
    typedef size_t size_type;
    typedef ptrdiff_t difference_type;

    pointer address(reference r) { return &r; }
    const_pointer address(const_reference r) { return &r; }
};
```

Carried to its logical conclusion, these definitions can be made into a traits class, which is what some of the more complex allocator templates on the Web do. This is also what the C++11 minimal allocator does, only the traits class works backward from normal. The traits class looks at the allocator template to see if it has any of these definitions, and provides a standard definition if the allocator does not. Then, the container code references the `allocator_traits` class, not the allocator, as in

```
typedef std::allocator_traits<MyAllocator<T>>::value_type value_type;
```

With the boilerplate out of the way, it's time to look at the important definitions (remember, the definitions for the minimal allocator discussed in "Minimal C++11 Allocator" on page 346 are also included):

void construct(pointer p, const T& val)

> This function copy-constructs an instance of T using placement new:

```
new(p) T(val);
```

> For C++11, this function can be defined so that an argument list can be given to the T constructor:

```
template <typename U, typename... Args>
    void construct(U* p, Args&&... args) {
        new(p) T(std::forward<Args>(args...));
    }
```

void destroy(pointer p);

> This function destroys a pointer to T, calling p->~T();.

rebind::value

> The declaration of struct rebind is at the very heart of allocators. It typically looks like this:

```
template <typename U> struct rebind {
    typedef allocator<U> value;
};
```

> rebind gives a formula for creating an allocator for a new type U, given an allocator<T>. Every allocator must provide this formula. It's how a container like std::list<T> allocates instances of std::list<T>::listnode<T>. It's important that in most containers, no nodes of type T are ever allocated.

Example 13-8 is a full C++98-style allocator equivalent to the C++11 minimal allocator in Example 13-7.

Example 13-8. C++98 allocator

```
template <typename T> struct my_allocator_98 :
    public std_allocator_defs<T> {
```

```
    template <typename U> struct rebind {
        typedef my_allocator_98<U, n> other;
    };

    my_allocator_98() {/*empty*/}
    my_allocator_98(my_allocator_98 const&) {/*empty*/}

    void construct(pointer p, const T& t) {
        new(p) T(t);
    }
    void destroy(pointer p) {
        p->~T();
    }
    size_type max_size() const {
        return block_o_memory::blocksize;
    }
    pointer allocate(
        size_type n,
        typename std::allocator<void>::const_pointer = 0) {
        return reinterpret_cast<T*>(::operator new(n*sizeof(T)));
    }
    void deallocate(pointer p, size_type) {
        ::operator delete(ptr);
    }
};

template <typename T, typename U>
    inline bool operator==(const my_allocator_98<T>&,
                           const my_allocator_98<U>&) {
    return true;
}

template <typename T, typename U>
    inline bool operator!=(const my_allocator_98<T>& a,
                           const my_allocator_98<U>& b) {
    return !(a == b);
}
```

When examining allocator code on the Internet, developers will encounter a variety of different spellings of the types. An extremely cautious and conformant developer will write the signature of the `allocate()` function as

```
pointer allocate(
    size_type n,
    typename std::allocator<void>::const_pointer = 0);
```

while a less cautious developer may write the same signature for an allocator strictly for use with standard library containers as

```
T* allocate(size_t n, void const* = 0);
```

The first signature is the most technically standard-conformant, but the second signature will compile successfully and has the advantage of brevity. This is the way things work in the wild and woolly world of templates.

Another issue with allocator code on the Internet is that `allocate()` must throw `std::bad_alloc` if the request cannot be fulfilled. So, for instance, the following code which calls `malloc()` to allocate memory is not standard-conforming because `malloc()` can return `nullptr`:

```
pointer allocate(
    size_type n,
    typename std::allocator<void>::const_pointer = 0) {
    return reinterpret_cast<T*>(malloc(n*sizeof(T)));
}
```

A Fixed-Block Allocator

The standard library container classes `std::list`, `std::map`, `std::multimap`, `std::set`, and `std::multiset` all create a data structure from many identical nodes. Such classes can take advantage of simple allocators implemented using the fixed-block memory manager described in "Fixed-Size-Block Memory Manager" on page 336. The partial definition in Example 13-9 shows the two functions `allocate()` and `deallocate()`. The other definitions are identical to those in the standard allocator shown in Example 13-8.

Example 13-9. Fixed-block allocator

```
extern fixed_block_memory_manager<fixed_arena_controller>
    list_memory_manager;

template <typename T> class StatelessListAllocator {
public:
    ...

    pointer allocate(
        size_type count,
        typename std::allocator<void>::const_pointer = nullptr) {
        return reinterpret_cast<pointer>
                (list_memory_manager.allocate(count * sizeof(T)));
    }
    void deallocate(pointer p, size_type) {
        string_memory_manager.deallocate(p);
    }
};
```

As previously mentioned, `std::list` never attempts to allocate nodes of type T. Instead, `std::list` uses Allocator template parameter to construct a `listnode<T>`, by calling `list_memory_manager.allocate(sizeof(<listnode<T>>))`.

The list allocator required a change to the memory manager previously defined. The implementation of std::list that comes with Microsoft Visual C++ 2015 allocates a special sentinel node that is a different size from the other list nodes. It happens to be smaller than a regular list node, so it was possible to make a small change to the fixed-block memory manager that allowed it to work. The modified version is shown in Example 13-10. The change is that instead of testing that the current request size is equal to the saved block size, allocate() only tests that it is not greater than the saved block size.

Example 13-10. Modified allocate() function

```
template <class Arena>
    inline void* fixed_block_memory_manager<Arena>
                ::allocate(size_t size) {
    if (empty()) {
        free_ptr_ = reinterpret_cast<free_block*>
                        (arena_.allocate(size));
        block_size_ = size;
        if (empty())
            throw std::bad_alloc();
    }
    if (size > block_size_)
        throw std::bad_alloc();
    auto p = free_ptr_;
    free_ptr_ = free_ptr_->next;
    return p;
}
```

Performance of the fixed-block allocator

I wrote a program to test the performance of the fixed-block allocator. The program is a loop that repeatedly creates a list of 1,000 integers, then deletes the list. Using the default allocator, it took 76.2 microseconds. The program created and destroyed a list using the block allocator in 11.6 microseconds, about 5.6 times faster. This is an impressive performance improvement, but it must be regarded with some suspicion. Only the creation and destruction of the list benefit from this optimization. Performance gains in a program that also processes the list will be far more modest.

I also built a map of 1,000 integer keys. Creating and destroying the map using the default allocator took 142 microseconds, versus 67.4 microseconds with the block allocator. This more modest 110% improvement shows the effect that additional activity in the program (in this case, rebalancing the tree in which the map is stored) has on the performance improvement achieved by the block allocator.

A Fixed-Block Allocator for Strings

`std::string` stores its contents in a dynamic array of char. Because the array is reallocated to a larger size as the string grows, it doesn't seem to be a candidate for the simple fixed-block allocator in the previous section. But sometimes even this limitation can be overcome. A developer who knows the maximum size a string can take in the program can create an allocator that always produces fixed-size blocks of the maximum size. This situation is surprisingly common, because the number of applications for million-character strings is limited.

Example 13-11 is a partial listing of the fixed-block allocator for strings.

Example 13-11. Fixed-block allocator for strings

```
template <typename T> class NewAllocator {
public:
    ...
    pointer allocate(
        size_type /*count*/,
        typename std::allocator<void>::const_pointer = nullptr) {
        return reinterpret_cast<pointer>
                (string_memory_manager.allocate(512));
    }

    void deallocate(pointer p, size_type) {
        ::operator delete(p);
    }
};
```

The important feature of this allocator is that `allocate()` completely ignores the size request, and returns a fixed-size block.

Performance of the string allocator

I tested the string allocator in a version of `remove_ctrl()` from Example 4-1 in Chapter 4. This function used `std::string` inefficiently, creating many temporary strings. Example 13-12 is the modified function.

Example 13-12. Version of remove_ctrl() using the fixed-block string allocator

```
typedef std::basic_string<
    char,
    std::char_traits<char>,
    StatelessStringAllocator<char>> fixed_block_string;

fixed_block_string remove_ctrl_fixed_block(std::string s) {
    fixed_block_string result;
    for (size_t i = 0; i<s.length(); ++i) {
```

```
        if (s[i] >= 0x20)
            result = result + s[i];
    }
    return result;
}
```

An experiment to time the original `remove_ctrl()` ran in 2,693 milliseconds. The improved version in Example 13-12 performed the same test in 1,124 milliseconds, about 1.4 times faster. This performance improvement is significant, but as we saw in Chapter 4, other optimizations performed even better.

Writing a custom memory manager or allocator can be effective, but it has less benefit than optimizations than remove calls to the memory manager altogether.

Summary

- *There may be more fruitful places to look for performance improvement than the memory manager.*
- *Whole-program performance improvements from replacing the default memory manager ranged from negligible to 30% in several large open-source programs.*
- *Memory managers for same-sized requests are particularly easy to write, and run efficiently.*
- *All allocation requests for instances of a particular class request the same number of bytes.*
- *`operator new()` can be overridden at the class level.*
- *The standard library container classes `std::list`, `std::map`, `std::multimap`, `std::set`, and `std::multiset` all create a data structure from many identical nodes.*
- *Standard library containers take an `Allocator` argument that allows the same ability to customize memory management as does a class-specific `operator new()`.*
- *Writing a custom memory manager or allocator can be effective, but it has less benefit than optimizations that remove calls to the memory manager altogether.*

Index

Symbols

#ifdef, 169
0mq library, 321
80/20 rule, 29
90/10 rule, 29
:: (global scope operator), 331
~ (tilde), 332

A

"A Toolbox of Strings Classes" (Panzer), 86
abstract base classes, 167
accuracy, 41
acquire semantics, 289
activity to be optimized
    dissecting, 205
    identifying, 204
addresses, 15
Advanced Configuration and Power Interface
    (ACPI), 48
algorithms (see also searching and sorting)
    changing/replacing, 206
    efficient search algorithms, 96-98
    efficient sort algorithms, 98-100
    impact of optimization, 91
    optimization patterns
        batching, 100, 102
        caching, 101, 103
        double-checking, 101, 105
        hashing, 101, 105
        hinting, 101, 105
        lazy computation, 100, 102
        optimizing the expected path, 101, 105
        precomputation, 100-102
        specialization, 101, 104

        taking bigger bites, 101, 104
    other costs of, 96
    parallelized, 96
    strategies for optimizing C++ code, 6-12
    time cost of, 92-96
    toolkit to optimize searching and sorting,
        96, 203-208
allocators
    C++98 allocators, 347
    consequences of reallocation, 237
    custom standard library allocators, 343
    dynamic variables and, 324
    fixed-block allocators, 352
    minimal C++11 allocator, 346
    reducing reallocation, 127-128
    selecting, 87
    templates for, 115
Amdahl's Law, 31, 323
amortized time cost, 95
arithmetic expressions (see expressions)
assignment operators, 129
associative containers, 230
<async> header, 296
asynchronous function calls, 293
asynchronous tasks, 295
<atomic> header, 301
atomicity, 289-291, 301-304
autogeneration of special member functions,
    141
automatic storage duration, 109

B

baseline measurements, 204
BasicLockable lock, 299

batching, 100, 102
The Better String Library (Hsieh), 86
big-endian computers, 20
big-O notation, 93
binary search, 97, 216-220
binary trees, 123
block arena, 338
block manager, 338
Boost libraries
    Boost Graph Library (BGL), 262
    Boost String Algorithms, 84, 87
    Boost.Container library, 262
    Boost.Coroutine, 320
    boost.heap library, 262
    Boost.Intrusive library, 262
    boost.lockfree library, 262
    Boost.MultiIndex library, 262
    Boost.Thread, 320
    boost::circular_buffer library, 261
    coroutines in, 305
    dynamic_bitset, 262
    Fusion, 262
    standard thread pools and task queues, 310
buffers
    capacity of, 237
    circular, 124
    creating large, 121
    using larger input buffers, 272

C

C++ AMP library, 321
C++ code
    behavior of variables in, 108-113
    C-style string keys, 210
    converting C string to std::string, 89
    dynamic variables in, 113-119
    for loop syntax, 149
    implicit function calls, 155
    optimization strategies, 6-12
    simple computer model followed by, 16
    statement behavior in, 24-25
C++ compilers
    ::operator new() version in, 333
    documentation for, 7
    enabling optimization in, 7
    move semantics and, 140
    precomputation in, 102
    profiler tools for, 37-40
    selecting, 7-8, 82

statement-level optimization and, 148
    string implementations, 69
C++ Concurrency TR working group, 305
C++ standard library
    concurrency facilities in, 291-305
    containers
        associative containers, 230
        benefits of, 229
        focus for optimization, 229
        optimization experiments, 231-236
        sequence containers, 230
        unordered associative containers, 231
    general uses of, 187
    issues in use of, 188-191
    optimizing sorting with, 226-228
    philosophy of, 188
    shared-memory thread support in, 280
C++ String Toolkit Library (StrTk), 84
C++03 Expression Templates (Henderson), 86
C++98 allocators, 347
cache memory
    algorithm optimization, 103
    capacity of, 20
    speed of, 19
    von Neumann bottleneck and, 18
caching
    benefits of, 19
    defined, 9
    goal of, 103
    loop end values, 149
    optimization patterns, 101
    variations on, 150
callable objects, 291
calling chains, 196, 269, 274
calloc(), 327
capacity, 237
character encodings, 89
check-and-update idiom, optimizing, 254
circular buffers, 124
class constructors/destructors, 115
class instances, creating statically, 119
class members, creating variables statically, 120
class-specific memory managers, 335
clocks, 42
    (see also software timers)
closed-form computations, 180
compilation firewalls, 171
concurrency, 279-321
    atomicity, 289

About the Author

Kurt Guntheroth has been a working software developer for over 35 years, and has developed heavy duty C++ code for 25 years. He has developed on Windows, Linux, and embedded devices.

Any time he can get away from the keyboard, Kurt loves to hang out with his wife and four active boys. Kurt lives in Seattle, Washington.

Colophon

The animal on the cover of *Optimized C++* is a Cape hartebeest (*Alcelaphus buselaphus caama*), which ranges over the plains and scrublands of southwestern Africa. The Cape hartebeest is a large antelope belonging to the taxonomic family *Bovidae*. Both males and females have distinctive twisty horns, which can reach 60 centimeters in length. Their hearing and sense of smell are excellent. They can run a zigzag evasive path at speeds up to 55 kilometers per hour. Although lions, leopards, and cheetahs occasionally prey upon the Cape hartebeest, they must usually go elsewhere for their meals. The Cape hartebeest may *look* like it was designed by a committee, but it has been carefully optimized.

Many of the animals on O'Reilly covers are endangered; all of them are important to the world. To learn more about how you can help, go to *animals.oreilly.com*.

The cover image is from *The Riverside Natural History*. The cover fonts are URW Typewriter and Guardian Sans. The text font is Adobe Minion Pro; the heading font is Adobe Myriad Condensed; and the code font is Dalton Maag's Ubuntu Mono.

Get even more for your money.

Join the O'Reilly Community, and register the O'Reilly books you own. It's free, and you'll get:

- $4.99 ebook upgrade offer
- 40% upgrade offer on O'Reilly print books
- Membership discounts on books and events
- Free lifetime updates to ebooks and videos
- Multiple ebook formats, DRM FREE
- Participation in the O'Reilly community
- Newsletters
- Account management
- 100% Satisfaction Guarantee

Signing up is easy:

1. Go to: oreilly.com/go/register
2. Create an O'Reilly login.
3. Provide your address.
4. Register your books.

Note: English-language books only

To order books online:
oreilly.com/store

For questions about products or an order:
orders@oreilly.com

To sign up to get topic-specific email announcements and/or news about upcoming books, conferences, special offers, and new technologies:
elists@oreilly.com

For technical questions about book content:
booktech@oreilly.com

To submit new book proposals to our editors:
proposals@oreilly.com

O'Reilly books are available in multiple DRM-free ebook formats. For more information:
oreilly.com/ebooks

O'REILLY®

Have it your way.

Lightning Source UK Ltd.
Milton Keynes UK
UKOW05f1309030516

273476UK00004B/8/P